Breaking Bad FAQ

Breaking Bad
FAQ

All That's Left to Know About Hustlers, Bunsen Burners, and Heisenberg

Rich Weidman

APPLAUSE
THEATRE & CINEMA BOOKS
An Imprint of Hal Leonard LLC

Published in 2018 by Applause Theatre & Cinema Books
An Imprint of Hal Leonard LLC
7777 West Bluemound Road
Milwaukee, WI 53213

Trade Book Division Editorial Offices
33 Plymouth St., Montclair, NJ 07042

The FAQ series was conceived by Robert Rodriguez and developed with Stuart Shea.

All images are from the author's collection unless otherwise noted.

Printed in the United States of America

Book design by Snow Creative

Library of Congress Cataloging-in-Publication Data is available upon request.

ISBN 978-1-4950-9489-7

www.applausebooks.com

Dedicated to the memory of my favorite author, Harry Crews (1935–2012), who once lamented the "dumbasses out there that are watching television until they are rotting in their souls."

Contents

Acknowledgments

F irst of all, I would like to thank my wife, Nadine, and kids, Hailey and Dylan. Fortunately, Nadine happens to be a big fan of both *Breaking Bad* and *Better Call Saul*, and happily endured endless days and nights of nonstop binge watching. A special thanks as always to my family—Mom, Dad, Boyd, and Tracy and her family—for all your support and enthusiasm. Thanks also to the McAuley clan—Jan; David, Kathy, and Kennedy; and Dan, Carrie, Joey, Kyle, and Caiden.

A big thanks as always to Jack Thompson, who has collaborated with me on many offbeat and rewarding Internet projects over the years such as Alternative Reel, Forgotten Movie Classics, and Pro Wrestlers: Dead or Alive. In fact, it was actually one of the first articles posted on Alternative Reel, "The Doors: A Retrospective," back in 1999 that eventually led to the writing of my first book in the FAQ series, *The Doors FAQ*. Back in the day, we also tore it up at pub trivia at such great venues as An Tobar, Bull & Bush, and Copper Rocket Pub, once the home of the legendary Mandaddy Trivia.

Thanks to Visit Albuquerque, the Albuquerque Film Office, and the New Mexico State Film Office for all of their support and assistance. A big note of thanks also to my good old friend Ben Parker for providing me with some great photos of *Breaking Bad* film locales throughout Albuquerque. In addition, a special shout-out goes to the Breaking Bad Wiki (breakingbad.wikia.com), an amazing collaborative website built by fans for *Breaking Bad* and *Better Call Saul*.

I'm truly grateful to Marybeth Keating from Applause Books for all her assistance throughout all of the production stages related to this book and for tolerating my frequent delays. In addition, I would like to extend my appreciation to Robert Rodriguez, the founder of the FAQ series and an inspiration to us all. Thanks as always to Robert Lecker of the Robert Lecker Agency for his persistence and assistance.

Thanks to Robert Jensen, who first introduced me to the concept of binge watching when he lent me the first four seasons of *The Sopranos* on DVD that I managed to knock out in a couple of weekends (one rainy Saturday night I actually polished off half a season of episodes!) back in 2005. A special mention goes to my boss, Denise Brookfield, who tolerated my frequent absences during the writing of this book, as well as Roland Szpond, coworker and drummer for the ska/punk band the Hoverounds, who is simply funny as shit and always makes me laugh.

For their ongoing inspiration, a special shout-out to Bill Chinaski, Jim Foley, Art "Barfly" Spackle, Doors expert and author Jim Cherry (*The Last Stage*), singer-songwriter Tony Brehm, Tony Fernandez of Peace Frog, Michael McCloud and the staff at Schooner Wharf Bar in Key West, Al Scortino (who I hope to see in concert someday soon), John Nixdorf (who actually has reportedly read or at least browsed through all of my previous books!), John "Hooch" Lewis, and my long-lost buddy Ben John Smith of HorrorSleazeTrash (and former Australian correspondent for Alternative Reel).

Last but certainly not least, a special shout-out to the memory of Leicester Hemingway (1915–1982), who idolized his famous older brother, wrote a great, highly recommended memoir called *My Brother, Ernest Hemingway* (which I carried around at all times to relieve stress during the writing of this book), and also founded the "island nation" of New Atlantis, stating that "there's no law that says you can't start your own country." Leicester, I lift a glass to you!

Introduction

> I hate entertainment. Entertainment is a thing of the past, now we got television.
>
> —*Archie Bunker, All in the Family*

Did you know . . .

- Two 1980s Hollywood icons, John Cusack (*The Sure Thing*) and Matthew Broderick (*Ferris Bueller's Day Off*), were both considered for the role of Walter White?
- After binge watching *Breaking Bad*, Anthony Hopkins wrote Bryan Cranston a fan letter comparing the series to a "great Jacobean, Shakespearian or Greek tragedy"?
- Marius Stan, who portrayed Walt's surly car wash boss, Bogdan, has a PhD in Chemistry and serves as Interim Director of the Systems Science Center in the Global Security Sciences division of Argonne National Laboratory?
- Jesse Pinkman (Aaron Paul) and Walter White Jr. (RJ Mitte) never shared a scene together during the entire series?
- Mark "Hector Salamanca" Margolis made his film debut (fully clothed!) as Unhappy Man in the XXX-rated classic *The Opening of Misty Beethoven* (1976)?

Welcome to *Breaking Bad FAQ*, a comprehensive and unorthodox exploration of the hit dramatic television series that not only provides readers with mind-bending trivia like the above tidbits and breaks down all sixty-two episodes with in-depth analysis, but also highlights the origins of the series, cast and crew, filming techniques and locales, television and film influences (such as Rod Serling's *The Twilight Zone*, Sergio Leone's Spaghetti Westerns like *The Good, the Bad, and the Ugly*, and Francis Ford Coppola's *The Godfather*), literary references, best songs on the soundtrack, fan theories, a Walter White vs. Tony Soprano tale of the tape, scientific allusions and accuracy, homages and parodies, *Better Call Saul*, and much more.

Simply one of the greatest dramatic television series of all time, *Breaking Bad* blended a totally original concept with a superb ensemble cast, along with the perfect locale in Albuquerque, New Mexico, great dialogue, dark humor, classic villains like Gus Fring and Tuco Salamanca, and some absolutely mind-blowing cinematography to create television magic, and *Breaking Bad FAQ* celebrates this stunning achievement from a fan's perspective.

One of the most critically acclaimed television series ever produced, *Breaking Bad* was created by Vince Gilligan and aired on AMC for five exhilarating seasons between 2008 and 2013 at a cost of approximately $3 million per episode. The series garnered an impressive nineteen Primetime Emmy Awards, eight Satellite Awards, two Golden Globe Awards, two Peabody Awards, two Critics' Choice Awards, and four Television Critics Association Awards. Cranston himself took home the Emmy for Outstanding Lead Actor in a Drama Series four times, while Aaron Paul captured the Outstanding Supporting Actor in a Drama Emmy three times and Anna Gunn won the Emmy for Outstanding Supporting Actress in a Drama Series twice.

In 2013, *TV Guide* ranked *Breaking Bad* as the ninth-greatest TV series of all time behind such long-established classics as *The Sopranos, Seinfeld, I Love Lucy, All in the Family, The Twilight Zone, The Wire, The Mary Tyler Moore Show,* and *M*A*S*H.* The 2014 edition of *Guinness World Records* featured *Breaking Bad* as the "Highest-Rated TV Series" after the show achieved an impressive 99 percent rating on MetaCritic.com. *Breaking Bad* ranked third on the *Rolling Stone* list of the "100 Greatest TV Shows of All Time" behind *The Sopranos* and *The Wire.* According to *Rolling Stone,* Walter White is "so frightening because he's so ordinary—any American loser who gets a chance to act on his most criminal fantasies, which in Walter's case is just the chance to finally be good at something . . . The more Walt transforms into Heisenberg, the deeper he digs into the grim side of the American dream." None other than the master of horror himself, Stephen King (*The Shining*), lauded the series, comparing it favorably to the likes of *Blue Velvet* and *Twin Peaks.*

I must confess that, prior to getting totally addicted to *The Sopranos* (*Miami Vice* being a rare exception!), I've never been a huge fan of any TV dramatic series. I always tended to gravitate more to sitcoms like *Cheers, Seinfeld,* and *The Office.* Believe it or not, I have yet to watch a single episode of the following shows: *Hill Street Blues, St. Elsewhere, Law & Order, NYPD Blue, ER,* or *CSI: Crime Scene Investigation.* However, antiheroes have always appealed to me and the arrival of such colorful characters onto the scene as Omar Little in *The Wire,* Tony Soprano in *The Sopranos,* Vic Mackey in *The Shield,* Dexter Morgan in *Dexter,* Don Draper in *Mad Men,* Jax Teller in *Sons of Anarchy,* Tyrion Lannister in *Game of Thrones,* and, of course, Walter White in *Breaking Bad* turned my television viewing habits upside down and became as addictive as Walt's blue meth.

Why are antiheroes so appealing in this day and age? Perhaps because the majority of us are caught in the monotonous grind of the nine-to-five workweek and secretly romanticize the idea of "breaking bad" now and then to declare our independence from the mind-numbing routine. In fact, most hardcore fans like myself shamelessly cheered Walt on even after he committed the most horrible deeds (what does that say about the status of our society?). Let's face it, when Walt dons the porkpie hat, dark sunglasses, and jacket as Heisenberg, the guy is totally badass and we are on his side no matter what—all the way up to his final revelation when he brazenly announces to Skyler, "I did it for me. I liked it. I was good at it. And, I was really . . . I was alive." With the arrival of *Breaking Bad*, it's obvious how far we had evolved (or devolved for that matter!) as a society since *Dragnet* first became the epitome of the crime drama in the 1950s.

In addition, Walter White differed from all of the other television antiheroes in that we actually got the opportunity to witness his stunning transformation through the length of the series (in comparison, Tony Soprano in *The Sopranos* was essentially the same sociopath from the first time we met him feeding ducks in his pool during the pilot episode to the guy eating onion rings in the diner during the series finale). For better or worse, Walt experiences an awakening, and we as viewers are totally enthralled by his journey and how it affects (and mostly destroys) the lives of those closest to him.

I have to admit that I avoided watching the first four seasons of *Breaking Bad* because I was busy working on two consecutive books, *The Doors FAQ: All That's Left to Know About the Kings of Acid Rock* (2010) and *The Beat Generation FAQ: All That's Left to Know About the Angelheaded Hipsters* (2015), and I had no free time to casually watch anything unrelated to those two topics. However, I had once browsed through an interview with series creator Vince Gilligan where he described *Breaking Bad* as transforming "Mr. Chips to Scarface," and that had always stuck in the back of my mind because the idea of a high school chemistry teacher turning into a drug kingpin seemed (and still seems to this day) so bizarre and original. So one day I was lounging on the couch channel surfing when by pure accident I came across the first episode ("Live Free or Die") of Season Five of *Breaking Bad*. Here was this slovenly character sitting alone in a Denny's rearranging bacon strips into the number 52. He then retreats to the restroom, where he meets with a sleazy arms dealer and purchases a machine gun. I didn't know what the hell was going on, but I was hooked from that moment on!

So I immediately ordered Season One of *Breaking Bad* on DVD and started doing some serious binge watching. The "Pilot" episode blew me away (if you haven't watched the series yet and aren't immediately hooked by the first episode, then I suggest you go back to watching reruns of *Glee*). So I worked my way through the first four seasons in just three weeks and managed to catch up to the fifth season already in progress.

In fact, *Breaking Bad* came at just the right time as our binge-watching culture was taking off. Viewers could catch up by streaming on Netflix and then participate in invigorating online discussions where many fan theories took shape. In the Introduction to *Breaking Bad: The Official Book* (2015), critic David Thomson remarked, "As a movie critic, I feel no American film of the twenty-first century has matched the achievement of *Breaking Bad*. Nothing on the 'big' screen has had its range and grandeur, or found a beauty that comes so organically from its subject . . . No theatrical movie has a fraction of its inventiveness, maintains such a high level of dialogue, or goes so deeply into character and acting." Just like Thomson and other critics have remarked, I truly believe that shows like *Breaking Bad*, along with other classic dramatic series like *The Wire*, *The Sopranos*, *Game of Thrones* (itself spawned from George R. R. Martin's series of fantasy novels, *A Song of Ice and Fire*), and others, serve as richly textured "novels" for the twenty-first century. In his article "Get a Life? No Thanks. Just Pass the Remote," which appeared in *The New York Times Sunday Review* (May 18, 2013), James Atlas wrote, "The most compelling thing about [*Breaking Bad*] . . . what makes it unique among TV series, is its depiction of how good and evil can coexist in one person . . . Like the characters in Dostoyevsky, Camus and Celine, Walt inhabits a world of moral ambiguity that TV has never been given the time to explore in depth until now. I watch 'Breaking Bad' for the same reason I read the classics: to discover why people act the way they do. (Also, it's colossally entertaining.)"

Over the last two decades, endless superhero movies have dominated the silver screen in all their increasingly bland glory, while much of the more sophisticated fare has gravitated to television, whether it be AMC, HBO, Amazon, or Netflix. So in the past, where viewers had to go out to movies every once in a while to escape the mindless junk churned out by the television networks, now they simply stay home to enjoy some intellectual stimulation away from the endless crap churned out by the movie studios (another *Captain America* sequel, anybody?). *Breaking Bad* directly and indirectly confronted some of the major issues facing Americans today such as fragmented families, the failure of the "war on drugs," exorbitant health-care costs, downward mobility, illegal immigration, and the growing militarization of our police force.

I must admit that I suffered serious withdrawal when *The Sopranos* ended in 2007 (has it really been more than eleven years?), but with *Breaking Bad* we still have the fourth season of its outstanding prequel, *Better Call Saul*, to look forward to along with the expectation that we can thrill to not only the further exploits of Saul Goodman but also cameos galore from many of our favorite characters that appeared in the original series.

Spoiler Alert: *Breaking Bad FAQ* serves as a comprehensive guide to the entire series, and therefore I assume that readers have already watched every episode. Spoilers abound in each and every chapter! In fact, the entire guide serves as an extended spoiler alert. Therefore, if you are not finished with the series, I suggest you either work your way through the episode-by-episode analysis at your leisure or simply close the book immediately, get to binge watching, and then resume reading when you are done. Either way, take time to enjoy the journey since you'll definitely regret when it's over!

This Is My Confession

Vince Gilligan and the Creation of *Breaking Bad*

> Even if the universe is chaotic—which I dearly hope it isn't—I have to believe that actions have consequences. If [Breaking Bad] was important, that was the way for me it was the most important.
>
> —*Vince Gilligan*

Behind every great TV series there lies a determined auteur, a true visionary whose creative influence and artistic control place a personal imprint on the entire production. Just think Rod Serling for *The Twilight Zone*, Carl Reiner for *The Dick Van Dyke Show*, Norman Lear for *All in the Family*, John Cleese for *Fawlty Towers*, Lorne Michaels for *Saturday Night Live*, Matt Groening for *The Simpsons*, Larry David for *Seinfeld*, David Lynch for *Twin Peaks*, Chris Carter for *The X-Files*, David Simon for *The Wire*, David Chase for *The Sopranos*, and Matthew Weiner for *Mad Men*, among others. For *Breaking Bad*, that creative visionary is Vince Gilligan.

The creator, head writer, director, and executive producer of both *Breaking Bad* and *Better Call Saul* (along with Peter Gould), Vince Gilligan has received widespread critical acclaim, including capturing two Primetime Emmy Awards, six Writers Guild of America Awards, two Critics' Choice Television Awards, two Producers Guild of America Awards, one Directors Guild of America Award, and a BAFTA (British Academy of Film and Television Arts). Quoted in David Bianculli's 2016 book *The Platinum Age of Television*, Gilligan remarked on *Breaking Bad*, "I love the idea of a good character, a good man, doing arguably bad things for a good reason."

Early Background

George Vincent "Vince" Gilligan Jr. was born on February 10, 1967, in Richmond, Virginia. He grew up in the small town of Farmville, Virginia (population: 8,216), the seat of Prince Edward County and less than thirty miles from Appomattox, site of Confederate General Robert E. Lee's surrender to Union General Ulysses S. Grant on April 9, 1865. Farmville also served as the birthplace of Confederate general Joseph E. Johnston, rapper The Lady of Rage (Robin Yvette Allen), and actor Chris Ashworth, who portrayed Sergei Malatov on *The Wire*. Gilligan's father, George Sr., worked as an insurance claims adjuster, while his mother, Gail, was a teacher (who had once reportedly been a wing walker!). His parents divorced in 1974. As a teenager, Gilligan and his younger brother, Patrick, used a borrowed Super 8 camera to make several science fiction films, including one titled *Space Wreck*. Gilligan also sought out film noir and classic Westerns on late-night television, as well as classic TV shows such as *The Untouchables* and *The Twilight Zone*. He was particularly enthralled with Sergio Leone's epic Spaghetti Westerns such as *The Good, the Bad and the Ugly* (1966) and *Once Upon a Time in the West* (1968).

Screenplays and Other Projects

Gilligan received a bachelor of fine arts degree in film production at NYU's Tisch School of the Arts. He was in good company since other notable Tisch alumni include Martin Scorsese (*Goodfellas*), Joel Coen (*Fargo*), Chris Columbus (*Home Alone*), Debra Granik (*Winter's Bone*), Ang Lee (*Brokeback Mountain*), Oliver Stone (*Born on the Fourth of July*), Jim Jarmusch (*Stranger Than Paradise*), Spike Lee (*Do the Right Thing*), Todd Phillips (*The Hangover*), M. Night Shyamalan (*The Sixth Sense*), Todd Solondz (*Welcome to the Dollhouse*), Jim Taylor (*Sideways*), Morgan Spurlock (*Super Size Me*), Billy Crystal (*City Slickers*), and Michael Arndt (*Little Miss Sunshine*), among many others.

One of Gilligan's NYU instructors was writer and producer Jesse Kornbluth, who scripted the insightful 1991 documentary, *Trump: What's the Deal?* While at NYU, Gilligan wrote the screenplay for *Home Fries*, which won the Virginia Governor's Screenwriting Award in 1989 and was turned into a 1998 film directed by Dean Parisot (*Galaxy Quest*) and starring Drew Barrymore, Luke Wilson, and Jake Busey. *Home Fries* was a box-office flop and received mixed reviews, with Stephen Holden of *The New York Times* commenting that although the film "evokes a cultural climate overheated with tabloid television and talk show melodrama, its humor lacks teeth." Gilligan also wrote the screenplay for *Wilder Napalm* (1993), which starred Debra Winger, Dennis Quaid, Arliss Howard, M. Emmet Walsh, and Jim Varney. Another box-office disaster (raking in an abysmal $84,859), the film received negative reviews, with Peter Rainer of *The Los Angeles Times* remarking that "most of the time you wish this film would self-incinerate."

A big fan of *The X-Files*, which was created by Chris Carter and originally ran from 1993 to 2002 (with a total of 202 episodes over its nine-season span), Gilligan submitted an unsolicited script to Fox that became

Breaking Bad creator Vince Gilligan has received widespread critical acclaim, including winning two Primetime Emmy Awards and six Writers Guild of America Awards.   *Gage Skidmore/Wikimedia Commons*

the second-season episode "Soft Light" and originally aired on May 5, 1995. "Soft Light" concerns "a guy whose shadow comes to life and sucks people in like a black hole and kills them," according to Gilligan in a July 6, 2011, *New York Times* interview. *Entertainment Weekly* gave "Soft Light" a "B-" and added that the episode "gains points for the obscure subject matter" but "loses them for the strained conspiratorial element."

Gilligan went on to write twenty-nine more *X-Files* episodes, as well as being co-executive producer of forty-four episodes, executive producer of forty episodes, co-producer of twenty-four episodes, and supervising producer of twenty episodes. He also served as co-creator of its spin-off, *The Lone Gunmen*, which only ran for one season of thirteen episodes in 2001. *The Lone Gunmen* focused on a trio of characters who had first appeared in *The X-Files*: Richard "Ringo" Langly (Dan Haglund), Melvin Frohike (Tom Braidwood), and John Fitzgerald Byers (Bruce Harwood). The name "lone gunmen" refers to the controversial conclusion reached by the Warren Commission that Lee Harvey Oswald was the lone gunman responsible for the assassination of President John F. Kennedy in Dallas, Texas, on November 22, 1963.

Gilligan also served as screenwriter for the 2008 film *Hancock*, a superhero comedy-drama directed by Peter Berg (*Friday Night Lights*) and starring Will Smith, Charlize Theron, and Jason Bateman. *Hancock* received mixed reviews, with Todd McCarthy of *Variety* calling it "an intriguing high concept" that "is undermined by low-grade dramaturgy . . . This misguided attempt to wring a novel twist on the superhero genre has a certain whiff of 'The Last Action Hero' about it." Gilligan's first draft of the script for *Hancock* was reportedly much darker than the finished product and sported the working title *Tonight, He Comes*.

Post-*Breaking Bad*, Gilligan co-created (with Peter Gould) the critically acclaimed *Breaking Bad* prequel, *Better Call Saul*, which premiered on AMC on February 8, 2015. The show stars Bob Odenkirk as Jimmy McGill/Saul Goodman, and has received a dedicated fan base just like its predecessor. *Better Call Saul* features a number of other *Breaking Bad* alumni, including Jonathan Banks (Mike Ehrmantraut), Raymond Cruz (Tuco Salamanca), Jesus Payan Jr. (Gonzo), Cesar Garcia (No-Doze), Maximino Arciniega (Krazy-8), Jim Beaver (Lawson), Mark Margolis (Hector "Tio"

Salamanca), Daniel and Luis Moncada (the Cousins), Giancarlo Esposito (Gustavo "Gus" Fring), Jeremiah Bitsui (Victor), Ray Campbell (Tyrus), Lavell Crawford (Huell Babineaux), and Laura Fraser (Lydia Rodarte-Quayle), among others. A ten-episode fourth season of *Better Call Saul* began during the fall of 2018. Gilligan lives in Los Angeles with his long-time girlfriend, Holly Rice.

"Mr. Chips into Scarface"

In 2004, Gilligan was chatting with fellow colleague (and future *Breaking Bad* writer and director) Thomas Schnauz regarding their unemployment (Schnauz had just read a story about a man cooking meth in an apartment complex) and joked that the solution was for them to set up a portable meth lab in the back of an RV, cruising across the country cooking up meth and raking in the cash. According to Schnauz in an interview that appeared in the article "The Dark Art of Breaking Bad," (*The New York Times Magazine*, July 6, 2011), "Neither of us were working . . . and we were like two seventy-year-old men who like to complain about the world. And somehow we spun off into the idea of driving around in a mobile lab, cooking meth. It was a joke and not something I would have ever thought about again. But a couple days later Vince called back and said: 'Remember we were talking about that mobile lab and meth? Do you mind if I run with that?'"

Gilligan thought it would be interesting to take the protagonist in a dramatic series and turn him into the antagonist, something unique in the annals of television history. In fact, Gilligan has stated that his ultimate goal with *Breaking Bad* was to turn "Mr. Chips into Scarface," a reference to both *Goodbye Mr. Chips*, a 1934 novella by James Hilton that was turned into a 1939 film that starred Academy Award-winning actor Robert Donat, and the brutal 1983 crime drama *Scarface*, which was directed by Brian De Palma (*Carlito's Way*) and starred Al Pacino chomping scenery in the title role. In essence, unlike the static leading man in the typical drama series (i.e., Don Draper in *Mad Men*), Walter White in *Breaking Bad* would undergo a startling transformation over the course of the series—from mild-mannered high school chemistry teacher to a ruthless drug kingpin. According to Gilligan in the "Dark Art of Breaking Bad" article, "Television is really good at protecting the franchise . . . It's good at keeping the Korean War going for 11 seasons, like 'M*A*S*H.' It's good at keeping Marshal Dillon policing his little town for 20 years. By their very nature TV shows are open-ended. So I thought, Wouldn't it be interesting to have a show that takes the protagonist and transforms him into the antagonist?"

Gilligan has remarked that if there is a "larger lesson" to *Breaking Bad*, it's that "actions have consequences." Elaborating on the show's philosophy, he stated, "If religion is a reaction of man, and nothing more, it seems to me that it represents a human desire for wrongdoers to be punished. I hate the idea of Idi Amin living in Saudi Arabia for the last 25 years of his life. That galls me to no end. I feel some sort of need for Biblical atonement, or justice or something. I like to believe there is some comeuppance, that karma kicks in at some point, even if it takes years or decades to happen." David Segal of *The New York Times* in turn referred to Gilligan as the "first true red-state auteur" whose "characters lead middle-American lives in a middle-American place, and they are beset with middle-American problems."

As with most other long-form dramatic TV series of the period, *Breaking Bad* owed a tremendous debt to *Twin Peaks*, which ran on ABC for just two seasons in 1990 and 1991. Totally original, *Twin Peaks* featured the trademark weirdness of creator David Lynch (*Eraserhead*) and involved a slew of eccentric characters in the Pacific Northwest. Another inspiration for the series was HBO's first long-form series, *Oz*, a revolutionary drama set in Oswald State Prison that ran from 1997 until 2003. In "The Great Oz" (*Esquire*, November 2017), Adrienne Westenfeld writes, "A man is branded with a swastika. Another is euthanized in bed with a hand over his nose and mouth. A third is sprayed with lighter fluid and set aflame. And that's just in the first episode . . . *Oz* redefined what you could do on non-network television—pretty much anything, it turned out—while fearlessly probing the unexplored tensions in American life. Without it, there would be no *Sopranos*, no *Breaking Bad*, no *Walking Dead*, no *Game of Thrones*."

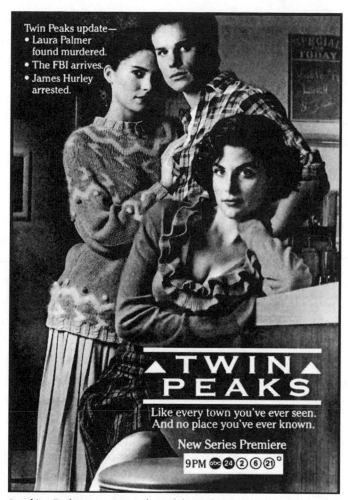

Twin Peaks update—
• Laura Palmer found murdered.
• The FBI arrives.
• James Hurley arrested.

▲TWIN▲
PEAKS
Like every town you've ever seen.
And no place you've ever known.
New Series Premiere
9PM abc 24 2 6 21

Breaking Bad owes a tremendous debt to the quirky early 1990's ABC drama *Twin Peaks*, which was created by David Lynch and featured a slew of eccentric characters in the Pacific Northwest.

Pitching the Show

While still pitching *Breaking Bad* to various networks, Gilligan was initially discouraged when he learned of the existing series *Weeds* on Showtime and its similarities to the premise of *Breaking Bad*. A black comedy, *Weeds*, which features a widowed mother, Nancy Botwin (Mary-Louise Parker), who lives in California and sells marijuana to support her family, debuted on Showtime in 2005 and ran for eight seasons. *Weeds* was the brainchild of Jenji Kohan, who later created the immensely popular comedy-drama *Orange Is the New Black* for Netflix. In fact, Showtime declined to meet with Gilligan due to the fact that *Weeds* was already an established show for the network. Gilligan later remarked that he would never have gone forward with *Breaking Bad* if he had known about *Weeds* during the initial stages of development.

After failing to persuade executives at HBO, Showtime, and TNT (FX showed some interest but eventually passed in favor of the short-lived and long-forgotten TV series *Dirt* starring Courteney Cox as the editor of a tabloid magazine), Gilligan turned to AMC, which had originally begun as American Movie Classics in 1984 and once offered a similar format to TCM (Turner Classic Movies)—airing classic films without commercial interruptions such as the silent version of *The Phantom of the Opera* (1925) starring Lon Chaney and *Duck Soup* (1933) starring the Marx Brothers. However, in 1998, AMC began running ads and the "classic" movies aired on the network started becoming few and far between (while *Die Hard* marathons became commonplace).

Gilligan made his *Breaking Bad* pitch to AMC executives in 2007, the same year that AMC's highly popular series *Mad Men* (which both HBO and Showtime had also passed on) made its debut. According to Gilligan, as quoted in Alan Sepinwall's 2013 book *The Revolution Was Televised*, Michael Lynton of Sony told him that *Breaking Bad* "is the single worst idea for a television series I've ever heard in my life." The network eventually ordered nine episodes for the first season (including the pilot), but the 2007–08 Writers Guild of America strike limited the production to just seven episodes (which included the pilot episode that was simply titled "Pilot"). Unique for a television series because of the added expense, *Breaking Bad* was shot primarily on 35-millimeter film and cost approximately $3 million per episode to produce.

According to Gilligan in *Breaking Bad: The Official Book*, "My biggest fear once AMC and Sony gave us the go-ahead to shoot the pilot, was that this character would quickly become so unlikable, and that first decision of his, the series engine—to cook crystal meth—would be so repulsive that we would not so much lose sympathy for him, but we would never have it at all."

Casting

According to Gilligan in a 2012 interview with *The Hollywood Reporter*, AMC executives preferred to cast the role of Walter White with an established star such as Matthew Broderick (*Ferris Bueller's Day Off*) or John Cusack (*The Sure Thing*). Thankfully, both actors turned down the role. Steve Zahn (*Happy, Texas*) and Christian Slater (*Heathers*) were also reportedly considered for the role. Although Bryan Cranston was then known primarily as a "sitcom dad" for his role as Hal Wilkerson in *Malcolm in the Middle* (as well as his memorable stint as dentist Tim Whatley on *Seinfeld*), Gilligan had remembered the actor's powerful performance as Patrick Crump in a 1998 episode of *The X-Files* that he had written called "Drive." For his part, Cranston jumped at the chance after reading the pilot script and hearing of Gilligan's plans to transform the character from good to bad during the duration of the series. Aaron Paul almost didn't get cast as Jesse Pinkman because some executives thought he was just too handsome for the role of a low-level meth dealer known as Cap'n Cook.

The Perfect Locale

Originally set in Riverside, California, which lies about sixty miles east of Los Angeles, *Breaking Bad* was moved to Albuquerque, New Mexico, to take advantage of tax breaks. Vince Gilligan has remarked in interviews that he considers Albuquerque itself to be a character within *Breaking Bad*. Albuquerque also serves as the locale for the *Breaking Bad* prequel, *Better Call Saul*.

Other notable television shows and movies shot in and around Albuquerque include *Walker, Texas Ranger* (1993–2001), *Earth 2* (1994–95), *Wildfire* (2005–08), *Crash* (2008–09), *Terminator: The Sarah Connor Chronicles* (2008–10), *In Plain Sight* (2008–12), *Dig* (2013), *Manhattan* (2014–15), *Gunslingers* (2014–16), *The Grapes of Wrath* (1940), *Ace in the Hole* (1951), *Butch Cassidy and the Sundance Kid* (1969), *Two-Lane Blacktop* (1971), *The Man Who Fell to Earth* (1976), *Silkwood* (1983), *No Country for Old Men* (2007), and *The Avengers* (2012), among many others.

2

Unknown Entities

The X-Files Helps Give Birth to the Series

> I wouldn't be in TV if it wasn't for Chris Carter and I wouldn't have been able to do *Breaking Bad* if not for what I learned on *The X-Files*.
>
> —*Vince Gilligan*

Breaking Bad creator Vince Gilligan worked for seven years as a writer and producer on *The X-Files* and later described the "television education" he got on the show as "priceless." Not only did Gilligan learn innovative storytelling and filming techniques from the cult sci-fi drama that would help him with *Breaking Bad*, but he also remembered the amazing performance of an actor portraying a multidimensional villain in a single episode of *The X-Files*—Bryan Cranston.

Origins of *The X-Files*

Created by Chris Carter, *The X-Files* aired on Fox for nine seasons between 1993 and 2002, featured 202 episodes, and became both a commercial and critical hit for the network. The longest-running science fiction series in U.S. television history, *The X-Files* also spawned two feature-length films: *The X-Files: Fight the Future* (1998) and *The X-Files: I Want to Believe* (2008). A tenth season of *The X-Files* consisting of six episodes was aired in 2016, followed by an eleventh season of ten episodes for the 2017–18 season.

 The X-Files focuses on two FBI special agents—Fox Mulder (David Duchovny) and Dana Scully (Gillian Anderson)—who investigate unsolved cases involving paranormal and extraterrestrial phenomena (with Mulder a true believer, while Scully is far more skeptical). *The X-Files* also featured

Mitch Pileggi as Special Agent Walter S. Skinner, Robert Patrick as Special Agent John Doggett, and Annabeth Gish as Special Agent Monica Reyes. In addition, *The X-Files* boasted a variety of eccentric recurring characters such as the Cigarette Smoking Man (William B. Davis), Scully and Mulder's main antagonist; as well as the Lone Gunmen (John Fitzgerald Byers, Melvin Frohike, and Richard Langly), Marita Covarrubias, Deep Throat, First Elder, Well-Manicured Man, Mr. X, and others. The show's tagline declared: "The Truth is Out There." Although *The X-Files* featured an ongoing story arc, approximately two-thirds of episodes were of the "Monster of the Week" variety with such memorable characters as the Flukeman, Great Mutato, Leonard Betts, Phyllis H. Paddock, Beggar Man, Robert Patrick Modell, Eve 9 and 10, Luther Lee Boggs, Peacock Family, and Leonard. During its first season, *The X-Files* got off to an extraordinarily slow start in a Friday night time slot and failed to crack the top one hundred shows in the ratings. However, by its second season, *The X-Files* had become a bona fide cult favorite.

Carter acknowledged such influences in the development of the series as *Alfred Hitchcock Presents* (1962–65), *The Twilight Zone* (1959–64), *Night*

Chris Carter, creator of *The X-Files*, has acknowledged such influences in the development of the series as *Alfred Hitchcock Presents*, *The Twilight Zone*, *Night Gallery*, *Tales from the Darkside*, and *Kolchak: The Night Stalker*.   *Gage Skidmore/Wikimedia Commons*

Gallery (1969–73), *Tales from the Darkside* (1983–88), and especially the lesser-known *Kolchak: The Night Stalker* (1974–75), which starred Darren McGavin (*A Christmas Story*) as a Chicago newspaper reporter who investigated mysterious crimes that often involved supernatural elements. *Kolchak: The Night Stalker* was created by Jeff Rice from his unpublished novel *The Kolchak Papers* and preceded by two television movies: *The Night Stalker* (1972) and *The Night Strangler* (1973). *The X-Files* itself influenced such immensely popular shows as *Lost, Fringe, Buffy the Vampire Slayer,* and *Breaking Bad,* among others. According to David Bianculli in *The Platinum Age of Television,* "Asked what he learned the most from his *X-Files* stint, Gilligan distilled it down to two major things: thinking cinematically and not revealing too much through dialogue."

The opening teasers (aka "cold opens") in *Breaking Bad* were influenced by *The X-Files,* according to Gilligan. Both series utilized a standard structure that featured the teaser followed by four acts. In a March 10, 2016, interview with *Creative Screenwriting,* Gilligan remarked,

> Chris Carter was—and is—a very visual storyteller. It was always important to him that each episode had a visual element that was very memorable and would stick in the heads of the viewers. So we were always looking for that opening teaser to really grab the viewers and make them want to keep watching . . . I learned from the best on that show and I took all these great lessons about how to break episodes and what format in which to write them, and the act breaks . . . all of that stuff. I took lock, stock and barrel from *The X-Files* when I started *Breaking Bad.*

Vince Gilligan's Role

The X-Files served as an excellent training ground for Gilligan that began when he submitted a script for the show that was turned into the twenty-third episode of the second season called "Soft Light," which first aired on May 5, 1995. "Soft Light" features Tony Shalhoub (best known for his portrayal of police detective Adrian Monk in the USA TV series *Monk*) as Dr. Chester Ray Banton, who is literally afraid of his own shadow. Gilligan went on to write twenty-nine more episodes of *The X-Files,* as well as serving as executive producer of forty-four episodes, co-executive producer of forty episodes, co-producer of twenty-four episodes, and supervising producer of twenty episodes. In addition, Gilligan served as co-creator and executive producer of the short-lived spin-off series of *The X-Files* called *The Lone Gunmen* (2001).

Bryan Cranston Episode

Bryan Cranston appeared in "Drive," the second episode of the sixth season of *The X-Files*, which was written by Gilligan and aired on November 15, 1998. A stand-alone "monster of the week" episode, "Drive" features Cranston as Patrick Crump, a totally abrasive racist loser with a constant piercing headache who kidnaps Mulder after a high-speed car chase and forces him to drive west. It turns out Crump's head will explode if the car stops (not kidding!). Regarding the casting of Cranston in a March 13, 2009, *New York* magazine article, Gilligan stated, "We needed a guy who could be scary and kind of loathsome but at the same time had a deep, resounding humanity." Gilligan later remarked that the episode served as a kind of homage to the 1994 film *Speed*, which starred Keanu Reeves, Sandra Bullock, and Dennis Hopper. During *Breaking Bad* casting, Gilligan reportedly screened the "Drive" episode for AMC executives who were only familiar with Cranston's work from the sitcom *Malcolm in the Middle*.

Actors in Both Series

Several actors have had the privilege of appearing in both *The X-Files* and *Breaking Bad*. For example, at the outset of his career, Aaron "Jesse" Paul appeared as David "Sky Commander Winky" Winkie in the 2001 episode (ninth season) of *The X-Files*, "Lord of the Flies," which was written by Thomas Schnauz, who went on to write, direct, and co-produce several *Breaking Bad* episodes such as "One Minute," "Shotgun," and "Say My Name." Dean "Hank" Norris starred as Marshal Tapia in "F. Emasculata," the twenty-second episode of the second season of *The X-Files*. Raymond

"Tuco" Cruz portrayed Eladio Buente, an illegal immigrant in "El Mundo Gira" (who may or may not be legendary monster El Chupacabra) in the eleventh episode of the fourth season of *The X-Files*. In *Breaking Bad* episode "Fifty-One," a photo of Tuco Salamanca is labeled as "Eladio Buente" in tribute to his stint on *The X-Files*.

Michael Shamus (as Black-Haired Man, cohort of the Cigarette Smoking Man), who appeared in *Breaking Bad* as Hank's DEA boss, ASAC George Merkert, appeared in two episodes of *The X-Files*—"The End" and "En Ami"—as well as the first *X-Files* film, *Fight the Future*. Adam Godley (Elliott Schwartz) appeared as Father Ybarra in the second *X-Files* movie, *I Want to Believe*. Michael "Uncle Jack" Bowen appeared as Dwight Cooper in the *X-Files* episode "Surekill." Danny Trejo (Tortuga) appeared as creepy murderer Cesar Ocampo in *The X-Files* episode "Redrum." Dale Dickey, who portrayed Spooge's old lady in *Breaking Bad* ("Breakage" and "Peekaboo"), actually appeared in *The X-Files* episode "Existence" as a game warden. Dan Desmond (Mr. Gardiner, Mr. and Mrs. Pinkman's attorney in "Down" and "Caballo Sin Nombre") appeared as salvage yard owner Harry Odell in *The X-Files* episode "Salvage." Javier Grajeda (Juan

The X-Files spawned two feature-length films: *The X-Files: Fight the Future* (1998) and *The X-Files: I Want to Believe* (2008).

Bolsa in "IFT," "I See You," and "Hermanos") appeared as Desk Sergeant in *The X-Files* episode "Tithonus." Jim Beaver (Lawson the arms dealer in "Live Free or Die" and "Thirty-Eight Snub") appeared as a doctor in *The X-Files* episode "Field Trip."

In addition, Jamie McShane (Train Conductor in "Dead Freight") appeared as an injured soldier in *The X-Files* episode "Providence." Michael Bryan French (Doctor in "I See You") appeared in *The X-Files* episode "Deep Throat." Ralph Alderman (Michael Kilbourne in "Open House") appeared as a motel manager in *The X-Files* episodes "Mind's Eye" and "The Pine Bluff Variant." John Koyama (Emilio Koyama in "Pilot" and "Cat's in the Bag") appeared as a stunt performer on *The X-Files*. Toby Holguin served as a stunt performer on both shows. *Better Call Saul's* Michael "Chuck" McKean appeared in four episodes of *The X-Files* as sleazy government agent Morris Fletcher.

In addition, director, writer, and producer John Shiban worked with Gilligan on *The X-Files* (seasons three to nine), as well as *The Lone Gunmen* and *Breaking Bad* (seasons two to four). Director and producer Michelle MacLaren first worked with Gilligan on *The X-Files* (2000–02) and later directed episodes of *Breaking Bad* and *Better Call Saul*, as well as *Game of Thrones*.

References to *The X-Files* in *Breaking Bad*

A fictional brand often used in movies and TV shows, Morley's served as the cigarette of choice for the Cigarette Smoking Man in *The X-Files*. In the "Pilot" episode of *Breaking Bad*, Emilio (John Koyama) is seen smoking a Morley cigarette and flicking it out of the RV window. In addition, Episode Four of Season One of *Breaking Bad* is titled "Cancer Man" in tribute to *The X-Files* villain. The fictional van rental company, Lariat, in *The X-Files* appears in the "To'hajiilee" episode of *Breaking Bad* as the van used to transport Walt's money barrels. The Cradock Marine Bank from *X-Files* episodes "Monday," "The Amazing Maleeni," and "Surekill" shows up in *Breaking Bad* ("Say My Name") as the bank that lawyer Dan Wachsberger (Chris Freihofer) uses to deposit hush money to Gus Fring's former associates.

In addition, "The Erlenmeyer Flask" is the title of an episode of *The X-Files* and gets several mentions in the *Breaking Bad* "Pilot" episode. Heisenberg is mentioned in Season Seven, Episode Nineteen of *The X-Files*, "Hollywood A.D." The name "Ehrmantraut" was used for a minor character in *The X-Files* in the episode "Tithonus," which was scripted by Vince Gilligan. Last but not least, the time on Gale Boetticher's potato clock reads 10:13 at the time of his death in the *Breaking Bad* episode "Box Cutter," a number that is used frequently in *The X-Files* in reference to Fox Mulder's birthday and also as a tribute to creator Chris Carter's birthday, October 13, 1956.

3

It Doesn't Compute

How *Breaking Bad* Got its Name

> Man, some straight like you, giant stick up his ass, all of a sudden at age what, sixty, he's just gonna break bad?
>
> —*Jesse Pinkman to Walter White*

According to *Breaking Bad* creator Vince Gilligan, the actual term "breaking bad" has its origins in the American South and means "to raise hell." As an example, Gilligan suggested, "I was out the other night at the bar . . . and I really broke bad." According to the top definition in the *Urban Dictionary*, to **break bad** means "to reject social norms for one's own gain or amusement. To give up on the typical moral and social norm and go one's own path, regardless of the legality or ethics." *The New Partridge Dictionary of Slang and Unconventional English* defines breaking bad as "to act in a threatening, menacing manner." In addition, the term is also defined in Wiktionary as "to turn toward immorality or crime."

In his 2016 autobiography, *A Life in Parts*, Bryan Cranston remarked, "I'm not sure I knew what the title meant then, but the script was oh-my-God superb, the best hour-long drama I'd ever read." In a 2013 Reddit AMA (Ask Me Anything), Cranston commented that he felt that "Walt broke bad in the very first episode. It was very subtle but he did because that's when he decided to become someone that he's not in order to gain financially. He made the Faustian deal at that point and everything else was a slippery slope."

Below is a sample of over a century of references related to the concept of breaking bad from a variety of diverse sources:

Saturday Evening Post (1905)

One of the earliest (if not the earliest) printed reference to "**broke bad**" can be found in a 1905 *Saturday Evening Post* article on baseball referenced at wordorigins.org: "He knows things are liable to '**break wrong**' for him some time and that he will be the object of criticism [. . .] Things broke bad, didn't they?"

The Barrier (1908) Rex Beach

Now almost totally forgotten, Rex Ellingwood Beach (1877–1949) wrote immensely popular adventure novels, many of which took place in Alaska, during the turn of the nineteenth century that were heavily influenced by Jack London, the legendary author of classic adventure novels such as *Call of the Wild* (1903), *The Sea-Wolf* (1904), and *White Fang* (1906). In *The Barrier*, Beach writes, "A woman came out from the East—Vermont, it was—and school-teaching was her line of business, only she hadn't been raised to it, and this was her first clatter at the game; but things had **broke bad** for her people, and ended in her pulling stakes and coming West all alone."

In his 1988 book *A Warm Past: Travels in Alaska History*, Stephen Haycox describes many of Beach's works as "mercifully forgotten today." In addition to his literary pursuits, Beach also competed on the water polo team that captured a silver medal in the 1904 Summer Olympics in St. Louis, Missouri. Two years after his wife Edith passed way, Beach died of a self-inflicted gunshot wound at the age of seventy-one on December 7, 1949, at his home in Sebring, Florida.

Crooked Trails and Straight (1913) William MacLeod Raine

In his 1913 Western novel *Crooked Trails and Straight*, William MacLeod Raine (1871–1954) writes, "Half the bad men are only coltish cowpunchers gone wrong through rotten whiskey and luck **breaking bad** for them." Raine was a prolific author of adventure stories about the Old West who also ghostwrote with legendary lawman Billy Breakenridge the 1928 book *Helldorado: Bringing Law to the Mesquite*, which provided a revisionist slant on the famous 1881 "Gunfight at O.K. Corral." In 1959, Raine was posthumously inducted into the Hall of Great Westerners of the National Cowboy and Western Heritage Museum in Oklahoma City, Oklahoma.

"The Hold-Out" (1917) Ring Lardner, published in *Ring Around the Bases: The Complete Baseball Stories of Ring Lardner* (2003) Matthew Joseph Bruccoli, editor

Several early baseball stories contain variations on "breaking bad" verbiage, including sports columnist and best-selling author Ring Lardner's short story "The Hold-Out," which first appeared in the *Saturday Evening Post* (March 24, 1917): "Hagedorn began to whine. 'Mr. Edwards,' he says, 'you got me entirely wrong. I wouldn't lay down on nobody. I've give you my best every minute, and if I haven't it was because things **broke bad** for me.'" Lardner (real name: Ringgold Wilmer Lardner) was apparently detailing behind-the-scenes salary negotiations long before the days of free agency.

Lardner's bibliography includes *You Know Me Al* (1916), *Champion* (1916), *Gullible's Travels* (1917), *Treat 'Em Rough* (1918), *The Real Dope* (1919), and *The Big Town* (1921), among others. His writings influenced a young Ernest Hemingway, and he was a good friend of F. Scott Fitzgerald. Lardner (1885–1933) was posthumously inducted into the Chicago Literary Hall of Fame in 2016. His son, Ring Lardner Jr., was a screenwriter blacklisted as a member of the so-called "Hollywood Ten" who refused to answer questions posed by the House Un-American Activities Committee. Lardner Jr. won screenwriting Oscars for both *Woman of the Year* (1942) and *M*A*S*H* (1970).

"Topics in Wall Street," *The New York Times* (May 18, 1919)

In an early overview of Wall Street that appeared in *The New York Times*, the writer uses **break bad** to describe volatile stock market activity: "the average speculator will not take a position in the highly speculative industrials for over Sunday, but because he can't stay out of the market altogether, gets into the rails at the end of the week in hope of making a successful turn and with confidence that if things '**break bad**' over Sunday rails will feel the shock less than the industrials."

Babe Ruth's Own Book of Baseball (1928) George Herman "Babe" Ruth

A year after hitting a career-high sixty home runs for the New York Yankees (a record that would stand for thirty-seven years until broken by fellow Yankee Roger Maris in 1961), George Herman "Babe" Ruth Jr. (1895–1948) made a "breaking bad" reference in his 1928 memoir, *Babe Ruth's Own Book of Baseball*: "What a friend he was, as I found out during 1924 and 1925 when things were **breaking bad** and I needed friends as I never had needed them before." Note that there is some controversy as to how much (if any) of the book Ruth actually wrote—with most baseball historians believing it was actually ghostwritten by Ford Frick, a sportswriter who later served as the Commissioner of Major League Baseball from 1951 to 1965.

Pylon (1935) William Faulkner

Known for his towering works such as *The Sound and the Fury* (1929), *As I Lay Dying* (1930), *Light in August* (1932), *Absalom, Absalom!* (1936), and others, literary giant William Faulkner received the Nobel Prize in Literature in 1948 "for his powerful and artistically unique contribution to the American novel." In one of Faulkner's lesser-known novels, *Pylon* (1935), he wrote a variation on the "breaking bad" theme: "If things **break**

right today, tonight I'll get you a bottle." An offbeat tale, *Pylon* concerns a group of barnstormers (stunt pilots performing tricks) in New Valois, a fictional version of New Orleans. In the May 30, 2015, *Daily Beast* article "William Faulkner's Tragic Air Circus," Nathaniel Rich remarked that *Pylon* "is drenched in an alcoholic haze that extends beyond the story to the characterization and the long, murky descriptive passages . . . As is often the case with Faulkner, it's not always exactly clear what is going on. But we can be sure it's depraved, gloomy, and at least moderately deranged." The novel served as the basis for a nearly forgotten 1957 film *The Tarnished Angels*, which was directed by Douglas Sirk (*Magnificent Obsession*) and starred Rock Hudson, Dorothy Malone, and Robert Stack. *Variety* referred to *The Tarnished Angels* as "a stumbling entry. Characters are mostly colorless, given static reading in drawn-out situations, and story line is lacking in punch."

Manchild in the Promised Land (1965) Claude Brown

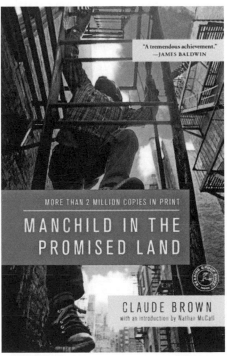

A classic of American literature, *Manchild in the Promised Land* is a brutal and uncompromising auto-biographical novel of Claude Brown's youth as an African American trying to survive the harsh, unforgiving streets of Harlem amid poverty and violence during the 1940s and 1950s. At one point, Brown (1937–2002) writes, "Down home, when they went to town, all the niggers would just **break bad**, so it seemed." *Manchild in the Promised Land* has sold more than four million copies and been translated into four-teen languages even though it has peri-odically appeared on banned book lists for "offensive language and violence."

Claude Brown's critically acclaimed 1965 novel *Manchild in the Promised Land* features one of the first references to "breaking bad" in American literature.

In a 1988 article for *The Los Angeles Times*, Brown writes, "In the New York City teenage gang fights of the 1940's and 50's we used homemade guns, zip guns and knives . . . Now America's inner cities have become the spawning grounds for adolescents who bear increasingly appalling resemblances to rabid, homicidal maniacs."

The Creation of Dangerous Violent Criminals (1992) Lonnie H. Athens

In his 1992 book *The Creation of Dangerous Violent Criminals*, criminologist Lonnie H. Athens, currently a professor of criminal justice at Seton Hall University, writes, "The subject has what is described in common parlance as '**broken bad**' and, as a result, has become a dangerous menace to others." A synopsis of the work states, "Lonnie Athens examines a problem that has long baffled experts and lay people alike: How does a person become a dangerous violent criminal? He explains how those who commit brutal crimes begin as relatively benign individuals who undergo lengthy, at times tortuous, development leading them to malevolence." According to Athens, "the process of violentization" encompasses four stages: "brutalization," "belligerency," "violent performance," and "virulency."

The New York Times (September 30, 1992)

In the article "Conversations/Isaac Fulwood Jr.: Washington's Departing Police Chief Laments the Sleep of Murderers," Fullwood remarks, "I don't want to make eye contact with this sucker because he may **break bad** on me." He was referring to citizens trying to stay safe on the mean streets of Washington, D.C., and particularly the random violence that could take place if motorists happen to simply look at someone the wrong way while driving.

Drylongso: A Self-Portrait of Black America (1993)— John Langston Gwaltney

In anthropologist, folklorist, and humanist John Gwaltney's critically acclaimed work, the oral history *Drylongso: A Self-Portrait of Black America*, a rural Missouri resident tells the author that "if a white man was to come over here and ask me anything, I wouldn't **break bad** with him." Drylongso is an old African American term that means "just the same old thing" or "ordinary." Gwaltney (1928–98), who lost his eyesight soon after birth, received his PhD in anthropology in 1967 from Columbia University, where he studied under legendary anthropologist Margaret Mead, who referred to him as "a most remarkable man . . . [who] manages his life and work with extraordinary skill and bravery."

Hoop Dreams (1994)

A critically acclaimed documentary directed by Steve James, *Hoop Dreams* follows the trials and tribulations of two African American high school basketball players—Arthur Agee and William Gates—in inner-city Chicago who both have dreams of getting college scholarships as stepping-stones to an NBA career. *Hoop Dreams* premiered at the 1994 Sundance Film Festival, where it won the Audience Award for Best Documentary. At about the fifty-nine-minute mark in the documentary, Arthur Agee's father, Bo, relates how he is trying to put his past troubles behind him: "And then Arthur, he was watching me. What move would I make now? Am I just being like this since I just come back . . . or am I gonna **break bad** again?" Tragically, Bo Agee, who managed to kick a drug habit and become an ordained minister, was shot to death in an alley in 2004 at the age of fifty-two—the apparent victim of a botched robbery attempt. Neither Agee nor Gates achieved their dream of making it to the NBA.

A Clash of Kings (1999) George R. R. Martin

In *A Clash of Kings*, the second novel of his epic fantasy series *A Song of Ice and Fire*, George R. R. Martin uses "**break bad**" in the context of abandoning a battlefield: "No man likes to look craven in the sight of his fellows, so they'll fight brave enough at the start, when it's all warhorns and blowing banners. But if the battle looks to be going sour they'll break, and they'll **break bad**. The first man to throw down his spear and run will have a thousand more trodding on his heels." In 2011, *A Song of Ice and*

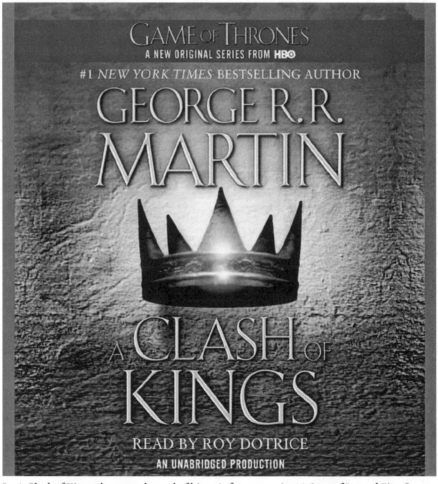

In *A Clash of Kings*, the second novel of his epic fantasy series, *A Song of Ice and Fire*, George R. R. Martin uses "break bad" in the context of abandoning a battlefield.

Fire was adapted into the award-winning HBO series *Game of Thrones*, and Martin himself would later become a *Breaking Bad* fan, calling it an "amazing series." In a September 16, 2013, blog entry, Martin remarked, "This is the final season of BREAKING BAD. I think GAME OF THRONES may have a shot at upsetting BB for this year's Emmy (only a shot, though, I think they are the clear favorite), which pits us against their previous season . . . but there's no way in hell that anyone is going to defeat BREAKING BAD next year, when their last season is the one in contention."

Inside Mrs. B's Classroom (2003) Leslie Baldacci

Subtitled "Courage, Hope, and Learning on Chicago's South Side," *Inside Mrs. B's Classroom* is a spellbinding memoir that documents the journey of former journalist Leslie Baldacci as she leaves the newsroom in 1999 after twenty-four years as a reporter and enters the classroom as a teacher in one of Chicago's toughest South Side neighborhoods. At one point, Baldacci remarks, "I swore I would never cry in front of my students, no matter how bad it got, just as I've never cried in front of a boss when things **broke bad**." She also compares her classroom to "just one deck chair on the *Titanic*." However, Baldacci perseveres and shows how a dedicated individual can make a difference even in the worst of circumstances.

The Unknown Darkness: Profiling the Predators Among Us (2004) Gregg O. McCrary

A twenty-five-year veteran of the FBI, McCrary profiles ten of his most compelling criminal investigations in his 2004 book, *The Unknown Darkness*. In one profile, McCrary, one of the most experienced serial killer profilers in the world, remarks, "Or could a monk have been unwittingly used by narcoterrorists to move drugs into the country and it somehow **broke bad**?"

The Glad River (2005) Will D. Campbell

A widely recognized preacher, writer, speaker and civil rights leader, Will D. Campbell (1924–2013) was awarded the National Humanities Medal in 2000. In his first novel, *The Glad River*, "the tale of three friends whose community survives war, persecution, and death," Campbell writes, "But somehow he **broke bad** when he was just a yearling boy, started running around at night with a bad crowd, drinking beer and wine, and fighting and getting in all kinds of trouble and wouldn't go to school."

The Racketeer (2012) John Grisham

Best-selling novelist John Grisham's twenty-seventh novel, *The Racketeer*, a legal thriller that revolves around the murder of a federal judge, features a "breaking bad" reference: "My nephew was **breaking bad**, getting deeper into the crack trade...."

Sports Talk: How it Has Penetrated Our Daily Language (2017) Colin McNairn

In his definitive guide to how many of our most common expressions are derived from the world of sports, Colin McNairn writes, "The expression 'get a [good] break' and the terms 'lucky break' and '**bad break**' may also come from pool, in particular from the opening shot in the game."

4

Say My Name

Meet the Principal *Breaking Bad* Cast and Characters

> I probably started with Walter White and fanned outward from him. I probably thought about who would a guy like that would be married to, so most likely Skyler was the second character I created.
>
> —*Vince Gilligan*

Can you imagine well-known Hollywood icons like Matthew Broderick or John Cusack in the role of Walter White? How about Colin Hanks as Jesse Pinkman? As talented as the above actors are, the total vibe of *Breaking Bad* as we know it would have been forever changed with these casting choices. Fortunately, the perfect cast came together for *Breaking Bad*.

In the case of Walter White, *Breaking Bad* creator Vince Gilligan stuck to his guns and remained committed to Bryan Cranston, who managed to deliver just the right amount of desperation, pathos, anger, and dark humor to excel in the role. Aaron Paul's character, Jesse Pinkman, was initially supposed to simply introduce Walt to the meth trade and then be killed off by the end of Season One, but the chemistry between the two actors led to Paul getting a permanent and most important role on the series. Anna Gunn's performance as Skyler White proved so effective that a negative and heavily misogynistic backlash formed on social media—how dare she try to prevent Walt from achieving his destiny as a drug kingpin? The rest of the major characters were also perfectly cast, leading to the development of arguably the greatest drama series in television history.

Walter White (Bryan Cranston)

A mild-mannered, underachieving high school chemistry teacher, Walter Hartwell White turns to cooking meth to pay his exorbitant medical expenses and support his family after being diagnosed with Stage IIIA lung cancer, and gradually evolves into the mysterious drug kingpin known only as Heisenberg. Walt's amazing (and often disturbing) transformation was described as "Mr. Chips to Scarface," according to series creator Vince Gilligan, who remarked in *Breaking Bad: The Official Book*, "Walter White is a brilliant man and an accomplished liar who lies best to himself." Indeed, Walt constantly rationalizes even his most abhorrent actions by reminding himself that he's doing it all for the good of his family. Cranston stated in his eminently readable 2016 autobiography, *A Life in Parts*, that he decided to totally immerse himself into the role of Walter White: "I dressed badly. I gained weight. Every aspect of Walt was an expression of the fact that he'd given up. The chinos, the Members Only jacket, the Wallabees, the pathetic hair and mustache. Tighty-whities fit into all that . . . He's missed so many opportunities in life . . . You can see that in every part of him . . . He blends into the background. Invisible. To society. To himself."

Bryan Lee Cranston was born on March 7, 1956, in Hollywood, California, to Audrey Peggy Sell, a radio actress, and Joe Cranston, an aspiring actor and former amateur boxer who walked out on the family when Bryan was just eleven years old. Cranston received his associate degree in police science from Los Angeles Valley College in 1976. Throughout the 1980s, Cranston could often be seen in bit roles in television shows such as *CHiPs*, *Airwolf*, *Hill Street Blues*, and *Baywatch*. He even supplied the voice of the villains Snizard and Twin Man during the first season of *Mighty Morphin Power Rangers* in 1993 (the last name of the first Blue Ranger, Billy Cranston, is named in his honor).

Seinfeld fans will no doubt remember Cranston as slightly pompous dentist Tim Whatley in five classic episodes of *Seinfeld*: "The Mom and Pop Store" (1994), "The Label Maker" (1995), "The Jimmy" (1995), "The Yada Yada" (1997), and "The Strike" (1997). In addition, Cranston portrayed astronaut Buzz Aldrin in HBO's 1998 miniseries *From the Earth to the Moon*. He also appeared (mostly in bit roles) in a variety of critically

Breaking Bad won the Peabody Award in 2008 and again in 2013. In addition, with four wins for *Breaking Bad*, Bryan Cranston is tied with Dennis Franz (*NYPD Blue*) for the most Emmy Awards in the "Outstanding Actor in a Drama Series" category.

Peabody Awards/Wikimedia Commons

acclaimed films such as *Saving Private Ryan* (1998), *Little Miss Sunshine* (2006), and *Argo* (2012), as well as *Drive* (2011) and *Godzilla* (2014). Cranston became well known for starring as goofy dad Hal Wilkerson in 151 episodes of the hit Fox sitcom *Malcolm in the Middle* between 2000 and 2006. During his stint as Hal, Cranston showed his adeptness at physical comedy and bold choices such as appeared in tighty-whities for the cause. For his stellar work as Walter White in *Breaking Bad*, Cranston won the Primetime Emmy Award for Outstanding Lead Actor in a Drama Series four times (2008–10, 2014).

Post-*Breaking Bad*, Cranston captured a Tony Award for Best Actor in a Play in 2014 for his critically acclaimed portrayal of President Lyndon Johnson in the Broadway play *All the Way* (he reprised the role in an HBO adaptation of the same name in 2016). He was also nominated for a Best Actor Oscar for his portrayal of blacklisted screenwriter Dalton Trumbo in *Trumbo* (2015). In a November 2017 *Esquire* interview, Cranston remarked, "In many ways, I think I have used my career as a therapy session of life . . . It has been, I think, tremendously beneficial for me to get into roles that are sometimes disturbing, and to be able to purge my darker side into the character and have a cathartic release."

Bryan Cranston Trivia

- Cranston's father, Joe, co-wrote the scripts for two sleazy and forgettable low-budget horror films: *The Crawling Hand* (1963) and *The Corpse Grinders* (1971). *The Crawling Hand* was billed as a "Jolting Space Shocker," while *The Corpse Grinders* was filmed in "Blood-Curdling Color!"
- Cranston appeared as car thief named Billy Joe in a 1982 episode of *CHiPs* titled "Return to Death's Door."
- In 1986, Cranston met his future wife, actress Robin Dearden, on the set of *Airwolf*, which starred Jan-Michael Vincent and Ernest Borgnine. The couple has one daughter, Taylor Dearden.
- He has "BrBa" (for *Breaking Bad*) tattooed on his ring finger.
- Cranston is best friends with actor John O'Hurley (best known as J. Peterman from *Seinfeld*) and served as the best man at both of O'Hurley's weddings.

- In the 1970s, Cranston and his brothers spent two years traveling via motorcycles around the United States.
- With four wins for *Breaking Bad*, Cranston is tied with Dennis Franz (*NYPD Blue*) for the most Emmy Awards in the Outstanding Actor in a Drama Series category.
- Cranston appeared in three movies that were nominated for the Best Picture Oscar: *Saving Private Ryan* (1998), *Little Miss Sunshine* (2006), and *Argo* (2012).
- He has named his favorite movie as *On the Waterfront* (1954), which starred Marlon Brando, Eva Marie Saint, and Rod Steiger, and his acting heroes include Steiger, Jack Lemmon, Dick Van Dyke, and Spencer Tracy.
- Just like Walter White, Cranston admitted during a Reddit AMA that he is indeed a Steely Dan fan! Incidentally, Steely Dan, which was founded by Donald Fagen and Walter Becker, took its name from a steam-powered dildo in William S. Burroughs's 1959 cult novel *Naked Lunch*.
- In 2013, Cranston selected two of his favorite *Breaking Bad* episodes to be screened during a special event for the Film Society of Lincoln Center in New York City: "Phoenix" (2.12) and "Fly" (3.10).

Jesse Pinkman (Aaron Paul)

One of Walter White's former students, Jesse Pinkman becomes his partner in crime as he attempts to enter the meth business. In a Q&A that appeared on amc.com, Aaron Paul described Jesse as "a lost soul—I don't think he's a bad kid, he just got mixed in the wrong crowd." Somewhat improbably, Jesse evolves from punk kid and low-level drug dealer to become the moral center of the entire series.

Born Aaron Paul Sturtevant on August 27, 1979, in Emmett, Idaho (population: 6,557), Paul made his way to Hollywood in the 1990s and found work as an usher at the Universal Studios Movie Theatre. In one of his earliest acting roles, Paul appeared as Chad on a single episode of *Beverly Hills, 90210* in 1999, followed by a stint as Frat Boy #2 in an episode of *Melrose Place* the following year. Interestingly, Paul auditioned for the role of Francis, the oldest son in *Malcolm in the Middle*, which starred his future costar Bryan Cranston (Christopher Kennedy Masterson eventually landed the role). Paul's early filmography includes *K-PAX* (2001)

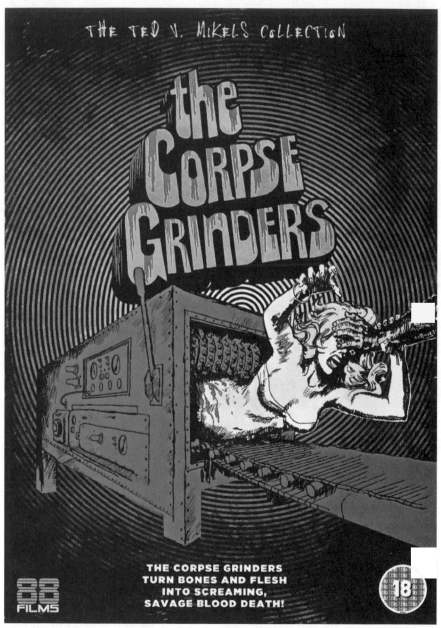

Bryan Cranston's father, Joe, cowrote the script for the low-budget horror film, *The Corpse Grinders* (1971), which was filmed in "BloodCurdling Color!"

and *Mission: Impossible III* (2006). He also appeared in the *Ghost Whisperer* episode "Fury" in 2006 with future *Breaking Bad* costar Giancarlo Esposito (Gus Fring). For *Breaking Bad*, Paul captured three Emmy Awards for Outstanding Supporting Actor in a Drama Series (2010, 2012, and 2014). Post-*Breaking Bad*, Paul has appeared in such films as *Need for Speed* (2014), *A Long Way Down* (2014), *Hellion* (2014), *Exodus: Gods and Kings* (2014), *Eye in the Sky* (2015), *Fathers and Daughters* (2015), *Triple 9* (2016), *Central Intelligence* (2016), *The 9th Life of Louis Drax* (2016), and *Come and Find Me* (2016). Paul and his wife, actress and director Lauren Parsekian, have a daughter.

Aaron Paul Trivia

- Paul appeared as a contestant on *The Price is Right* in 2000, during which he lost by overbidding on the showcase by $132. During a 2017 appearance on *The Late Late Show with James Corden*, Paul remarked, "When I did [*The Price is Right*], I was struggling, had no money and it was really a source of possible income. When I lost that damn car, I was so depressed for so long."
- In an August 13, 2013, Reddit AMA, Paul revealed that he has never taken acting lessons: "I always thought, 'Hey, pretend like you're being someone else and that's all there is to it.'"
- A fan of nu metal band Korn, Paul appeared in the band's 2002 music video for "Thoughtless."
- Paul claims that the 1985 adventure comedy *The Goonies*, which was directed by Richard Donner (*Lethal Weapon*), inspired him to become an actor.
- He has "No Half Measures" tattooed on his arm in reference to Mike's comment to Walt in Episode 3.12, "Half Measures."
- Paul's original audition tape for the role of Jesse Pinkman can be found on YouTube.
- During a humorous interview on *Jimmy Kimmel Live!*, Paul claimed that he probably holds the Guinness World Record for getting cursed out in public: "I think I've been called 'bitch' more than anyone on the planet . . . I'm proud of that."

Skyler White (Anna Gunn)

Walt's long-suffering wife, Skyler, is about ten years younger than her husband, an aspiring writer who is pregnant with the couple's second child at the outset of the series. According to Vince Gilligan in *Breaking Bad: The Official Book*, "Skyler is a pragmatist who will do pretty much anything to keep her family together." Gunn has referred to the character she portrayed as "grounded, tough, smart, and driven." Frustrated by Walt's secrecy, Skyler retaliates by embarking on a brief fling with her sleazy boss, Ted Beneke (Christopher Cousins). Initially disgusted after finding out about Walt's meth operation, Skyler eventually persuades him to buy a car wash to help him launder the massive amounts of incoming drug money. Skyler's independence and ability to call out her husband on his various misdeeds earned her an inexplicable amount of hatred from a disturbing segment of *Breaking Bad* fans, and an "I Hate Skyler White" Facebook page generated tens of thousands of "likes."

Born on August 11, 1968, Gunn actually grew up in Santa Fe, New Mexico, and studied drama at Northwestern University. She portrayed Jean Ward in the ABC drama series *The Practice* and Martha Bullock in the HBO series *Deadwood*. Gunn also has appeared in episodes of *Seinfeld* (see Chapter 24), *Six Feet Under*, *ER*, *Boston Legal*, and *Law & Order*. Her film credits include *Nobody's Baby* (2001), *Enemy of the State* (1998), *Without Evidence* (1995), *Red State* (2011), *Little Red Wagon* (2012), and *Sassy Pants* (2012), for which she received a nomination for Best Supporting Actress at the 2012 Milan Film Festival.

Anna Gunn Trivia

- Gunn portrayed a junkie named Kimmy on an episode of *NYPD Blue* titled "Dead and Gone" in 1994.
- She played one of Jerry's many ill-fated girlfriends, Amy, in the 1993 *Seinfeld* episode "The Glasses."

Walter White Jr. (RJ Mitte)

Walt and Skyler's son, Walt Jr. is a typical good-natured, and slightly rebellious, teenager who just happens to have cerebral palsy. Early in the series, Walter Jr. asserts his independence by demanding to be called "Flynn," echoing the legendary movie swashbuckler and lothario Errol Flynn (1909–59), who starred in such classics as *Captain Blood* (1935), *The Charge of the Light Brigade* (1936), *The Adventures of Robin Hood* (1938), and *They Died with Their Boots On* (1941). In addition to craving big breakfasts, Walter Jr. idolizes his Uncle Hank and remains totally oblivious to his father's criminal activities until informed very late in the series. In fact, besides getting caught trying to buy a six-pack beer, Walt Jr. remains a consistently decent character throughout the entire series, unlike just about everyone else in the cast. He even creates a cheesy but heartfelt personal website, SaveWalterWhite.com, as a way to raise money for his father's medical expenses (which Walt and Saul end up corrupting by turning it into just another money laundering opportunity). According to Vince Gilligan in a September 25, 2013, *Rolling Stone* interview, "[Walt Jr. has] been a sweet character without much edge to him, and in hindsight, because everyone on the show gets corrupted one by one, the writers and I liked keeping Walt Jr. as an oasis of innocence. I wish we'd had time to do something more interesting with Walt Jr., but I guess we didn't."

Born on August 21, 1992, in Lafayette, Louisiana, Mitte has cerebral palsy, although a milder form than the character he portrays. As a youngster, Mitte appeared as an extra (listed as School Jock) on the *Hannah Montana* TV show and at one time was linked romantically to the show's star, Miley Cyrus. Mitte was featured as one of the emerging artists in Gap Inc.'s 2014 "Lived-In" global marketing campaign and appeared in the 2015 crime drama *Dixieland*.

RJ Mitte Trivia

- In an August 22, 2016, interview with *The Telegraph*, Mitte remarked, "My character was actually based on a real person, a college friend of Vince Gilligan, and one of the reasons he cast me was because I apparently look very much like him."

- In 2017, Mitte appeared on the *Celebrity Island with Bear Grylls* TV series.

Hank Schrader (Dean Norris)

A wisecracking, rather rednecky DEA agent, Walt's brother-in-law is married to Skyler's sister, Marie. In his 2016 memoir, *A Life in Parts*, Bryan Cranston described Hank as Walt's "dickish, emasculating brother-in-law." Hank has an affinity for illegal Cuban cigars and creating homemade brew, which he refers to as "Schraderbrau." He suffers from post-traumatic stress disorder after witnessing a particular gruesome incident involving drug informant Tortuga (Danny Trejo) while briefly serving as a member of the El Paso drug task force. Hank becomes one of the first DEA agents to take an interest in the Heisenberg legend and obsessively follows lead after lead (to the detriment of the advancement of his law-enforcement career) until he finally discovers the truth about his brother-in-law, ultimately leading to his tragic death in the desert at the hands of neo-Nazi Uncle Jack Welker. According to Vince Gilligan in a September 25, 2013, *Rolling Stone* interview, "Hank loves his brother-in-law but he thinks the guy is an egghead. He feels a bit sorry for him. Hank doesn't think of Walt as a real man. It was right under his nose, which does lead folks to think Hank was dumb. It would be a hard thing to suddenly realize that your ineffectual, milquetoast brother-in-law is the Keyser Söze-like criminal genius you've been tracking for almost a year."

Born in South Bend, Indiana, on April 8, 1963, Dean Joseph Norris graduated from Harvard College and also attended the Royal Academy of Dramatic Art in London, England, for a year. His film credits include *Lethal Weapon 2* (1989), *Hard to Kill* (1990), *Gremlins 2: The New Batch* (1990), *Total Recall* (1990), *Terminator 2: Judgment Day* (1991), *The Firm* (1993), *Gattaca* (1997), and *Little Miss Sunshine* (2006), among many others.

Dean Norris Trivia

- Norris was the valedictorian of his graduating class at Clay High School in South Bend, Indiana.

- Norris appeared as Cop in the eminently forgettable *Police Academy 6: City Under Siege* (1989).
- In *Total Recall* (1991), Norris portrayed Tony the Mutant, who utters the line: "You got a lot of nerve showing your face around here, Hauser." Arnold Schwarzenegger's character replies, "Look who's talking."
- Norris appeared in *Terminator 2: Judgment Day* (1991) as SWAT Team Leader and in two episodes of the TV series *Terminator: The Sarah Connor Chronicles* (2008): "Automatic for the People" and "Goodbye to All That."

Marie Schrader (Betsy Brandt)

Hank's loving wife, the purple-obsessed nurse with a penchant for kleptomania, has been described by Bryan Cranston as Walter White's "passive-aggressive sister-in-law." In a Q&A that appeared on amc.com, Brandt referred to her character as "an unpleasant bitch."

Born on March 14, 1973, in Bay City, Michigan, Brandt received a bachelor of fine arts in acting at the University of Illinois in 1996. In addition, she studied at the Moscow Art Theater Institute at Harvard and the Royal Scottish Academy of Music and Drama in Glasgow.

Betsy Brandt Trivia

- Brandt was pregnant during the filming of Season Two of *Breaking Bad*, roughly coinciding with Skyler White's pregnancy.

Saul Goodman (Bob Odenkirk)

A sleazy lawyer who operates out of a strip mall, Saul Goodman is one of the most colorful *Breaking Bad* characters, often providing some much-needed comic relief. He is often decked out in neon-bright colors, emphasizing his inner gaudiness. At one point, Walt refers to Saul as "a two-bit bus bench lawyer." The interior of Saul's tacky office features fake columns and Constitution wallpaper. The roof is adorned with—just what you would expect—an inflatable Statue of Liberty. In *Breaking Bad: The Official Book*, Vince Gilligan remarked, "Saul Goodman is like a cockroach—even after the apocalypse hits, he's going to find a way to survive." In a Q&A that appeared on amc.com, Odenkirk stated that legendary movie producer Robert Evans (*The Godfather*) served as an inspiration for his Saul Goodman portrayal: "Saul likes to talk. He likes to go on and on and pontificate and lecture. One of the things I was concerned with is how do I make these monologues and these runs really fun to hear? I thought about Robert Evans because I've listened to *The Kid Stays in the Picture* [Evans's 1994 autobiography] on CD. He's constantly switching up his cadence and delivery. He emphasizes interesting words. He has loads of attitude in almost every line that he says. So when I rehearse the scenes alone I do my impression of Robert Evans to find those moments and turns. Then I go out and I do Saul."

Born on October 22, 1962, in Berwyn, Illinois, Odenkirk attended Marquette University before transferring to Southern Illinois University. Odenkirk worked as a writer for *Saturday Night Live* (*SNL*) between 1987 and 1991. During this period, he created Chris Farley's iconic Matt Foley, Motivational Speaker character, who was "thirty-five years old, thrice divorced and living in a van down by the river." Odenkirk also appeared in several *SNL* skits, including the memorable "Bad Idea Jeans" parody commercial in 1991. He also wrote for both *The Dennis Miller Show*, which only lasted seven months in 1992, and *The Ben Stiller Show* (1992–93), which won a Primetime Emmy Award for Outstanding Writing for a Variety Series. In addition, Odenkirk wrote for *Late Night with Conan O'Brien* during 1993–94, appeared on *The Larry Sanders Show* as Larry's agent Stevie Grant, and collaborated with fellow comedian David Cross on the HBO series *Mr. Show with Bob and David*. Odenkirk also wrote the screenplay for *Run Ronnie Run* (2002) and directed the films *Melvin Goes to Dinner* (2003), *Let's Go to Prison* (2006), and *The Brothers Solomon* (2007). He has made guest appearances on many television sitcoms over the years such as *Seinfeld, Just Shoot Me!, 3rd Rock from the Sun, Curb Your Enthusiasm, Ed, Everybody Loves Raymond, Less Than Perfect, Arrested Development, How I Met Your Mother,* and *Weeds*.

Bob Odenkirk Trivia

- In addition to Robert Evans, Odenkirk revealed during a NPR "Fresh Air" interview that notorious Hollywood agent Ari Emanuel inspired his Saul Goodman character.
- Odenkirk portrayed Concert Nerd in *Wayne's World 2* (1993).
- He has acknowledged his comedic influences as Monty Python's Flying Circus, Steve Martin, Woody Allen, and Bob and Ray.
- In 2004, Odenkirk appeared in a series of Miller Lite commercials.
- Odenkirk's younger brother, Bill, is also a comedy writer who has written and executive produced several episodes of *The Simpsons*. He holds a PhD in inorganic chemistry from the University of Chicago.

Gustavo "Gus" Fring (Giancarlo Esposito)

A meth kingpin, meticulous businessman Gustavo "Gus" Fring uses a popular fast-food chain, Los Pollos Hermanos, as a cover for his drug empire. Gus, who conceals a mysterious past in Chile, carries a personal grudge against the Mexican drug cartel for killing his former partner (and possible lover), Maximino Arciniega (James Martinez). A complete sociopath who prides himself on self-discipline, Gus once informs Walt that one of his tenets is to "never make the same mistake twice." According to Esposito in a Q&A that appeared on amc.com, "Gus is the coolest cucumber that ever walked the Earth. I think about Eddie Olmos way back in *Miami Vice*. He was like dead—he was hardly breathing. I thought, how is this guy just standing in this fire and doing nothing? Gus has totally allowed me that level of flexibility and relaxation—not because he has ultimate power and he knows he can take someone's life. He's just confident."

Giancarlo Giuseppe Alessandro Esposito was born on April 26, 1958, in Copenhagen, Denmark. He portrayed Agent Mike Giardello on the TV series *Homicide: Life on the Street* in 1998. Esposito's filmography includes *Mo' Better Blues* (1990), *Harley Davidson and the Marlboro Man* (1991), *Malcolm X* (1992), *The Usual Suspects* (1995), *Ali* (2001), *A Killer Within*

(2004), *Carlito's Way: Rise to Power* (2005), and *Maze Runner: The Scorch Trials* (2015).

Giancarlo Esposito Trivia

- Esposito can be heard as one of the chorus of children who sang the theme song for *The Electric Company*. He also appeared on *Sesame Street*.
- He made his film debut as Puerto Rican Teenager in the drama *Running* (1979), which starred Michael Douglas.
- Esposito's early film credits include Cadet Captain JC Pierce in *Taps* (1981), Cellmate in *Trading Places* (1983), and Buggin' Out in Spike Lee's *Do the Right Thing* (1989).

Mike Ehrmantraut (Jonathan Banks)

An all-purpose "cleaner" and hitman, Mike Ehrmantraut takes care of the dirty work for both Gus Fring and Saul Goodman. Disciplined and unemotional (although he dotes on his granddaughter Kaylee), Banks's character has been compared to Harvey Keitel's Winston Wolf from the 1994 Quentin Tarantino film *Pulp Fiction*. However, in a Q&A that appeared on amc.com, Banks remarked, "I immediately tried to put it out of my mind, quite honestly. [Keitel's] cleaner ain't my cleaner. But throughout this world, you would suspect there had been a great many cleaners, whether government-run or individual contractors."

A former Philadelphia police officer, Mike's backstory is revealed in the *Breaking Bad* spin-off, *Better Call Saul*. When Saul first meets Mike, he is working as a parking attendant at the Albuquerque Courthouse, but economic realities force him to engage in criminal activities to support his widowed daughter-in-law and granddaughter. It is Mike who warns Walt not to take "half measures," advice that comes back to haunt him when Heisenberg tracks him down to get the names of the prison inmates who are still on Gus's payroll. According to Vince Gilligan in *Breaking Bad: The Official Book*, "Mike is a man who knows he's lost a good chunk of his soul, and seems sad and world-weary about it. But he goes on none-theless because he knows his strengths as well as his weaknesses."

Born in Washington, D.C., on January 21, 1947, Jonathan Ray Banks attended Indiana University Bloomington. Banks portrayed Frank McPike in the TV crime series *Wiseguy*, which ran from 1987 to 1990. Banks has received five Primetime Emmy Award nominations for Outstanding Supporting Actor in a Drama Series. His filmography includes *Honeymoon Academy* (1990), *Freejack* (1992), *Boiling Point* (1993), *Under Siege 2: Dark Territory* (1995), *Let the Devil Wear Black* (1999), *Trash* (1999), *Crocodile Dundee in Los Angeles* (2001), *Dark Blue* (2002), *Reign Over Me* (2007), *Proud American* (2008), *Identity Thief* (2013), and *Mudbound* (2017).

Jonathan Banks Trivia

- Banks acted in a production of *The Threepenny Opera* with classmate Kevin Kline while attending Indiana University Bloomington.
- Banks made a rather inauspicious film debut as Marine at Party in the critically acclaimed 1978 drama *Coming Home*, which starred Jane Fonda, Jon Voight, and Bruce Dern.
- Banks's early film credits include Zack in *Beverly Hills Cop* (1984) and Clyde Klepper in Ar*med and Dangerous* (1986).

Lydia Rodarte-Quayle (Laura Fraser)

A high-ranking employee of Madrigal Electromotive and former associate of Gus Fring, the forever uptight Lydia Rodarte-Quayle reluctantly helps Walter White expand his meth operation overseas. Asked about her por-trayal of Lydia in a September 5, 2013, interview with *Metro World News*, Fraser remarked, "I didn't know how demented she was in the beginning. She seems to vibrate at a very high-pitched frequency—constantly in a fight-or-flight mode, you know? I feel like she's gone from being rather cold to completely glacial. She's almost like a little Nazi in these last episodes."

In a startling transformation from "Mr. Chips" to "Scarface," bland high school chemistry teacher Walter White gradually evolves into the mysterious drug kingpin known only as Heisenberg.

Born on July 24, 1976, in Glasgow, Scotland, Laura Fraser attended the prestigious Royal Scottish Academy of Music and Drama. Her film credits include *Left Luggage* (1998), *Divorcing Jack* (1998), *Virtual Sexuality* (1999), *Titus* (1999), and *Coney Island Baby* (2003).

Laura Fraser Trivia

- Billed as The Future, Fraser voiced the last line in *Vanilla Sky* (2001): "Relax, David. Open your eyes."
- In 1996, Fraser appeared in the BBC adaptation of Neil Gaiman's *NeverWhere*.
- Fraser portrayed American suffragist Doris Stevens in the critically acclaimed HBO drama *Iron Jawed Angels* (2004).

Todd Alquist (Jesse Plemons)

A creepy employee of Vamonos Pest Control (the front business for Walt and Jesse's meth operation) who learns how to cook meth under Walt's tutelage, Todd Alquist is arguably the most deranged character in the entire series as evidenced by his nonchalantly killing an innocent kid who stumbles upon the train heist in the episode "Dead Freight" and his cold-blooded killing of Jesse's girlfriend, Andrea. After both Mike and Jesse quit on Walt in disgust, Todd becomes his new assistant in the meth lab. He also brings his neo-Nazi "Uncle Jack" into the picture—precipitating the downfall of Heisenberg. In fact, before anyone even knows about Todd's connection to white supremacists, Jesse dubs him "Ricky Hitler." In addition, Todd becomes obsessed with Lydia Rodarte-Quayle, a situation that she briefly uses to her advantage.

Born Jesse Lon Plemons on April 2, 1988, in Dallas, Texas, he appeared in the TV series *Friday Night Lights* (the only member of the cast who had actually played high school football). His film credits include *Paul* (2011), *Battleship* (2012), and *Black Mass* (2015), a crime drama about Boston mobster Whitey Bulger based on the 2001 book *Black Mass: The True Story of an Unholy Alliance Between the FBI and the Irish Mob* by Dick Lehr and Gerard O'Neill.

Jesse Plemons Trivia

- Plemons got engaged to actress Kirsten Dunst (*Marie Antoinette*) in 2017.
- He is related to Stephen F. Austin (1793–1836), known as the "Father of Texas."
- Plemons sings in the alternative folk band Cowboy and Indian.
- He was considered for the role of Finn in *Star Wars: The Force Awakens* (2015) that went to John Boyega.
- Due to his resemblance to Matt Damon, Plemons was dubbed "Meth Damon" by a demented portion of the *Breaking Bad* online fanbase.
- IGN named Todd Alquist as 2013's "Best TV Villain."

5

No Honor Among Thieves

Essential Minor Characters in *Breaking Bad*

"Hey, man, I'm slingin' mad volume and fat stackin' benjis, you known what I'm sayin'?"

—*Skinny Pete*

There are scores of memorable minor characters in *Breaking Bad* that add colorful new dimensions to the series, as well as being responsible for some of the most humorous comic relief when it's needed most. For example, who can forget Badger and Skinny Pete discussing a galactic pie-eating contest as the basis for a *Star Trek* script, debating video game zombies, or trying to determine the amount of stress Darth Vader underwent in trying to complete the Death Star? How about lab assistant Gale Boetticher singing karaoke to Peter Schilling's 1983 hit "Major Tom (Coming Home)"? Or Huell Babineaux channeling Scrooge McDuck as he lounges on a stack of $80 million in Walt's drug money inside the storage unit? Scenes like these add up to create some of the most memorable comic moments in *Breaking Bad* history.

Huell Babineaux (Lavell Crawford)

Saul Goodman's rather dim-witted personal bodyguard (and sometime pickpocket), Huell Babineaux provides some much-need comic relief like when he lies atop that mountain of drug money and exclaims, "Mexico. All's I'm saying." Huell handles such dirty work as intimidating Ted and lifting the

A stand-up comedian, Lavell Crawford made his television debut on *Def Comedy Jam* and finished second on *Last Comic Standing* in 2007.

ricin from Jesse so Walt could poison Andrea's son Brock and convince his partner to help him eliminate Gus Fring. Huell appears in eleven episodes of *Breaking Bad*: "Box Cutter," "Open House," "Hermanos," "Crawl Space," "End Times," "Hazard Pay," "Blood Money," "Buried," "Confessions," "Rabid Dog," and "To'hajiilee." He also makes a reappearance in Season Three of *Better Call Saul*.

A stand-up comedian whose father was a bodybuilder, Lavell Crawford was born on November 11, 1968, in St. Louis, Missouri. He made his television debut on *Def Comedy Jam* and finished second on *Last Comic Standing* in 2007 (losing out to Jon Reep). Crawford has been a featured performer on *Comedy Central Presents*, *Showtime at The Apollo*, and *Comics Unleashed*. In 2011, he recorded the comedy video *Lavell Crawford: Can A Brother Get Some Love?* Crawford also has appeared in several films, including *American Ultra* (2015) and *Mike and Dave Need Wedding Dates* (2016).

Ted Beneke (Christopher Cousins)

Skyler's sleazy boss at Beneke Fabricators, Ted Beneke, not only has a brief affair with Skyler but she ends up giving him $617,000 in drug money (he thinks it's from a long-lost relative) so he can get out of IRS trouble (Ted had enlisted Skyler's assistance to "cook the books" to keep the business alive). Instead of paying off the IRS, Ted uses the money to buy an expensive Mercedes and prepares to reopen his business. After Skyler confronts Ted and he attempts to blackmail her, she turns to Saul Goodman, who enlists Huell Babineaux and Patrick Kuby to persuade him to send the check to the IRS. The hapless Ted tries to escape, trips on a rug, smashes his head into some furniture, and ends up in the hospital in a coma. When Ted wakes from his coma, Skyler visits him and he promises her he will never reveal anything to the authorities. Ted appears in thirteen episodes of *Breaking Bad*: "Negro Y Azul," "Over," "Mandala," "Phoenix," "Caballo Sin Nombre," "I.F.T.", "Green Light," "Mas," "Kafkaesque," "Bug," "Salud," "Crawl Space," and "Live Free or Die."

Christopher Cousins was born on September 27, 1960, in New York City. Prior to *Breaking Bad*, Cousins was perhaps best known for his acting stint as con artist Cain Rogan on the soap opera *One Life to Live* in the 1990s. In 2013–14, he portrayed Victor Doyle in the NBC series *Revolution*. His film credits include *Wicker Park* (2004), *Grudge 2* (2006), and *Untraceable* (2008).

Gale Boetticher (David Costabile)

A chemist hired by Gus Fring to work as Walter's lab assistant, Gale Boetticher is the polar opposite of Jesse Pinkman. He was the recipient of the Max Arciniega College Scholarship, which was set up by Gus. A vegan and self-proclaimed nerd and libertarian, Gale justifies his role in the meth trade: "There's crime and then there's *crime* . . . Consenting adults want what they want. And if I'm not supplying it they will get it someplace else. At least with me they're getting exactly what they pay for—no added toxins or adulterants." A specialist in X-ray crystallography, Gale holds an MS degree in organic chemistry. In addition, he often reveals a quirky side as evidenced in his karaoke tune of choice—"Major Tom (Coming Home)," which he recorded during a visit to Thailand. Gale quotes Walt Whitman's "When I Heard the Learn'd Astronomer" to Walt and greatly admires his new mentor's chemistry skills. Gale appears in seven episodes of *Breaking Bad*: "Sunset," "One Minute," "I See You," "Full Measure," "Box Cutter," "Bullet Points," and "Problem Dog." Incidentally, the name "Boetticher" serves as a tribute to famous Hollywood director Budd Boetticher, who was best known for such low-budget Westerns as *The Tall T* (1957), *Decision at Sundown* (1957), *Buchanan Rides Alone* (1958), *Ride Lonesome* (1959), and *Comanche Station* (1960).

David Costabile was born on January 9, 1967, in Washington, D.C. He graduated from New York University's Master of Fine Arts program in Acting in 1998. His Broadway credits include *Titanic* (1997), *The Tempest* (1995), and *Translations* (2007). In addition, Costabile has appeared on several TV series in addition to *Breaking Bad* such as *The Wire* (as Managing Editor Thomas Kelbanow), *Flight of the Conchords*, *Damages*, and *Suits*, among others. His film credits include *Solitary Man* (2009), *The Bounty Hunter* (2010), *Lincoln* (2012), *Side Effects* (2013), and *13 Hours: The Secret Soldiers of Benghazi* (2016).

Bogdan (Marius Stan)

Simply known as Bogdan (aka Eyebrows), Bogdan Wolynetz is the Romanian owner of the A1 Car Wash and Walt's boss. After his lung cancer diagnosis in the "Pilot" episode, Walt makes a public display of quitting his job in front of Bogdan, who was frequently demeaning to him: "Fuck you and your eyebrows!" Bogdan reappears later in the series when Skyler gets the idea to purchase the car wash as a way of laundering Walt's drug money. In order to get Bogdan to sell the car wash, Saul Goodman sends a fake inspector to discover a fabricated environmental issue, forcing Bogdan to sell out for the price of $800,000. After taking over the car wash, Walt rips Bogdan's framed dollar from the wall and buys a Coke with it from the vending machine. Bogdan appears in five episodes of *Breaking Bad*: "Pilot," "Abiquiu," "Thirty-Eight Snub," "Open House," and "Cornered."

Believe it or not, the actor who portrayed "Bogdan," Marius Stan, actually has a PhD in chemistry. "Bogdan" was his first acting role. Stan is currently Interim Director of the Systems Science Center in the Global Security Sciences division at Argonne National Laboratory. He formerly worked as a scientist at Los Alamos National Laboratory.

Andrea Cantillo (Emily Rios)

Jesse's second girlfriend, Andrea Cantillo is a recovering drug addict with a young son named Brock. Jesse meets Andrea at a Narcotics Anonymous meeting (he was there, along with Badger and Skinny Pete, for the sole purpose of finding new customers for the blue meth he pilfered from Gus Fring's meth superlab) and later finds out that it was her younger brother, Tomas, who killed Combo. Tomas was later killed by rival dealers. Walt poisons Brock in order to get Jesse to believe it was actually Gus (he needs Jesse's help to eliminate the drug kingpin). Andrea is ultimately killed by Todd as punishment for Jesse's escape attempt from Uncle Jack and his gang's meth compound. Andrea appears in nine episodes of *Breaking Bad*: "Abiquiu," "Half Measures," "Thirty-Eight Snub," "Hermanos," "Crawl Space," "End Times," "Hazard Pay," "To'hajiilee," and "Granite Space."

Born on April 27, 1989, in Los Angeles, California. Rios portrayed Magdalena in the critically acclaimed 2006 film *Quincenera* and has appeared in recurring roles in several TV series, including *Friday Night Lights*, *Men of a Certain Age*, *The Bridge*, *From Dusk till Dawn: The Series*, and *Snowfall*. She was raised as a Jehovah's Witness.

Ed (Robert Forster)

A "new identity specialist" who operates undercover as a vacuum cleaner repairman, Ed (aka the Disappearer) successfully relocates both Walter White (to a cabin in New Hampshire) and Saul Goodman (to a Cinnabon in Omaha, Nebraska). Walt had originally requested Ed's services through Saul when Gus threatened his entire family, but the plan backfired when Walt discovered that Skyler gave the money ($600,000 in all!) to Ted to help settle his IRS issues. Jesse also considers using Ed's services to disappear, but backs out at the very last minute. At one point, Ed reveals to Walt, "You are the hottest client I have ever had. By far." Ed visits Walt several times at his remote New Hampshire cabin to bring him necessary supplies (at one point Walt becomes so desperate for company that he pays Ed $10,000 just to play cards with him). Ed appears in one episode of *Breaking Bad*: "Granite State."

Robert Forster was born Robert Wallace Foster Jr. on July 13, 1941, in Rochester, New York. He received a BA in Psychology from the University of Rochester in 1963. Interestingly, as a struggling actor, Forster reportedly worked as a door-to-door vacuum cleaner salesman. He made his film debut as Private L. G. Williams in *Reflections in a Golden Eye* (1967), which was directed by John Huston (*The Maltese Falcon*) and starred Marlon Brando and Elizabeth Taylor. Forster's film credits include *The Stalking Moon* (1968), *Medium Cool* (1969), *Justine* (1969), *The Black Hole* (1979), *Vigilante* (1982), *Walking the Edge* (1986), *The Delta Force* (1986), and *Maniac Cop III: Badge of Silence* (1993). Interestingly, Bryan Cranston served as a production assistant in the special-effects department on the low-budget 1980 horror film *Alligator*, which starred Forster as a world-weary police officer named David Madison.

Forster's career was reinvigorated in 1997 after he was cast as bail bondsman Max Cherry opposite Pam Grier in Quentin Tarantino's *Jackie Brown*—a role for which he received an Academy Award nomination for Best Supporting Actor (losing out to Robin Williams for *Good Will Hunting*). More recently, Forster has appeared in such films as *Me, Myself & Irene* (2000), *Mulholland Drive* (2001), *The Descendants* (2011), *Olympus Has Fallen* (2013), and *London Has Fallen* (2016), among others. For his performance as Ed in the "Granite State" episode of *Breaking Bad*, Forster received the Saturn Award for Best Guest Starring Role on Television.

Steven "Gomie" Gomez (Steven Michael Quezada)

Hank's DEA partner and best friend, Steven "Gomie" Gomez reluctantly helps his colleague with his Heisenberg obsession, even though he initially believes that they should be focusing on other, more pertinent drug investigations. Gomie has an extensive knowledge of Mexican gangs and frequently engages in lighthearted banter with Hank. He is tragically killed during the gunfight in the desert with Uncle Jack Welker and his gang. Gomie appeared in thirty-three episodes of *Breaking Bad*, starting with "Pilot" and ending with "Ozymandias."

Born on February 15, 1963, Steven Michael Quezada is the only Albuquerque, New Mexico, native in the *Breaking Bad* cast. He studied theater at Eastern New Mexico University. A stand-up comedian, Quezada is a five-time recipient of the New Mexico Hispanic Entertainers Association Comedian of the Year Award. His TV credits include *Wildfire*, *Crash*, and *In Plain Sight*.

Tyrus Kitt (Ray Campbell)

Along with Mike Ehrmantraut, Tyrus Kitt serves as Gus Fring's enforcer in Season Four of *Breaking Bad* (replacing Victor, who was murdered by Gus in front of Walt and Jesse). Tyrus, who is rather mysterious and rarely speaks, gets killed in the explosion at Casa Tranquila Nursing Home that also takes the life of Gus. Tyrus appears in ten episodes of *Breaking Bad*: "Thirty-Eight Snub," "Open House," "Bullet Points," "Shotgun," "Cornered," "Bug," "Salud," "Crawl Space," "End Times," and "Face Off."

In addition to *Breaking Bad*, Ray Campbell has appeared in several other television series over the years such as *Angel*, *The District*, *Haunted*, *Cold Case*, *Girlfriends*, *The Shield*, *The Unit*, *NCIS*, *The Cleaner*, *Parenthood*, and *For Better or Worse*, among others.

Patrick Kuby (Bill Burr)

A former Boston police officer and hired con man for Saul Goodman, Patrick Kuby takes on a variety of roles (often alongside Huell Babineaux), including helping out with the train heist, threatening Ted Beneke, posing as a fake environmental auditor, and loading up Walt's barrels of drug money into a rented van. Patrick appears in five episodes of *Breaking Bad*: "Open House," "Crawl Space," "Dead Freight," "Buried," and "Rapid Dog."

A graduate of Emerson College, Burr is a well-known stand-up comedian, actor, and writer from Canton, Massachusetts. He was the first stand-up comedian to perform on *The Tonight Show with Conan O'Brien*. Burr created and starred in the Netflix animated sitcom *F is for Family*. He also records a weekly podcast, *Bill Burr's Monday Morning Podcast*. Burr ranked No. 17 on the *Rolling Stone* list of the "50 Best Stand-Up Comics of All Time," with the magazine calling him "the undisputed heavyweight champ of rage-fueled humor." Burr has cited his comedic influences as George Carlin, Bill Cosby, Sam Kinison, Patrice O'Neal, and Richard Pryor.

According to Burr in a January 19, 2012, interview with *Austinist*, "I've never missed one [*Breaking Bad*] episode, and it was the most surreal thing that I got to do. It's like, if you were into *Star Wars*, and they made another *Star Wars*, and you got to play Boba Fett or a Stormtrooper . . . All of a sudden, I was somehow inserted into the storylines of these characters . . . It's like if you booked a scene, like you're watching *The Sopranos* and you're following the story and all of a sudden you are in it and you're standing next to Paulie and you got a scene with him, and you're just like, how the fuck did this happen?"

Bill Burr was the first stand-up comedian to perform on *The Tonight Show* with Conan O'Brien and ranks No. 17 on *Rolling Stone*'s list of the "50 Best Stand-Up Comics of All Time."

Lawson (Jim Beaver)

An Albuquerque arms dealer, Lawson provides Walter White with the title weapon in the episode "Thirty-Eight Snub," as well as the machine gun he later uses to gun down Uncle Jack Welker and his crew in "Live Free or Die." Lawson also first appears in the Season Two episode of *Better Call Saul*, "Gloves Off," showing Mike several rifles (Mike ends up walking away without purchasing any weapons). Lawson appears in two episodes of *Breaking Bad*: "Live Free or Die" and "Thirty-Eight Snub."

James Beaver Jr. was born on August 13, 1950, in Laramie, Wyoming. He served as a radio operator with the 1st Marine Division in Vietnam. Beaver has appeared in several TV series, including as Bobby Singer in *Supernatural*, Whitney Ellsworth in *Deadwood*, and Sheriff Shelby Parlow in *Justified*. Beaver published a memoir, *Life's That Way*, in 2009. His film credits include *In Country* (1989), *Sister Act* (1992), *Sliver* (1993), *Magnolia* (1999, as Smiling Peanut Patron No. 1), *Joy Ride* (2001), *Adaptation* (2002), and *Dark and Stormy Night* (2009).

Donald Margolis (John de Lancie)

Jane's father, Donald Margolis, serves as an air traffic controller. He discourages Jane's relationship with Jesse, believing that Jane will relapse into addiction (which she promptly does). During a chance meeting at a bar with Walt the night that Jane overdoses, Donald offers him the following advice: "You can't give up on family. Never. I mean, what else is there?" Mourning Jane's death, Donald inadvertently causes an airplane collision, which leads to the death of 167 people. In a subsequent episode, Walt hears over the radio that Donald has been rushed to the hospital from a self-inflicted gunshot wound. Donald appears in four episodes of *Breaking Bad*: "No Mas," "ABQ," "Phoenix," and "Over."

John de Lancie was born on March 20, 1948, in Philadelphia, Pennsylvania. He is well known by Trekkies for portraying Q in *Star Trek: The Next Generation*, *Star Trek: Deep Space Nine*, and *Star Trek: Voyager*. He also supplies the voice of Discord in *My Little Pony: Friendship Is Magic*. His father, John Sherwood de Lancie, served as principal oboist for the Philadelphia Orchestra between 1954 and 1977.

Jane Margolis (Krysten Ritter)

Jesse's apartment manager and girlfriend, Jane Margolis, is a talented tattoo artist and recovering heroin addict. Jane tries to hide her relationship with Jesse from her father, who correctly fears that she will relapse if she hangs out with him (however, for the record, it is Jane who ultimately turns Jesse on to heroin). She also tries to blackmail Walt into giving Jesse his share of the money (Walt has insisted that Jesse get clean before he gives him his share). After receiving Jesse's share, the couple makes somewhat dubious plans to get clean and run away to New Zealand, where she will "paint, like, the local castles and shit" and he will become "a bush pilot."

Tragically, the couple decides to finish off their remaining heroin that night, and Jane later overdoses (with Walt standing by her side doing nothing). A devastated Jesse resorts to nonstop drug use in an unsuccessful attempt to ease his pain. Several critics have noted the resemblance of Jane to both the title character in the song "Jane Says" by Jane's Addiction and Uma Thurman's character Mia Wallace from *Pulp Fiction* (1994). In addition, the last name "Margolis" references actor Mark Margolis, who portrays Hector Salamanca in *Breaking Bad*. Jane appears in nine episodes of *Breaking Bad*: "Breakage," "Negro Y Azul," "Better Call Saul," "4 Days Out," "Over," "Mandala," "Phoenix," "ABQ," and "Abiquiu."

Krysten Alyce Ritter was born on December 16, 1981, in Bloomsburg, Pennsylvania. She stars as the title character in the Netflix series *Jessica Jones*. Ritter is a member of the band Ex Vivian. Her film credits include *Mona Lisa Smile* (2003), *What Happens in Vegas* (2008), *27 Dresses* (2008), *Confessions of a Shopaholic* (2009), *She's Out of My League* (2010), *Veronica Mars* (2014), and *Big Eyes* (2014). She also has appeared in several other television series, including *Gravity*, *'Til Death*, *Veronica Mars*, *Gossip Girl*, and *The Blacklist*.

Brandon "Badger" Mayhew (Matt L. Jones)

One of Jesse's dim-witted buddies and a fellow drug dealer, Badger often provides comic relief —whether pitching an imaginary *Star Trek* script about a "pie-eating contest" or discussing Darth Vader's responsibilities in the creation of the Death Star. After he first tries Walt's fabled blue meth, Badger exclaims, "That is awesome, Jesse! I feel like somebody took my brain out and boiled it in, like, boiling hot, like . . . like, Anthrax." Badger appears in twelve episodes of *Breaking Bad*: "Gray Matter," "Bit by a Dead Bee," "Breakage," "Negro Y Azul," "Better Call Saul," "Sunset," "Kafkaesque," "Abiquiu," "Thirty-Eight Snub," "Hazard Pay," "Blood Money," and "Felina."

Matthew Lee "Matt" Jones was born in Sacramento, California, on November 1, 1981. His film credits include *Red State* (2011), *Mom* (2013), and *Home* (2015). Jones also portrayed Special Agent Ned Dorneget in the television series, *NCIS*.

Christian "Combo" Ortega (Rodney Rush)

Another one of Jesse's drug-addled buddies, Christian "Combo" Ortega also serves as a meth dealer when Walt and Jesse decide to expand their turf after the death of Tuco Salamanca. He is killed under the instigation of a rival gang who use a kid to do the dirty work. In a Season Three flashback, it is revealed that Combo provided Jesse with the mobile meth lab RV after Jesse and his buddies blow Walt's money at a strip club. Jesse later finds out that Combo was actually killed by his girlfriend Andrea's little brother, Tomas (who himself is later eliminated by the same crew). Combo appears in five episodes of *Breaking Bad*: "Cancer Man," "Breakage," "Negro Y Azul," "Mandala," and "Mas."

In addition to *Breaking Bad*, Rodney Rush has appeared in *Bad Buddha* (2014) and *Cadillac Respect* (2017). In a June 29, 2012, interview that appeared on bettercallsaulfans.blogspot.com, Rush remarked,

> In the beginning I was supposed to just be in one episode. I had never acted before this . . . It was a little intimidating I have to admit . . . I originally went to be an extra. They asked me to audition the next day . . . In the second season they decided to give my character the name Combo and write me into the show because the creator of the show Vince Gilligan really liked me . . . I was hoping it would go a little further than it did at the time I found out I would get killed off. I was a little sad at the time. Like

Bryan Cranston said though, "If you gotta go then that's the way to go." But looking back I am just amazed at all that's come from it. I mean my whole Identity changed. I am now Combo from *Breaking Bad*. Which is dope!

Hector Salamanca (Mark Margolis)

A former high-ranking member of the Juarez Cartel and a cold-blooded killer, Hector Salamanca is the "tio" (uncle) of Tuco Salamanca, as well as the Cousins—Marco and Leonel Salamanca. Extremely loyal, Hector previously spent seventeen years in San Quentin Prison and never informed on anyone in the cartel. Because he suffered a stroke, Hector communicates with the help of a bell strapped to his wheelchair. According to Vince Gilligan in *Breaking Bad: The Official Book*, "Tio came to us as a way to . . . lay a really nasty surprise on Walt and Jesse and really get them in Dutch with Tuco, this very scary character. When we cast Mark Margolis to play this part, though, we said to ourselves, 'Man, this actor is great! This is a guy we're lucky to be working with; what more can we do with this character? Can we bring him back in a subsequent episode?" In a flashback, it is revealed that Hector had killed Gus Fring's partner (and possible lover), Max Arciniega. Hector loathes Gus (and the feeling is quite mutual!), referring to him as "chicken man" and a "dirty South American." Walt uses Hector's intense hatred for Gus to assist him in setting up the drug kingpin's murder (which also kills Hector in the process of course). Hector appears in eight episodes of *Breaking Bad*: "Grilled," "Bit by a Dead Bee," "Caballo sin Nombre," "I.F.T.," "One Minute," "Hermanos," "Crawl Space," and "Face Off." He reappears in several episodes of *Better Call Saul*.

A self-described "journeyman actor," Mark Margolis was born on November 26, 1939, in Philadelphia, Pennsylvania. He studied drama with Stella Adler at the legendary Actors Studio in New York City. Margolis made his acting debut (fully clothed!) as Unhappy Guy on Plane in the classic XXX-rated film *The Opening of Misty Beethoven* (1976) with a single line: "Excuse me, but I had one blowjob and I haven't got my brandy yet." He also turned in a memorable performance as sinister hitman Alberto the Shadow in *Scarface* (1983). Margolis's film credits include *Requiem for a Dream* (2000), *The Fountain* (2006), *The Wrestler* (2008), *Black Swan* (2010), and *Noah* (2014)—all of which were directed by Darren Aronofsky. He also appeared as Antonio Nappa in the critically acclaimed HBO prison drama *Oz*. Margolis is the only *Breaking Bad* cast member to receive an Emmy nomination for Outstanding Guest Actor in a Drama Series. True to the villains he has portrayed in his most memorable roles, Margolis once remarked, "You don't play villains like they are villains. You play them like you know exactly where they are coming from. Which hopefully you do."

Leonel and Marco Salamanca (Daniel and Luis Moncada)

Known simply as the Cousins, nephews of Hector Salamanca and relentless hitmen for the Juarez Cartel, twin brothers Leonel and Marco Salamanca cross the border to avenge the killing of their cousin Tuco. Gus Fring manages to hold them off because he needs Walt as his meth cook and he finally redirects their wrath to Walt's brother-in-law Hank, who had actually killed Tuco. Leonel and Marco appear in the *Breaking Bad* episodes "No Mas," "Caballo sin Nombre," "I.F.T.," "Sunset," and "One Minute." Leonel also appears in "I See You." The Cousins also make a reappearance in *Better Call Saul*.

Daniel and Luis Moncada are actual brothers, but they were born three years apart in Honduras. Luis is a Muay Thai fighter who has "FU" tattooed on his eyelids.

Tuco Salamanca (Raymond Cruz)

A total psychopath, Tuco Salamanca briefly serves as Walter and Jesse's meth distributor and main antagonist in Season Two of *Breaking Bad*. He is the nephew of Hector Salamanca and the cousin of Leonel and Marco Salamanca. Tuco's penchant for extreme violence becomes evident to Walt and Jesse after they witness him beat his associate No-Doze to death in the junkyard for no apparent reason. Tuco's first name is a homage to the character Tuco Ramirez, the "Ugly" in Sergio Leone's groundbreaking 1966 Spaghetti Western *The Good, the Bad, and the Ugly*. Tuco also reappears in *Better Than Saul*, getting thrown into jail after beating the shit out of Mike Ehrmantraut. Tuco appears in four episodes of *Breaking Bad*: "Grilled," "Seven Thirty-Seven," "A No-Rough-Stuff-Type Deal," and "Crazy Handful of Nothin'."

Raymond Cruz was born on July 9, 1961, grew up in East Los Angeles, and attended East Los Angeles College. Cruz portrayed another total psychopath known as Sniper in a brief but very memorable and disturbing scene in *Training Day* (2001), which starred Denzel Washington and Ethan Hawke. His film credits also include *Clear and Present Danger* (1994), *Out for Justice* (1991), *Under Siege* (1992), *The Rock* (196), and *Alien: Resurrection* (1997). He left *Breaking Bad* to assume the role of Detective Julio Sanchez in the TV series *The Closer*.

Gretchen and Elliot Schwartz (Jessica Hecht and Adam Godley)

The co-owners of Gray Matter Technologies, Gretchen and Elliot Schwartz founded the company along with Walter White. In fact, Gretchen was once romantically linked to Walter, but the couple had a major falling out. Gretchen appears in five episodes of *Breaking Bad*: ". . . And the Bag's in the River," "Gray Matter," "Peekaboo," "Granite State," and "Felina." Elliott appears in three episodes: "Gray Matter," "Granite State," and "Felina."

Jessica Anne Hecht was born on June 28, 1965, in Princeton, New Jersey. She received her bachelor of fine arts in drama at the NYU Tisch School of the Arts (where *Breaking Bad* creator Vince Gilligan studied filmmaking) in 1987. When she first arrived in Los Angeles in the early 1990s, Hecht served as a nanny to the three children of actor George Wendt (Norm from *Cheers*). Her film credits include *Sideways* (2004), *The Forgotten* (2004), and *Dan in Real Life* (2007). Hecht was nominated for a Tony for Best Featured Actress in a Play for her performance in *A View from the Bridge* in 2010. She is married to film director Adam Bernstein, who has directed eight *Breaking Bad* episodes: "Cat's in the Bag . . ." (2008), ". . . And the Bag's in the River" (2008), "Mandala" (2009), "ABQ" (2009), "Caballo Sin Nombre" (2010), "Half Measures" (2010), "Box Cutter" (2011), and "Hazard Pay" (2012).

Adam Godley was born on July 22, 1964, in Amersham, England. He was nominated for an Olivier Award for Best Actor for *Rain Man* at the Apollo Theatre in London (2008). Godley also received a Tony Award nomination for Best Supporting Actor in a Musical for *Anything Goes* (2011).

Skinny Pete (Charles Baker)

One of the most memorable members of Jesse's posse, Skinny Pete (last name unknown) often hangs out with Badger, and the duo's typically inane dialogue always serves as comic relief. After Skinny Pete's infamous encounter with Spooge, Jesse exclaims, "Spooge? Not Mad Dog? Not Diesel? So lemme get this straight, you got jacked by a guy named Spooge?" Skinny Pete manages a surprising rendition of C. P. E. Bach's "Solfeggietto" in the music shop in the episode "Hazard Pay" (5.03). Skinny Pete appears in fifteen episodes of *Breaking Bad*: "Cancer Man," "Crazy Handful of Nothin'", "Breakage," "Peekaboo," "Negro Y Azul," "Mandala," "Mas," "Sunset," "I See You," "Kafkaesque," "Abiquiu," "Thirty-Eight Snub," "Hazard Pay," "Blood Money," and "Felina."

Charles Baker was born on February 27, 1971, in Washington, D.C. The son of an Army colonel, Baker was originally a music major who also worked as a recreational therapist. His film credits include *Splinter* (2008), *To the Wonder* (2011), and *Wild* (2014). Baker currently has a recurring role on the NBC series *The Blacklist*.

Tortuga (Danny Trejo)

A Mexico cartel member and DEA informant, Tortuga lives according to the motto: "There are two kinds of men in this world, those who drink and those who pour." However, the boastful, wisecracking thug succumbs to a particularly disturbing death—his head is chopped off by the Cousins and attached to a tortoise. Tortuga appears in two episodes of *Breaking Bad*: "I.F.T." and "Negro Y Azul."

Dan Trejo was born on May 16, 1944, in Echo Park, Los Angeles, California. After a troubled childhood, Trejo served time in San Quentin State Prison in California on armed robbery and drug offenses. He made his film debut in *Runaway Train* (1985), which was directed by Andrei Konchalovsky and starred Jon Voight, Eric Roberts, Rebecca De Mornay, and John P. Ryan. Trejo portrayed "Trejo" in Michael Mann's *Heat* (1995), and he is the only actor to appear in all three of the *From Dusk to Dawn* movie series (Trejo and director Robert Rodriguez are second cousins). He has named his all-time favorite films as *The Searchers* (1956), *Once Upon a Time in the West* (1968), *Dirty Harry* (1971), *Death Wish* (1974), and *Animal Factory* (2000).

Victor (Jeremiah Bitsui)

One of Gus Fring's loyal enforcers, Victor (last name unknown) gets spotted by witnesses at Gale Boetticher's apartment shortly after the lab assistant's murder, making him a liability. Victor informs Walt and Jesse that, after watching them at work in the superlab, he can cook a whole batch of meth by himself, and he promptly does so. Gus arrives at the lab and promptly murders Victor with a box cutter, seemingly to send a message to Walt and Jesse, who are forced to dispose of Victor's body using hydrofluoric acid. However, Walt later reflects that there may have been another reason for Victor's murder: "Victor trying to cook that batch on his own, taking liberties that weren't his to take. Maybe he flew too close to the sun and got his throat cut." Victor appears in eight episodes of *Breaking Bad*: "Mandala," "Caballo Sin Nombre," "Green Light," "I See You," "Kafkaesque," "Half Measures," "Full Measure," and "Box Cutter" (which is also the weapon Gus uses to kill him). Victor reappears in *Better Call Saul*.

Bitsui has appeared in *Natural Born Killers* (1994), *Brothers* (2009), and *Drunktown's Finest* (2014).

Don Eladio Vuente (Steven Bauer)

The ruthless boss of the Juarez Cartel, Don Eladio Vuente served as one of Gus Fring's main antagonists (years earlier he had instructed Hector Salamanca to murder Gus's partner, Maximino Arciniega). Vuente is ultimately killed by Gus using poisoned tequila, and he collapses dead into his own swimming pool. Vuente appears in two episodes of *Breaking Bad*: "Hermanos" and "Salud." He also reappears in Season Three of *Better Call Saul*.

Steven Bauer was born Esteban Ernesto Echevarria in Havana, Cuba, on December 2, 1956. He studied in the Department of Theater Arts at the University of Miami. Bauer made his inauspicious film debut in the 1983 teen comedy *Valley Girl* as Guy in Pink Shirt. However, he received his big acting break when he starred as Manolo Ribera alongside Al Pacino in *Scarface* (1983), for which he was nominated for a Golden Globe for Best Supporting Actor (losing out to Jack Nicholson for *Terms of Endearment*). Bauer also appeared in the Eurythmics music video "Would I Lie to You" (1985). His film credits include *Thief of Hearts* (1984), *Running Scared* (1986), *Wildfire* (1988), *Raising Cain* (1992), *Primal Fear* (1996), and *Kickboxing Academy* (1997), among many others. He also portrayed Michael Santana in the 1980s TV series *Wiseguy*.

Jack Welker (Michael Bowen)

Todd Alquist's uncle and the leader of a white supremacist gang, Uncle Jack Welker helps Walt by arranging the synchronized murder of ten prison inmates, but later turns against him—killing Walt's brother-in-law Hank and stealing most of Walt's drug money. Uncle Jack appears in seven episodes of *Breaking Bad*: "Gliding Over All," "Buried," "Confessions," "To'hajiilee," "Ozymandias," "Granite State," and "Felina."

Michael Bowen was born on June 21, 1953, in Houston, Texas. Fans of 1980s teen comedies may find it hard to believe that Bowen appeared in *Valley Girl* (1983) as Tommy, the douchebag boyfriend of Julie (Deborah Foreman) and the main antagonist of Randy (Nicolas Cage). Bowen also portrayed Vince in *The Wild Life* (1984) and Larry Dupree in *Night of the*

Comet (1984). He also has appeared in several Quentin Tarantino films, including *Jackie Brown* (1997), *Kill Bill Vol. 1* (2003), and *Kill Bill: Vol. 2* (2004). Bowen is the half-brother of actors Keith and Robert Carradine. He has appeared in two films that were nominated for Best Picture Oscars: *The Godfather: Part III* (1990) and *Django Unchained* (2012).

Wendy (Julia Minesci)

A meth-addicted prostitute who turns tricks in the parking lot of the Crossroads Motel, "Wendy the Whore" is used by Hank to scare Walt Jr. about the effects of drug use. She also hooks up with Jesse on several occasions and even takes part in his failed plot to use tainted hamburgers to poison the drug dealers who ordered the death of Combo. Wendy appears in three episodes of *Breaking Bad*: ". . . And the Bag's in the River," "Bit by a Dead Bee," and "Half Measures."

Minesci, who appeared in the short film *Me & My Deadbeat Husband* (2012), has competed in numerous marathons over the years, as well as Hawaii and German Ironman events. As an interesting side note, Minesci so looked the part of a meth-addicted prostitute that she was even propositioned by a passing motorist at one point during the filming of a *Breaking Bad* episode.

6

I Am the One Who Knocks

A Profile of Walter White

I thought of [Walt] as a nice guy who had this chaotic senseless world arrayed against him. A world that didn't care whether he existed or not. And in the process of coming to grips with that—and despite our liking to think there's a point to our existence—perhaps there really isn't."

—*Vince Gilligan*

Full Name: Walter Hartwell White

Date of Birth: September 7, 1959

Alias: Heisenberg (named after German theoretical physicist and Nobel Prize in Physics recipient Werner Karl Heisenberg, 1901–76)

Family: Wife, Skyler; Son, Walt Jr. (aka "Flynn"); Daughter, Holly

Address: 308 Negra Arroyo Lane, Albuquerque, New Mexico

Pets: None

Education: California Institute of Technology (aka Caltech), where he conducted research on proton radiography and assisted a team that won the 1985 Nobel Prize in Chemistry.

Work History: Research chemist, cofounder of Gray Matter Technologies (with Elliott and Gretchen Schwartz; settled for a $5,000 buyout), chemistry teacher at J. P. Wynne High School, car wash attendant at A1 Car Wash, meth cook, car wash owner, drug kingpin

Teaching Salary: $43,700/year

Drug-Related Earnings: $80 million

Medical History: Stage IIIA lung cancer

Cars: 2004 Pontiac Aztek, 2012 Chrysler 300

Favorite Poet: Walt Whitman (1819–92)

Favorite Book: *Leaves of Grass* (1855)

Walt's alias, Heisenberg, refers to Werner Karl Heisenberg, an acclaimed German theoretical physicist who was considered one of the most important physicists of the twentieth century.

Max Lobrich/Smithsonian Institution/Wikimedia Commons

Favorite Musicians: Boz Scaggs, Steely Dan, America

Favorite Movie: *Scarface* (1983), directed by Brian De Palma, scripted by Oliver Stone, and starring Al Pacino as Tony Montana

Favorite Meal of the Day: Breakfast

Murders: Emilio Koyama (phosphorus gas), Krazy-8 (strangled with bike lock), Jane Margolis (watches her die while she chokes on her own vomit), two unnamed drug dealers (runs over in car and shoots one in head to protect Jesse), Gale Boetticher (forces Jesse to shoot in head),

Gus Fring and Tyrus Kitt (attaches pipe bomb to Hector's wheelchair in Casa Tranquila nursing home), Mike Ehrmantraut (shoots to death), ten prisoners (hires Uncle Jack and his white supremacist gang to orchestrate simultaneous murders), Uncle Jack and associates (eliminates using a remotely controlled machine gun in trunk car), Lydia Rodarte-Quayle (poisons with ricin)

On Tuco Salamanca: "an insane degenerate piece of filth."

On Life: "I have spent my whole life scared—frightened of things that could happen, might happen, might not happen. Fifty years I spent

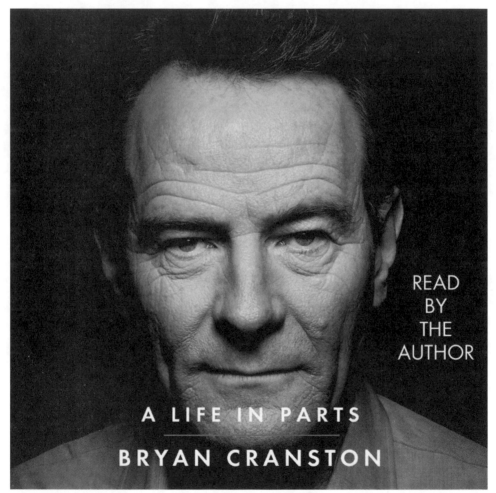

In 2012, Bryan Cranston published his critically acclaimed autobiography, *A Life in Parts*, which Vince Gilligan called "just the right mixture of funny, sad, and heartfelt."

like that. Finding myself awake at three in the morning. But you know what? Ever since my diagnosis, I sleep just fine."

On Fear: "What I came to realize is that fear, that's the worst of it. That's the real enemy. So, get up, get out in the real world and you kick that bastard as hard as you can right in the teeth."

On His Blue Meth: "It is impeccable. It is the purest, most chemically sound product on the market, anywhere."

On SaveWalterWhite.com: "Cyber-begging, that's all that is. Just rattling a little tin cup to the entire world."

On Criminality: "I'm making a change in my life is what it is, and I'm at something of a crossroads and it's brought me to a realization: I'm not a criminal. No offense to any people who are, but . . . this is not me."

On Chemistry: "I simply respect the chemistry. The chemistry must be respected."

On Mike Ehrmantraut: "grunting dead-eyed cretin."

On the Universe: "My God, the universe is random; it's not inevitable, it's simple chaos. It's subatomic particles and endless pings, collision—that's what science teaches us."

On Danger: "I am *not* in danger . . . *I am the danger!* A guy opens his door and gets shot and you think that of me? No. I am the one who knocks!"

On Consequences: "I have lived under the threat of death for a year now. And because of that, I've made choices . . . I alone should suffer the consequences of those choices, no one else. And those consequences . . . they're coming. No more prolonging the inevitable."

On Saul Goodman: "a two-bit, bus-bench lawyer."

On Business: "You asked me if I was in the meth business or the money business." Neither. I'm in the *empire* business."

On Squandered Potential: "Being the best at something is a very rare thing. You don't just toss something like that away. And what? You want to squander that potential—*your* potential? Why? To do what?"

On Hell: "If you believe that there's a Hell—I don't know if you're into that—but we're already pretty much going there. But I'm not gonna lie down until I get there."

On Starting Over: "Whole lifetime ahead of you, with a chance to hit the reset button. In a few years, this might all feel like nothing more than a bad dream."

Date of Death: September 7, 2011

Cause of Death: Gunshot wound

Final Resting Place: Sunset Memorial Park (Albuquerque), "New Mexico's Most Beautiful Cemetery"

Epitaph: "Beloved Husband, Father, Teacher & Entrepreneur"

Other Notable TV Antiheroes: Jack Bauer (*24*), Don Draper (*Mad Men*), Rick Grimes (*The Walking Dead*), Omar Little (*The Wire*), Vic Mackey (*The Shield*), Dexter Morgan (*Dexter*), Tony Soprano (*The Sopranos*), Al Swearengen (*Deadwood*), Jax Teller (*Sons of Anarchy*)

7

Some Worthless Junkie

A Profile of Jesse Pinkman

Ever since I met you, everything I ever cared about is gone! Ruined, turned to shit, dead, ever since I hooked up with the great Heisenberg! I have never been more alone!

—Jesse Pinkman to Walter White

Full Name: Jesse Bruce Pinkman

Date of Birth: September 14, 1984

Alias: Cap'n Cook

Family: Father, Adam Pinkman; Mother, Mrs. Pinkman; Brother, Jake Pinkman; Aunt, Ginny (deceased)

Girlfriends: Jane Margolis (dies of overdose while Walter White stands over her and does nothing to save her), Andrea Cantillo (murdered by Todd Alquist as a lesson to Jesse after he escapes from Uncle Jack's compound)

Posse: Christian "Combo" Ortega, Skinny Pete, Brandon "Badger" Mayhew

Education: J. P. Wynne High School, studied data systems management at DeVry University

Work History: Crystal meth cook and dealer

Cars: 1982 Monte Carlo (with "Cap'n Cook" vanity plate), 1986 Toyota Tercel

Interests: His MyShout page lists "fine herbage," "keepin' it real," "bangin' the skins with my smokin' band TwaughtHammer," "MILFs, MILFs, MILFs"; also art and go-karting

Favorite Word: "Bitch" (which he says a total of fifty-four times over the course of the series)

Second Favorite Word: "Yo"

Favorite TV Show: *Ice Road Truckers* (History Channel)

Favorite Musician: Jethro Tull

Aaron Paul almost didn't get cast as Jesse Pinkman because some executives thought he was just too handsome for the role of a low-level meth dealer known as "Cap'n Cook."

Anders Krusberg/Peabody Awards/Wikimedia Commons

Favorite Eatery: Dog House Drive In

Favorite Junk Food: Funyuns

Secret Meth Ingredient: chili powder

Murders: Gale Boetticher (shot in the face at the instigation of Walter White), Joaquin Salamanca (shot to death in Mexico), Todd Alquist (strangled to death in season finale)

On Meth Cooking: "This ain't chemistry—this is art. Cooking is art. And the shit I cook is the bomb . . . "

On His Parents: "greedy kleptomaniac douchebags."

On Ambition: "This is our city, alright? All of it. The whole damn place. Our territory. We're staking our claim. Yo, we sell when we want, where we want. We're gonna be kings, understand?"

On Making Money: "Gonna make some mad cheddar, yo . . . Fat stacks. Dead Presidents. Cash money. We're gonna own this city."

On Hiring Saul Goodman: "Seriously, when the going gets tough, you don't want a criminal lawyer. All right, you want a *criminal* lawyer. You know what I'm saying?"

On Future Ambitions: "Right on. New Zealand, that's where they, uh, that's where they made *Lord of the Rings*! I say we just move there, yo! I mean, you could do your art, right? Like, you could like paint the local castles and shit, and I can be a bush pilot!"

On DEA Harassment: "This is my own private domicile and I will not be harassed . . . bitch!"

On the Drudgery of Work: "Been working a lot . . . It's in a laundromat. It's totally corporate . . . It's like rigid, all kinds of red tape, my boss is a dick, the owner, super dick, don't know if we're ever going to meet him, everybody's scared of the dude. Place is full of dead-eyed douchebags, the hours suck, and nobody knows what's going on."

On Responsibility: "What's the point of being an outlaw when you got responsibilities?"

On Quality: "Did you know that there's an acceptable level of rat turds that can go into candy bars? . . . Even government doesn't care that much about quality. You know what is okay to put in hot dogs? Pig lips and assholes."

On Adapting: "For what it's worth, getting the shit kicked out of you? Not to say you get used to it, but you do kinda get used to it."

The site of many days and nights of nonstop debauchery, Jesse Pinkman's house is located in the upscale Albuquerque Country Club neighborhood.   *Courtesy of Ben Parker*

On Math: "So, what if this is like math or algebra? And you add a plus douchebag to a minus douchebag, and you get, like zero douchebags?"

On Ingenuity: "Yeah, bitch! Magnets!"

On Walter White: "Mr. White . . . he's the devil. You know, he is—he is smarter than you, he is luckier than you. Whatever—whatever you think is supposed to happen—I'm telling you, the exact reverse opposite of that is going to happen, okay?"

On Walt's Ambitions: "Is a meth empire really something to be that proud of?"

Whereabouts: Unknown

8

She Stood by You

The Inexplicable Fan Hatred Toward Skyler White

> I haven't been myself lately, but I love you. Nothing about that has changed, nothing ever will. So right now, what I need is for you to climb down out of my ass . . . Will you do that for me, honey?
>
> —*Walt to Skyler*

A disturbing subsection of *Breaking Bad* fans took to Facebook, Twitter, blogs, and other various social media over the course of the series to express their total hatred for Skyler White, amazingly portrayed by Anna Gunn, who was even forced to take protective steps at one point to ensure her safety. For example, an "I Hate Skyler White" Facebook page numbered more than thirty thousand likes, while an even more vicious "Fuck Skyler White" page garnered more than twenty-nine thousand likes. The most vocal of these Skyler White "critics" were simply misogynistic cretins who felt that Skyler was somehow holding her sociopathic meth cook husband from realizing his drug empire dreams. How dare she try to keep her family together in the wake of Walt's strange behavior and frequent disappearances!

In a September 5, 2013, *Esquire* article, Jen Chaney stated,

> By extension, as a culture, we also tend to be less forgiving of women who do wrong and more understanding of men who cheat, or over-tweet, or do a whole host of much worse things. Why? Because men, supposedly, have a harder time resisting temptation. They deserve some slack and we should all just climb down out of their asses, for God's sake. None of this is fair, mind you. These preconceived but deeply ingrained notions are insulting to both men and women. But they're there, felt unconsciously even if not spoken out loud. We

want Skyler to do the clear-cut, black-and-white right thing because that's
what women are supposed to do.

At the outset of *Breaking Bad*, we learn that Skyler is approximately
eleven years younger than Walt, as well as pregnant with the couple's
second child. Skyler met Walt at a diner where she worked as a host-
ess close to his former place of work, near the Los Alamos National
Laboratory. An aspiring writer of short stories, Skyler sells miscellaneous
items on eBay for extra cash. When Walt is diagnosed with lung cancer,
he acts strangely and disappears for hour on end without telling Skyler
his whereabouts. He also initially rejects chemotherapy until strongly
persuaded by Skyler and the rest of the family during the infamous
"Talking Pillow" intervention. To add to all her existing stress, Skyler has
to deal with the dramatics of her kleptomaniac sister, Marie.

When Walt simply disappears for a couple of days (he and Jesse are
kidnapped by Tuco Salamanca), Skyler organizes a search party and
hangs up missing posters. She also encourages Walt Jr.'s online campaign
to raise money for her husband's medical expenses (SaveWalterWhite.
com), even though Walt discourages the effort. When Skyler gives birth
to Holly, Walt is nowhere to be found because he's desperately attempting
to orchestrate a meth transaction with Gus Fring.

Skyler is eventually forced to take a job as a bookkeeper with her
old employer, Beneke Fabricators, to help make ends meet (as well as
a way to spend time away from Walt). She later has an affair with her
boss, Ted Beneke (Christopher Cousins), mostly as a way to get back at
Walt. After finding out about Walt's meth business, she first demands
a divorce in exchange for being quiet about his various criminal enterprises. However, when that strategy fails (Walt defiantly returns to the
house), Skyler orchestrates the purchase of the A1 Car Wash and becomes
heavily involved in laundering his drug money. She also invents Walt's
fake gambling addiction as a way to explain the car wash purchase. In
addition, Skyler reluctantly helps Ted cover up his ongoing tax fraud.

In perhaps her worst "Lady Macbeth" moment, Skyler actually urges
Walt to kill Jesse: "For us, what's one more?" When Hank discovers the
true identity of Heisenberg, Skyler refuses to testify against Walt. After
Walt simply disappears, Skyler is threatened in her home by creepy Todd

In response to the inexplicable and irrational hatred generated toward Skyler White, actress Anna Gunn (pictured with Aaron Paul at the Peabody Awards) wrote a 2013 op-ed for *The New York Times* titled "I Have a Character Issue."

Peabody Awards/Wikimedia Commons

Alquist and his gang. She has to abandon the house, move to a rundown apartment, and take a job as a taxi dispatcher. After Walt visits Skyler one last time and admits he did it all for himself, she even lets him see his daughter, Holly, one last time.

In a May 12, 2013, *Vulture* magazine interview, Vince Gilligan remarked, "I like Skyler a little less now that she's succumbed to Walt's machinations, but in the early days she was the voice of morality on the show. She was the one telling him, 'You can't cook crystal meth.' She's got

Anna Gunn has referred to her character Skyler White as "grounded, tough, smart, and driven."   *Gage Skidmore/Wikimedia Commons*

a tough job being married to this asshole." Just the reverse of what most of Skyler's critics were spewing in most of the online venom, Gilligan admitted that he lost sympathy for Skyler only after "she started being co-opted by Walt." Prior to that, she was doing whatever possible to shield the rest of the family from Walt's evil machinations. In fact, Gilligan at one point refers to Skyler's more hardcore critics as "misogynists, pure and simple."

In a widely read August 23, 2013, op-ed for *The New York Times* titled "I Have a Character Issue," Gunn wrote,

> My character, to judge from the popularity of Web sites and Facebook pages devoted to hating her, has become a flash point for many people's feelings about strong, nonsubmissive, ill-treated women. As the hatred of Skyler blurred into loathing for me as a person, I saw glimpses of an anger that, at first, simply bewildered me . . . As the one character who consistently opposes Walter and calls him on his lies, Skyler is, in a sense, his antagonist. So from the beginning, I was aware that she might not be the show's most popular character. But I was unprepared for the vitriolic response she inspired.

According to Gunn, the harsh online comments devolved into "outright personal attacks" on not only the character but the actress as well. One post actually went so far as to threaten violence: "Could somebody tell me where I can find Anna Gunn so I can kill her?" According to Gunn, "Because Skyler didn't conform to a comfortable ideal of the archetypical female, she had become a kind of Rorschach test for society, a measure of our attitudes toward gender. I can't say that I have enjoyed being the center of the storm of Skyler hate. But in the end, I'm glad that this discussion has happened, that it has taken place in public and that it has illuminated some of the dark and murky corners that we often ignore or pretend aren't still there in our everyday lives."

9

Finding Myself Awake

Pilot Episode (January 20, 2008)

You and I will not make garbage. We will produce a chemically pure and stable product that performs as advertised. No adulterants, no baby formula, no chili powder.

—Walter White

Written and directed by series creator Vince Gilligan, the pilot episode of *Breaking Bad*, simply titled "Pilot," aired on AMC on January 20, 2008. Gilligan remarked in a commentary on the first DVD of the series that he wanted the show to be about "a good man who loves his family, and who decides to become a criminal." In his 2016 autobiography, *A Life in Parts*, Bryan Cranston described the pilot as "great characterizations, complex plots, nuanced story elements, surprises that left you thinking: What on earth is going to happen next?"

The "Pilot" episode opens with an extended and disorienting flashback featuring a frantic individual wearing a gas mask and clad in tighty-whities recklessly driving a battered RV in the middle of the desert. As sirens seemingly close in on him, the individual records a strange confession: "My name is Walter Hartwell White. I live at 308 Negra Arroyo Lane, Albuquerque, New Mexico. 87104. To all law enforcement entities, this is not an admission of guilt. I am speaking to my family now. Skyler, you are the love of my life, I hope you know that. Walter junior, you're my big man. There are . . . there are going to be some things, things that you'll come to learn about me in the next few days. I just want you to know that, no matter how it may look, I only had you in my heart. Goodbye."

Next, viewers learn all about how this desperate individual ended up in the middle of the desert making this strange confession. Once a brilliant chemist with a promising future (a framed award on his wall acknowledges his contribution to work that was awarded the 1985 Nobel Prize), Walter Hartwell White (Cranston) now watches helplessly as his students at J. P. Wynne High School doze off during his lectures. "Chemistry is, well technically, chemistry is the study of matter. But I prefer to see it as the study of change," he informs the indifferent, unresponsive class. In addition, Walt is forced to work a demeaning second job at the A1 Car Wash to make ends meet. On his fiftieth birthday, he is presented with a

Vince Gilligan remarked in a commentary on the first *Breaking Bad* DVD that he wanted the show to be about "a good man who loves his family, and who decides to become a criminal."

breakfast plate full of veggie bacon spelling out the number fifty. Later that night, he sits through a rather sedate surprise party, after which his pregnant wife Skyler (Anna Gunn) "gives him the least sexy hand job in the history of mankind," according to Cranston in his autobiography. Skyler even scolds Walt for using the wrong credit card for a $15.88 purchase at Staples. A truly ordinary individual who blends into the background, the out-of-shape Walt wears very muted colors at the outset of the series and sports an "impotent" moustache that looks like "a dead caterpillar," according to Cranston.

According to Vince Gilligan in a September 25, 2013, *Rolling Stone* interview, "In the first few episodes of *Breaking Bad*, you immediately establish how emasculated Walter White is. His wife serves him veggie bacon and nags him to take his Echinacea. His son calls him a 'pussy.' His students ignore him. His macho brother-in-law mocks him." In essence, here is a guy having the "world's worst midlife crisis," according to Gilligan.

Shortly after his rather uneventful birthday, Walt learns that he has inoperable lung cancer. In an effort to make long-term provisions for

The A1 Car Wash, where Walt worked a demeaning second job, was filmed at the Octopus Car Wash, which is today known as Mister Car Wash.   *Courtesy of Ben Parker*

Skyler and son Walt Jr. (RJ Mitte), who has cerebral palsy, Walt partners with former student Jesse Pinkman (Aaron Paul) to cook meth. He notices Jesse escaping from a drug bust during a ride-along with his brother-in-law, DEA agent Hank Schrader (Dean Norris). The self-proclaimed "Cap'n Cook," Jesse adds chili powder to his meth as a kind of signature. Walt gives Jesse the choice of partnering with him or he will turn him in to the authorities (although at this point he does not fill him in on his reason for wanting to cook meth). Jesse replies, "Some straight like you, giant stick up his ass all a sudden at age, what, sixty, he's just gonna break bad?" In a not-so-bright move, Walt even hands over his life savings of $7,000 to Jesse to purchase a rundown Bounder RV to use as a mobile meth lab, and even steals supplies such as beakers and gas masks from his chemistry lab at the high school to help with the first meth cook.

Walt and Jesse head to a remote desert location and cook up their first batch of meth, which Jesse claims to be the purest meth he has ever seen. Unfortunately, Jesse leads two tough drug dealers, Krazy-8 (Max Arciniega) and Emilio Koyama (his former partner, portrayed by John Koyama) to the meth lab, and they take Walt and Jesse hostage by gunpoint (recognizing him from the drug bust, Emilio believes that Walt is an informant). Krazy-8 unwittingly causes a brushfire after flicking a lit cigarette out of the RV. Under the guise of showing Krazy-8 and Emilio how he cooks meth, Walt manages to escape the RV after filling it with phosphorus gas, trapping the two drug dealers inside. Walt then proceeds to crash the RV into a ditch. When he hears sirens, he tape-records the confession, thinking he is about to be nabbed by the police. However, to his relief, it is simply fire engines driving by in response to the brushfire. Walt and Jesse make it back to Jesse's house with the RV that contains the two drug dealers in the back—Emilio dead and Krazy-8 barely alive. Emboldened by his new status as an "outlaw," Walt initiates passionate sex with Skyler, who exclaims, "Walt, is that you?"

Indications of Walt's emerging dark side (the Heisenberg persona that will be revealed later) in the "Pilot" episode include how he manhandles a teenager who makes fun of Walt Jr. in the clothing store and how he berates his boss when he quits his job at the car wash ("Fuck you! And your eyebrows!").

"Pilot" Episode Trivia

- Believe it or not, the tighty-whities Walt wears in this episode were actually sold at auction for $9,900.
- Cranston won a Primetime Emmy Award for Outstanding Lead Actor in a Drama Series for this episode. Gilligan was nominated for Outstanding Directing for a Drama Series (losing out to Greg Yaitanes for *House*).
- Gilligan won the Writers Guild of America Award for Television: Episodic Drama for the "Pilot" episode.
- During a 2013 interview on *The Colbert Report*, Gilligan recalled the "Pilot" episode getting under one million viewers due to the fact "we went up against some big football game, and we got crushed."
- Cranston learned some chemistry basics from a professor at the University of Southern California and sat in on many classes at Rio Rancho High School (where much of the actual high school filming took place) to help develop his bland chemistry teacher persona. In addition, an actual DEA agent was recruited on set to show the cast and crew how to make crystal meth.
- A plaque on the wall of the White household indicates that Walt did research that contributed to the 1985 Nobel Prize for Chemistry. The actual Nobel laureates in chemistry that year were Herbert A. Hauptman (1917–2011) and Jerome Karle (1918–2013) "for their outstanding achievements in developing direct methods for the determination of crystal structures."

10

A Series of Very Bad Decisions

Season One (2008)

We got new players in town. We don't know who they are, where they come from, but they possess an extremely high skill-set.

—*Hank Schrader*

After the exhilarating "Pilot" episode (see Chapter 9), the rest of Season One of *Breaking Bad* focused on Walt and Jesse trying to resolve their initial missteps involving Emilio and Krazy-8, and also introduced a new villain for them to deal with—the psychopathic Tuco Salamanca (portrayed with gusto by Raymond Cruz!). Originally intended for a total of nine episodes, Season One was shortened to just seven episodes due to the 2007–08 Writers Guild of America strike.

Episode 1.02: "Cat's in the Bag . . . " (January 27, 2008)

Walt and Jesse attempt to dispose of the bodies of Emilio and Krazy-8 in the RV. However, they discover to their horror that Krazy-8 is still alive, and they are forced to imprison him in Jesse's basement using a bike lock around his neck and attached to a pole. Skyler grows suspicious of Walt's frequent absences and strange behavior. However, Walt tells her that he loves her and that he needs her "to climb down out of my ass." Walt and Jesse end up flipping a coin to see which of them will have to dispose of Emilio's body and which will have to kill Krazy-8 (Walt loses). Jesse sets about disposing of Emilio's body with hydrofluoric acid, but ignores Walt's instructions to use a plastic bin and opts for the upstairs bathtub—turning the entire affair into a grotesque, bloody spectacle as the acid leaks through the ceiling onto the first floor hallway below. Walt informs Jesse, "After we finish cleaning up this mess, we will go our separate ways. Our paths will never cross and we will tell this to no one. Understood?"

The episode was written by Vince Gilligan and directed by Adam Bernstein, who is married to Jessica Hecht (Gretchen Schwartz). The episode's title comes from the 1957 film noir *Sweet Smell of Success*, which was directed by Alexander Mackendrick and starred Burt Lancaster, Tony Curtis, Susan Harrison, and Martin Milner. Lancaster portrays J. J. Hunsecker, a sleazy New York City columnist, who at one point asks Manhattan press agent "Sidney Falco" (Tony Curtis) if he can deliver on his plan. Falco replies, "The cat's in the bag and the bag's in the river." Vince Gilligan has stated that *Sweet Smell of Success* is his all-time favorite movie.

Episode 1.03: ". . . And the Bag's in the River" (February 10, 2008)

After Walt and Jesse clean up from the hydrofluoric acid debacle, Jesse exclaims, "How am I supposed to live here now, huh? My whole house smells like toe cheese and dry cleaning." However, Walt is torn over whether or not he should kill Krazy-8. On his way to deliver food to Krazy-8, Walt passes out on the basement steps and the plate shatters. When Walt wakes up, he tells Krazy-8 about his lung cancer, and the captor and captive bond over things they have in common. Walt soon decides to release Krazy-8, but when he disposes of the broken plate he notices that a shard is missing and realizes that Krazy-8 intends to kill him with it. When Walt confronts Krazy-8, he gets attacked immediately. Walt is forced to strangle Krazy-8 with the bike lock. Meanwhile, Marie has suspicions that Walt Jr. is smoking marijuana and pleads with Hank to intervene and scare him straight. Hank takes Walt Jr. to the Crossroads Motel to show him what drugs lead to, and they encounter the perfect example—Wendy the Whore (Julia Minesci).

During filming of the Crossroads Motel scene in episode 1.03, a bystander—unaware that they were filming—tried to pick up actress Julia Minesci, believing she was an actual prostitute.

Courtesy of Ben Parker

The episode was written by Vince Gilligan and directed by Adam Bernstein. The episode's title continues the line from *Sweet Smell of Success* (1957) that started in the title of the previous episode, "Cat's in the Bag," and refers to Walt finally killing Krazy-8. During filming of the Crossroads Motel scene, a bystander—unaware that they were filming—tried to pick up Minesci, believing she was an actual prostitute. Note that the 1988 drama *Rain Man* is referenced by Gomie as he jabs with Hank: "Yeah, you're like Rain Man. Retarded."

Episode 1.04: "Cancer Man" (February 17, 2008)

Hank becomes aware of a new and mysterious drug kingpin in Albuquerque, unaware it is his own brother-in-law Walt, who reveals that he has lung cancer at a family barbecue. Jesse visits his family, but they remain distant and finally kick him out of the house after they discover a pot pipe (ironically, Jesse takes the rap for his younger brother, who is considered the golden child of the family). Jesse visits Walt at his house, refers to Skyler as a "ball buster," tells him "how much everybody digs that meth we cooked," and gives him his share of the meth cook totaling $4,000. Also in this episode, Walt gets revenge on an arrogant yuppie with a vanity license plate that reads "KEN WINS" who steals his parking space.

The episode was written by Vince Gilligan and directed by Jim McKay. The episode's title refers to Walt's condition and also to Jesse as a "cancer" to his family that they are trying to desperately expunge out of their lives because of his drug use and lies. In addition, the episode pays homage to the Cigarette Smoking Man (played by William B. Davis), the main antagonist from *The X-Files*. Note that Hank makes a crude reference to country music superstar Shania Twain: "Yeah, I want Shania Twain to give me a tuggy. Guess what. It ain't happening either." KEN WINS will later make a reappearance in *Better Call Saul* (Episode 2.01) as the victim of one of Jimmy McGill's scams.

Episode 1.05: "Gray Matter" (February 24, 2008)

Walt and Skyler visit the mansion of his former business partners at Gray Matter Technologies, Elliott and Gretchen Schwartz, to celebrate Elliott's birthday. Briefed by Skyler about Walt's condition, Elliott offers him a position in the company, but Walt can easily read through the situation and declines their "charity." Desperately looking for work, Jesse turns down a job as a local bank mascot (as a teenager, Aaron Paul worked briefly as a frog mascot for a radio station). Jesse starts cooking meth again, but discovers the quality of his product is inferior to Walt's. Meanwhile, Walt Jr. gets caught trying to buy beer at a convenience store. Walt refuses chemotherapy, telling Skyler, "Sometimes I feel like I never actually make any of my own. Choices, I mean. My entire life, it just seems I never . . . you know, had a real say about any of it. Now this last one, cancer . . . all I have left is how I choose to approach this." Walt's family stages an intervention (complete with an infamous "Talking Pillow") in an effort to persuade him to undergo chemotherapy. He adamantly refuses at first, but gradually relents. After burning the bridge with Elliott and Gretchen, Walt drops by Jesse's house and asks to resume their partnership with the simple words, "Wanna cook?"

The episode was written by Patty Lin and directed by Tricia Brock, who previously directed the 2004 film *Killer Diller*, and also has directed episodes of *The Walking Dead*, *Grey's Anatomy*, *Gossip Girl*, *30 Rock*, *Hellcats*, *White Collar*, *Smash*, and *Ugly Betty*, among others.

Episode 1.06: "Crazy Handful of Nothin'" (March 2, 2008)

Walt and Jesse resume their meth operation with the agreement that Walt will cook and Jesse will sell the product. In addition, Walt insists that he doesn't want any interaction with the clientele: "As far as the customers go, I don't want to know anything about them. I don't need to see them.

Java Joe's coffee shop served as the filming location for Tuco Salamanca's hideout, where Walt causes an explosion using fulminated mercury that actually impresses the psychotic drug dealer.

Courtesy of Ben Parker

I don't want to hear from them." Jesse discovers that Walt has lung cancer, telling him, "I get it now. That's why you're doing this. You want to make some cash for your people before you check out." Hank traces the recovered respirator that Walt ditched in the desert to the chemistry lab at J. P. Wynne High School. Walt starts losing his hair from chemotherapy and decides to shave his head, beginning his gradual transformation into the Heisenberg persona. Walt Jr. even calls him a "badass." The next batch of

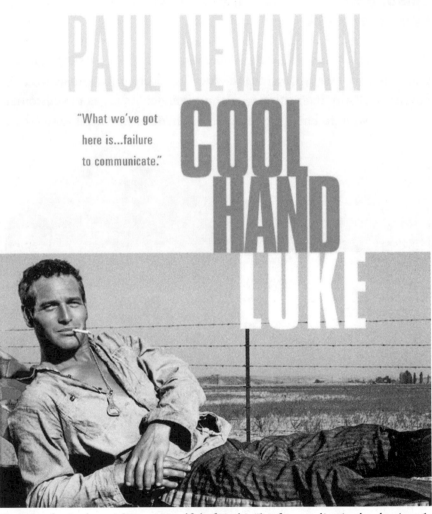

The title of episode 1.06 ("Crazy Handful of Nothin'") refers to a line in the classic 1967 prison drama *Cool Hand Luke*: "Oh Luke, you wild, beautiful thing. You crazy handful of nothin'."

meth only yields $2,600, so Walt demands that Jesse find a new distributor. Unfortunately, through Skinny Pete, Jesse contacts Tuco Salamanca, the psychotic drug dealer who took over Krazy-8's turf. When Jesse visits Tuco's hideout and tries to make a deal, Tuco gives him a severe beating and steals all his meth as well. Undaunted, Walt fearlessly visits Tuco's hideout as Heisenberg and puts his chemistry knowledge to good use by causing an explosion using fulminated mercury. The reckless and totally out-of-character action by Walt actually impresses Tuco enough for him to make a deal: "You got balls, I'll give you that."

The episode was written by George Mastras and directed by Bronwen Hughes. The episode's title refers to a line in the classic 1967 prison drama *Cool Hand Luke* addressed to the title character Lucas "Luke" Jackson (Paul Newman) from Dragline (George Kennedy): "Oh Luke, you wild, beautiful thing. You crazy handful of nothin'." Kennedy won a Best Supporting Actor Oscar for his outstanding performance. *Cool Hand Luke* was based on a 1965 novel of the same name by Donn Pearce, who had spent two years on a chain gang in Raiford Penitentiary in Florida after getting arrested for burglary in 1949 at the age of twenty. Walt's Heisenberg persona alludes to German theoretical physicist and Nobel Prize winner Werner Heisenberg (1901–76), one of the most important physicists of the twentieth century. Also listen for former Vermont Governor Howard Dean's infamous scream during the explosion at Tuco's hideout. During his 2004 presidential candidacy, Dean let out the high-pitched shriek during a rally (aka the "I Have a Scream" speech), and the reverberations led to the collapse of his campaign.

Episode 1.07: "A No-Rough-Stuff-Type Deal" (March 9, 2008)

Walt and Jesse run into some major difficulties as they try to keep up with Tuco's increasing demand for their immensely popular product. They decide to break into a warehouse and steal a large barrel of methylamine, allowing them to produce a greater quantity of meth more quickly. Hank and Walt have a discussion about the former procuring illegal Cuban cigars, with Walt asking if they were illegal. Hank replies, "Yeah, well, sometimes forbidden fruit tastes the sweetest." Walt challenges that notion, asking, "It's funny, isn't it? How we draw the line? . . . What's legal—what's illegal . . . I'm just saying it's arbitrary." Meanwhile, Skyler confronts Marie about her kleptomania after she discovers her sister has stolen an expensive tiara from a jewelry store as a baby shower gift. Walt and Jesse are able to deliver the promised amount of meth, but they witness Tuco's savagery as he brutally beats an associate, No Doze (Cesar Garcia), to death in front of them.

The episode was written by Peter Gould and directed by Tim Hunter. The episode's title alludes to a comment by conniving car salesman Jerry Lundegaard (William H. Macy) in the 1996 Coen brothers' cult film *Fargo* regarding the kidnapping of his wife: "This was supposed to be a no-rough-stuff type deal." Note that Walt starts wearing his porkpie hat in this episode, further descending into his Heisenberg persona. In a bit of much-needed comic relief, Walt gets criticized by both Jesse and Tuco for his choice of a junkyard for the drug meet. Jesse remarks that it is a "non-criminal's idea of a drug meet" and suggests in the future either the Gap in the mall or the fast-food chain Taco Cabeza, since "Nobody ever gets shot at Taco Cabeza." No Doze's death in this episode will later be foreshadowed in the *Better Call Saul* episode "Mijo" (1.02) when Tuco warns his associate to "stop helping."

11

A Bit of a Learning Curve

Season Two (2009)

I have spent my whole life scared—frightened of things that could happen, might happen, might not happen. Fifty years I spent like that. Finding myself awake at three in the morning. But you know what? Ever since my diagnosis, I sleep just fine.

—*Walter White*

The second season of *Breaking Bad* premiered on March 8, 2009, consisted of thirteen episodes, and features the demise of one villain—the ruthless, psychotic Tuco Salamanca—and the arrival of his exact opposite, the cunning, diabolical fast-food entrepreneur/drug kingpin Gustavo "Gus" Fring (Giancarlo Esposito). Jesse Pinkman also embarks on a doomed relationship with his next-door neighbor/landlord Jane Margolis (Krysten Ritter). Another major character introduced in Season Two is sleazy lawyer Saul Goodman (Bob Odenkirk), who helps keep Badger out of jail and quickly ingratiates himself into Walt's inner circle when he gets a whiff of the cash potential of his meth operation. Also note that the first, fourth, tenth, and thirteenth episodes (titled "Seven Thirty-Seven"/"Down"/"Over"/"ABQ" respectively) contain mysterious black-and-white teaser intros that foreshadow the horrifying airplane crash in the season finale, "ABQ."

For its second season, *Breaking Bad* was showered with nominations and awards, including five Primetime Emmy Award nominations with two wins: Outstanding Lead Actor in a Drama Series (Bryan Cranston) and Outstanding Single-Camera Picture Editing for a Drama Series (Lynne Willingham for "ABQ"). Cranston also captured the Television Critics Association Award for Individual Achievement in Drama and his second consecutive Satellite Award for Best Actor in a Drama Series. Paul won the

Season Two of *Breaking Bad* featured the demise of one villain—the ruthless, psychotic Tuco Salamanca—and the arrival of his exact opposite: the cunning, diabolical Gus Fring.

Saturn Award for Best Supporting Actor on Television. None other than the "Master of the Macabre" himself, horror novelist Stephen King, lavished praise on the series, comparing it favorably to *Twin Peaks* and *Blue Velvet*. In a March 6, 2009, article that appeared in *Entertainment Weekly*, King wrote, "*Breaking Bad* invites us into another world, just as *The Shield* and *The Sopranos* did, but Walt White could be a guy just down the block, the one who tried to teach the periodic table to your kids before he got sick. The swimming pool with the eye in it could be right down the block too. That's exactly what makes it all so funny, so frightening, and so compelling. This is rich stuff."

Episode 2.01: "Seven Thirty-Seven" (March 8, 2009)

A car falls on Tuco Salamanca's associate Gonzo (Jesus Payan Jr.) in the junkyard, killing him instantly as he tries to dispose of the body of

No-Doze, who was brutally beaten to death by Tuco Salamanca. Hank Schrader reviews the grainy surveillance of Walt and Jesse's rather inept but ultimately successful break-in at the chemical warehouse. Walt and Jesse come to the conclusion that Tuco is simply too dangerous to deal with, and they plot to eliminate him by somehow getting him to snort ricin, a poison found naturally in castor beans. Meanwhile, Skyler rants about having to deal with her "spoiled, kleptomaniac bitch sister" Marie— even though she is also pregnant, has a husband with lung cancer "who disappears for hours on end," along with a "moody son," and an "over-drawn checking account." At the end of the episode, a totally unhinged Tuco kidnaps both Jesse and Walt.

The only season premiere not scripted by Vince Gilligan, "Seven Thirty-Seven" was written by J. Roberts and directed by Bryan Cranston. The episode's title refers to $737,000, Walt's calculation of the amount of money he will need to raise in order to provide for his family ("eleven more drug deals"), and also a number that foreshadows the Wayfarer 515 disaster (Boeing 737) that takes place in the season finale. Note that Skyler's later love interest, Ted Beneke, can be viewed in one of her old photos in this episode although he doesn't make his first appearance until the episode "Negro y Azul" (2.07).

Episode 2.02: "Grilled" (March 15, 2009)

"Grilled" features the first appearance of Tuco Salamanca's uncle, the frequently grimacing Hector Salamanca (Mark Margolis), who communicates via a bell attached to his wheelchair after he is sidelined with a stroke. Tuco holds Walt and Jesse hostage in a remote desert hideout that is home to Hector, a former high-level soldier in the Mexican cartel. Tuco mistakenly believes that Walt and Jesse may have ratted him out to the DEA. As Hector intently watches *El Mago* (*The Magician*), a 1949 Mexican film starring Mexican comedian Cantinflas (Mario Moreno), Jesse refers to it as one of those "telenovelas" with "all those ripe honeys." In the meantime, Hank attempts to track down Jesse, believing him to be Walt's marijuana connection and therefore a lead to finding his brother-in-law. Skyler distributes missing flyers with Walt's photo (along with a partial view of

Several *Breaking Bad* scenes used Taco Sal, a local landmark that first opened its doors in 1961, as a backdrop—such as when Skyler and Marie handed out missing flyers of Walt in the episode "Grilled."
Courtesy of Ben Parker

Junior's face) and listing his height as 5′11″ and weight as 165 lbs: "Last seen April 25th near the corner of Black Volcano Rd. and 67th St. in Albuquerque, New Mexico, and may be suffering from confusion or dizzy spells."

Back at the desert hideout, Walt tries to poison Tuco's burrito with ricin, but he is caught by the observant Hector. Tuco takes Walt and Jesse outside the hideout with plans to kill them after Walt confesses to him, "We tried to poison you. We tried to poison you because you are an insane, degenerate piece of filth and you deserve to die." However, Walt and Jesse manage to wound Tuco and then hightail it into the desert. Hank tracks down Jesse's car (a Monte Carlo that has been converted into a low-rider) at the hideout and kills Tuco after a gunfight, while Walt and Jesse escape undetected.

The episode was written by George Mastras and directed by Charles Haid. As Tuco Salamanca, Raymond Cruz was supposed to have a larger role as Walt's main antagonist throughout Season Two. However, due to a scheduling conflict (a role as Detective Julio Sanchez on the TNT crime drama *The Closer*), Cruz had to be written out of the series. Fortunately, Cruz would return to portray Tuco in several episodes of *Better Call Saul*.

Episode 2.03: "Bit by a Dead Bee" (March 22, 2009)

In order to cover his whereabouts in the desert, Walt ends up wandering naked in a grocery store, claiming no memory of the past few days. After being hospitalized and given a series of tests, Walt confides to his doctor, "My wife is seven months pregnant with a baby we didn't intend. My fifteen-year-old son has cerebral palsy. I am an extremely overqualified high school chemistry teacher. When I can work, I make $43,700 per year. I have watched all of my colleagues and friends surpass me in every way imaginable. And within eighteen months, I will be dead. And you ask why I ran?" Skyler asks Walt if he has a second cell phone, and he adamantly denies it. Hank is presented with Tuco's grill in a glass cube as a trophy for killing the drug kingpin (the prop grill actually sold at auction for $20,250 in 2013!). As an alibi, Jesse tells authorities he has been shacked up with "Wendy the Meth-Addicted Whore" at the Crossroads Motel for the weekend, claiming his car had been stolen. The DEA attempts to get Hector to identify Jesse, but the aging gangster refuses to cooperate (in a most disturbing manner!).

"Bit by a Dead Bee" was written by Peter Gould and directed by Terry McDonough. The episode's title comes from *To Have and Have Not*, a 1944 Humphrey Bogart film very loosely based on the 1937 novel of the same name by Ernest Hemingway. Directed by Howard Hawks (*Scarface*, 1932), *To Have and Have Not* also featured Lauren Bacall in her film debut. The line in question is delivered by Bogie's sidekick, Eddie (Walter Brennan), who asks, "Say, was you ever bit by a dead bee?" The idea is that an antagonist can continue to do you harm from beyond the grave.

Episode 2.04: "Down" (March 29, 2009)

Frustrated with his drug abuse and continual lies, Jesse's parents take drastic action and evict him from his Aunt Ginny's former home. Jesse tells Walt in turn that his parents are "being greedy kleptomaniac douche-bags." Walt and Jesse appear to be in the clear following the debacle with Tuco Salamanca, but Jesse is broke and Walt can't leave the house without arousing Skyler's suspicion. Jesse eventually finds himself without a place to stay and with no friends who will even put him up for the night. In desperation, he breaks into the lot where the RV is being stored (accidentally falling through a portable toilet in a disgusting but hilarious scene). After a negative encounter with Clovis (Tom Kiesche), Badger's cousin who owns the lot, Jesse breaks into the lot again and steals the RV. Meanwhile, Walt's strategy of blending back into family life backfires as Skyler starts playing Walt's game of disappearing and not telling him where she is going. At one point, Skyler confronts Walt, exclaiming, "Shut up and say something that isn't complete bullshit! . . . You have to tell me what's really going on right now—today! No more excuses, no more apologies, no more of these . . . these obvious desperate breakfasts!"

The second episode in Season Two that foreshadows the Wayfarer 515 tragedy, "Down" was written by Sam Catlin and directed by John Dahl. Regarding the rather disgusting Port-a-Potty scene, Vince Gilligan remarked in a July 10, 2011, *New York Times* article, "The original version was that [Jesse] was going to get bit by a guard dog . . . But the guard dog would have cost us $25,000, and we didn't have the money. So we came up with the $5,000 outhouse gag. Which is quite a bit more memorable."

Episode 2.05: "Breakage" (April 5, 2009)

"Breakage" serves to introduce Jane Margolis (Krysten Ritter) to the cast of characters. Jesse starts to reestablish himself and moves into a new apartment managed by Jane, a recovering drug addict who lives next door. She gives him a simple warning: D.B.A.A. ("Don't Be an Asshole"). Walt and Jesse start cooking meth again, with Walt admitting to "a bit of a learning curve" after all the missteps the duo has taken so far in regard to their meth-cooking operation. Jesse establishes a network of meth dealers consisting of his slacker buddies Combo (Rodney Rush), Badger (Matt L. Jones), and Skinny Pete (Charles Baker). Meanwhile, the DEA has come across the name "Heisenberg" being bandied about in drug circles, and

MISSING

HAVE YOU SEEN THIS MAN?
Walter White
Age: 50   Height: 5'11   Weight: 165

LAST SEEN APRIL, 25TH NEAR THE CORNER OF BLACK VOLCANO RD. AND 67TH ST.
IN ALBUQUERQUE, NEW MEXICO AND MAY BE SUFFERING FROM CONFUSION OR DIZZY SPELLS.

IF YOU HAVE ANY INFORMATION OR HAVE SEEN WALTER PLEASE CONTACT
THE POLICE IMMEDIATELY. AT 505-145-4331 OR CALL 911

PLEASE - INFORMATION NEEDED

After Walt and Jesse get kidnapped by Tuco, a frantic Skyler distributes this missing poster throughout Albuquerque.

Hank and his fellow agents aren't sure if he is a real person or if it's just another "tweaker urban legend." Hank gets promoted and appointed to the tri-state drug task force headquartered in El Paso, and proceeds to have a panic attack in the elevator. He throws his trophy of Tuco's grill into the Rio Grande in disgust. Finally, Skinny Pete gets ripped off by a drug addict named Spooge and his old lady. Walt insists that Jesse take care of Spooge or they will have trouble making collections. Illegal immigrants crossing the Rio Grande discover Tuco's grill.

The episode was written by Moira Walley-Beckett and directed by Johan Renck. In this episode, Hank takes up home brewing (Schraderbräu) and even sings the 1970s ad jingle for Lowenbrau. Note that the towing company where the RV is being stored is named Crank It Up (crank being a popular street name for meth).

Episode 2.06: "Peekaboo" (April 12, 2009)

Easily one of the most disturbing episodes (as well as one of the most critically acclaimed) in the entire series, "Peekaboo" involves Jesse breaking into Spooge's filthy house and finding no one home except the couple's neglected young son (actually played by twins Brandon and Dylan Carr), sitting on a couch in total squalor and staring blankly at a home shopping show running endlessly on the television. When Spooge (David Ury) and his Old Lady (Dale Dickey) return home, Jesse tries to intimidate them, but gets overpowered by the couple, who have stolen an ATM, which lies in their living room. As Spooge works to open the ATM, his old lady tips the machine over and crushes his head in retaliation for his repeatedly calling her a "skank." Jesse manages to eventually recover the meth and cash from the ATM, calls the police in order to get assistance for the boy, and flees the scene. Meanwhile, a somewhat bewildered Gretchen Schwartz pays a visit to the White household after Skyler thanks her for paying for Walt's cancer treatment. Gretchen covers for Walt, but when she meets with him privately, his bitterness at their past relationship resurfaces, as well as his belief that they cut him out of their billion-dollar enterprise, Gray Matter Technologies. Gretchen remarks, "What happened to you? Really, Walt? What happened? Because this isn't you."

The episode was written by J. Roberts and Vince Gilligan, and directed by Peter Medak. It is one of the few episodes where Cranston and Paul do not share any scenes together. Paul was nominated for an Emmy Award for Outstanding Supporting Actor in a Drama Series for "Peekaboo." In 2009, *TV Guide* ranked "Peekaboo" on its list of the "100 Greatest Episodes." Note that at one point in the episode Walt uses the phrase "yada, yada, yada," which was popularized on *Seinfeld* in an episode ("The Yada Yada," 8.19) that Cranston appeared in as slightly sleazy dentist Tim Whatley. The depressing "Peekaboo" episode also contains several humorous moments courtesy of Skinny Pete, such as when Jesse berates him for getting ripped off by a guy named Spooge and for spelling "street" with an "a".

Episode 2.07: "Negro y Azul" (April 19, 2009)

"Negro y Azul" opens with a lively "narcocorrido" (a drug ballad) by the band Los Cuates de Sinaloa with colorful lyrics highlighting a "gringo boss" named Heisenberg who is disrespecting the Mexican drug cartel by cornering the Albuquerque market with high-quality blue crystal. The word on the street is that Jesse killed Spooge, so drug payments continue flowing due to the fear of a similar fate. Skyler decides to get a bookkeeping job and returns to her old employer, Beneke Fabricators, run by the sleazy Ted Beneke (Christopher Cousins), who Marie refers to as "Mr. Grabby Hands." Hank embarks on his new job with the task force in El Paso where his fellow employees totally disrespect him. Tortuga (Danny Trejo) is a DEA informant whose severed head ends up on the back of a tortoise (Tortuga is Spanish for "turtle"). When Hank backs away from the disturbing scene, DEA agent Vanco (J. D. Garfield) exclaims, "What's the matter, Schrader? You act like you've never seen a severed human head on a tortoise before!" Just then a bomb on the tortoise goes off, killing one of the agents and severely wounding several others (Hank is physically unscathed but mentally affected by the ordeal).

Meanwhile, Walt has trouble getting in touch with Jesse, who's been laying low since his disturbing visit to the Spooge household. So Walt arranges to deliver product directly to Jesse's dealers—Badger, Combo, and Skinny Pete—in an effort to keep the meth operation going. Jesse's crew informs Walt that since Jesse has developed a rep as a cold-blooded killer, they are having no problem at all collecting payments. Therefore, Walt decides it's time to expand their territory. Meanwhile, Jesse and Jane embark on a romantic relationship (they have a shared love for both art and drugs). Walt catches up to Jesse and tells him about expanding their territory with the strange analogy that he is a "blowfish." Jesse finally jumps onboard, exclaiming, "I'm a blowfish, yeah!" Once his crew is onboard, Jesse tells Walt, "Gonna make some mad cheddar, yo. Cheddar, Mr. White. Fat stacks. Dead Presidents. Cash money. We're gonna own this city."

The episode was written by John Shiban and directed by Felix Alcala. "Negro y Azul" is Spanish for "Black and Blue"—a reference to Walt's black Heisenberg attire (sunglasses, windbreaker, and porkpie hat) and the distinctive blue meth he cooks. Tortuga appears during the teaser nar-cocorrido video, which also foreshadows a dead Heisenberg at the end: "But the homie's dead/he just doesn't know it yet." During the end credits, a whistling instrumental rendition of "Negro y Azul" can be heard. When Walt meets Jesse's dealers at the National Museum of Nuclear Science & History, the 1950s civil defense video "Duck and Cover" is playing and features a cartoon turtle named Burt followed by the image of an atomic bomb (foreshadowing the "Tortuga" explosion). As Jesse enters the National Atomic Museum, he walks past a photo of an atomic bomb explosion and the words "headed by Werner Heisenberg."

Episode 2.08: "Better Call Saul" (April 26, 2009)

Badger gets arrested by the Albuquerque Police for dealing meth on a street corner. Walt and Jesse decide to hire sleazy strip-mall lawyer Saul Goodman (Bob Odenkirk in his first appearance in the series) to make Badger's legal problems go away. According to Jesse, "Seriously, when the going gets tough, you don't want a criminal lawyer. All right, you want a *criminal* lawyer. You know what I'm saying?" Following the Juarez bombing, Hank returns to Albuquerque and resumes his old job at the DEA, but suffers from post-traumatic stress disorder (PTSD). Meanwhile, Jesse and Jane's relationship deepens.

The episode was written by Peter Gould and directed by Terry McDonough. Note that Saul requests the money order for his services to be made out to a fictional entity called Ice Station Zebra Associates. A Cold War suspense thriller, *Ice Station Zebra* (1968) was directed by John Sturges from a 1963 novel of the same name by Alistair MacLean and starred Rock Hudson, Patrick McGoohan, Ernest Borgnine, and Jim Brown. *Ice Station Zebra* was a favorite of reclusive billionaire Howard

Hughes, who reportedly watched it 150 times on a continuous loop in his private hotel suite at the Desert Inn in Las Vegas. Legendary film critic Roger Ebert called *Ice Station Zebra* "a dull, stupid movie." When Walt and Jesse take Saul out to the desert, he references the Weather Underground: "Take the ski masks off, I feel like I'm talking to the Weather Underground here." Saul also blurts out, "it wasn't me, it was Ignacio," referencing Nacho, a character who makes an appearance in *Better Call Saul*. In addition, Saul jokes about finding D. B. Cooper (the mysterious 1970s skyjacker) when Walt shows up in disguise and also references *The Godfather* (1972): "What did Tom Hagen do for Vito Corleone?" When Walt responds, "I'm no Vito Corleone," Saul exclaims, "No shit! Right now you're Fredo!" Also in this episode, Saul reveals that his real name is McGill and that his Jewish-sounding name is just "for the homeboys." Also look for DJ Qualls as Getz, the Albuquerque police officer who busts Badger. Qualls made his film debut as Kyle Edwards in *Road Trip* (2000), in which he consumes a particularly unappetizing plate of French toast. Last but not least, note that before he is busted, Badger sits on a bench that features an advertisement for Saul's lawyering services.

Episode 2.09: "4 Days Out" (May 3, 2009)

Walt and Jesse head out to the desert for an epic cook that turns into a total disaster that nearly costs the duo their lives. After a couple of days, they cook up an estimated $1.2 million of meth. When the RV's battery dies during the cook after Jesse leaves the key in the ignition by mistake, Walt and Jesse fight for survival in the desert. Jesse manages to contact Skinny Pete via cell phone, but he never shows up. Walt finally manages to create a makeshift battery that jumpstarts the RV, and they somewhat miraculously escape their predicament once again. Later, Walt and his family find out that his cancer is in remission. However, Walt is not elated by the news—he has become obsessed with creating a drug empire and realizes it will now have to come to an end.

The critically acclaimed episode was written by Sam Catlin and directed by Michelle MacLaren. Aaron Paul later remarked that "4 Days Out" was his favorite *Breaking Bad* episode. Note that after Walt receives his test results, Hank quotes from Michael Corleone in *The Godfather: Part III* (1990), "Just when I thought I was out . . . they pull me back in!"

Episode 2.10: "Over" (May 10, 2009)

Skyler throws a party for Walt, who has mixed feelings when he finds out his cancer is in remission. During the bash, Walt forces Junior to drink so much alcohol that he pukes in the swimming pool. Agitated by not being able to cook meth and expand his empire, Walt soon grows increasingly obsessed over a home improvement project (the rot underneath the house possibly symbolizing the deteriorating family life in the White household). Meanwhile, Jane hides her relationship with Jesse when her concerned father, Donald Margolis (John de Lancie), comes to visit. She later gives Jesse a drawing of a superhero, "Apology Girl," as a way to ask for his forgiveness (interestingly, Krysten Ritter would go on to star as a superhero in the Netflix series *Jessica Jones*). Outside a home improvement store (filmed at RAKS Building Supply in Los Lunas, New Mexico), Walt threatens two aspiring meth cooks, warning them to stay out of his territory.

The episode was written by Moira Walley-Beckett and directed by Phil Abraham. The episode's title is the third of four that foreshadow the Wayfarer 515 crash in the season finale, "ABQ."

Episode 2.11: "Mandala" (May 17, 2009)

After Combo gets murdered on a street corner by a young kid working for a rival gang, Saul suggests to Walt that they work with an established meth distributor. So he puts Walt in touch with Gustavo "Gus" Fring (Giancarlo Esposito, in his first appearance on the series), who uses a fast-food chain, Los Pollos Hermanos (Spanish for "the Chicken Brothers"), as cover for his major drug enterprise. However, Gus has his doubts about working with Walt due to the unreliability of his sidekick, Jesse. Walt replies that he sticks with Jesse because "he does what I say. Because I can trust him." Meanwhile, Skyler discovers that her boss, Ted Beneke

(Christopher Cousins) has been embezzling from his firm and she performs a cringe-inducing imitation of Marilyn Monroe singing "Happy Birthday, Mr. President," in front of Ted and the rest of the somewhat aghast Beneke Fabricators employees. Skyler ends up going into labor. Meanwhile, Jane introduces Jesse to heroin: "There's a chill. Don't freak out, it passes. And then . . . you'll see. I'll meet you there."

The episode was written by George Mastras and directed by Adam Bernstein. The episode's title, "Mandala," means "circle" in Sanskrit. Look for Sam McMurray, who played Dr. Kennedy in *The Sopranos*, as Dr. Victor Bravenec, a cancer surgeon.

Episode 2.12: "Phoenix" (May 24, 2009)

Although Walt delivers his first meth shipment to Gus Fring in time, he misses the birth of his daughter, Holly. Walter Jr. has set up a cheesy and amateurish but heartfelt website, SaveWalterWhite.com, to garner donations for his father's medical expenses. However, Saul reengineers the website to serve as a vehicle to launder Walt's drug money. Jane blackmails Walt into giving Jesse his share of the drug earnings: "Do right by Jesse tonight or I'll burn you to the ground." Jesse and Jane have vague plans of relocating to New Zealand and starting a new life once Walt hands over Jesse's share of the drug money: "New Zealand, that's where they, uh, that's where they made *Lord of the Rings*! I say we move there, yo! I mean, you could do your art, right? Like, you could like paint the local castles and shit, and I can be a bush pilot!" Jane's father discovers her drug relapse and insists she goes to rehab (she manages to convince him that she will definitely go to rehab the next day). Walt and Jane's father have a chance encounter at a bar (filmed at Quarters, located at 801 Yale Boulevard SE in Albuquerque). Walt visits Jesse and finds his partner and Jane passed out in bed after a drug-fueled binge. Jane starts to suffocate on her own vomit, but Walt makes no attempt to save her.

The critically acclaimed episode, which was written by John Shiban and directed by Colin Bucksey, begins with a birth, Holly, and ends with a death, Jane. In fact, Jane's death was foreshadowed in the script, when she remarks, "I think I just threw up in my mouth a little" and "Lie on your side or you might choke." Also, when Jesse attempts to surprise Jane with breakfast in bed, he says, "You weren't supposed to wake up," to which she replies, "Ever?" Note that Walt and Jane's father discuss the Phoenix Mars Lander, which landed on the Red Planet in 2008. In his 2016 autobiography, *A Life in Parts*, Bryan Cranston admitted he was greatly affected by Jane's death scene and wept afterward: "I'd put everything, *everything*, into that scene. All the things I was and all the things I might have been: all the side roads and the missteps. All the stuttering successes and the losses I thought might sink me. I was murderous and I was capable of great love. I was a victim, moored by my circumstances and I was the danger. I was Walter White. But I was never more myself." Aaron Paul added in a 2013 Reddit AMA that "When that day was over, I couldn't be happier that it was over because I really, truly felt I was living those tortured moments with Jesse." By the way, SaveWalterWhite.com is an actual website that is still live to this day, and visitors who click the Donate button get redirected to the official *Breaking Bad* site on amc.com. Last but not least, Baby Holly was named after Vince Gilligan's longtime girlfriend, Holly Rice.

Episode 2.13: "ABQ" (May 31, 2009)

After discovering Jane dead, an anguished Jesse contacts Walt, who in turn gets in touch with Saul. A "cleaner" named Mike Ehrmantraut (Jonathan Banks, in his first appearance in the series) arrives on the scene quickly and coaches Jesse as to what to say when the authorities arrive: "I woke up. I found her. That's all I know." Fueled with guilt and despair, Jesse heads immediately to a crack house. Distraught about his daughter's death, Jane's father, an air traffic controller, causes a midair collision, resulting in the death of 167 passengers. Human remains and debris from the crash—including the mysterious pink teddy bear—rain down on the White residence.

The episode was written by Vince Gilligan and directed by Adam Bernstein. The episode's title is the final of four clues used to foreshadow the plane crash: "Seven Thirty-Seven—Down—Over—ABQ" (the airport code for Albuquerque International Airport). According to Vince Gilligan in Alan Sepinwall's 2012 book *The Revolution Was Televised*, "In simple terms . . . we just wanted a giant moment of showmanship to end the season. And what better way than to have a rain of fire coming down around our protagonist's ears, sort of like the judgment of God? It seemed like a big showmanship moment, and to visualize, in one fell swoop, all the terrible grief that Walt has wrought upon his loved ones, and the community at large." Note that when Jane's father visits her room, a falling teddy bear can be seen in the mural on her wall.

12

That Blue Stuff

Season Three (2010)

> It's methamphetamine. But I'm a manufacturer, I'm not a dealer.
> —*Walter White, Confessing to Skyler*

Season Three of *Breaking Bad* premiered on March 21, 2010, consisted of thirteen episodes, and portrayed Walt and Jesse getting ensnared deeper and deeper into the lair of Gus Fring's sinister drug empire. New characters added to the cast in Season Three include Walt's new lab assistant Gale Boetticher (David Costabile) and silent hitmen for the Mexico cartel, Leonel and Marco Salamanca (Daniel and Luis Moncada).

Episode 3.01: "No Más" (March 21, 2010)

The entire city is devastated by the horrifying plane crash. In the wake of the tragedy, Walt decides to burn his ill-gotten drug money in the backyard grill, but changes his mind just in the nick of time. Meanwhile, Leonel and Marco Salamanca (Daniel and Luis Moncada, in their first appearance in the series) make their way up from Mexico to Albuquerque in a quest to avenge their cousin Tuco Salamanca's death. We first see them literally crawling with others in an eerie procession that culminates at the foot of a candlelit shrine to Santa Muerte, the Mexican folk saint of death. One of the twins pins a sketch of Heisenberg to the shrine. Once over the border, the twins blow up a truck full of illegal immigrants and walk away unscathed. At a high school assembly designed to assuage the students' grief over the plane crash, Walt flippantly suggests that it could have been a lot worse (much to the horror of fellow faculty members): "Look on the bright side. . . . " Walt

In Season Three, Walt and Jesse find themselves unwittingly getting ensnared deeper and deeper into the lair of Gus Fring's sinister drug empire.

later confesses to Skyler that he is simply a meth "manufacturer," not a dealer. Skyler replies that she won't tell anyone as long as "you grant me this divorce and stay out of our lives." Walt turns down Gus Fring's offer to do business, telling him, "I'm not a criminal. No offense to any people who are, but . . . that is not me."

The episode was written by Vince Gilligan and directed by Bryan Cranston, who had also directed the premiere episode of Season Two titled "Seven Thirty-Seven." The episode's title, "No Más," is Spanish for "no more." Cranston's daughter, Taylor, portrays Sad Faced Girl in this episode, while his wife, Robin Dearden, appears as Emotional Woman. Note that one of the students at the assembly brings up the bogus urban legend that colleges automatically give an automatic A to any student whose roommate dies (the premise of the 1998 comedy *Dead Man on Campus*).

Episode 3.02: "Caballo Sin Nombre" (March 28, 2010)

Most viewers remember this episode for the uncut pizza Walt heaves onto the roof in disgust after Skyler sends him away. Amazingly, Cranston managed to throw the uncut pizza onto the roof during the very first take, which Vince Gilligan called a "one-in-a-million shot." Jesse's parents, who appear in the series for the last time in this episode, unknowingly sell his home back to him at a bargain price of $400,000 arranged by Saul Goodman. The Cousins visit their "tio" Hector and symbolically utilize a Ouija board to find out from him that Walter White is their target. They pay a visit to the White household with axe in hand and sit on his bed, waiting for him to get out of the shower (until they make a hasty exit when one of them receives a text simply reading "POLLOS"). Meanwhile, Hank and Marie discuss the possibility that Walt may be having an affair, with Hank remarking, "Look, a guy like Walt? Nice guy. Decent. Smart. Let's face it: underachiever—dead-end life. He gets cancer, time is running out. He steps out."

The episode was written by Peter Gould and directed by Adam Bernstein. The episode's title is Spanish for "horse with no name," referring to the hit 1971 song of the same name from the band America that

The filming locale for Los Pollos Hermanos is known in Albuquerque as Twisters, a Southwestern fast-food chain that serves burritos and burgers—but not fried chicken!

John Phelan/Wikimedia Commons

Walt sings along with during the cold open and later in the shower when he's totally oblivious to the invasion of the axe-wielding cousins into his house (Vince Gilligan had reportedly originally chosen the Crosby, Stills & Nash song "Southern Cross").

Episode 3.03: "I.F.T." (April 4, 2010)

The cold open in "I.F.T." features a flashback of the doomed Tortuga (Danny Trejo) in a rundown Mexican cantina (actually filmed at the Sandia Bar in Corrales, New Mexico). His Spanish dialogue with the bartender translates as "There are two kinds of people in this world: those who pour drinks and those who drink. Now shut up and fill my glass." Revealed to be a DEA informant, Tortuga is decapitated with a machete by the Cousins. Back to the present, Skyler decides to take drastic action and embarks on a sexual relationship with her boss, Ted Beneke, after Walt refuses to move out of the house. Meanwhile, Hank and Gomie hang out in a dive bar (filmed at Leo's Bar at 1119 Candelaria Road NW in Albuquerque), where Hank gets into an ill-advised altercation with two "dirtbags." In an attempt to get him out of the house for good, Skyler confesses to Walt that she "fucked Ted."

The episode was written by George Mastras and directed by Michelle MacLaren. The episode's title, "I.F.T." refers to Skyler's shocking confession to Walt: "I fucked Ted." Trejo, whose character, Tortuga, was killed with a machete, appeared in the films *Machete* (2010) and *Machete Kills* (2013), both of which were directed by his second cousin, Robert Rodriguez (*Once Upon a Time in Mexico*).

Episode 3.04: "Green Light" (April 11, 2010)

Walt refuses to move out of the house, even after hearing Skyler's confession: "You think this will get me to move out? You can screw Ted, you can screw the butcher, the mailman, whoever you want!" Walt discovers that Saul Goodman has been bugging his house and promptly fires him. Mike informs Gus that Walt is a "disaster" mentally and that the Cousins have been to his house. Hank discovers a new lead at a remote gas station after he uses the camera at an ATM to view an image of Walt and Jesse's meth lab RV (Jesse had traded some blue meth to the rather naïve young cashier in exchange for gas).

The episode was written by Sam Catlin and directed by Scott Winant. Note that Walt listens to "In the Valley of the Sun" by jazz singer Buddy Stewart (aka Stuart) on the radio. Tragically, Stewart was killed in a car accident in Deming, New Mexico, on February 1, 1950, at the age of twenty-eight.

Episode 3.05: "Más" (April 18, 2010)

Hank humiliates himself by climbing onto the roof of what he believes is the "meth RV" and peers through the vent to discover an elderly couple playing cards. Gomie informs a demoralized Hank that he has been promoted and heads out to El Paso to join the drug task force. Gus Fring gives Walt a tour of the state-of-the-art meth superlab hidden under an industrial laundry facility. Walt confesses to Gus, "I have made a series of very bad decisions and I cannot make another one." However, Walt eventually ends up agreeing to cook meth again for Gus. Hank is made aware of another registered RV fitting the description of the mobile meth lab. He visits the former owner, Mrs. Ortega, and finds out it was her deceased son, Combo, who stole the family RV. Hank checks out Combo's old bedroom and views a photo of him and Jesse at the strip club the night they blew the money Walt gave them to buy the RV.

"Más" was written by Moira Walley-Beckett and directed by Johan Renck. The episode was dedicated to Gwyn Savage, a casting director for *Breaking Bad*, who died of cancer on January 21, 2010.

Episode 3.06: "Sunset" (April 25, 2010)

Gale Boetticher (David Costabile), a specialist in X-ray crystallography and nerdy vegan libertarian, makes his series debut as Walt's new lab assistant. Gale shares with Walt his enthusiasm for the poetry of Walt Whitman, even reciting "When I Heard the Learn'd Astronomer" to him and giving him an inscribed copy of *Leaves of Grass* (which will later come back to haunt Walt). Old Joe (Larry Hankin) runs the junkyard where the RV is to be destroyed. However, Hank shows up just in time, trapping Walt and Jesse in the RV. Through some ingenuity at the expense of Hank's emotions, they manage to find a way out of the dilemma. Meanwhile, Gus Fring informs the cartel that it was Hank that pulled the trigger that killed Tuco Salamanca, not Walt: "May his death satisfy you."

The episode was written and directed by John Shiban. Hankin appeared on *Seinfeld* in two episodes of the fourth season: *The Pilot, Part*

1 and *The Pilot, Part 2* (see Chapter 24). Note that Walt cuts off the crust while making a sandwich just as Krazy-8 did when he was being held hostage in Jesse's basement (a popular fan theory features Walt assuming character traits of his victims throughout the series).

Episode 3.07: "One Minute" (May 2, 2010)

Enraged that Jesse somehow tricked him into believing his wife Marie was in the hospital after a car accident, Hank promptly goes to Jesse's house and severely beats him up. Walt visits Jesse in the hospital and gets informed that his "scumbag brother-in-law" will "be scrubbing toilets in Tijuana for pennies and I'll be standing over him to get my cut . . . I'll haunt his crusty ass forever until the day he sticks a gun up his mouth and pulls the trigger just to get me out of his head." In the hospital, Walt confides to Jesse, "Your meth is good. As good as mine." In the episode's tense final few minutes, Hank gets a mysterious phone call, warning him, "Two men are coming to kill you . . . You have one minute." At first he thinks Gomie is playing a cruel gag on him, but quickly realizes his life is in danger. Hank gets wounded but manages to ram his car into one of the cousins, pinning him between two cars. The other cousin makes the fateful decision that killing Hank with a gun is just too easy, so he retrieves an axe from his trunk. Hank manages to get a single bullet into his gun just in time to shoot the cousin in the head.

The episode was written by Thomas Schnauz and directed by Michelle MacLaren. Note that when Hank receives the mysterious phone call, the clock reads 3:07—"One Minute" is the seventh episode of Season Three of *Breaking Bad*. Gale's comment to Walt, "This might be the beginning of a beautiful friendship," is a direct line of dialogue from the classic 1942 film, *Casablanca*, which was directed by Michael Curtiz (*Angels with Dirty Faces*) and starred Humphrey Bogart and Ingrid Bergman. Last and most certainly least, Saul tackily references the Beatles when he looks at Jesse's battered face in the hospital and tells Walt, "You're now officially the cute one in the group. Ringo, meet Paul. Paul, meet Ringo."

Episode 3.08: "I See You" (May 9, 2010)

As Jesse leaves the hospital, Hank arrives in an ambulance after his alter-cation with the Cousins, much to Jesse's delight. Gus Fring runs into Walt at the hospital and tells him, "I hide in plain sight, same as you." Gus makes a move against the Mexican cartel. Now that Jesse is back, Walt terminates Gale Boetticher's apprenticeship at the lab, arguing that "I'm classical, but you are more jazz."

The episode was written by Gennifer Hutchison and directed by Colin Bucksey. The episode's title is a play on "ICU" (Intensive Care Unit), where both Jesse and Hank end up at different times. In the waiting room of the hospital, Walt Jr. shows his father a copy of the 2001 book *Killing Pablo: The Hunt for the World's Greatest Outlaw* by Mark Bowden, a gift from his Uncle Hank. "I See You" features the last appearance of Leonel Salamanca, who is apparently murdered by Mike Ehrmantraut in his hospital room.

Episode 3.09: "Kafkaesque" (May 16, 2010)

The opening montage in "Kafkaesque" features a variation of the "Bolivia Theme" from the soundtrack of *Scarface* (1983) that takes place when Tony Montana (Al Pacino) travels to South America to meet drug kingpin Alejandro Sosa (Paul Shenar) in Bolivia. In his rehab group, Jesse sarcasti-cally describes his work environment: "It's in a Laundromat, it's totally corporate . . . It's like rigid, all kinds of red tape, my boss is a dick, the owner, super dick, don't know if we're ever going to meet him, everybody's scared of the dude. Place is full of dead-eyed douchebags, the hours suck, and nobody knows what's going on." When Jesse asks what the point of being an outlaw is if you've got responsibilities, Badger replies "Darth Vader had responsibilities. He was responsible for the Death Star." Skyler comes up with an elaborate lie involving Walt's "gambling addiction" in order to convince Marie that they will help pay for Hank's medical expenses.

The episode was written by Peter Gould and George Mastras, and directed by Michael Slovis. The episode's title refers to the word that the leader of the group therapy meeting uses to describe Jesse's humorous description of his work environment. In another *Seinfeld* connection, Mark Harelik, who portrays an unnamed doctor in this episode, also played Milosh, the awful tennis player who runs the pro shop and taunts Jerry about his tennis game in "The Comeback" (8.13), which originally aired on January 30, 1997.

Episode 3.10: "Fly" (May 23, 2010)

An episode that *Breaking Bad* fans either love or hate (there is no middle ground here, folks), "Fly" is a so-called "bottle episode" that takes place entirely in the meth superlab as Walt obsessively tries to get rid of the "contaminant"—a simple housefly. Jesse panics for a second, believing Walt is talking about "an Ebola leak or something . . . Yeah, it's a disease on the Discovery Channel where all your intestines sort of just slip right out of your butt." An exhausted Walt later confides to Jesse that he met Jane's father at a bar the night she died: "Think of the odds. Once I tried to calculate them, but they're astronomical. I mean, think of the odds of me going in and sitting down that night, in that bar, next to that man."

The episode, which came about due to budget restrictions, was written by Sam Catlin and Moira Walley-Beckett, and directed by Rian Johnson. Except for the appearance of some laundromat extras, Bryan Cranston and Aaron Paul are the only actors in the episode (in fact, it is the only episode in the entire series not to feature Anna Gunn, although her voice can be heard at one point). According to Vince Gilligan in a July 29, 2013, *Vulture* interview, "We were hopelessly over budget . . . And we needed to come up with what is called a bottle episode, set in one location." James Poniewozik of *TIME* referred to it as "the most unusual and very possibly the best episode of *Breaking Bad* so far" and compared it favorably to the legendary "Pine Barrens" episode of *The Sopranos*.

Other memorable bottle episodes" in TV history include "Balance of Terror" in *Star Trek*, "Two's a Crowd" in *All in the Family*, "Johnny Be Gone" from *Married . . . with Children*, "Ice" in *The X-Files*, "The Edge of Destruction" from *Doctor Who*, "The Chinese Restaurant" from *Seinfeld*," "The Conversation" from *Mad About You*, "Vision Quest" in *Archer*, and "Brian & Stewie" from *Family Guy*, among many others.

Episode 3.11: "Abiquiu" (May 30, 2010)

The opening flashback in "Abiquiu" features Jesse and Jane wandering through the Georgia O'Keeffe Museum in Santa Fe and discussing the artist's painting "My Last Door." In the present day, Jesse comes up with the strategy of selling meth he has smuggled out from Gus Fring's superlab at a Narcotics Anonymous meeting where he meets recovering addict Andrea Cantillo (Emily Rios), a single mother who lives with her son, Brock. Jesse soon discovers that it was Andrea's little brother, Tomas, who killed Combo. Meanwhile, Gus invites Walt over to his house for dinner and gives him some sound advice: "Never make the same mistake twice."

The episode was written by John Shiban and Thomas Schnauz, and directed by Michelle MacLauren. At one point, Saul Goodman refers to Skyler as "Yoko Ono" after she suggests buying the car wash (Saul had suggested they invest in a laser tag business).

Episode 3.12: "Half Measures" (June 6, 2010)

An obsessed Jesse attempts to avenge Combo's death. First, Jesse uses Wendy the Whore (in her last appearance in the series) to try to poison the drug dealers responsible using a tainted hamburger. However, his ill-conceived plan is thwarted by Gus Fring's enforcers, Mike and Victor. Gus calls a meeting to keep the peace, and the rival drug dealers agree to no longer use kids in their operation. Mike relates a story to Walt about the time he let a wife abuser off the hook and sometime later the guy killed his wife, telling him that he learned a valuable lesson from the tragic incident: "No more half measures." Jesse finds out that the rival drug dealers have killed Tomas because he is of no more value to them. On a mission of pure revenge, Jesse goes after the two drug dealers that killed Tomas with a gun. He is saved from certain death when Walt appears from nowhere and plows over the two drug dealers in his car, shoots the surviving one in the head, and tells Jesse to "run."

The episode was written by Sam Catlin and Peter Gould, and directed by Adam Bernstein. The title comes from Mike's anecdote to Walt: "The moral of the story is I chose a half measure when I should have gone all

The opening flashback in "Abiquiu" features Jesse and Jane wandering through the Georgia O'Keeffe Museum in Santa Fe and discussing the artist's painting, *My Last Door*. Considered the Mother of American Modernism, O'Keeffe was known for her close-ups of flowers, as well as her New Mexico landscapes.   *Carl Van Vechten/Library of Congress/Wikimedia Commons*

the way. I'll never make that mistake again. No more half measures."
According to Vince Gilligan in a June 13, 2010, *AV/TV Club* interview, "I
think [Walt] running over the two guys is a sign of the end for him, morally or ethically . . . But I can see the point . . . for that moment to be . . .
him standing up for his partner in a way that he has never done before."
Paul received the Primetime Emmy Award for Outstanding Supporting
Actor in a Drama Series for his performance in "Half Measures." In a
Men's Health interview (January-February 2018), Jonathan Banks said that
after his "no half measures" monologue, "I remember walking off the set
and I said, 'Man, this is about as good as it gets.'" At the end of the series,
Paul got "No Half Measures" tattooed on his bicep.

Episode 3.13: "Full Measure" (June 13, 2010)

In "Full Measure," Gale Boetticher returns as Walt's meth-cooking partner, much to the latter's chagrin. Victor keeps a close eye on both of them.
Walt believes that he will be killed by Gus Fring once Gale masters his
meth-cooking procedure. Walt is heading over to Gale's apartment to kill
him when Victor summons him to the superlab, where Mike is waiting
for him. Walt pleads for his life, and as a last resort he calls Jesse and
desperately urges him to eliminate Gale immediately. Jesse arrives at
Gale's apartment, and when the confused lab assistant opens the door, he
shoots him in the face, killing him instantly.

The season finale was the first episode since "Pilot" to be written and
directed by Vince Gilligan. Cranston captured his third consecutive
Primetime Emmy Award for Outstanding Lead Actor in a Drama Series
for his performance in "Full Measure."

13

Never Give Up Control

Season Four (2011)

I'm doing quite well. I'm good . . . It's over. We're safe . . . I won.
—*Walter White*

Season Four of *Breaking Bad* premiered on July 17, 2011, features a total of thirteen episodes, and showcases a battle of wits between Walter White and Gus Fring for the control of the meth empire (Vince Gilligan apparently was unsure if the show would be renewed for a fifth season, so he wrote Season Four like it could possibly be the last). Although the fourth season received an astounding thirteen Primetime Emmy Award nominations, Aaron Paul won the only award for Outstanding Supporting Actor in a Drama Series. In addition, Bryan Cranston was nominated for his second consecutive Golden Globe Award for Best Actor in a Drama Series (losing out to Kelsey Grammer for *Boss*). Gilligan received his first nomination for a Directors Guild of America Award for Outstanding Directing—Drama Series for "Face Off" (losing out to Patty Jenkins for *The Killing*).

Episode 4.01: "Box Cutter" (July 17, 2011)

In the cold open, a flashback reveals Gale Boetticher excitedly opening up lab equipment with a box cutter in anticipation of creating Gus Fring's meth superlab. Gale reassures Gus that Walt is creating a superior product. In the present, Skyler breaks into Walt's apartment and discovers the teddy bear's plastic eyeball, which has always seemed to symbolize Walt's moral degradation over the course of the series. (Appropriately, Skyler starts becoming a more willing participant in Walt's illegal activities from then on, later helping him launder money through the car wash, for instance.) Following Gale's death, Gus arrives at the superlab, changes into a red hazmat suit, coldly and deliberately cuts Victor's throat with a box cutter in front of Walt and Jesse, and then calmly tells them to "get back to work."

The episode was written by Vince Gilligan and directed by Adam Bernstein. Gilligan received the Writers Guild of America Award for Best Episodic Drama for his work on "Box Cutter." The episode also marks the first appearance of Lavell Crawford as Saul's bodyguard, Huell Babineaux. Note that the box cutter used to kill Victor is apparently the same one Gale used to set up equipment in the meth superlab during the cold open. Giancarlo Esposito was profoundly affected by the disturbing scene where he kills Victor, and in a July 18, 2011, *Vulture* interview stated that he worried about "coming out of it unscathed, without really hurting my spirit and my soul." Concerning Esposito's chilling performance in the Victor murder scene, Bryan Cranston remarked, "When he plays that bad character, his eyes go dead, and all it takes is to look into his eyes." Actor Jeremiah Bitsui sprained his ankle during the scene where Walter and Jesse dispose of Victor's corpse into a barrel full of hydrofluoric acid.

Note that Gale's apartment is decorated with several Persian rugs reminiscent of those used in the Coen brothers' 1998 cult comedy *The Big Lebowski*, which starred Jeff Bridges in the title role. Gale's apartment also contains a copy of Stephen King's 2002 collection of short stories titled *Everything's Eventual*, which includes such relevant story titles as "Autopsy Room Four," "The Man in the Black Suit," "In the Deathroom," and "Riding the Bullet." (Incidentally, King himself is a huge fan of *Breaking Bad*.) In addition, the diner scene with Walt and Jesse dressed in identical Kenny Rogers T-shirts after cleaning up the superlab following Victor's death pays homage to a similar scene in Quentin Tarantino's 1994 film *Pulp Fiction* with Vincent and Jules in a diner after they clean up following Marvin's death. Obsessed with his newfound rock-collecting hobby, Hank visits MineralEmporium.com to bid on magnesite crystal (even to this day the fictional site redirects visitors to sonypictures.com/tv/breakingbad).

Gale Boetticher's apartment contains a copy of Stephen King's 2002 collection of short stories *Everything's Eventual*, which includes such relevant story titles as "Autopsy Room Four," "The Man in the Black Suit," "In the Deathroom," and "Riding the Bullet."

Episode 4.02: "Thirty-Eight Snub" (July 24, 2011)

Fearing that Gus Fring will make a move against him and his family, Walt meets with an illegal arms dealer, Lawson (Jim Beaver), who sells him the weapon that names this episode's title. The scene recalls Travis Bickle (Robert De Niro) meeting gun salesman Easy Andy (Steven Prince) in *Taxi Driver* (1976), which was directed by Martin Scorsese (*Raging Bull*). Later in the episode, Walt practices drawing the gun in another scene reminiscent of *Taxi Driver*. During an endless party at Jesse's house, Skinny Pete and Badger explain why the pizza joint delivers uncut pizzas, hearkening back to Walt heaving the uncut pizza onto the roof in the episode "Caballo Sin Nombre" (3.02).

To numb the pain from having to kill Gale Boetticher, Jesse embarks on an endless round of partying. (Note that when Jesse exclaims "Wake up and party!" the guest he rouses is none other than Bryan Cranston in a wig and different glasses.) Meanwhile, Badger and Skinny Pete engage in a humorous discussion about "Nazi zombies" in video games. Walt visits Mike Ehrmantraut in a dive bar and tries to enlist the enforcer's aid in eliminating Gus, but instead Mike punches him in the face and kicks him a few times for good measure as he writhes on the floor. Skyler attempts to purchase the car wash, but Bogdan proves to be a tough negotiator after discovering that she is married to his former employee, Walt.

The episode was written by George Mastras and directed by Michelle MacLaren. The party scenes at Jesse's house feature a lively soundtrack that includes Flavor Flav ("Unga Bunga Bunga"), M.O.P. ("Raise Hell"), and Honey Claws ("Digital Animal") blaring from his new sound system. Critic Melissa Maerz of *Entertainment Weekly* compared the episode with the films of legendary director Sergio Leone: "Those extreme close-ups of Walt's face mimicked the opening shots of *The Good, the Bad and the Ugly*. Those tense silences before Walt drew his gun were straight out of *Fistful of Dollars*. So much of it felt like a Western." The episode also serves as the first appearance of Ray Campbell as Tyrus Kitt.

Episode 4.03: "Open House" (July 31, 2011)

Eventually even Badger and Skinny Pete abandon the house party, and Jesse ultimately sits all alone in his trashed house. He later rides a go-kart to relieve stress in a cool montage (filmed at Albuquerque Indoor Karting at 5110 Copper Avenue NE). Depressed by Hank's lack of interest to get moving again, Marie attends various open houses and starts stealing items off the shelves. Skyler enlists Saul Goodman's aid in her scheming to purchase the car wash from Bogdan.

The episode was written by Sam Catlin and directed by David Slade. A British filmmaker, Slade's filmography includes *Hard Candy* (2005), *30 Days of Night* (2007), and *The Twilight Saga: Eclipse* (2010). Comedian Bill Burr makes his first appearance as Patrick Kuby, who poses as an environmental inspector to help with the car wash purchasing scheme. The episode's soundtrack includes "If I Had a Heart" by Swedish musician Fever Ray.

Episode 4.04: "Bullet Points" (August 7, 2011)

The episode's cold open features a Los Pollos Hermanos truck full of meth being riddled with bullets during an attempted hijacking that is thwarted by Mike Ehrmantraut. Meanwhile, Walt and Skyler create an elaborate backstory that concerns Walt's online "gambling addiction" to explain their purchase of the A1 Car Wash from Bogdan. Hank shows Walt a note he found in Gale Boetticher's lab notebook: "To W.W. My Star, My Perfect Silence." Hank throws out a couple of ideas of who he thinks the initials "W.W." could stand for: "Willy Wonka ... Woodrow Wilson ... Walter White?" Walt replies jokingly, "You got me!" However, Walt quickly flips through the notebook some more and finds a Walt Whitman poem and shows it to Hank: "Walt Whitman ... your W.W." A 2008 "Ron Paul for President" sticker can also be glimpsed in Gale's lab notebook (the deceased lab assistant was a self-proclaimed libertarian who did not believe in the "war on drugs").

The episode was written by Moira Walley-Beckett and directed by Colin Bucksey, who had previously worked on the episodes "Phoenix" in Season Two and "I See You" in Season Three. Gale shows up in this episode (back from the dead!) singing Peter Schilling's "Major Tom (Coming Home)" in a hilarious karaoke video with Thai subtitles. Also look for Jeremy Howard as a drug addict named Sketchy, who provides a humorous rant about radiation:

> I'm not even kidding, because if you really think about it, you can't see it so how can you know just how bad radio frequencies and microwaves and cell phones and stuff are getting you. I mean, you can be strolling through security at the airport on your way to see your grandma and then you get waved through a full body x-ray scanner and the next day you can be dead or dying or at least dying from all the radiation that they say is safe which there's no way it could because they have to deliver a concentrated dose, OK?

Last but not least, Walt refers to Mike as a "grunting dead-eye cretin."

Episode 4.05: "Shotgun" (August 14, 2011)

Jesse and Mike drive around hitting dead drops at the instigation of Gus Fring, while a very disgruntled Walt is forced to cook meth alone. Hank learns about Walt's so-called "gambling addiction" and dubs him "Nick the Greek." Hank tries to imagine Gale Boetticher as the drug kingpin based on the rather mundane contents of his lab notebook: "It's like Scarface had sex with Mister Rogers or something." Walt does not like to see Gale getting credit for the meth operation, so he casually suggests to Hank that the real kingpin must still be at large. Regarding a Los Pollos Hermanos menu found in Gale's apartment, Hank ponders, "Since when do vegans eat fried chicken?" Hank's suspicions quickly turn to fast-food king Gus Fring as the possible meth kingpin. The episode was written by Thomas Schnauz and directed by Michelle MacLaren.

Episode 4.06: "Cornered" (August 21, 2011)

Similar to the "Bullet Points" episode, "Cornered" opens with one of Gus Fring's trucks being hijacked. Meanwhile, Walt takes over the car wash and then uses the first dollar Bogdan ever earned to buy a soda from the machine. Skyler visits Four Corners Monument (a popular tourist attraction marking the point where Arizona, Colorado, New Mexico, and Utah meet) and ponders whether to leave Walt (she decides to return home). Walt buys Junior a new Dodge Challenger (one of the few vanity purchases he ever makes with the drug money besides buying himself a new car as well). The episode was written by Gennifer Hutchison and directed by Michael Slovis.

Episode 4.07: "Problem Dog" (August 28, 2011)

Hank turns his suspicions of Albuquerque's meth distributor to Gus Fring, who he believes would not only have "the money to finance this operation" but perhaps the connections as well. However, Hank can't convince any of his colleagues that "Gus as kingpin" is feasible (even though his fingerprints were found in Gale's apartment). Gomie tells Hank sarcastically, "If your guy had his meeting at KFC, you wouldn't immediately assume that he's sitting down with Colonel Sanders." Skyler demands that Walt Jr.'s new Dodge Challenger be returned (and replaced with a PT Cruiser!), prompting Walt to freak out and blow up the car in a rage. Walt enlists Jesse's aid in poisoning Gus with ricin. The Mexican cartel delivers an ultimatum to Gus, which he rejects outright. The episode was written and directed by Pete Gould. The title comes from Jesse referring to shooting a "problem dog" (actually Gale Boetticher) during his rehab meeting. Note that at one point Jesse can be seen playing the video game RAGE, which describes Walt's state in this episode.

Episode 4.08: "Hermanos" (September 4, 2011)

Gus Fring continues to taunt Hector Salamanca at the Casa Tranquila nursing home, describing in detail the death of his nephews, Marco and Leonel, as well as the murder of Juan Bolsa: "This is what comes of blood for blood, Hector. Sangre por sangre." A flashback reveals Gus and his partner Max Arciniega (James Martinez) attempting to get Don Eladio (Steven Bauer) to enter the meth business with them. Don Eladio refers to meth as "poor man's cocaine. Only bikers and hillbillies use it. There's no money in it." Gus replies, "This product is the drug of the future." Hector ends up killing Max in front of Gus, casually remarking, "My advice . . . stick to chicken."

The episode was written by Sam Catlin and George Mastras, and directed by Johan Renck. The title means "Brothers" in Spanish, referring to Gus and Max, founder of Los Pollos Hermanos ("the Chicken

The Casa Tranquila nursing home scenes, including Gus Fring's explosive death finale, were filmed at the former Valle Norte Caring Center (now the site of the Medical Resort at Fiesta Park).

Courtesy of Ben Parker

Brothers"). According to Vince Gilligan, Gus and Max "probably were lovers." The episode features two actors who appeared in *Scarface* (1983): Steven Bauer (Manny Ribera) and Mark Margolis (Alberto the Shadow). Both characters are killed by the movie's title character, Tony Montana (Al Pacino). Gus's death is foreshadowed in the elevator scene when a "ding" sound can be heard repeatedly (similar to the bell on Hector's wheelchair). Also note that a young Hector in a flashback sits on a chair with wheels.

Episode 4.09: "Bug" (September 11, 2011)

Hank continues his surveillance of Gus Fring. Ted Beneke informs Skyler that he is being investigated for tax fraud. After Ted is ordered by the IRS to pay back taxes along with a fine, Skyler decides to cover the $600,000 (which Walt has stashed in the crawl space of the couple's home) he will need to resolve his tax issues. Gus invites Jesse to his house and asks him if he can produce Walt's formula by himself. Jesse replies that if Gus kills Walt, "you're gonna have to kill me, too!" However, Gus informs Jesse that he will simply be sent to Mexico to teach the cartel how to cook the legendary blue meth. Walt confronts Jesse about visiting Gus's house and not poisoning him. A fight ensues, and Jesse warns a battered Walt to leave his home and never return. The episode was written by Moira Walley-Beckett and Thomas Schnauz, and directed by Terry McDonough.

Episode 4.10: "Salud" (September 18, 2011)

Walt misses Junior's sixteenth birthday party. Gus takes Jesse to Mexico with him and manages to poison everyone in the cartel (including himself). Jesse guns down Hector's grandson, Joaquin Salamanca. According to Vince Gilligan in *Breaking Bad: The Official Book*, the initial concept for the elimination of the Mexican cartel was to bring "an army of guys down there with machine guns, sort of like at the end of *Scarface* . . . And then you think to yourself, 'That's using a sledgehammer when it might be more interesting and more subtle to go with the scalpel . . . [Gus] is a guy willing to poison himself along with his nemeses in order to kill them. We chose that idea because it presented Gus as the biggest badass in the world: that's why we went with it." The episode was written by Peter Gould and Gennifer Hutchison, and directed by Michelle MacLaren. The episode's title is a word used to toast in Spanish and means "health."

Episode 4.11: "Crawl Space" (September 25, 2011)

Gus Fring and Jesse pay a visit to Hector Salamanca, so Gus can taunt him about the deaths of the cartel members, which included Hector's grandson, Joaquin. Gus threatens Walt: "If you try to interfere, this becomes a much simpler matter. I will kill your wife. I will kill your son. I will kill your infant daughter." Fearing for the safety of his family, Walt requests that Saul Goodman contact the individual who "could disappear me." Saul tells him that the "deluxe service" will cost him $500,000 for his family to disappear without a trace. When Walt goes to retrieve the money under the floorboards, he discovers that Skyler has given all the money to Ted Beneke to help with his IRS troubles.

The episode was written by George Mastras and Sam Catlin, and directed by Scott Winant. With his bruised face, Walt looks like "Macho Camacho," according to Hank. A world champion boxer from Puerto Rico, Hector "Macho" Camacho held the WBC Super Featherweight Title from 1983 to 1984, the WBC Lightweight Title from 1985 to 1987, and the WBO Junior Welterweight Title from 1989 to 1992. Tragically, Camacho was shot in the face during a drive-by shooting in 2012 and died four days later at the age of fifty. When Gus and Jesse visit Hector, the bell ringer is glued to a broadcast of *The Bridge on the River Kwai*, the 1958 Best Picture Oscar winner that features a huge explosion (foreshadowing Gus's demise). Directed by David Lean (*Lawrence of Arabia*), the film stars Alec Guinness, William Holden, Jack Hawkins, and Sessue Hayakawa. Jesse and Brock can be seen playing the classic SEGA game *Sonic the Hedgehog* in this episode.

Episode 4.12: "End Times" (October 2, 2011)

Jesse confronts Walt and accuses him of poisoning Brock with ricin. Walt adamantly denies the accusation and persuades Jesse to help him focus on the elimination of Gus Fring. Walt plants a homemade bomb under Gus's car, but misses his opportunity after a cautious Gus grows suspicious of the situation. The episode was written by Thomas Schnauz and Moira Walley-Beckett, and directed by Vince Gilligan (the third episode he directed and the only one that he directed but did not write). Aaron Paul captured the Primetime Emmy Award for Outstanding Supporting Actor in a Drama Series at the 64th Primetime Emmy Awards for his performance in "End Times."

Episode 4.13: "Face Off" (October 9, 2011)

Believing that Hector Salamanca has become a DEA informant, Gus Fring and Tyrus travel to the nursing home with the intention of killing the aging gangster with a poison-filled syringe. However, Walt has rigged an explosive to Hector's wheelchair that can be triggered by him ringing his bell. Walt had told Hector, "I know you despise me and I know how much you want to see me dead. But I'm willing to bet there's a man that you hate even more. I'm offering you an opportunity for revenge." When Gus visits Hector, he baits him one more time: "What kind of man talks to the DEA? No man. No man at all. A crippled little rata. What a reputation to leave behind. Is that how you want to be remembered? Last chance to look at me, Hector?" Just then, Hector rings the bell maniacally and stares directly at Gus with an expression of pure hatred. Gus immediately realizes at the last second that he has fallen into a trap, but it is too late and the explosion goes off. Gus calmly exits the room with half of his face blown off, stares straight ahead, adjusts his tie, and collapses dead onto the floor. After watching the explosion reported on the local news, Skyler asks Walt what happened and he replies, "I won."

The episode was written and directed by Vince Gilligan (the third episode to be both written and directed by him after "Pilot" and "Full Measure"). "Face Off" is the third highest-rated episode of the entire series

The filming locale for the underground meth lab where Walt and Jesse memorably chased after an errant fly for an entire episode actually serves as Delta Uniform & Linens.   *Courtesy of Ben Parker*

on IMDb, just behind "Ozymandias" and "Felina." The title refers to Gus's condition after the explosion and also alludes to the fact that his secret identity as a drug kingpin behind the façade of fast-food entrepreneur has been exposed forever. In addition, it serves as a small tribute to the 1997 John Woo thriller *Face/Off*, which starred Nicolas Cage and John Travolta. Gus Fring was the first major character to die in the series. Note that the dying Fring bears a startling resemblance to the Batman villain Two-Face. The *Breaking Bad* crew turned to the special effects team from AMC's other hit show, *The Walking Dead*, to help with the makeup and visual effects related to Gus Fring's death.

"Goodbye" by Apparat plays on the soundtrack as Gus approaches Casa Tranquila for the final time. The soundtrack also includes "Black" by Danger Mouse and Daniele Luppi featuring Norah Jones and "Freestyle" by Taalbi Brothers. "Face Off" was nominated for six Primetime Emmy Awards. *TV Guide* named it among the best episodes in 2011 after "Flu Season" (*Parks and Recreation*) and "Always" (*Friday Night Lights*), calling it a "jaw-dropping finale that will go down as one of TV's best. For one, there's the indelible, gross and awesome image of Gus' half-disfigured face after he emerged ostensibly from a bomb blast. But the ultimate 'holy crap!' came in the final, game-changing seconds when we learn that Walt had poisoned Brock—a reveal that tested the limits of our sympathy for him and showed that he had no ethical limits anymore. Walt is indeed the one who knocks." By the way, the Whites' neighbor, Rebecca Simmons, was portrayed by Vince Gilligan's mother, Gail.

14

Falling Apart Like This

Season Five (2012–13)

If that's true—if you don't know who I am—then maybe your best course would be to tread lightly.

—*Walter White to Hank*

Season Five of *Breaking Bad* premiered with "Live Free or Die" on July 15, 2012, and consisted of a total of sixteen episodes split into two mini seasons, each composed of eight episodes. Both halves of Season Five won the Primetime Emmy Award for Outstanding Drama Series. In addition, Anna Gunn won a Primetime Emmy for Outstanding Supporting Actress in a Drama Series, and another Primetime Emmy was awarded to the show for Outstanding Single-Camera Picture Editing for a Drama Series.

Six of the episodes in Season Five of *Breaking Bad* were the most-watched episodes in the entire series: "Felina" (10.28 million viewers), "Granite State" (6.58 million viewers), "Ozymandias" (6.37 million viewers), "Blood Money" (5.92 million viewers), "Say My Name" (2.98 million viewers), and "Live Free or Die" (2.93 million viewers). In addition, a live talk show hosted by Chris Hardwick called *Talking Dead* made its debut during the second half of the season. *Talking Dead* featured interviews with Vince Gilligan and cast members, along with superfans such as actor Samuel L. Jackson.

According to Aaron Paul, in a Q&A that appeared on amc.com, "I found out [the Season Five plot] just like our fans are going to find out, one episode at a time. So all I can say about the final eight is that every *Breaking Bad* fan knows that each season gets progressively darker. And the final eight hours are just a brutal sprint to the finish line. I never wanted the show to end, but after reading the final eight hours, I couldn't think of a better way to end it."

Episode 5.01: "Live Free or Die" (July 15, 2012)

In the opening flash-forward, Walter White appears extremely disheveled with a full head of hair (for the first time since early in the first season) as he sits alone in a Denny's restaurant and arranges the number "52" with bacon to mark his fifty-second birthday. He is using the alias "Lambert," which is Skyler's maiden name. Walt is driving a Volvo (which is incidentally the same car Gus drove) with a New Hampshire license plate that features the state motto, "Live Free or Die" (hence the episode title). He meets with arms dealer Lawson in the restroom and is handed keys to a car that contains an M60 machine gun and ammunition in the trunk.

In the present day, Walt, Jesse, and Mike try to figure out how to destroy the evidence on Gus Fring's laptop that lies in storage at the police station. Ironically, it is actually Jesse, not Walt, who comes up with the brilliant idea that a powerful magnet may just do the job. Mike suggests that they all need to simply flee the city and go their separate ways,

An Albuquerque institution, the Dog House, served as the backdrop of several *Breaking Bad* scenes, most notably as the place where Jesse doles out cash to the homeless guy in "Blood Money."

Courtesy of Ben Parker

but he is overruled by Walt and Jesse. So they equip an old truck with an industrial electromagnet purchased from junkyard owner Old Joe (Larry Hankin). The magnet works more effectively than they ever imagined, and they barely escape after being forced to abandon the truck. Ironically, the laptop was encrypted, and therefore the DEA had no access to its information. However, the magnet causes such destruction in the evidence room that it unearths a hidden list of Gus Fring's accounts, allowing the DEA to freeze the money set aside to prevent Mike's associates from squawking to the Feds. Meanwhile, Skyler visits Ted Beneke in the hospital, and he tells her he will never reveal anything related to the causes of his injury.

The episode was written by Vince Gilligan and directed by Michael Slovis. At just forty-two minutes, "Live Free or Die" is the shortest episode in the entire series. At the time of its airing, it was the most-watched episode in the series with 2.93 million viewers. Note that when Saul Goodman has the gall to actually bring up ethics, Walt compares him unfavorably to legendary lawyer Clarence Darrow: "You're a two-bit, bus-bench lawyer." Darrow (1857–1938) became nationally known after defending Nathan Leopold and Richard Loeb in 1924, and for opposing William Jennings Bryan in the so-called Scopes "Monkey" Trial in 1925. By the way, "Live Free or Die" was also the title of an episode of *The Sopranos* (6.06), which originally aired on April 16, 2006.

Episode 5.02: "Madrigal" (July 22, 2012)

The episode opens at Madrigal Electromotive in Germany and features a very disturbing scene where the company's executive, Peter Schuler, electrocutes himself in a bathroom using an automatic defibrillator as authorities close in on him. According to Vince Gilligan in a July 23, 2012, *Entertainment Weekly* interview, "We always like to surprise our viewers, and the idea of suddenly opening in Germany seemed like fun. We also wanted to start showing you the business of Madrigal, the company that financed Gus Fring. Is Madrigal all corrupt? Or was it just a couple of executives?" Meanwhile, Hank interrogates Mike about his connection to Gus Fring's drug empire. Mike informs him that he was simply in charge of "corporate security," with Hank replying sarcastically, "Like, uh, guarding the special sauce?" Mike admits to being a former Philadelphia cop, and Hank exclaims, "I mean, given your history, doing background checks on pimple-faced fry cooks seems like overkill."

The episode was written by Vince Gilligan and directed by Michelle MacLaren. "Madrigal" is the first episode to feature a location outside of the United States or Mexico. Note that Mike watches *The Caine Mutiny* (1954) on television at one point. The film, which was reportedly one of Vince Gilligan's childhood favorites, stars Humphrey Bogart as paranoid Lieutenant Commander Phillip Queeg. Also, Jesse refers to the RV as "the Crystal Ship," which is the name of a song by the Doors that appears on the band's self-titled debut album from 1967 and can also be found as the B-side of the band's No. 1 hit single "Light My Fire." According to rock critic Greil Marcus in his 2013 book *The Doors: A Lifetime of Listening to Five Mean Years*, the opening lines of the song, "Before you slip into unconsciousness/I'd like to have another kiss," could represent "sleep, it could be an overdose, inflicted by the singer or the person he's addressing; it could be murder suicide, or a suicide pact."

Episode 5.03: "Hazard Pay" (July 29, 2012)

Walt and Jesse set up a new mobile meth lab that utilizes Vamonos Pest Control as a cover. To Skyler's total dismay, Walt moves back into the White household. She even arrives from work to find Walt and Junior watching *Scarface* (1983) on television, and Walt comments somewhat prophetically, "Everyone dies in this movie, don't they?" Later, Mike admonishes Walt: "Just because you killed Jesse James . . . don't make you Jesse James." In quite a character anomaly, Skinny Pete plays "Solfeggietto No. 2 in C Minor" by Carl Philipp Emanuel Bach on the keyboard (filmed at the now-defunct Grandma's Music & Sound in Albuquerque). Mike visits all of Gus's former associates in prison, assuring them that they will still receive their "hazard pay" as long as they remain quiet. The episode was written by Peter Gould and directed by Adam Bernstein. "Hazard Pay" features the first appearance of creepy Todd Alquist (Jesse Plemons). The scene where Walt and Jesse drink beer on the couch was parodied on the "What Animated Woman Want" episode (24.17) of *The Simpsons* in 2013.

Episode 5.04: "Fifty-One" (August 5, 2012)

Walt sells his shoddy 2004 Pontiac Aztek for $50 and buys himself a new car, a brand-new Chrysler 300, for his birthday. A frustrated and depressed Skyler jumps in the deep end of the swimming pool in a scene reminiscent of Benjamin Braddock (Dustin Hoffman) in *The Graduate* (1967). The end of the episode reveals Walt's watch ticking—time is running out for him and his drug enterprise.

"Fifty-One" is actually the fiftieth episode in the series. It was written by Sam Catlin and directed by Rian Johnson, who won the Directors Guild of America Award for Outstanding Directing—Drama Series for the episode. In addition, Anna Gunn captured the Primetime Emmy Award for Outstanding Supporting Actress in a Drama Series for her performance in "Fifty-One." The episode's title refers to Walt's age. In a foreshadowing of the train heist in the subsequent episode, "Dead Freight," Walt declares, "The methylamine keeps flowing no matter what. We are not ramping down . . . Nothing stops this train." Note that Jesse gives Walt a Tag Heuer Monaco watch, which was made famous by actor Steve McQueen (aka "the King of Cool") in the 1977 movie *Le Mans*. McQueen's classic antihero persona shined through in such classic films as *The Magnificent Seven* (1960), *The Great Escape* (1963), *Bullitt* (1968), *The Getaway* (1972), and *Papillon* (1973), among others. He died of a rare form of inoperable cancer at the age of fifty in 1980.

Episode 5.05: "Dead Freight" (August 12, 2012)

Walt and his partners decide to boost methylamine from a freight train. Jesse remarks that stealing the methylamine from the train will be just like "Jesse James." Everything goes pretty well during the train heist until Todd Alquist casually kills a young kid on a dirt bike who innocently stumbles upon the scene. The episode was written and directed by George

Mastras (his directorial debut on the series). He was nominated for a Primetime Emmy Award for Outstanding Writing for a Drama Series for scripting "Dead Freight." The train heist itself took four days to film. The locale of the heist just outside of Santa Fe, New Mexico, was also used as a filming location for *Butch Cassidy and the Sundance Kid* (1969), which was directed by George Roy Hill (*The Sting*) and starred Paul Newman and Robert Redford in the title roles.

At one point in the episode, Hank asks Walt Jr. if he has ever watched the 1995 Michael Mann film *Heat*, which stars Robert De Niro and Al Pacino, and features an elaborate bank heist that goes wrong (and costars Danny Trejo, who appears in *Breaking Bad* as Tortuga). Note that Walt bugs Hank's office with the same lamp model that the FBI used to bug Tony's Soprano's basement in the episode "Mr. Ruggerio's Neighborhood" (3.01) from *The Sopranos*.

Episode 5.06: "Buyout" (August 19, 2012)

After the train heist, the partners dispose of the evidence. Jesse punches Todd out after he casually states "shit happens" in reference to killing the kid on the dirt bike. Mike and Jesse decide to take their share ($5 million apiece) and ditch the meth enterprise. Walt tells Jesse about his history with Gray Matter Technologies, a now-billion-dollar company that Walt left long ago for a paltry $5,000 buyout. Walt remarks to Jesse, "You asked me if I was in the meth business or the money business. Neither. I'm in the empire business." The episode was written by Gennifer Hutchison and directed by Colin Bucksey. Aaron Paul was nominated for a Primetime Emmy Award for Outstanding Supporting Actor in a Drama Series for his performance in "Buyout."

Episode 5.07: "Say My Name" (August 26, 2012)

At a desert meeting, Walt establishes a new partnership with meth distributor Declan (Louis Ferreira), to whom he arrogantly says, "What I produce is 99.1 percent pure . . . So it's grade-school T-ball versus the New

York Yankees. Yours is just some tepid, off-brand, generic cola. What I'm making is Classic Coke." He demands that Declan call him Heisenberg (hence the episode title). As the DEA searches Mike's house, he calmly sits watching *The Big Heat*, a 1953 film noir directed by Fritz Lang and starring Glenn Ford, Gloria Grahame, Lee Marvin, and Jocelyn Brando (Marlon's older sister). The film's tagline exclaims, "Somebody's going to pay . . . because he forgot to kill me . . . ." Walt ends up killing Mike when he refuses to divulge the names of the ten prisoners who are receiving hush money. Mike's final words are directed toward Walt: "Shut the fuck up and let me die in peace."

The episode, which had a working title of "Everybody Wins," was written and directed by Thomas Schnauz. Mike Ehrmantraut is the second major character to die in the series after Gus Fring. While filming "Say My Name," the entire crew wore black armbands to mark the final episode of Jonathan Banks. However, Banks would soon reprise the character in *Better Call Saul*. In a May 30, 2013, *Empire* interview, Vince Gilligan referred to Mike's death scene as "a sad moment, beautifully written and directed by one of my oldest friends, a writer named Thomas Schnauz, who I've known since NYU film school, and in his first professional directing gig he just did a fantastic job with that episode and that scene."

Episode 5.08: "Gliding Over All" (September 2, 2012)

Walt considers retiring from the meth-making business. Skyler and Walt visit the storage unit containing the huge pile of money and Skyler remarks, "There is more money here than what we could spend in ten lifetimes . . . Please tell me . . . how much is enough? How big does this pile have to be?" Through Uncle Jack Welker's connections, Walt manages to take out all of Gus Fring's legacy members in a horrifying two-minute montage. During a family get-together at the White household, Hank uses the bathroom and finds the copy of Walt Whitman's *Leaves of Grass* that Gale Boetticher gifted to Walt with the dedication, "To my other favorite W.W. It's an honor working with you. Fondly G.B." Hank immediately makes the connection that his brother-in-law is drug kingpin Heisenberg.

"Gliding Over All" served as the mid-season finale of Season Five. It was written by Moira Walley-Beckett and directed by Michelle MacLaren, who received a nomination for a Primetime Emmy Award for Outstanding Directing for a Drama Series for the episode. "Gliding Over All" is the first episode featuring Todd's Uncle Jack Welker (Michael Bowen), the leader of a white supremacist gang. The prison killings recall the string of murders at the end of *The Godfather* (1972) as Michael Corleone (Al Pacino) takes out the other heads of the New York mob families, thereby solidifying his power. The episode's title is also the name of a famous Walt Whitman poem, "Gliding O'er All." Believe it or not, the inscribed copy of *Leaves of Grass* used in this episode fetched $65,500 at auction in 2013. The episode's soundtrack features the 1968 Tommy James and the Shondells song "Crystal Blue Persuasion," which plays during the meth-making montage.

Episode 5.09: "Blood Money" (August 11, 2013)

In the cold open of "Blood Money," Walt breaks into his former house, which is now abandoned and fenced off. The interior of the house has been vandalized (with "HEISENBERG" spray-painted in yellow on one of the walls). Walt manages to scare the hell out of his neighbor Carol in the process. In the present, Walt confronts Hank, who exclaims, "You bombed a nursing home. Heisenberg. Heisenberg. You lying, two-faced sack of shit." When Hank tells Walt, "I don't even know who I'm talking to," Walt warns him, "If that's true—if you don't know who I am—then maybe your best course would be to tread lightly."

In a bit of comic relief to a very tense episode, Skinny Pete and Badger discuss the finer points of *Star Trek*: "So you're telling me every time Kirk went into the transport he was killing himself? So over the whole series, there was, like one-hundred-forty-seven Kirks?" Badger tells Skinny Pete about his rather surreal *Star Trek* script: "The Enterprise is five parsecs out of Rigel XII. Nothing's going on. Neutral Zone is quiet, the crew is bored, so they put on a pie-eating contest."

The episode was written by Peter Gould and directed by Bryan Cranston. It was the third episode Cranston directed after "Seven

Thirty-Seven" and "No Más." The episode was dedicated to sixteen-year-old superfan Kevin Cordasco, who was terminally ill with cancer and sadly passed away before the episode aired. Note that in the cold open, Carol drops a bag of groceries and oranges roll out, a possible reference to the presence of oranges in *The Godfather* (1972) that signal the future death of characters.

Episode 5.10: "Buried" (August 18, 2013)

Hank meets with Skyler in a diner and tries to get her to testify against Walt, but she refuses. Walt places his drug money (about $80 million in cash) in eight separate barrels, which he buries in the desert. He cleverly disguises the GPS coordinates (N 34, 59′, 20″, W 106, 36′, 52) where the barrels of money are located in the desert on a lottery ticket that he pins to the refrigerator door. Saul Goodman suggests to Walt that Hank gets sent to "Belize" (a casual way of saying just eliminate him). Walt replies that he's going to send Saul to Belize instead. Uncle Jack's crew emerges victorious after an (off-camera) shootout with Declan's men.

At one point, Saul suggests to Walt that Hank get "sent to Belize" (eliminate him). Due to the negative Belize reference in this episode, the Belize Tourism Board actually offered free vacations for the entire *Breaking Bad* cast and crew.

The episode was written by Thomas Schnauz and directed by Michelle MacLaren. Schnauz was nominated for a Writers Guild of America Award for Television: Episodic Drama for "Buried." The shootout was reportedly filmed off-screen due to budget constraints for the episode. Due to the negative Belize reference in this episode, the Belize Tourism Board actually offered free vacations for the entire *Breaking Bad* cast and crew to the Central American country. A popular vacation destination, Belize (formerly British Honduras) is known for its ecotourism, jungles, Mayan ruins, cave tours, black howler monkeys, Ambergris Caye, extensive barrier reef, and famous dive site the Blue Hole. Also in this episode, Marie asks Hank, "What are you, Lone Wolf McQuade?"—referencing the cheesy 1983 action movie starring Chuck Norris. By the way, the GPS coordinates are actually those of Q Studios in Albuquerque where many scenes from the show were filmed.

Episode 5.11: "Confessions" (August 25, 2013)

Hank confronts Jesse with his newfound discovery that Heisenberg is Walt and offers him a deal. In true Jesse-like fashion, he responds with "Eat me." Walt brilliantly and diabolically creates a "confessional" video that directly implicates Hank as the true drug kingpin with Walt as his reluctant meth cook. The episode was written by Gennifer Hutchison and directed by Michael Slovis. Hutchison won a Writers Guild of America Award for Television: Episodic Drama for "Confessions." In addition, Aaron Paul captured an Emmy for Outstanding Supporting Actor in a Drama Series for his performance in this episode.

Note that by the end of "Confessions," both Skyler and Walt Jr. have wished death on Walt. The song "Gonna Romp and Stomp" by Slim Rhodes plays in the background when the Neo-Nazis are in the diner. The opening line of Walt's fake video confession hearkens back to his original confession in the "Pilot" episode. Todd relates the train heist to Uncle Jack, who compares his leap from the train to a similar stunt from the 1978 action movie *Hooper*, which was directed by Hal Needham (*Smokey and the Bandit*) and starred Burt Reynolds, Sally Field, and Jan-Michael Vincent. Also look for former J.Crew and Gap CEO Mickey Drexler in a cameo as a car wash customer who informs Skyler that she has given him a $5 bill instead of a single (making him the only honest character on the show, according to some fans).

Episode 5.12: "Rabid Dog" (September 1, 2013)

Jesse decides to burn the White household to the ground, but is intercepted by Hank, who enlists him to record a confession detailing his involvement in Walt's meth operation. Hank and Gomie convince Jesse to wear a wire and meet with Walt, but he backs out at the last minute with a new plan to get revenge on his former partner. In true Lady Macbeth manner, Skyler casually urges Walt to eliminate Jesse. Meanwhile, Patrick Kuby bugs Skinny Pete and Badger's apartment to determine Jesse's whereabouts and informs Walt they spent three hours talking about *Babylon 5*. The episode was written and directed by Sam Catlin. The title refers to the scene where Saul Goodman compares Jesse to a rabid dog that needs to be put down just like in the 1957 Walt Disney film *Old Yeller*, which was based on the 1956 novel of the same name by Fred Gipson and starred Tommy Kirk, Dorothy McGuire, Fess Parker, and Beverly Washburn.

Episode 5.13: "To'hajiilee" (September 8, 2013)

Jesse's warning to Hank (which later becomes prophetic) about Walt goes unheeded: "Whatever—whatever you think is supposed to happen—I'm telling you, the exact reverse opposite of this is going to happen, okay?" Hank and Jesse trick Walt into divulging where his money barrels are located in the desert. Jesse calls Walt "a lying, evil scumbag." Hank arrests Walt, but Uncle Jack and his crew arrive just in time and a firefight ensues. The episode was written by George Mastras and directed by Michelle MacLaren. A Navajo Indian reservation in New Mexico, To'hajiilee was the site of Walt and Jesse's first cook in the "Pilot" episode and the burial site of his eight barrels of money in "Buried." Note that Todd's ringtone for Walt is English musician Thomas Dolby's 1982 hit "She Blinded Me with

Science" from his debut album, *The Golden Age of Wireless*. VH1 named the song No. 20 on its list of the "100 Greatest One-Hit Wonders" (for the record, "Macarena" by Los Del Rio placed No. 1).

Episode 5.14: "Ozymandias" (September 15, 2013)

Tragically, Gomie gets killed during the firefight with Uncle Jack's crew. Despite Walt's strenuous objections, Uncle Jack then proceeds to murder Hank in cold blood and helps himself to seven of Walt's barrels, leaving him one barrel containing about $11 million. Considered by critics as one of the best, if not the best, episode in the entire series, "Ozymandias" was written by Moira Walley-Beckett and directed by Rian Johnson. Walley-Beckett captured the Emmy for Outstanding Writing for a Drama Series for the "Ozymandias" screenplay. In addition, Bryan Cranston and Anna Gunn both won Emmy Awards for Lead Actor and Supporting Actress respectively for this episode. Vince Gilligan remarked during a *Breaking Bad Insider* podcast, "'Ozymandias' is the best episode we ever have had or ever will have." In a September 16, 2013, blog entry on livejournal.com, author George R. R. Martin (known for his best-selling series of novels *A Song of Fire and Ice*, the basis for the hit HBO series *A Game of Thrones*) stated after watching "Ozymandias" that "Walter White is a bigger monster than anyone in Westeros."

The episode title refers to Percy Bysshe Shelley's 1818 sonnet "Ozymandias," which highlights the transient nature of all human endeavors (and indeed Walt ends up losing everything and everyone he ever cared about). The episode's soundtrack features "Take My True Love by the Hand" by the Limeliters. In a 2013 trailer for the series, Cranston recites Shelley's entire poem (which can be heard on YouTube). Note that as Walt rolls the money barrel, he passes a pair of pants that appear to be the very ones he lost in the "Pilot" episode. Knowing its significance to the entire series, acclaimed director Guillermo del Toro (*Pan's Labyrinth*) reportedly expressed a strong desire to direct this episode, but eventual director Rian Johnson joked with him, "Yeah, sorry, I'm the one who gets to fuck the prom queen."

Episode 5.15: "Granite State" (September 22, 2013)

Walt goes into hiding, assuming a new identity in a snowy cabin in New Hampshire with the assistance of an expert relocator (portrayed by legendary character actor Robert Forster). Uncle Jack and his crew hold Jesse as their prisoner and force him to cook meth for them. After Jesse tries to escape, Todd casually kills his girlfriend Andrea in front of him as punishment. Walt cringes as he hears Gretchen and Elliott Schwartz disparage him during a TV interview with Charlie Rose. He also places a phone call to Walt Jr., whose final words to him are: "Why don't you just die already?" The episode was written and directed by Peter Gould, who was nominated for a Writers Guild of America for Television: Episodic Drama. Bob Odenkirk made his final appearance in *Breaking Bad* as Saul Goodman in this episode as he heads to Omaha, Nebraska, to manage a Cinnabon (he would reprise his Saul Goodman/Jimmy McGill role in *Better Call Saul*). The episode's title refers to New Hampshire's nickname, "The Granite State." Forster's guest appearance as Ed garnered him a Saturn Award for Best Guest Starring Role on Television. Ex-PBS talk show host Charlie Rose makes a cameo appearance as himself in the

Walt gets whisked away to his new identity after waiting for the "vacuum cleaner repairman" at the John B. Robert Dam, which features eerie rows of cement blocks that resemble tombstones.
Courtesy of Ben Parker

episode (Rose's television career abruptly ended in 2017 following allega-
tions of sexual harassment).

"Granite State" is the only episode in the entire series that contains a
full version of the "Breaking Bad Theme" by Dave Porter. The snowy New
Hampshire scenes in "Granite State" were actually filmed in the Sandia
Mountains that surround Albuquerque. Walt is stuck in the cabin with
not one but two copies of the critically maligned 2007 film *Mr. Magorium's
Wonder Emporium*, which was directed by Zach Helm and starred Dustin
Hoffman and Natalie Portman. After the film was referenced in a negative light in "Granite State," Helm remarked to TMZ, "Having myself
endured the ignominy of watching the Technicolor train-wreck that is
Mr. Magorium's Wonder Emporium multiple times every day for over a
year, I can attest to it being the perfect Kafkaesque Hell for a character
of such moral ambiguity as Walter White." Earlier in the episode, Saul
tells Walt that if he stays in Albuquerque he will be considered the "John
Dillinger of Metropolitan Detention Center." By the way, Michael Bowen
and Robert Forster both appeared in Quentin Tarantino's 1997 film *Jackie
Brown*, which also starred Pam Grier, Samuel L. Jackson, Robert De Niro,
and Bridget Fonda.

15

I Was Alive

Series Finale (September 29, 2013)

> Just get me home . . . I'll do the rest.
> —*Walter White*

The sixty-second episode of *Breaking Bad*, "Felina" also served as the series finale. The fifty-five-minute episode was written and directed by Vince Gilligan. Unlike the series finale of *The Sopranos*, which cut to black and left viewers wondering what the hell had just happened, *Breaking Bad* managed to tie up all of the loose ends, and allowed Walt to settle scores and make amends to an extent, while also making sure he was punished in the end for his transgressions. In *Breaking Bad: The Official Book*, Gilligan remarked, "When it came down to it, it seemed most fitting for Walt's end that it wasn't the cancer that got him, but a death of his own making. It seemed appropriate for the character, and the journey we had taken him on, for Walt to have an active hand in his mortality."

As "Felina" opens, Walter White listens to the classic country ballad "El Paso" by Marty Robbins as he heads back to New Mexico in a stolen Volvo (the same make of car that Gus Fring once drove) and somehow manages to evade a nationwide manhunt. A disheveled Walt sports a scraggly beard, the lines in his face magnified—evoking a truly ghostly apparition. Once he hits Albuquerque, Walt retrieves the ricin from his abandoned house. He later crashes a meeting between Todd Alquist and Lydia Rodarte-Quayle, and offers them a formula for making methylamine-free meth (as a way to gain access to Uncle Jack's compound). Lydia agrees to hear the pitch as a way to lure Walt to his death.

Walt then pays a final visit to Skyler and gives her the GPS coordinates where authorities can find the burial sites of both Hank and Gomie.

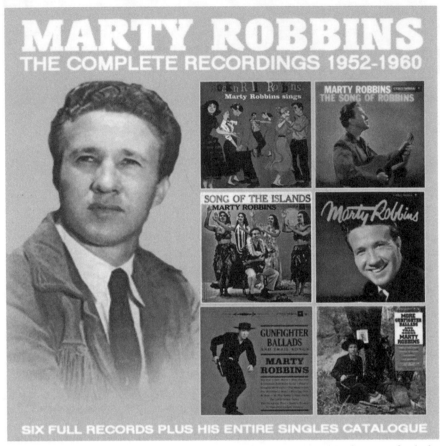

As Walt makes his way back to New Mexico to settle various scores in the series finale, he listens to the classic country and western ballad "El Paso" by Marty Robbins.

Significantly, Walt finally confesses to her that he created the whole meth empire for himself, not his family: "I did it for me. I liked it. I was good at it. And . . . I was . . . really . . . I was alive." Even after all Walt has put her through, Skyler allows him to hold Holly one more time. Walt later tracks down his old partners Gretchen and Elliott Schwartz, and orders them to "make things right" by giving his remaining $9.72 million to Walt Jr. once he reaches the age of eighteen. To make sure that the Schwartzes uphold their end of the deal, Walt has "two of the best hitmen west of the Mississippi" from outside the house train their weapons on them (viewers soon discover that it was actually Badger and Skinny Pete aiming red laser pointers).

Lastly, Walt visits Uncle Jack's compound and uses a remote-control machine gun rigged within the trunk of his car to wipe out the entire gang (he takes a gunshot for Jesse as well). Jesse strangles Todd in revenge for killing his girlfriend, Andrea. Walt urges Jesse to kill him, but he refuses. Todd's phone rings and Walt answers to hear Lydia's voice. He tells her that he poisoned her tea with ricin. Walt's last words are "Goodbye, Lydia." Walt and Jesse share a knowing glance before Jesse jumps into Todd's El Camino and breaks through the fence, tears of joy streaming down his face. Totally exhilarated, he is free at last. Walt stumbles into the meth superlab and nostalgically admires the equipment. Badfinger's "Baby Blue" plays during the final scene (symbolizing Walt's one true love, his signature blue meth): "Guess I got what I deserved/Kept you waiting there, too long my love."

According to Gilligan in a Q&A that appeared on amc.com, "We wanted the right balance of Walt paying for his sins and yet we wanted some sort of a note of triumph at the end of it all. He got a whole lot of money to his family; trouble is he's destroyed his family in the meantime. Even the pick of the final song of the series reflects that—the Badfinger song has got a tinge of sadness to it and yet the chord structure is almost kind of triumphant." Cranston added in his 2016 memoir, *A Life in Parts*, "Walter White was more alive in the last years of his life than he had been

The Grove Café and Market is where Walt notoriously slips ricin in Lydia's tea during a classic act of revenge in the series finale, "Felina."   *Courtesy of Ben Parker*

in the previous fifty. He went from utter failure to great power . . . I don't agree with the decisions Walt made or the actions he took, of course. But I feel for him. If you have two years to live, you don't let them cut your balls off. You go out fighting. That's what he did. He was alive."

"Felina" Trivia

- "Felina" was the fourth episode that Gilligan both wrote and directed (the other three being "Pilot," "Full Measure," and "Face Off").
- First released on Marty Robbins's 1959 album, *Gunfighter Ballads and Trail Songs*, "El Paso" captured a Grammy Award for Best Country & Western Recording in 1961. The song features a character named "Feleena." The episode title was changed to "Felina" as an anagram of "finale."
- "Felina" also can be broken down to represent the symbols of three chemical elements found in the periodic table: iron (Fe), lithium (Li), and sodium (Na). Some trenchant observers interpreted this to mean "blood, meth, and tears"—but that's quite a stretch.
- "Felina" drew 10.28 million viewers, making it the most-watched episode in *Breaking Bad* history (beating out the previous episode, "Granite State," which drew 6.58 million viewers).
- Gilligan has acknowledged John Ford's classic 1956 Western *The Searchers*, which starred John Wayne, as inspiration for the final standoff between Walt and Jesse. (See Chapter 22 for more information on *The Searchers* along with other major film and TV influences on *Breaking Bad*.)
- During a 2017 Reddit AMA, someone asked Gilligan, "Is Walter White really dead?" He replied, "Sure looked that way to me!"
- Walt appears to be wearing the same clothes in "Felina" that he first wore in the "Pilot" episode.
- Sirens can be heard as Walt lies dying in the lab at the end, just as sirens can be heard at the beginning of the "Pilot" episode as Walt awaits his destiny in the desert.
- One fan theory popularized by stand-up comedian and actor Norm MacDonald is that Walt never even left New Hampshire, and the

Walt is stuck in the New Hampshire cabin with not one but two copies of the critically maligned 2007 film *Mr. Magorium's Wonder Emporium*, which starred Dustin Hoffman and Natalie Portman.

entire finale is his dying fantasy about how he would have wanted to have closure (see Chapter 27 for this and other fan theories). However, Vince Gilligan vehemently denied this theory.

- Saul Goodman does not appear in "Felina" (he must be on his way to Omaha, Nebraska, to manage that Cinnabon!).

16

Here in the Real World

Breaking Bad Filming Locales

> Me personally? I'm thinking Albuquerque just might have a new kingpin.
> —*Hank Schrader*

B*reaking Bad* was originally set in Riverside, California, but fortunately the filming locale was changed to Albuquerque, New Mexico, after the production received some significant tax rebates. According to Nick Maniatis, director of the New Mexico State Film Office, in a September 28, 2013, *New York Times* article, "'Breaking Bad' became such a phenomenon that it helped in other areas such as tourism . . . You wouldn't think that would be the case for a show about meth. But it was shot so beautifully. They did such a great job showing different areas of our state."

During an interview by *Local IQ*, series creator Vince Gilligan exclaimed, "I can't imagine the show would be nearly as interesting as it is if it were set anywhere else. Just the cinematography and the look of the show. When I think of Albuquerque, I think of clouds, just those beautiful floating cumulus clouds. The skies. These are skies you just don't see in Southern California. You really get the depth and the sense of scale in the desert in Albuquerque." According to Bryan Cranston in his 2016 memoir, *A Life in Parts*, "Albuquerque was as central to the show as any person or character. Shooting there, I got to know the place well; its friendly people, stark beauty, and quirky charms will always have a place in my heart." Aaron Paul added in an amc.com Q&A, "I fell in love with that city during the first season and fell in love with the entire state in the seasons after that. I own a place there and I'm going to keep it, so I'll go back." In an interview with the *Albuquerque Journal*, Giancarlo Esposito remarked, "There's something very wonderful to be surrounded by the mountains and good air. It's a wonderful place to work and it feels like home."

With the beautiful Sandia Mountains as a backdrop, Albuquerque (elevation: 5,312 feet) boasts 559,000 residents, making it New Mexico's largest city. Albuquerque is nicknamed "The Duke City" since it was named for the Duke of Albuquerque, while New Mexico itself is known as the "Land of Enchantment." A fun and informative way to get around and catch many major *Breaking Bad* landmarks throughout Albuquerque is to book a reservation with Breaking Bad RV Tours (breakingbadrvtours. com). For the definitive guide to *Breaking Bad* and *Better Call Saul* filming locales throughout Albuquerque, pick up a copy of the meticulously detailed *A Guidebook to Breaking Bad Filming Locations* (2016) by Marc P. Valdez.

Note: Addresses have been redacted on private residences, which can easily be found during a quick search of the Internet anyway. If you do visit any of these locations, please respect the privacy of the inhabitants (and absolutely refrain from throwing uncut pizzas onto rooftops!).

A1 Car Wash
(9516 Snow Heights Circle NE)

"Have an A1 day!" The A1 Car Wash is where Walt works a demeaning second job to make ends meet in the "Pilot" (1.01) episode. Later, Skyler negotiates the purchase of the A1 Car Wash for the purpose of laundering Walt's drug money. At the time of filming, it was known as the Octopus Car Wash (motto: "Many hands to serve you."). Today, it's part of a chain of car washes known as Mister Car Wash ("Have a dirty car? We can help").

Albuquerque Rail Yards (1100 2nd Street SW)

Numerous *Breaking Bad* scenes were filmed in the Albuquerque Rail Yards. In addition, the Rail Yards were used as a backdrop during the photo shoot for the "All Hail the King" poster campaign to promote Season Five of *Breaking Bad*. The Rail Yards also served as a filming locale for *The Avengers* (2012), the sixth film in the Marvel Cinematic Universe.

Albuquerque Studios
(5650 University Boulevard SE)

Many *Breaking Bad* and *Better Call Saul* sets were built on the sound-stages at Albuquerque Studios (aka Q Studios), including the dungeon-like meth superlab. Films shot at Q Studios include *The Spirit* (2008), *Terminator Salvation* (2009), *Gamer* (2009), *Passion Play* (2010), *Let Me In* (2010), *Due Date* (2010), *The Book of Eli* (2010), *The Resident* (2011), *Fright Night* (2011), *Cowboys & Aliens* (2011), *The Avengers* (2012), and *The Lone Ranger* (2013).

Albuquerque's Civic Plaza
(1 Civic Plaza)

In the episode "Rabid Dog," (5.12), Hank and Gomie convince Jesse to wear a wire and meet Walt at the Civic Plaza, but he backs out at the last minute, informing them that he has a better plan. Ideally located in the heart of downtown Albuquerque, the Harry E. Kinney Civic Plaza was constructed in 1974 to host a variety of outdoor events. It was named for Harry E. Kinney (1924–2006), who served as Mayor of Albuquerque for two terms—1974–77 and 1981–85.

Buried Bus Meth Lab
(South Valley, adjacent to Pueblo of Isleta)

In the episode "Buried" (5.10), Declan and his gang operate an underground meth lab at this location until Uncle Jack Welker and his crew kill them all and take over the drug operation.

Many *Breaking Bad* and *Better Call Saul* sets were built on the soundstages at Albuquerque Studios (aka Q Studios), including the dungeon-like meth superlab.   *AllenS/Wikimedia Commons*

Candy Lady
(424 San Felipe St NW)

Visitors to the Candy Lady, a legendary New Mexican candy restaurant, can purchase blue rock candy that resembles the infamous blue meth cooked up by Walt and Jesse. In fact, the candy was actually used as a prop during the first two seasons of *Breaking Bad*. The Candy Lady also offers "classic sweets, custom confections, and modern delights."

Casa Tranquila Nursing Home
(8820 Horizon Blvd. NE)

"Tio" Hector Salamanca resides at Casa Tranquila (translation: "Quiet House") nursing home, and it is here where Walt convinces him to lure Gus Fring to his explosive death in the episode "Face Off" (4.13). The Casa Tranquila scenes were filmed at the former Valle Norte Caring Center (now the site of the Medical Resort at Fiesta Park).

"Combo's Corner"
(Corner of 1st, 2nd and Atlantic Streets SW)

Jesse Pinkman's drug-addled buddy Combo is casually dealing drugs at this corner when he gets gunned down by a kid working for a rival gang (later identified as Jesse's girlfriend Andrea's little brother, Tomas). It's also the spot where Walt runs down two rival drug dealers in his Pontiac Aztec before they have a chance to kill Jesse.

Crossroads Motel
(1001 Central Avenue NE)

Known as the "Crystal Palace," the infamous Crossroads Motel is where meth-addicted hooker Wendy turns tricks and occasionally entertains Jesse. It's also where Hank warns Walt Jr. about the danger of drugs in the episode ". . . And the Bag's in the River" (1.03).

Denny's
(2608 Central Avenue SE)

Two memorable *Breaking Bad* scenes were shot at this now-defunct Denny's: Walt and Jesse ate breakfast here wearing identical Kenny Rogers T-shirts after cleaning up the superlab following Victor's murder by Gus Fring in the episode "Box Cutter" (4.01). The breakfast scene serves as a homage to a similar scene involving Vincent Vega (John Travolta) and Jules Winnfield (Samuel L. Jackson) in Quentin Tarantino's *Pulp Fiction* (1994). At the beginning of Season Five, Walt enjoys a lonely fifty-second breakfast here and purchases a machine gun from arms dealer Lawson in the process in the episode "Live Free or Die" (5.01). The former Denny's site is now occupied by a Chipotle, Verizon store, and Jersey Mike's Subs.

Dog House Drive In
(1216 Central Ave. NW)

An Albuquerque institution, the Dog House served as the backdrop of several *Breaking Bad* scenes, most notably as the place where Jesse doles out cash to the homeless guy in the episode "Blood Money" (5.09). The Dog House also appears in the 2007 thriller *First Snow*, which starred Guy Pearce (*Memento*).

Garduno's Restaurant
(2100 Louisiana Boulevard NE)

Garduno's is the Mexican eatery that specializes in tableside guacamole where Walt, Skyler, Hank, and Marie have a very awkward lunch in the episode "Confessions" (5.11). Immediately after the episode aired, Garduno's reported a 5 percent increase in tableside guacamole orders.

Georgia O'Keeffe Museum
(217 Johnson Street, Santa Fe)

In a flashback that takes place in the cold open of the episode "Abiquiu" (3.11), Jane and Jesse visit the Georgia O'Keeffe Museum in Santa Fe and discuss the finer points of O'Keeffe's painting *My Last Door*. Jesse asks, "Why would anyone paint a picture of a door, over and over again, like, dozens of times?" Jane replies, "Why not a door? Sometimes you get fixated on something, and you might not even get why. You open yourself up and go with the flow, wherever the universe takes you." Considered the "Mother of American Modernism," O'Keeffe (1887–1986) was known for her close-ups of flowers, as well as her New Mexico landscapes. In her 1976 book *Some Memories of Drawings*, O'Keeffe writes, "The unexplainable thing in nature that makes me feel the world is big far beyond my understanding—to understand maybe by trying to put it into form. To find the feeling of infinity on the horizon line or just over the next hill."

Gertrude Zachary Jewelry
(3300 Central Ave. SE)

Gertrude Zachary Jewelry served as the locale for the jewelry store where Marie shoplifts the tiara she ends up gifting at Skyler's baby shower in the episode "No-Rough-Stuff-Type Deal" (1.07).

The Grove Café and Market
(600 Central Ave SE)

The Grove Café and Market is where Walt often met with the usually frazzled Lydia Rodarte-Quayle. She later met Mike Ehrmantraut and Todd Alquist there. In addition, Walt notoriously slips ricin in Lydia's tea here in the series finale, "Felina" (5.16), leading to her inevitable demise ("Goodbye, Lydia").

Gus Fring's House
(Private Residence)

Fast-food entrepreneur Gus Fring hosted both Walt and Jesse at this modest ranch house (the perfect cover for the careful drug kingpin) at separate times.

Gus Fring's Laundry Business & Meth Lab
(1617 Candelaria Road NE)

The filming locale for the underground meth lab where Walt and Jesse memorably chased after an errant fly for an entire episode (3.10) actually serves as Delta Uniform & Linens.

Hank and Marie's House
(Private Residence)

Hank and Marie live in a spacious house located at the foothills of the Sandia Mountains in the outskirts of town. It's also here in the garage where Walt and Hank have a memorable confrontation after Hank discovers his brother-in-law is none other than the notorious Heisenberg in the episode "Blood Money" (5.09): "You bombed a nursing home. Heisenberg. *Heisenberg!* You lying, two-faced sack of shit!" Most importantly, this is where Hank displays his mineral collection and homebrews his infamous Schraderbrau! Both exterior and interior shots were reportedly filmed here.

Isleta Casino and Resort
(11000 Broadway Blvd. SE)

In the episode "ABQ" (2.13), Jesse's stint in rehab was filmed here. The Isleta Casino and Resort also served as the hotel where Walt, Skyler, and

Hank and Marie live in a spacious house located at the foothills of the Sandia Mountains where the former displays his mineral collection and homebrews his infamous Schraderbrau.

Courtesy of John Parker

Junior fled after Jesse dumped gasoline all over their carpet in the episode "Rabid Dog" (5.12).

J. P. Wynne High School
(301 Loma Colorado NE, Rio Rancho)

Walt is employed as a chemistry teacher at J. P. Wynne High School (named after a school Vince Gilligan attended while growing up in Farmville, Virginia). The high school scenes were originally filmed at Rio Rancho High School and also at Central New Mexico Community College (Westside Campus), Eldorado High School, and Highland High School.

Jesse and Jane's Rental Apartment
(Private Residence)

Forced out of his aunt's former house by his parents and temporarily homeless living in the RV, Jesse ends up renting at this duplex, where he embarks on a brief, intense, and ultimately tragic relationship with his landlord, Jane, who lives next door.

Jesse Pinkman's House
(Private Residence)

The site of many days and nights of nonstop debauchery (as well as the killing of Krazy-8 and the "disposal" of Emilio), Jesse Pinkman's house is located in the upscale Albuquerque Country Club neighborhood. The house was initially used for both exterior and interior shots until it was remodeled and sold. From then on, it was only used for exterior shots.

The John B. Robert Dam
(Corner of Juan Tabo Blvd and Osuna Rd NE)

Both Jesse and Walt wait for "vacuum cleaner repairman" (Robert Forster) here to be whisked off to unknown whereabouts with new identities. Jesse changes his mind at the last minute, while Walt relocates briefly to a cabin in New Hampshire. Note that the dam's eerie rows of cement blocks resemble a graveyard (foreshadowing Walt's demise?).

Loyola's Family Restaurant
(4500 Central Ave.)

Mike and Jesse eat at this popular local diner in Season Four in the episode "Cornered" (4.06). An Albuquerque landmark, Loyola's has also been used as a filming locale for *Better Call Saul, In Plain Sight* (2008–12), and *Terminator: The Sarah Connor Chronicles* (2008–09).

Marble Brewery
(111 Marble Avenue NW)

Bryan Cranston reportedly hung out here on occasion to relax and unwind after long days of filming *Breaking Bad*. Founded in 2008 and located in the heart of downtown Albuquerque, the Marble Brewery occasionally sells *Breaking Bad* tribute beers such as Walt's White Lie and Heisenberg's Dark.

National Museum of Nuclear Science & History
(601 Eubank SE)

The scene in the episode "Negro y Azul" (2.07) where Walt meets with Jesse's dealers—Badger, Skinny Pete, and Combo—at the National Museum of Nuclear Science & History was actually shot at the museum's old location at 1905 Mountain Road NW. The current location of the museum is at 601 Eubank SE. However, many exhibits shown in the background of the "Negro y Azul" episode can still be viewed at the new address.

New Hampshire Bar
(10676 South Highway 14/337, Tijeras)

In the series finale, "Felina" (5.16), Walt calls Junior and then catches Elliott and Gretchen Schwartz being interviewed on *The Charlie Rose Show* at a New Hampshire dive bar, which was actually filmed at the former Ponderosa Eatery and Saloon in Tijeras, New Mexico.

La Palomita Park
(La Sala Grande)

La Palomita Park is where Mike Ehrmantraut enjoyed spending his time with his granddaughter, Kaylee, when not getting harassed by DEA agents.

Los Pollos Hermanos
(4257 Isleta Boulevard SW)

The filming locale for Los Pollos Hermanos (Spanish for "the Chicken Brothers") is known in Albuquerque as Twisters, a Southwestern fast-food chain that serves burritos and burgers—but not fried chicken! Los Pollos Hermanos made its first appearance in the *Breaking Bad* episode "Mandala" (2.11). Even after the series ended, the fictional Los Pollos Hermanos logo remained inside the restaurant and according to Vince Gilligan, "I hope it stays there forever."

Rebel Donut
(400 Gold Ave.)

A novelty shop, Rebel Donut makes immensely popular "Blue Sky" doughnuts using blue frosting and blue rock candy (the first batch was reportedly created here as a gift to Aaron Paul in 2012).

Saul Goodman's Office
(9800 Montgomery Boulevard NE)

Saul Goodman's sleazy strip-mall office with its inflatable Statue of Liberty and tacky interior (complete with an oversized copy of the Constitution plastered on the wall) is now home to Duke City Sports Bar.

Savoy Bar & Grill
(10601 Montgomery Boulevard Northeast)

Billed as "a sun-filled, unpretentious but sophisticated, wine-friendly restaurant," the Savoy served as the filming locale for the upscale restaurant where Walt and Gretchen Schwartz meet for an awkward lunch in the episode "Peekaboo" (2.06).

Taco Sal
(9621 Menaul Boulevard NE)

Several *Breaking Bad* scenes used Taco Sal, a local landmark that first opened its doors in 1961, as a backdrop such as when Skyler and Marie handed out missing flyers of Walt in the episode "Grilled" (2.06).

A true mecca for hardcore *Breaking Bad* fans, the White residence has become so popular over the years that Vince Gilligan was forced to publicly urge fans to stop throwing pizzas on the roof.
Courtesy of John Parker

To'hajiilee Indian Reservation

To'hajiilee (a Navajo word that means "place near water") is where Walt and Jesse take the RV for their first meth cook in the "Pilot" episode, where Walt buries his money barrels in "Buried" (5.10), where Walt gets tricked into revealing the location of the barrels in the aptly named "To'hajiilee" (5.13), and where Hank gets murdered in "Ozymandias" (5.14).

Tuco's Hideout
(906 Park Ave. SW)

Java Joe's coffee shop served as the filming location for Tuco Salamanca's hideout, where Walt causes an explosion using fulminated mercury that impresses Tuco and convinces him to work with the mysterious Heisenberg.

Walt and Skyler's House
(Private Residence)

A true mecca for hardcore *Breaking Bad* fans, the White residence (located at the fictional address of 328 Negro Arroyo) has become so popular over the years that things were truly getting out of hand. Fans were not only stealing rocks and other "souvenirs" from the property, but also heaving uncut pizzas on the roof. In fact, things got so bad that Vince Gilligan was forced to publicly urge fans to stop throwing pizzas on the roof.

17

All This Brilliance

Innovative Filming Techniques in *Breaking Bad*

> I am showing the Old West as it really was. Cinema takes violence from life. Not the other way around. Americans treat Westerns with too much rhetoric.
>
> —*Sergio Leone*

Often referred to as a modern Western, *Breaking Bad* evokes a cinematic feel and incorporates many filming techniques patterned after legendary director Sergio Leone's epic Spaghetti Westerns, most notably *The Good, the Bad, and the Ugly* (1966) and *Once Upon a Time in the West* (1968), as well as William Friedkin's crime thriller *The French Connection* (1971). Many of the visual tricks Vince Gilligan picked up during his stint as writer and producer of *The X-Files* between 1995 and 2002 also can be found throughout *Breaking Bad*, which was shot on 35-millimeter film instead of digitally—giving the show a much more cinematic quality than the average television drama series (at a significantly higher cost as well!).

The decision to film *Breaking Bad* in Albuquerque served to enhance the cinematographic quality of the series, with Gilligan remarking in a May 16, 2010, *New York* magazine article that "the big skies and stark beauty of New Mexico have become characters all their own." According to Director of Photography Michael Slovis in *Breaking Bad: The Official Book*, "The place of action (location) in film is not arbitrary; it's intentional and is therefore a character in the show, and we gain a lot by seeing our actors move through these spaces. Vince always regarded the show as a Western, so whenever we spoke about approach, the go-to references were Sergio Leone's films. If you look at them, you will see how our show is an homage." The goal of both

Gilligan and Slovis in regard to the cinematography of *Breaking Bad* was to reach the level of quality that appears in feature films throughout its rigorous, twelve-hour-per-day, eight-day-per-episode shooting schedule. Everything is integrated perfectly to give the show a consistent look and feel.

Breaking Bad evokes a cinematic feel and incorporates filming techniques patterned after Sergio Leone's epic Spaghetti Westerns, most notably *The Good, the Bad, and the Ugly* (1966) and *Once Upon a Time in the West* (1968).

Michael Slovis, Director of Photography

Much of the bold visual style of *Breaking Bad* can be credited to award-winning cinematographer Michael Slovis. Starting with Season Two, Slovis served as Director of Photography on fifty episodes of *Breaking Bad* and also directed "Kafkaesque," "Cornered," "Live Free or Die," and "Confessions," as well as a *Better Call Saul* episode, "Bali Ha'i." According to Slovis in an August 6, 2012, wired.com interview, "My job is not just to merely record the time; my job is to interpret the scripts . . . That said, I never want to overwhelm them, and I never want it to be about the photography so I'm lucky that the performers are so strong and the writing is so strong. It allows me to take more chances."

Slovis graduated from New York University's Tisch School of the Arts. A cinematographer since 1995, Slovis has worked on such films as *Party Girl* (1995), the first feature film to be shown in its entirety on the Internet, as well as *Halloweentown* (1998), *The Thirteenth Year* (1999), *Ready to Run* (2000), and *Half Past Dead* (2002). Slovis also has directed episodes of *Ed*, *CSI: Crime Scene Investigation*, *Rubicon*, *Law & Order: Special Victims Unit*, *30 Rock*, *Royal Pains*, *Running Wilde*, and *Hell on Wheels*. In addition, Slovis has worked on the hit HBO series *Game of Thrones*. Gilligan has praised Slovis as "an innate storyteller" who "goes for substance over surface always." In 2010, Slovis joined the American Society of Cinematographers. Over the years, Slovis has received four Primetime Emmy Award nominations for Outstanding Cinematography for a One Hour Series and Outstanding Cinematography for a Single-Camera Series.

Close-ups and Wide Shots

Breaking Bad made innovative use of both close-ups and wide shots, which have become more popular in television now that large-screen TVs tend to dominate household living rooms. The utilization of wide shots in *Breaking Bad* emphasizes how small and insignificant the characters seem amid the backdrop of the vast New Mexico horizons and to a larger extent, an indifferent universe. According to Vince Gilligan in the previously referenced *New York* magazine article, "I love these images that you find in old Westerns of a solitary man against the sky, against this wide empty backdrop ... It's wonderful to pull our cameras back and have our actors be tiny little dark figures against this endless landscape."

The use of both close-ups and wide shots in *Breaking Bad* was strongly influenced by Sergio Leone's classic Western *The Good, the Bad, and the Ugly* (1966). Leone collaborated with cinematographer Tonino Delli Colli (1923–2005) on that film, as well as on *Once Upon a Time in the West* (1968) and *Once Upon a Time in America* (1984). In a March 2005 interview with *American Cinematographer*, Delli Colli remarked,

> Sergio was a real go-getter, a very meticulous artist who paid attention to everything he did, right down to the smallest details ... For the images, he asked for things that were truly effective: full light for long shots because he wanted the details to be visible on screens of all sizes, and close-ups

The decision to film *Breaking Bad* in Albuquerque served to enhance the series' cinematographic quality, with Vince Gilligan stating that "the big skies and stark beauty of New Mexico have become characters all their own." *Courtesy of Ben Parker*

with the individual hairs of the characters' beards visible. It was impossible in Spain—he wanted deep, long shadows, the deepest and longest we could get, and the [sun went] down late. On the set, we prepared in the morning, and then we just died waiting for the right light . . . He wanted to shoot the actors' eyes in every scene. I told him we could shoot 100 meters of eyes—looking here, looking there—and then use them whenever he wanted. But he wasn't having any of that. And that's how it went for the entire shoot.

A nice representative selection of *Breaking Bad* wide shots compiled by film/video editor Jorge Luengo Ruiz and titled "The Breaking Bad Wide Shot" can be found on Vimeo.

Cold Opens

Breaking Bad made effective use of cold opens/opening teasers throughout the entire series from the very beginning when the "Pilot" episode totally disorients the viewer with the image of Walt in his tighty-whities and gas mask frantically driving the beat-up RV in the middle of the desert. One of the most unusual cold opens involves the narcocorrido (aka drug ballad) music video "Ballad of Heisenberg" by Los Cuates de Sinaloa in the episode "Negro y Azul" (2.07).

Other memorable cold opens in *Breaking Bad* include Badger's arrest in "Better Call Saul" (2.08), the Cousins crawling through the dirt on their way to the shrine of Santa Muerte (Mexican Saint of Death) in "No Mas" (3.01), the Los Pollos Hermanos commercial in "Kafkaesque" (3.09), the bittersweet flashback of Jesse and Jane visiting the Georgia O'Keeffe Museum in "Abiquiu" (3.11), the day-in-the-life of Wendy the Hooker montage set to the Association's hit 1967 song "Windy" in "Half Measures" (3.12), the tribute to *Taxi Driver* (1976) as Walt purchases an illegal handgun from Lawson in "Thirty-Eight Snub" (4.02), Mike thwarting the attempted hijacking of the Los Pollos Hermanos truck in "Bullet" (4.04), the doomed kid on the dirt bike capturing the tarantula in a glass jar in "Dead Freight" (5.05), and Walt totally intimidating Declan in classic Heisenberg mode during a desert confrontation in "Say My Name" (5.07), among others.

In Season Two, the repeated motif of the pink teddy bear's floating eyeball foreshadowing the plane crash turns up in the ominous, black-and-white cold opens of "Seven Thirty-Seven" (2.01), "Down" (2.04), "Over" (2.10), and "ABQ" (2.13). In addition to *Breaking Bad*, a variety of other television shows have used cold opens to various effect, including *The X-Files*, *Malcolm in the Middle*, *The Office*, *The Walking Dead*, *Fear the Walking Dead*, and *Preacher*, among others.

Light and Color

Vince Gilligan has acknowledged the influence of American painter Edward Hopper (1882–1967) when it comes to the light and color choices used in *Breaking Bad*. Hopper is best known for his frequently parodied 1942 painting *Nighthawks*, which portrays the loneliness and isolation of an all-night diner. The painting was sold that same year to the Art Institute of Chicago for $3,000. A profile of *Nighthawks* on the Art Institute of Chicago website states, "Hopper denied that he purposefully infused this or any other of his paintings with symbols of human isolation and urban emptiness, but he acknowledged that in *Nighthawks* 'unconsciously, probably, I was painting the loneliness of a large city.'"

According to Gilligan in a March 21, 2016, vulture.com article, "We've been ripping off Edward Hopper shamelessly over the last two years, at least. We love that image of an island of light surrounded by an ocean of darkness, two lonely people sitting at a counter drinking coffee at an all-night diner surrounded by loneliness and gloom. We've emulated that shot a great many times." Slovis has remarked that the *Breaking Bad* crew made a conscious decision to embrace the landscape of New Mexico with its gold, brown, orange, and yellow hues. According to Gilligan, "We are not afraid of the dark in terms of story or photographically . . . We are really swinging for the fences and taking chances and putting exposures on film and on TV that would probably scare the hell out of executives at other television networks."

Point-of-View Shots

Breaking Bad is full of unique point-of-view shots, originating from toilet bowls, wine glasses, ATMs, and even from the bottom of a pool. All different types of lenses were used by the production crew to capture innovative shots as well. In addition, moving objects were used for effective point-of-view shots such as the "Roomba vacuum cam," "gas can cam," and "shovel cam." In the episode "Live Free or Die" (5.01), an out-of-the-trunk camera shot in which Walt views the M60 machine gun pays homage to similar shots in both Quentin Tarantino's *Reservoir Dogs* (1992) and *Pulp Fiction* (1994). According to Michael Slovis in an interview that appeared on creativeCOW.net, "We use Technocranes, Condors and scissor lifts to get the camera up high and snorkel lenses to get the camera low. Our rule is to tell the story organically, to be filmmakers and make it cinematic."

18

Hide in Plain Sight

Top Ten Enemies of Walter White

I am not in danger, Skyler. I am the danger! A guy opens his door and gets shot and you think that of me? No. I am the one who knocks!

—*Walter White*

Walter White made a lot of enemies during his rise from mundane high school chemistry teacher to ruthless meth kingpin. From the downright psychopathic Tuco Salamanca and the cold, brutal, and sociopathic Gustavo Fring to the conniving Lydia Rodarte-Quayle and the neo-Nazi Uncle Jack Welker, Walt somehow manages to outsmart them all (albeit at a terrible cost). However, it is ultimately the persistent detective work of Walt's own brother-in-law, Hank Schrader, that ultimately leads to the downfall of "Heisenberg."

Interestingly, in 2013 *Bustle* ranked *Breaking Bad* characters from "Least to Most Evil" and this is what they came up for their Top 10 most evil characters in the series: 10) Krazy-8; 9) Huell Babineaux; 8) Lydia Rodarte-Quayle; 7) Walter White; 6) Gus Fring; 5) the Cousins; 4) Hector Salamanca; 3) Todd Alquist; 2) Tuco Salamanca; and 1) Uncle Jack Welker.

Todd Alquist

"Man, shit happens, huh?" Creepy Todd Alquist (Jesse Plemons), a sociopath who lacks even the remotest trace of humanity, works for Vamonos Pest Control, which is appropriated by Walt and Jesse as a cover for their meth-cooking operation. Todd first catches Walt's attention when he draws his attention to a nanny-cam in one of the houses that will be tented and used for the meth-cooking operation. On the surface, Todd seems like the all-American kid (he always politely addresses Walt as "sir" and goes to great lengths to try to please him), but his callous cruelty rises to the surface very quickly, and viewers almost immediately sense that something is seriously off with this character. During the infamous train heist, Todd casually shoots an innocent kid, Drew Sharp, who happens to come across the scene on his dirt bike. In Todd's warped mind he was just following Jesse's instructions prior to the heist that "no one other than us can ever know that this robbery went down." He later shrugs it off as "shit happens," leading Jesse to punch him out. It's later revealed that Todd had even kept the kid's tarantula as a sort of trophy (similar to Hank's fellow DEA agents giving him Tuco's grill).

Todd gradually becomes Walt's lab apprentice after Jesse quits the business in disgust, and even introduces Walt to his repugnant Uncle

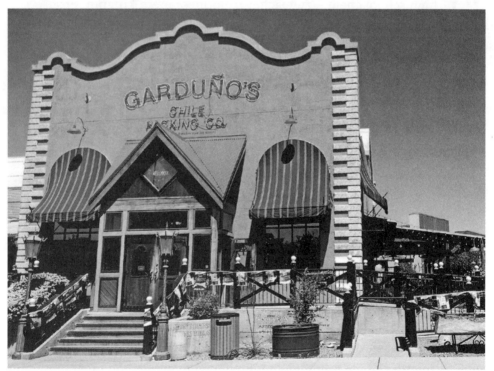

Garduno's is the Mexican eatery that specializes in tableside guacamole where Walt, Skyler, Hank, and Marie have a very awkward lunch in "Confessions."   *Courtesy of Ben Parker*

Jack Welker, a neo-Nazi, who implements Walt's idea of simultaneously assassinating ten prison inmates who are still receiving hush money. In addition, Todd is infatuated with Lydia Rodarte-Quayle, the only time in the series that he shows even the slightest bit of affection for anyone. His ringtone for Lydia is "Lydia, the Tattooed Lady," a song written by Yip Harburg and Harold Arlen made famous when Groucho Marx sang it in the film *At the Circus* (1939).

After Uncle Jack steals most of Walt's money, Todd shamelessly convinces him to keep the meth-operation running with Jesse as a slave meth cook: "This is millions, Uncle Jack. No matter how much you got, how do you turn your back on more?" After Jesse tries to escape the compound, Todd flippantly kills his girlfriend, Andrea Cantillo, execution style in front of him as a punishment. When Walt disappears to New Hampshire, Todd and his cronies break into the White household and threaten Skyler to not to go to the authorities. Jesse gets his revenge in the final episode by strangling Todd to death (for the record, the only character Jesse willingly kills during the entire series).

Mike Ehrmantraut

"You are a time bomb, tick-tick-ticking. And I have no intention of being around for the boom." A former Philadelphia cop and parking lot attendant (as we later learn from the *Breaking Bad* prequel, *Better Call Saul*), Mike Ehrmantraut (Jonathan Banks) works as a fixer/enforcer for both Gus Fring and Saul Goodman. In fact, we first meet Mike when he arrives at Jesse's apartment to give him specific instructions on how to deal with the authorities following Jane's death from an overdose. Mike is cautious, well prepared, and extremely professional no matter whom he is working for or what difficult job he has taken on. In addition, he is cool under questioning, and the presence of DEA agents showing up at his front door at a moment's notice doesn't seem to faze him one bit. He even tries to teach Jesse the ropes at one point and becomes somewhat a mentor to him for a brief period.

At best, Mike tolerates Walt and oftentimes shows disgust for his actions and his unbridled ego. Walt in turn refers to Mike as a "grunting dead-eye cretin." However, Mike ends up saving Walt's life by contacting Gus Fring when he observes the axe-wielding cousins entering the White household while Walt is in the shower, totally oblivious. On the other hand, Mike is perfectly willing to eliminate Walt at the instigation of Gus at the superlab, but the plan is thrown awry when Walt gets Jesse to kill Gale Boetticher.

Mike at times even shows some compassion, especially when he dotes on his granddaughter, Kaylee, and sets up a trust fund for her. After Walt kills Gus, Mike reluctantly agrees to team up with Walt and Jesse to continue the meth-cooking operation. However, Walt confronts Mike in an attempt to get the names of Gus's former associates who are still receiving "hazard pay." After shooting Mike, Walt realizes it wasn't necessary after all—he could have simply asked Lydia Rodarte-Quayle for the names. Mike retreats to the riverbank to die. His last words to Walt: "Shut the fuck up and let me die in peace."

Gustavo "Gus" Fring

"Never make the same mistake twice." The polar opposite of raging psychopath Tuco Salamanca, Gus Fring (Giancarlo Esposito) is just as dangerous, but he is more of a deliberate and cunning sociopath who conceals his identity behind that of a dedicated fast-food entrepreneur (he cofounded Los Pollos Hermanos), philanthropist, and community activist. According to Vince Gilligan in an October 10, 2011, interview with the *Los Angeles Times*, "I don't think Gus is a good man, but he's not an entirely bad man. He's infinitely pragmatic. When he does something awful, it's not with any pleasure or joy. He's out to accomplish a goal and make a point." Gus lives in a bland suburban neighborhood and drives a 1998 Volvo.

However, Gus's true cold-blooded nature is revealed sporadically as when he casually and deliberately slits Victor's throat with a box cutter and when he later takes Walt out to the desert and threatens the life of his family: "If you try to interfere, this becomes a much simpler matter. I will kill your wife. I will kill your son. I will kill your infant daughter." A native of Chile, Gus has a mysterious past and may very well have been

Fast-food entrepreneur Gus Fring hosted both Walt and Jesse at this modest ranch house (the perfect cover for the careful drug kingpin) at separate times.   *Courtesy of Ben Parker*

connected to the brutal regime of Augusto Pinochet, who was dictator of Chile between 1973 and 1990. Gus is all business (he sets up a thriving meth superlab), except for one significant weakness: He seeks personal vengeance from the Mexican cartel for killing his business partner (and possible lover) Maximino Arciniega. In fact, Gus is willing to poison himself to get rid of Don Eladio Vuente and his crew. According to Vince Gilligan, "Gus is an empire-builder and a great inspiration and motivation to Walter White—whether Walt would admit it or not."

Curiously, it is Walt's brother-in-law Hank who actually suspects that Gus is the drug kingpin of Albuquerque (his fellow DEA agents won't possibly believe that he is anything other than an upstanding citizen of the community). Walt and Jesse try to eliminate Gus on several occasions, but he is way too clever and careful to fall prey to their assassination attempts. However, Walt finally comes up with the clever plan of using Gus's only remaining rival, Hector Salamanca, to help bring down the meth kingpin (Hector had actually been the one who pulled the trigger on Gus's partner Max). As Gus and Tyrus visit Hector at the Casa

Portrayed by Giancarlo Esposito, Gus Fring is a deliberate and cunning sociopath who conceals his identity behind that of a dedicated fast-food entrepreneur, philanthropist, and community activist.

Genevieve/Wikimedia Commons

Tranquila nursing home preparing to eliminate him (they believe he has become a DEA informant), Hector simply rings the bell on a wheelchair rigged to an explosive device. Gus walks out of Hector's room seemingly unscathed, but then viewers notice that half his face has been blown off. He casually straightens his tie and then collapses dead onto the floor in front of several aghast nursing home employees.

Vince Gilligan reportedly got the idea for Gus's gruesome death from reading the 2006 book *Strange Angel: The Otherworldly Life of Rocket Scientist John Whiteside Parsons* by George Pendle. A legendary rocket engineer and occultist, Parsons (1914–52) was killed in a mysterious laboratory explosion that tore a hole through the right side of his face.

Emilio Koyama

"I say we cap 'em both." Walt's first victim (and the first character to die in the entire series), Emilio Koyama (John Koyama) was Jesse's former meth-cooking partner and Krazy-8's cousin. Jesse indicates that he has known Emilio since elementary school. We first meet Emilio when he gets arrested during a DEA raid in which Hank and Walt were present, while Jesse escapes through a window. Emilio makes bail and heads out with Krazy-8 to find Jesse, who he mistakenly believes informed on him. After confronting Jesse and Walt (whom he recognizes from the drug raid) at their mobile meth lab in the desert, Emilio suggests killing them both. However, Walt manages to buy time by convincing Emilio and Krazy-8 that he will teach them how to create the formula for his signature blue meth. Walt then causes an explosion in the mobile meth lab and manages to trap both Emilio and Krazy-8 in the RV. Emilio dies from inhaling phosphine gas. Jesse later botches the disposal of Emilio's corpse using hydrofluoric acid that eats through both the bathtub and the floor of his home.

Krazy-8

"You're not cut out for this line of work, Walter. You should get out, while you still can." The former partner and cousin of Emilio Koyama, Domingo Gallardo "Krazy-8" Molina (Max Arciniega) manages to survive the phosphine gas that kills his cousin. Held hostage in Jesse's basement and secured by a bike lock around his neck and attached to a pole, Krazy-8 tries to negotiate his freedom with Walt, who lost the coin toss and must kill the prisoner. Walt even confides to Krazy-8 (the first person outside his immediate family) that he is dying of lung cancer. Walt, who has not yet been consumed by his Heisenberg persona, is genuinely looking for valid reasons to let Krazy-8 free until he notices a glass shard from a broken plate missing (indicating Krazy-8 plans to kill him). After Krazy-8 reaches for the shard of glass, Walt chokes him with the bike lock. Walt and Jesse later find out that Krazy-8 was an informant.

Lydia Rodarte-Quayle

"You are tying up loose ends, and I don't want to be one of them." A long-time employee of Madrigal Electromotive (she rises to the position of Head of Logistics out of the German company's Houston, Texas, office) and single mom, the high-strung and paranoid but ultimately ruthless Lydia Rodarte-Quayle (Laura Fraser) served as the methylamine supplier for Gus Fring's drug empire until Walt eliminated him. She then reluctantly continues to supply methylamine to Walt, Jesse, and Mike's operation, and finally to Uncle Jack and his gang. In fact, it is Lydia who directs Walt to committing the train heist, which results in the stealing of one thousand gallons of methylamine. Discussing Lydia's possible involvement in the meth operation with Gomie, Hank remarks, "What about that Lydia what's her name? Lady Banjo-Eyes at the warehouse?" Gomie responds, "No way. Too uptight. Too together." Lydia is totally devious and at one point or another plots (or at least suggests) the death of Gus Fring's former associates, as well as Mike, Declan and his gang, Skyler, and Walt as a way to cover the tracks of her nefarious activities at Madrigal Electromotive. In the season finale, Walt serves Lydia ricin-laced tea, ensuring her demise. "Goodbye Lydia," he exclaims over the phone. For the record, Lydia is Walt's final victim, as well as the last character to be killed in the series.

Asked about her character's "awful, hyphenated surname" in a September 16, 2013, *Rolling Stone* interview, Fraser commented, "I know! Vince, what did you do to me? She couldn't very well turn into a nice, balanced person with that kind of name. A Rodarte-Quayle isn't gonna be easygoing and laidback. She was fucked from the start." Fraser went on to describe Lydia as "a clean-cut, bonkers sociopath . . . She takes herself so seriously, which is deeply unattractive, and she always thinks she's right, which is another nightmarish characteristic."

Marco and Leonel Salamanca

"We've waited long enough. We won't wait any longer." The silent, ruthless nephews of Hector Salamanca, Marco and Leonel Salamanca (Luis and Daniel Moncada) travel across the border from Mexico to avenge the death of their cousin, Tuco. Dressed in matching sharkskin suits and distinctive cowboy boots tipped with silver skulls, the Cousins appear to worship Santa Muerte, the Mexican deity of death. Once they arrive over the border, they casually kill everyone on the truck and set the vehicle ablaze. In a flashback, it is also revealed that the Cousins decapitated Tortuga on orders from Juan Bolsa. Waiting to get the green light to murder Walt, the Cousins eventually redirect their wrath toward Hank based on information given to them by Gus Fring, leading to deadly consequences for the brothers. Ultimately, the Cousins meet their match in Hank, who smashes Leonel with his car (Mike later finishes him off in the hospital) and shoots Marco in the head during a gunfight in a store parking lot (Hank had received a mysterious warning just one minute prior to the appearance of the Cousins).

Tuco Salamanca

"This kicks like a mule with its balls wrapped in duct tape!" A complete psychopath, Tuco Salamanca (Raymond Cruz) nearly kills off Walt and Jesse before they even get their feet wet in the meth-cooking business. Walter later refers to Tuco as a "degenerate piece of human filth." Tuco refuses to abide by the famous lesson set forth in *Scarface* (1983): "Don't get high on your own supply." In addition, Tuco's mood swings and violent outbursts lead him to beat Jesse badly and later kill his associate, No-Doze, for no apparent reason and with absolutely no remorse. He then kidnaps Walt and Jesse, takes them to his desert hideout, and tries to kill them after he discovers from his uncle, Hector Salamanca, that they were planning to eliminate him with a ricin-laced burrito. It is actually Hank who arrives on the scene at the hideout and kills Tuco after Walt and Jesse have escaped into the desert.

Interestingly, Tuco was intended to be Walt's main antagonist throughout Season Two of *Breaking Bad*, but he was forced to get killed off after landing a role as LAPD detective Julio Sanchez on the TNT police drama *The Closer*. Gus Fring was soon introduced as the polar opposite of Tuco in terms of manner (but just as cold-bloodedly ruthless!).

Hank Schrader

"I'm thinking Albuquerque just might have a new kingpin." Walt's brother-in-law, Hank Schrader (Dean Norris) initially comes off as a good-natured buffoon, but it is his obsessive determination to uncover the identity of Heisenberg that leads to Walt's ultimate downfall. In fact, it is Hank who believes that Gus Fring is the meth kingpin of Albuquerque even though all of his fellow DEA agents scoff at the notion of the good-natured fast-food entrepreneur being involved in a criminal enterprise.

Hank can indeed be a formidable opponent, as when he takes out Tuco Salamanca and coolly gets the best of Marco and Leonel Salamanca during a firefight in a store parking lot (even though he got tipped off to the assassins). However, Hank can also be cruel, impulsive, and erratic, as when he beats Jesse in one instance and takes out the bikers in the dive bar. When he gets transferred to the El Paso Task Force, Hank is truly a fish out of water and disrespected by his colleagues. He later suffers from post-traumatic stress disorder after witnessing the Tortuga incident that results in the death and injury of several DEA agents. In addition, Hank and his partner, Steven "Gomie" Gomez, provide a lot of comic relief with their banter throughout the series. Hank finally arrests Walt in the desert and would have been deemed a hero if not for the fact that Uncle Jack and his gang arrive on the scene just in time to "rescue" Heisenberg. Despite Walt's frantic pleas, Uncle Jack methodically kills Hank and buries him in the desert.

Jack Welker

"Jesus, what's with all the greed here? It's unattractive." Walt first encounters Uncle Jack Welker (Michael Bowen) when he enlists his help in arranging the murder of ten prison inmates who were Gus Fring's former associates. The leader of a white-supremacist gang, Jack is the uncle of Todd Alquist. The personification of total evil, Uncle Jack later murders Declan and his gang (at the instigation of Lydia Rodarte-Quayle) and then takes over his remote meth-cooking compound.

During a desert confrontation, Uncle Jack kills Gomie during a firefight, shoots Hank execution style, and steals most of Walt's money, leaving him with one barrel worth approximately $11 million. At the suggestion of Todd, Uncle Jack turns Jesse into a slave meth cook. In the series finale, "Felina," Walt gets revenge on Uncle Jack and his gang by sneaking a remote-control-operated machine gun into his compound.

19

Tread Lightly

Walter White's Most Evil Acts

Mr. White . . . he's the devil. You know, he is—he is smarter than you, he is luckier than you. Whatever—whatever you think is supposed to happen— I'm telling you, the exact reverse opposite of that is gonna happen, okay?

—*Jesse Pinkman*

Highly acclaimed science fiction writer J. G. Ballard (1930–2009) once described suburbs as "the death of the soul," an endless void of cul-de-sacs, strip malls, and fast-food restaurants. It's a place where "one's almost got to get up in the morning and make a *resolution* to perform some deviant or antisocial act, some perverse act, even if it's just sort of *kicking the dog*, in order to establish one's own freedom . . . Suburbs are very sinister places, contrary to what many people imagine." Ballard may as well have been describing the Albuquerque of *Breaking Bad* and its resident sociopath, Walter Hartwell White.

By the end of the series, Walt was directly or indirectly responsible for the following deaths: Emilio Koyama (phosphine gas), Krazy-8 (strangled with bike lock), Jane Margolis (does nothing while she overdoses), 167 airline passengers (Jane's grieving father, an air traffic controller, makes a fatal error on the job), two drug dealers (runs over them and shoots one in the head), Gale Boetticher (instructs Jesse to shoot), Gus Fring (rigs Hector Salamanca's wheelchair with explosives), Tyrus (blown up with Gus), two guards at the meth superlab (shoots to death), Mike Ehrmantraut (shoots to death), ten prisoners (coordinates their simultaneous deaths with the help of neo-Nazis), Steven Gomez (killed in desert firefight with neo-Nazis), Hank Schrader (shot by Uncle Jack Welker), Andrea Cantillo (killed by Todd Alquist to punish Jesse for trying to escape the meth compound), Uncle Jack and his crew (remote-control machine gun), Uncle Jack (shot in the head), and Lydia Rodarte-Quayle (ricin poisoning). In addition, Walt has helped destroy the lives of countless meth addicts who have abused his product.

Believe it or not, in a September 16, 2013, blog entry on livejournal.com, author George R. R. Martin (known for his best-selling series of novels *A Song of Fire and Ice*, the basis for the hit HBO series *A Game of Thrones*) stated after watching the critically acclaimed *Breaking Bad* episode "Ozymandias" (5.14) that "Walter White is a bigger monster than anyone in Westeros." In addition, the Bulgarian title for *Breaking Bad*

Author George R. R. Martin (known for his best-selling series of novels, *A Song of Fire and Ice*) stated after watching "Ozymandias" that "Walter White is a bigger monster than anyone in Westeros." *Yerpo/Wikimedia Commons*

(*V Obukvite na Satanana*) literally translates as "In the Shoes of Satan," which pretty well sums up Walt's path of destruction throughout the series.

In a September 25, 2013 *Rolling Stone* interview, Vince Gilligan remarked,

> I'm sad the show's over, because I miss the crew and the cast and the work. But there were times I was looking forward to it being over. Walter White is a hard guy to keep in your head 24 hours a day for six years. He wasn't so hard to have around in the early going, but late in season two or season three, when he was lying so effortlessly to his family and doing awful things, it started to affect my outlook on life. You start to see the world as Walter White sees the world, and Walt's world is a dark place of suspicion and paranoia.

Going through the following list of Walt's most vile deeds, it's always a bit surprising that a vast chunk of the *Breaking Bad* viewing audience (myself included!) actually rooted for this guy for so long (up to the very end in my case, I must confess):

Deciding to Cook Meth in the First Place

Faced with daunting health-care bills, how many rational human beings would take Walt's course of action and resort to cooking meth? Indeed, Walt possessed a brilliant scientific mind and could very well have come up with a creative solution to attack his mounting debt or at least exhaust every possible option before resorting to a life of crime. With everything to lose, Walt could have even swallowed his pride and accepted the generous offer made by his former partner, Elliott Schwartz, to join Gray Matter Technologies. However, of course, his vanity and jealousy got in the way. By the end of the "Pilot" episode, Walt and Jesse are in way over their heads out in the desert, and there is no turning back from there.

Strangling Krazy-8

Walt loses a coin toss and has to decide whether he can kill Krazy-8, a low-level drug dealer held prisoner in Jesse's basement. He even establishes a rapport with Krazy-8, who it turns out possesses a college degree and could possibly turn his life around if given a second chance. However, when Walt notices that Krazy-8 is hiding that glass shard from the broken plate, he comes to the realization that the only alternative is to strangle him with the bike lock ("And the Bag's in the River," 1.03). Walt has reached a crucial point where he could have released Krazy-8 and/or gone to the authorities and confessed his crimes up to that point. Probably for the last time in his journey toward drug kingpin, Walt actually feels some remorse for killing Krazy-8 (his alter ego Heisenberg would never have had any doubts about what to do in this instance). The cycle of violence started with the killing of Emilio and Krazy-8 would continue to snowball through the progression of the series.

Assaulting Skyler

In the episode "Seven Thirty-Seven" (2.01), Walt returns from a particularly insane encounter with Tuco Salamanca at the junkyard, enters the kitchen, and sexually assaults Skyler in one of the most disturbing scenes in the entire series. Many of Walt's most ardent fans tend to block this early incident out of their minds. However, rape is rape and Skyler says "no" to Walt multiple times during the ordeal.

According to Anna Gunn in a Q&A that appeared on amc.com, the scene was very difficult to shoot,

> But Bryan [Cranston] was directing and he had so clearly done his homework. He knew what the scene had to be, and we choreographed it, and then we actually never rehearsed. He turned on the cameras and we just did what we did, and that's what it turned out to be. It was extremely upsetting—at one point when we got to the point where my face hits the refrigerator, I actually was off a little bit and I hit my face on the corner. I kind of cracked myself and went down on the floor, and Bryan was just mortified. But when you're in that environment you feel completely safe, and that's what gives us the feeling that we can make it as real and as ugly as it has to be.

Letting Jane Die

A recovering drug addict, Jane relapses with Jesse and attempts to blackmail Walt into turning over Jesse's share of the drug money. The couple has delusions of starting a new life in New Zealand where Jane will flourish as an artist and Jesse will start a new career as a bush pilot. However, Walt stands by and does absolutely nothing when he stops by Jesse's apartment and watches Jane overdose and asphyxiate on her own vomit in the episode "Phoenix" (2.12). Jane's death ultimately leads to the demise of 167 passengers and crew in the airline collision due to a major miscalculation by her grieving father after he returns to his job as an air traffic controller too soon.

Forcing Jesse to Kill Gale

Gus Fring cleverly utilizes Gale Boetticher to absorb all of Walt's meth-cooking skills so he can eventually be eliminated. Realizing that Mike

Jesse briefly ends up renting at this duplex, where he embarks on a brief, intense, and ultimately tragic relationship with his landlord, Jane, who lives next door.   *Courtesy of Ben Parker*

has been ordered to kill him, Walt tricks him into allowing him to call Jesse and pleads with his partner to go to Gale's apartment and kill him in the episode "Full Measure" (3.13). Jesse is faced with the agonizing choice of either killing Gale or letting Walt die. The guilt he feels in shooting Gale in the face causes Jesse to relapse in a major way.

Poisoning Brock

In the episode "End Times" (4.12), Jesse's girlfriend Andrea's son, Brock, is admitted to the hospital with mysterious flu-like symptoms. Realizing his cigarette containing the ricin is missing, Jesse confronts Walt and accuses him of poisoning Brock. Walt eventually convinces Jesse that only someone as diabolical as Gus Fring would be willing and able to pull off the poisoning of a child. In the subsequent episode, "Face Off," viewers realize that Walt did indeed poison Brock after the lily of the valley plant is shown in his backyard. When Jesse later finds out the truth from Saul Goodman, Walt informs him somewhat glibly, "Yes, I am sorry about Brock! But he's alive, isn't he? He's fine, just as I planned it! Don't you think I knew exactly how much to give him? That I had it all measured out? Come on! Don't you know me by now?"

Planting a Bomb in a Nursing Home

In the episode "Face Off" (4.13), Walt devises the suicide bomb attached to Hector's wheelchair that is triggered by the ringing of his bell and directed toward Gus Fring (and his henchman Tyrus Kitt) at Casa Tranquila nursing home. That's right, Walt decided the best way to eliminate Gus Fring was by bombing a nursing home! Although the explosive went off exactly as planned, Walt could have had no way of knowing if any innocent staff or patients would get in the way as collateral damage. However, it's quite doubtful that Walt even agonized for a second over this possibility in his desire to eliminate Gus.

Killing Mike

Mike Ehrmantraut didn't deserve to die at the hands of Walt of all people in the episode "Say My Name" (5.07). During a quite heated argument, Mike tells Walt, "You and your pride and your ego! You just had to be the man! If you'd known your place, we'd all be fine right now!" In fact, after shooting Mike, Walt realizes that he could have gotten the names of Gus Fring's former associates from Lydia, so Mike's death was totally unnecessary.

Orchestrating the Murder of Ten Prisoners

Walt hires Uncle Jack and his neo-Nazi cohorts to help orchestrate the murders of ten prisoners throughout three prisons in a synchronized killing spree in the episode "Gliding Over All" (5.08). He feels absolutely no remorse and in fact revels in the precision killing that went off like clockwork. It's clear that Walt has totally entered the dark side of his Heisenberg persona and there will be no return.

Handing Jesse Over to Neo-Nazis

In "Ozymandias" (5.14), Walt, angered by Jesse's "betrayal," hands him over to Uncle Jack and his gang of white supremacists. Just to rub it in, Walt confesses to Jesse, "I watched Jane die. I was there. And I watched her die. I watched her overdose and choke to death. I could have saved her. But I didn't." Little does Walt realize that Todd will convince Uncle Jack that it would be better to keep Jesse as a meth-cooking slave than kill him.

20

Cooking Is Art

Breaking Bad and the Crystal Meth Industry

Meth used to be legal—sold it over every pharmacy counter in America.
Thank God they came to their senses over that one, right?
—*Hank Schrader to Walt*

U sing his substantial chemistry skills, Walter White eventually
conquers the Southwestern drug market with his signature "blue
meth"—99.1 percent chemically pure and also known as "Blue Sky," "Big
Blue," and "Blue Magic." Jesse informs a cynical Tuco Salamanca, "It may
be blue, but it's the bomb." Here is a brief glossary of how meth cooking as
portrayed in *Breaking Bad* compares to the sad realities of the actual meth
industry in the United States:

Blue Meth

Contrary to *Breaking Bad*, pure meth is typically white or clear rather than
blue. According to Dr. Donna Nelson, *Breaking Bad*'s science consultant and
a chemistry professor at the University of Oklahoma, "when you crystallize
anything that's colorless, which methylamine crystals are, they usually
come out with a yellow tinge because of impurities." By the way, the blue
meth used in the first two seasons of *Breaking Bad* was actually rock candy
provided by The Candy Lady, a popular Albuquerque candy restaurant. In
addition, Bryan Cranston reportedly learned the exact process for cooking
meth from DEA chemists to help him prepare for the role. Believe it or not,
as *Breaking Bad* became more popular, some actual meth dealers started
adding blue dye to their meth in an effort to brand their product.

Hallucinations

Strung out on meth, Jesse believes that two badass bikers are heading toward his house to kill him (viewers discover they are actually two Mormon missionaries on bicycles) in the episode "Cancer Man" (1.04). However, meth does not reportedly create the type of vivid hallucinations that Jesse experienced.

Hydrofluoric Acid

Walt's preferred method of disposing of a body is actually quite common among the Mexican drug cartels and is even referred to as the "guiso" (or "stew").

Meth History

A respected Japanese chemist named Nagai Nagayoshi (1844–1929), first synthesized methamphetamine using ephedrine in 1893. A protégé of Nagayoshi's named Akira Ogata (1887–1978) developed a new method of synthesizing the crystalline form of methamphetamine in 1919, creating crystal meth. During World War II, methamphetamine tablets (branded "Pervitin") were allegedly distributed to German troops as a way to reduce fatigue and increase aggression. Adolf Hitler himself reportedly received daily injections of methamphetamines as well. During the early 1960s, both actress Marilyn Monroe (*Some Like It Hot*) and President John F. Kennedy, as well as author Truman Capote (*Breakfast at Tiffany's*), allegedly received shots of methamphetamine by Max "Dr. Feelgood" Jacobson.

Meth in Popular Culture

One of the first movies to address the scourge of amphetamine addiction, *Death in Small Doses* (1957) was billed as "the picture that crosses the forbidden territory . . . of THRILL PILLS!" A campy little B-movie (think *Reefer Madness* but with speed), *Death in Small Doses* features Peter Graves (*Mission: Impossible*) as Tom Kaylor, a federal agent who goes undercover to track down a drug ring providing illegal amphetamines to truck

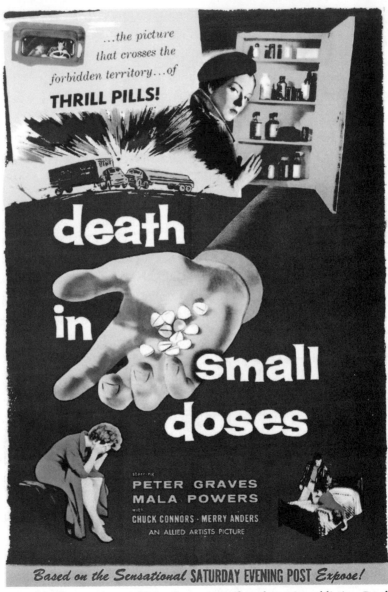

One of the first movies to address the scourge of amphetamine addiction, *Death in Small Doses* (1957) was billed as "the picture that crosses the forbidden territory . . . of THRILL PILLS!"

drivers. Chuck Connors (*The Rifleman*) chews the scenery as frenzied, pill-popping junkie Mink Reynolds (for some reason he reminded me of Willem Dafoe's Bobby Peru character from David Lynch's 1990 film *Wild at Heart*, sans the bad teeth). Just watching the maniacal Reynolds popping "bennies" (he also refers to them as "co-pilots") as he barrels his truck down the highway or channels his inner hepcat at the roadside diner is worth the price of admission alone. Directed by Joseph M. Newman (*This Island Earth*), *Death in Small Doses* was based on a 1956 article published in *The Saturday Evening Post*. The film opens with a disclaimer stating that "Nothing in this picture is intended to minimize the importance of the drug 'Amphetamine' when properly used under a doctor's prescription."

In Martin Scorsese's gritty 1976 drama *Taxi Driver*, Travis Bickle (Robert De Niro) intends to purchase an illegal firearm from Easy Andy (Steven Prince), who tells him, "Crystal meth. I can get ya crystal meth. Nitrous oxide. How about that? How about a Cadillac? I get ya a brand new Cadillac. With the pink slip for two grand." In the otherwise dismal 2006 holiday film *Deck the Halls* (2006), Dr. Steven Finch (Matthew Broderick) exclaims to his wife, "Who moves in the middle of the night? A meth lab?" In the sitcom *The Big Bang Theory*, Penny (Kaley Cuoco) remarks, "I, myself, grew up in Nebraska. Small town, outside of Omaha. Yeah, a nice place, mostly family farms, a few meth labs." During a 2010 interview on *Larry King Live*, comedian and social commentator Bill Maher exclaimed, "I don't hate America. I love America. I want it to be better. The only way we can get it to be better is to realistically criticize what's wrong with it . . . Always waving the big foam number one finger; we're not number one in most things. We're number one in military. We're number one in money. We're number one in fat toddlers, meth labs, and people we send to prison." Last but not least, Jennifer Digori (Olivia Luccardi) in the TV series *Orange Is the New Black* comments, "I would never do blue meth. That color ain't natural."

Meth Slang

Street terms for meth include crystal meth, speed, crystal, crystal glass, ice, pookie, shards, crank, shabu, shaboo, side, glass, coffee, gak, jib, crank, batu, tweak, piko, rock, tina, fast, cold, Christina, puddle, Tina, hillbilly crack, Chris, Cristy, go fast, cookies, chalk, dust, speed, white bitch, geep, trash, Smurf dope, sniff, spindarella, rocket fuel, garbage, tick tick, white cross, cotton candy, dunk, go-go juice, twack, spaceman, no doze, pookie, Scooby snax, peanut butter, stove top, yammer bammer, albino poo, got anything, peanut butter, hippy crack, eraser dust, gak, cheebah, chicken feed, white crunch, and shit, among many others.

Methylamine

Although Walt prefers the harder-to-obtain methylamine, most meth production utilizes pseudoephedrine, an active ingredient in

The blue meth used in the first two seasons of Breaking Bad was actually rock candy provided by The Candy Lady, a popular Albuquerque candy restaurant.   *Courtesy of Ben Parker*

over-the-counter cold medicines such as Sudafed. Low-level meth producers utilize so-called "smurfs," who go from drugstore to drugstore buying small amounts of Sudafed since there are restrictions on its sale. In fact, the only two states—Oregon and Mississippi—that have implemented laws making pseudoephedrine prescription-only have virtually eliminated their meth labs. By the way, methylamine is reportedly not too hard to make—therefore the robbery of the warehouse and the infamous train heist that scored all that methylamine for Walt and his crew were probably totally unnecessary (but made for great television!).

Money Laundering

It's absolutely true that many large-scale meth manufacturers use legitimate businesses to launder money just like Walt and Skyler accomplish with the A1 Car Wash.

Odes to Meth

Songs written about amphetamine include "St. Ides Heaven" by Elliott Smith, "Semi Charmed Life" by Third Eye Blind, "Amphetamine" by Everclear, "Amphetamine" by Three Souls in My Mind, "20 Dollar Nose Bleed" by Fall Out Boy, and "Headfirst for Halos" by My Chemical Romance, among others. For a feeling of true, crushing depression, seek out Bruce Springsteen's "Sinaloa Cowboys," which relates the saga of a Mexican immigrant who dies in a meth lab explosion. It can be heard on Springsteen's critically acclaimed 1995 album *The Ghost of Tom Joad*.

Purity

Although as a perfectionist, Walt boasts of his meth's purity, the market for "pure meth" is really not that significant since, according to one theory, the typical customer for meth uses the drug for increased energy to work multiple low-skilled service jobs. Therefore, especially in impoverished rural areas, the actual quality of the meth is less important than the price and availability of the drug. In fact, most of the meth currently on the market is reportedly diluted.

"Shake and Bake" Operations

Most meth operations in the United States are of a much lower level than the massive operation south of the border (or for that matter Gus Fring's superlab) and can be found in more rural areas. These are called "shake and bake" operations (and much less prone to violence than the massive Mexican meth operations) such as portrayed in the critically acclaimed 2010 drama *Winter's Bone*, which was directed by Debra Granik.

In *Winter's Bone*, Jennifer Lawrence stars as Ree Dolly, an impoverished teenager living in a dirt-poor rural area of the Missouri Ozarks with her mentally ill mother, brother, and sister. Desperate meth addicts populate the ravaged landscape like zombie refugees from *Night of the Living Dead*. The film also stars Dale Dickey, who portrays Spooge's Old Lady in the haunting "Peekaboo" episode (2.06) of *Breaking Bad*. Ree embarks on a harrowing journey to track down her father Jessup, a meth cook out on bail, before the rest of the family gets evicted from their home. John Hawkes turns in a powerful performance as Ree's meth-addicted uncle, Teardrop. *Winter's Bone* captured the Grand Jury Prize for Dramatic Film at the 2010 Sundance Film Festival.

Side Effects

According to the National Institute on Drug Abuse (NIDA), short-term side effects of meth include increased wakefulness and physical activity; decreased appetite; increased breathing, heart rate, blood pressure, and temperature; and irregular heartbeat. Long-term side effects of meth include anxiety, confusion, insomnia, mood problems, violent behavior, paranoia, hallucinations, delusions, weight loss, severe dental problems ("meth mouth"), and intense itching leading to skin sores from scratching. In addition, meth users risk HIV, hepatitis, and other infectious diseases from shared needles. Like any other highly addictive drug, meth leads to a craving for more meth. The devastating side effects of meth can clearly be seen in the ragged, forlorn face of Wendy the Meth Addict, who turns tricks at the Crossroads Motel (interestingly, Jesse never shows any signs of meth teeth or any of the other side effects related to abusing the drug). In the 2010 memoir *Loss of Innocence: A Daughter's Addiction, A Father's Fight to Save Her*, by Carren Clem and Ron Clem, the former remarks, "I had an overwhelming sense of loss and depression and all I wanted to do was die when I couldn't get my new best friend—meth."

Superlabs

Although meth superlabs like the one that Gus Fring built under the laundry facility are actually somewhat common among meth manufactured associated with Mexican cartels and in Central America, many low-level meth manufacturers in the United States cook much smaller batches in mini labs like Walt and Jesse's RV due to fact that it's harder to gain access to the necessary chemicals.

21

Nothing More Than a Bad Dream

Breaking Bad Symbols and Motifs

> So no matter what I do, hooray for me because I'm a great guy? It's all good?
> No matter how many dogs I kill, I just, what, do an inventory and accept?
> —*Jesse Pinkman*

One of the most intriguing aspects of *Breaking Bad* is the recurring symbols and motifs found throughout the series that encourage multiple viewings to unlock their meaning. For instance, who can forget the pink teddy bear with one eye ending up in the pool that appears throughout Season Two? Or the way that the colors of a character's clothing can bring out their personality (example: Marie = purple)? Or how the vehicle that a character drives also reflects on their identity (example: Gus = Volvo)? A glimpse of the ubiquitous symbolism of *Breaking Bad* can unearth layers of complexity that are often missed with just a casual viewing of the series.

Animals

Even though the White household is fairly typical of a lower-middle-class demographic (before Walt decides to cook meth, that is!), it is interesting to note that the Whites do not own any pets. In fact, none of the characters in the series seem to enjoy the company of pets. Ironically, one of the few references to an actual pet is by Jesse's drug-addled buddy Badger, who turns down Jesse's offer to crash at his place after three days of nonstop partying:

"Yeah, that's cool and all, but I think I got like this cat? Think I'm like supposed to feed it." However, animal symbolism can be found throughout the series and even in several of the episode titles such as "Cat's in the Bag" (1.02), "Bit by a Dead Bee" (2.03), "Fly" (3.11), "Problem Dog" (4.07), and "Rabid Dog" (5.12).

The episode "Peekaboo" (2.06) opens with Jesse examining a beetle make its way across the sidewalk and along comes Skinny Pete who casually squashes the beetle (later in the episode Spooge will face a similar fate as his Old Lady squashes his head with an ATM). In the episode "Negro Y Azul" (2.07), Hank confronts the DEA informant Tortuga, who asks him, "Hey white boy, my name's Tortuga. You know what that means?" Hank replies, "If I have to guess, I'd say that's Spanish for asshole." Tortuga responds, "Tortuga means turtle, and that's me. I take my time but I always win." Tortuga's severed head later shows up on the head of a tortoise along with the writing "Hola DEA."

In "Fly," the entire episode revolves around Walt's obsessive quest to rid the meth superlab of a pesky housefly. The quest to rid the superlab of the "contaminant" is simply Walt's attempt to regain some of the control and freedom he has lost by working under the employ of Gus Fring. A frustrated Jesse exclaims, "So, you're chasing a fly, and in your world I'm the idiot." Note that Walt and Jesse later take over the company Vamonos Pest Control as a cover for their meth-cooking operation (Walt getting rid of a major pest in Gus Fring before taking over the business). In "Problem Dog," Jesse attends his support group and tells the attendees about a "problem dog" he had to put down (actually referring to his killing of Gale Boetticher). "Dead Freight" opens with the kid, Drew Sharp, on the dirt bike scooping up a tarantula and placing it into a glass jar. After Todd casually kills Sharp, who innocently comes upon the freight train heist, he takes the tarantula with him as a trophy of sorts (perhaps foreshadowing how Todd later persuades Uncle Jack to keep Jesse as a meth slave in the compound). In "Rabid Dog" (5.12), Skyler suggests somewhat akin to Cersei Lannister in *Game of Thrones* that Walt needs to eliminate Jesse ("What's one more?"), while Walt exclaims, "Jesse isn't just some—some—some rabid dog. This is a person."

Cars

The vehicles they drive definitely bring out the true personality of each character in *Breaking Bad*. For example, at the outset of the series, Walt drives a boring, pathetic 2004 Pontiac Aztek, which has been featured on several "Ugliest Cars of All Time" lists. The car is perfect for the bland high school chemistry teacher who has reached a dead end in life. (As a side note, one of the totaled Azteks used in the show was put up for auction in 2013 and sold for $7,800.) As he totally morphs into the Heisenberg persona, Walt dumps the Pontiac Aztek for a brand-new 2012 Chrysler 300. In his early "gangsta" phase, Jesse drives a 1982 Monte Carlo converted into a lowrider with the vanity plate "THE CAPN" (this is the car that Hank manages to trace to Tuco's remote desert hideout). Jesse later opts for a more sedate, anonymous 1986 Toyota Tercel. The mobile meth lab itself is a broken-down 1986 Fleetwood Bounder RV (dubbed "the Crystal Ship" by Jesse) scored by Combo after Jesse and his crew manage to blow all of Walt's savings during an all-night strip club excursion.

Gus Fring, who always plays it safe and "hides in plain sight," prefers to drive a 1998 Volvo V70. Interestingly, Walt is seen driving a Volvo when he returns to Albuquerque from New Hampshire in the season finale, "Felina." Other cars that appear in the series include Skyler's 1991 Jeep Grand Wagoneer (the ultimate family vehicle), Walt Jr.'s 2009 Dodge Challenger (soon replaced at Skyler's insistence with a PT Cruiser), Mike's 1988 Chrysler Fifth Avenue (totally old school!), and Saul's 1997 Cadillac DeVille (complete with a vanity plate that reads "LWYRUP").

Colors

Just like the cars that they drive, the colors the characters in *Breaking Bad* wear reflect on their individual personalities. At the outset of the series, Walt prefers muted colors and green shirts. As he gets more involved in the meth trade, he starts wearing blue (symbolizing his blue meth) and darker colors. He inevitably adopts the Heisenberg look—complete with black porkpie hat, black jacket, and black sunglasses. During the brief periods that Walt backs out of the drug operation, the color of his clothes

Jesse refers to the beat-up RV as "the Crystal Ship," referencing the name of a song by the Doors that appears on the band's self-titled debut album from 1967 and can also be found as the B-side of their No. 1 hit single, "Light My Fire."

reverts once again to more neutral tones. According to *Breaking Bad* costume designer Kathleen Detoro in *Breaking Bad: The Official Book*, "Here is a man who has been beaten down by life; even his name illustrates his blandness . . . a milquetoast kind of character. He always wore the most conservative khaki pants, plaid shirt, and crewneck sweater: a boring teacher . . . Green becomes symbolic of rebirth and life, for Walt . . . Walt's color palette and silhouette becomes darker as he advances through chemo and into the meth-dealing world."

Jesse gradually ditches his gaudy "hip-hop" apparel for darker, more serious tones, especially when he is recovering from one of his frequent drug binges. Skyler typically wears blue, although her clothing also gradually gets darker as she gets more involved in the money-laundering aspects of Walt's criminal enterprise. Marie is almost always seen in purple (however she starts wearing black during her kleptomania phase). Jesse's girlfriend, Jane, the recovering addict, almost exclusively wears black (also foreshadowing her fate). In the superlab, Walt and Jesse wear bright yellow hazmat suits (representing caution and impending danger) in the red superlab (representing danger). Significantly, Gus Fring is wearing a red hazmat suit when he kills Victor with the box cutter in the superlab. Yellow shows up again with the spray-painted graffiti "HEISENBERG" inside the abandoned White home. Last but not least, the White household is located at 308 Negra Arroyo Lane (Spanish for "black creek").

The Desert

The fortunate decision to move the setting of *Breaking Bad* from Riverside, California, to Albuquerque, Mexico, enabled the series to take full advantage of the remarkable (and quite symbolic) desert locale. Many of the most important scenes in the entire series take place amid the bleak landscape of the desert—which brings to mind isolation and danger—such as the initial cook in the "Pilot" episode, the confrontation with Tuco in "Grilled," the senseless killing of Drew Sharp in "Dead Freight," and the tragic murder of Hank in "Ozymandias," among others.

The desert itself is unforgiving and indifferent to the fates of the characters, such as when Walt and Jesse get stuck for four days with a broken-down RV during an epic meth-cooking session in the episode "4 Days Out." It is in the desert that Walt totally absorbs his Heisenberg persona, such as when he confronts the rival drug dealer Declan and tells him to "say my name." Walt also places his drug money into barrels and buries it in the desert. Ironically, the desert setting has typically been used in films and television series to represent American individuality, freedom, and self-reliance such as in the classic John Ford-John Wayne Westerns like *Stagecoach* (1939), *She Wore a Yellow Ribbon* (1949), and *The Searchers* (1956). However, in *Breaking Bad*, often considered a "postmodern Western," the desert is foreboding, desolate, and symbolic of Walt's moral degradation over the course of the series. In a July 23, 2012, interview with *Entertainment Weekly*, Vince Gilligan remarked, "One of the main ways we view the show is a portrait of decay. Walt in particular . . . thinks his business is expanding, but he's also decaying before our eyes—certainly morally."

Names

Just about every hardcore *Breaking Bad* fan knows that the name "Heisenberg" alludes to German theoretical physicist and Nobel Prize in Physics recipient Werner Karl Heisenberg (1901–76), who is known for his "uncertainty principle." Both of the names "Walter White" and "Jesse Pinkman" pay homage to Quentin Tarantino's 1992 movie *Reservoir Dogs*, in which each of the group of criminals is given a color codename, including "Mr. Pink" and "Mr. White." Tarantino, in turn, reportedly took the color codename idea from the 1974 thriller *The Taking of Pelham One Two Three*, which was directed by Joseph Sargent and starred Robert Shaw, Walter Matthau, Martin Balsam, and Hector Elizondo. The name "White" also brings to mind bland, average, and everyman—which certainly describes Walt's persona at the outset of the series. Believe it or not, Jesse's original name in the pilot script was "Marion Alan Dupree."

According to Vince Gilligan in a May 6, 2011, *Vulture* interview, "Character names are a situation where you know it's right when you hear it, and 'Walter White' appealed to me because of the alliterative sound of it and because it's strangely bland, yet sticks in your head nonetheless—you know, white is the color of vanilla, of blandness." In addition, the name "Skyler" is of Danish origin and means "fugitive, giving shelter." Hank and Marie Schrader's surname alludes to German chemist Gerhard Schrader (1903–90), who is notoriously known as the "father of the nerve agents" for his accidental discovery of tabun and sarin. As for Walt's former partner, Elliott, his surname "Schwartz" means "black" in German. Combined with White, the duo created Gray Matter Technologies.

Pink Teddy Bear

One of the most widely discussed symbols in *Breaking Bad* is the pink teddy bear with the missing eye that shows up ominously in several cold

WALTER MATTHAU   ROBERT SHAW   HECTOR ELIZONDO
MARTIN BALSAM

THE TAKING OF PELHAM
ONE TWO THREE

Both the names "Walter White" and "Jesse Pinkman" pay homage to Quentin Tarantino's 1992 movie, *Reservoir Dogs*. Tarantino reportedly took the color codename idea from the 1974 thriller, *The Taking of Pelham One Two Three*.

opens as black-and-white flashbacks during Season Two in the episodes "Seven Thirty-Seven," "Down," "Over," and "ABQ," and foreshadows the horrific plane crash that occurs in the latter episode (2.13). The pink teddy bear ends up in the Whites' pool after the plane crash. In *Breaking Bad:*

The Official Book, Vince Gilligan remarked that the teddy bear's eyeball "probably represented some form of the eye of the universe, the eye of God, the eye of morality, I suppose, judging Walter White." Clearly, the pink teddy bear is also associated with death (perhaps the death of innocence?). For example, the pink teddy bear also shows up as part of a mural on Jane's bedroom wall after her death from an overdose, and its half-destroyed face foreshadows the fate of Gus Fring. Curiously, Walt ends up saving the teddy bear's eyeball for some unknown reason.

Rowboat Painting

The infamous "rowboat painting" first appears in the episode "Bit by a Dead Bee" (2.03) after Walt is hospitalized and again in "Gliding Over All" (5.08) after Walt first meets Uncle Jack Welker and his gang. The rowboat painting depicts a man rowing away from his family, who are left stranded on the shore, and heading toward stormy seas and a ship anchored in the distance. One critic referred to the rowboat painting as a "cheap Winslow Homer knockoff." The rowboat painting symbolizes Walt's isolation from his family as he embarks on his meth empire and also foreshadows his fate—the journey into rough seas symbolizing his eventual path into oblivion.

Swimming Pools

Normally swimming pools symbolize middle-class status and domestic bliss, but in *Breaking Bad* pools serve as the backdrop of disillusionment, violence, destruction, and death. For instance, Gus Fring's partner, Max, is murdered next to Don Eladio's pool. Gus in turn gets revenge on Don Eladio and his crew by poisoning them (and himself!) by the same pool. The plane crash scatters debris, including the charred pink teddy bear, into the Whites' swimming pool. Walt Jr. vomits into the pool after getting goaded into taking multiple shots by Walt. Skyler wades into the pool with the intent to drown herself until Walt fishes her out. Walt starts burning his drug money poolside and then changes his mind and throws the entire grill into the pool. The lily of the valley plant used to poison Brock is located next to the pool in Walt's backyard.

In fact, no one in the entire series seems to spend any time just relaxing and enjoying their time poolside. One of the most enduring images in the entire series is when Walt visits his abandoned house and discovers kids skateboarding in the empty swimming pool—he has truly lost everything, and his dreams of empire have turned to ashes.

22

No Vito Corleone

Breaking Bad Film and TV Influences

Hank: I wanted to be the one to slap the handcuffs on him, that kind of shit. Popeye Doyle waving to Frog One.

Walt: If I recall, at least from the first *French Connection*, Popeye Doyle never actually caught him.

Hank: Ha. Yeah, I guess me and old Popeye, huh? A day late and a dollar short.

In an April 3, 2015, *Yahoo TV* interview, Vince Gilligan stated, "I was inspired by classic movies and wonderful novels, as well . . . As far as television goes, I watched quite a bit of it growing up, probably too much. I watched a lot of classic TV shows." Indeed, *Breaking Bad* wears its many influences like a badge of honor, and references to well-known (and sometimes extremely obscure!) films and television shows have been cleverly woven into the narrative of the series for the astute viewer to discover—ranging from legendary classics like *The Searchers*, *The Twilight Zone*, *Once Upon a Time in the West*, and *The Godfather* to 1990s cult films such as *Reservoir Dogs*, *Pulp Fiction*, *American Beauty*, and *Fight Club*.

Goodbye, Mr. Chips (1939)

"I know the world's changing . . . I've seen the old traditions die, one by one. Grace, dignity, feeling for the past—all that matters here today is a fat banking account." Vince Gilligan has stated that his original concept for *Breaking*

Bad was to transform "Mr. Chips into Scarface." While "Scarface" clearly alludes to cocaine-addled kingpin Tony Montana (Al Pacino) from the cult 1983 movie of the same name, "Mr. Chips" refers to kindly Charles Chipping, the fictional British schoolteacher in James Hilton's 1934 novella *Goodbye, Mr. Chips*. Originally a stern taskmaster at Brookfield School, Chipping transforms into one of the institution's most respected teachers with the help of his beloved wife Katherine. The sentimental story was turned into a somewhat hokey but endearing 1939 film starring Robert Donat (*The 39 Steps*) in the title role. Directed by Sam Wood (*A Night at the Opera*), *Goodbye, Mr. Chips* also starred Greer Garson as Katherine. Donat won a Best Actor Oscar for his performance, beating the likes of Clark Gable (*Gone With the Wind*), James Stewart (*Mr. Smith Goes to Washington*), Laurence Olivier (*Wuthering Heights*), and Mickey Rooney (*Babes in Arms*). A less successful but reasonably enjoyable musical version of *Goodbye, Mr. Chips* appeared in 1969 with Peter O'Toole in the title role. Hilton also wrote the 1933 bestseller *Lost Horizon*, which depicts the fictional utopia Shangri-La. He won an Academy Award for his screenplay for *Mrs. Miniver*, a 1942 war drama that also starred Greer Garson.

To Have and Have Not (1944)

"Was you ever bit by a dead bee?" The title of Episode 2.03 of *Breaking Bad*—"Bit by a Dead Bee"—refers to a line from *To Have and Have Not*, which was directed by Howard Hawks and starred Humphrey Bogart as American expatriate Harry Morgan and Lauren Bacall in her film debut as Marie "Slim" Browning. *To Have and Have Not* was very loosely based on the 1937 novel of the same name by American literary icon Ernest Hemingway. In the film, Harry's sidekick Eddie (Walter Brennan) frequently asks the nonsensical question, "Say, was you ever bit by a dead bee?" Hawks also directed the original 1932 *Scarface* (aka *Scarface: The Shame of the Nation*), which starred Paul Muni in the title role, as well as Ann Dvorak, Karen Morley, Osgood Perkins, and Boris Karloff. The film was based on a 1929 novel of the same name by Armitage Trail and inspired by the exploits of legendary gangster Al "Scarface" Capone. The

1983 remake of *Scarface* heavily influenced Vince Gilligan in creating the concept of *Breaking Bad*.

Ikiru (1952)

"I don't know what I've been doing with my life all these years." Directed by legendary Japanese director Akira Kurosawa (*Seven Samurai*), *Ikiru* details the last days of a Tokyo bureaucrat (Takashi Shimura), who gets diagnosed with terminal stomach cancer and goes on a quest for the meaning of existence. The screenplay was partly influenced by the 1886 novella *The Death of Ivan Ilyich*, by Leo Tolstoy. In a 2011 radio interview on NPR's *Fresh Air*, Vince Gilligan remarked, "There's a wonderful Kurosawa movie from the 50s in which a man, a mid-level, very much a Walter White . . . finds out he's dying of cancer. And in the last months of his life what he chooses to do is a very good thing. It's to build a playground, a small playground in Tokyo for the children in his neighborhood."

Bigger Than Life (1956)

"Portrait of a man with a habit!" Directed by Nicholas Ray (*Rebel Without a Cause*), *Bigger Than Life* stars James Mason as Ed Avery, a schoolteacher and all-around family man who becomes addicted to a "miracle drug" (cortisone) and begins to lose his sanity. The film's tagline exclaimed, "The story of the handful of hope that becomes a fistful of hell!" Extremely controversial for its time and a box-office disaster, *Bigger Than Life* also starred Barbara Rush and Walter Matthau. However, the film's reputation grew over time and none other than legendary French director Jean-Luc Godard (*Breathless*) hailed *Bigger Than Life* as one of the ten best American sound films of all time. For the record, Godard's Top Ten list also included the likes of *Scarface* (1932), *The Great Dictator* (1940), *Vertigo* (1958), *The Searchers* (1956), *Singin' in the Rain* (1952), *The Lady from Shanghai* (1947), *Angel Face* (1953), *To Be or Not to Be* (1942), and *Dishonored* (1931). In "The 7 Movies That Influenced Breaking Bad," (*Esquire*, September 26,

2013), Calum Marsh writes that *Bigger Than Life* paints "a sobering portrait of a very particular strain of American psychosis, telling the story of a good man's slow transformation into a monster, and it's not hard to see the kernel of Walter White in there . . . As in *Breaking Bad*, *Bigger Than Life* shows us how a person can love their family so intensely that their efforts to help keep them together ultimately tear them apart, alienating loved ones and making them blind to their own insanity."

The Searchers (1956)

"That'll be the day." Vince Gilligan has credited the classic 1956 John Ford Western *The Searchers* as the inspiration for the final standoff between Walt and Jesse in the series finale, "Felina." In an September 30, 2013, interview with *Entertainment Weekly*, Gilligan stated, "A lot of astute viewers who know their film history are going to say, 'It's the ending to *The Searchers*.' And indeed it is . . . It just gets me every time—the ending of that movie just chokes you up, it's wonderful. In the writers room, we said, 'Hey, what about *The Searchers* ending?' So, it's always a matter of stealing from the best." Based on the 1954 novel of the same name by Alan Le May, *The Searchers* stars John Wayne as Civil War veteran Ethan Edwards, who obsessively searches for his niece, Debbie (Natalie Wood), who has been abducted during a Comanche raid. In 2008, the American Film Institute named *The Searchers* as the greatest American Western of all time. In his 2011 memoir, *Life Itself*, Roger Ebert remarked that Wayne "wasn't a cruel and violent action hero. He was almost always a man doing his job. Sometimes he was other than that, and he could be gentle, as in *The Quiet Man*, or vulnerable, as in *The Shootist*, or lonely and obsessed, as in *The Searchers*."

Sweet Smell of Success (1957)

"It's a dirty job, but I pay clean money for it." Titles from Episode 1.02 ("Cat's in the Bag . . .") and Episode 1.03 (". . . and the Bag's in the River") of *Breaking Bad* allude to *Sweet Smell of Success*, a 1957 film noir Vince

Gilligan has cited as his all-time favorite movie—particularly for its eminently quotable dialogue (for example, "I'd hate to take a bite outta you. You're a cookie full of arsenic."). In *Guide for the Film Fanatic* (1986), Danny Peary describes the film as a "[s]avage glimpse at the sleazy New York show-biz scene . . . It's an ugly world full of paranoia, hatred, hustling, squirming, backbiting, lying, blackmailing, sex traded for favors, schemes, threats, broken dreams, ruined lives, money, and power." Directed by Alexander Mackendrick (*The Ladykillers*), *Sweet Smell of Success* stars Burt Lancaster, Tony Curtis, Susan Harrison, and Martin Milner. The film's tagline exclaimed, "The Motion Picture That Will Never Be Forgiven . . . Or Forgotten!"

The Twilight Zone (1959–64)

"You are about to enter another dimension. A dimension not only of sight and sound, but of mind." A groundbreaking anthology series created by Rod Serling, *The Twilight Zone* featured a total of 156 episodes during its initial five-year run. Although each episode of *The Twilight Zone* features a different cast, the typical plot focuses on ordinary people thrown into extraordinary situations (dare we say, Kafkaesque?). In his book *Cult TV*, Stan Beeler comments that *The Twilight Zone* "provided socially relevant, well-written plots masked from the censor's hand through the use of metaphor." On its list of the "60 Best Series of All Time," *TV Guide* listed *The Twilight Zone* at No. 5 behind *The Sopranos*, *Seinfeld*, *I Love Lucy*, and *All in the Family* (*Breaking Bad* placed No. 9). In 2013, the Writers Guild of America ranked *The Twilight Zone* as the third best-written TV series ever (behind *The Sopranos* and *Seinfeld*). In a September 30, 2013, interview with *The Guardian*, Vince Gilligan stated, "You want your work to be remembered. You want it to outlive you. My favorite show ever was *The Twilight Zone* and I think about Rod Serling . . . [The show] long outlived him—he passed away in 1975—but there's kids who haven't been born yet who will know the phrase 'the twilight zone,' and hopefully will be watching those wonderful episodes. I can't say that's what will happen [with *Breaking Bad*], but you wanna have that kind of immortality through your work."

The Flight of the Phoenix (1965)

"If there's just one chance in a thousand that he's got something . . . I'd rather take it than just sit around here waiting to die." Directed by Robert Aldrich (*Kiss Me Deadly*), *The Flight of the Phoenix* concerns an aircraft that has to make an emergency landing in the Sahara Desert, forcing the survivors to struggle to survive and eventually create a new aircraft out of the wreckage. The film, which was a box-office disaster but has gained a cult following over the years, features an all-star cast that includes James Stewart, Richard Attenborough, Peter Finch, Hardy Kruger, Ernest Borgnine, Ian Bannen, Ronald Fraser, Christian Marquand, Dan Duryea, and George Kennedy. *The Flight of the Phoenix* was based on a 1964 novel of the same name by Elleston Trevor. In 2004, a mediocre remake of the film starring Dennis Quaid and Giovanni Ribisi quickly faded into obscurity. The ninth episode of the second season of *Breaking Bad*, "4 Days Out," owes inspiration to *The Flight of the Phoenix* as Walt and Jesse get stuck in the desert with a dead RV battery and have to use their own ingenuity and available materials to get the vehicle working again.

The Good, the Bad, and the Ugly (1966)

"You see, in this world there's two kinds of people, my friend: Those with loaded guns and those who dig. You dig." Vince Gilligan has frequently cited Italian director Sergio Leone's Spaghetti Westerns as inspiration for *Breaking Bad*, most notably the stunning cinematography of the films (especially the effective combination of long shots and close-ups). In fact, Tuco Salamanca (Raymond Cruz), the show's villain in the latter half of Season One and beginning of Season Two of *Breaking Bad*, was named after the "Ugly" in *The Good, the Bad, and the Ugly*—Mexican bandit Tuco Benedicto Pacifico Juan Maria Ramirez (aka "the Rat"). Tuco was effectively portrayed by Eli Wallach, who starred alongside Clint Eastwood (the "Good," aka "the Man with No Name"), and Lee Van Cleef (the "Bad," aka "Angel Eyes"). The film was complemented by a powerful score by frequent Leone collaborator Ennio Morricone that featured such memorable compositions as "The Ecstasy of Gold" and "The Story of a Soldier." *The*

Good, the Bad, and the Ugly serves as the final installment of the so-called "Dollars Trilogy," which includes *A Fistful of Dollars* (1964) and *For a Few Dollars More* (1965). According to Gilligan in a March 27, 2013, interview with *Local iQ*, "After the first *Breaking Bad* episode, it started to dawn on me that we could be making a contemporary Western. So you see scenes that are like gunfighters squaring off, like Clint Eastwood and Lee Van Cleef—we have Walt and others like that."

Seconds (1966)

"The years I've spent trying to get all the things I was told were important—that I was supposed to want! Things! Not people ... or meaning. Just things." Bleak, disturbing, and uncompromising, this intense existential science fiction/horror flick was directed by John Frankenheimer (*Birdman of Alcatraz*) and based on a 1963 novel of the same name by David Ely. Boring middle-aged banker Arthur Hamilton (John Randolph) is living a drab, empty suburban existence. Through a mysterious call from Charlie Evans (Murray Hamilton)—a long-lost pal who is supposedly dead!—Arthur gets hooked up with a secret organization simply known as "the Company" that allows customers to be "reborn" by faking their deaths and setting up new, more exciting lives for them. After extensive surgery, Arthur transforms into Tony Wilson (now portrayed by Rock Hudson), relocates to a Malibu beach house, begins a new life as an "artist," and embarks on a relationship with a neighbor, "Nora Marcus," (Salome Jens). However, Arthur/Tony has trouble adjusting, and everything begins to go terribly wrong. Strong performances abound, especially from Hudson, Randolph, and Will Geer as the grandfatherly, ultimately sinister Old Man—the brains behind the Company. The nightmarish final scene is very disturbing—one of the bleakest endings in movie history. The film's amazing claustrophobic black-and-white cinematography by James Wong Howe (*The Rose Tattoo*) was nominated for an Academy Award. According to Calum Marsh in the *Esquire* article, "The 7 Movies That Influenced Breaking Bad" (September 26, 2013), *Seconds* "more or less invented the sort of hyper-subjective cinematography for which *Breaking Bad* is so often praised ... Cockeyed extreme close-ups, trippy rapid-fire montages, all manner of fish-eyed lens—it's *Breaking Bad's* bread and butter and Frankenheimer got to it first." *Seconds* serves as the final film in Frankenheimer's so-called "Paranoia Trilogy" along with *The Manchurian Candidate* (1962) and *Seven Days in May* (1964).

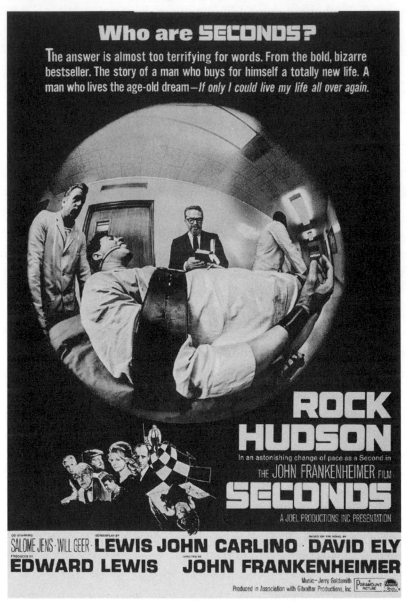

The bleak and intense existential science fiction/horror film *Seconds* (1966) served as an influence on *Breaking Bad* for its main character's startling transformation, as well as its surreal cinematography courtesy of James Wong Howe.

Cool Hand Luke (1967)

"Yeah, well, sometimes nothin' can be a real cool hand." The title of Episode 1.06 of *Breaking Bad*, "Crazy Handful of Nothing," pays tribute to this classic prison drama, which Vince Gilligan has acknowledged as one of his favorites. Directed by Stuart Rosenberg (*The Amityville Horror*), the film takes place in a Florida chain gang prison and stars Paul Newman in the title role of classic antihero Lucas "Luke" Jackson, along with George Kennedy (who won a Best Supporting Actor Oscar for his performance as Dragline), Strother Martin, Jo Van Fleet, Luke Askew, Dennis Hopper, and Harry Dean Stanton. It is Dragline who remarks, "Oh Luke, you wild, beautiful thing. You crazy handful of nothin'." Just like Walter White, Luke serves as an antihero who breaks all the rules, and the audience ends up rooting for him anyway. *Cool Hand Luke* was based on the 1965 novel of the same name by Donn Pearce, who had spent two years in the Florida penal system, including stints at Raiford Prison and Tavares Prison Camp No. 48, after getting arrested for burglary in 1949 at the age of twenty. Pearce, who described his experience on the chain gang as "a chamber of horrors," appeared in a cameo in the film as a convict named Sailor.

Once Upon a Time in the West (1968)

"The future don't matter to us. Nothing matters now—not the land, not the money, not the woman." Vince Gilligan has frequently cited the influence of this classic Sergio Leone Spaghetti Western (especially the tension-filled opening fifteen minutes) on the visual style of *Breaking Bad*. In fact, *Breaking Bad* composer Dave Porter has referred to the series as "a postmodern Western." *Breaking Bad* frequently uses filming techniques popularized by Leone such as close-ups, wide shots, and flashbacks (see Chapter 17). In his definitive Leone biography, *Sergio Leone: Something to Do with Death*, author Christopher Frayling remarks, "It is no accident that [Leone's] films usually feature an elaborate flashback, which only comes into focus, piece by piece, as the story progresses." *Once Upon a Time in the West* stars Charles Bronson as a mysterious stranger (Harmonica),

Henry Fonda (cast against type as blue-eyed villain Frank), Jason Robards (as the likable outlaw Cheyenne), and Claudia Cardinale (as the beautiful widowed homesteader Jill McBain). The film is punctuated by an incredibly powerful and haunting Ennio Morricone score. By the way, Clint Eastwood was originally offered the role of Harmonica but turned it down.

The French Connection (1971)

"There are no rules and no holds barred when Popeye cuts loose!" Based on Robin Moore's 1969 nonfiction book *The French Connection: A True Account of Cops, Narcotics, and International Conspiracy*, this groundbreaking, Academy Award-winning crime thriller exerted a major influence on *Breaking Bad*. Directed by William Friedkin (*The Exorcist*), *The French Connection* details the exploits of New York Police Department detectives Jimmy "Popeye" Doyle (Gene Hackman) and Buddy "Cloudy" Russo (Roy Scheider) in pursuit of French heroin smuggler Alain Charnier (Fernando Rey). The first R-rated movie to capture a Best Picture Oscar, *The French Connection* also won Academy Awards for Best Director, Best Actor (Hackman), Best Film Editing, and Best Adapted Screenplay (Ernest Tidyman). Hackman and Rey both reprised their roles for the 1975 sequel, *The French Connection II*. Just like Popeye Doyle, Walt dons a porkpie hat (whenever he assumes his Heisenberg persona). At one point in the "Bullet Points" episode of *Breaking Bad*, Hank remarks that he dreams of waving to Heisenberg "like Popeye Doyle" before he handcuffs him. Walt replies, "If I recall, at least, from the first *French Connection*, Popeye Doyle never actually caught him."

The Godfather (1972)

"I believe in America." At one point early in *Breaking Bad*, Saul Goodman offers his legal services to Walt—comparing himself to Tom Hagen (the "consigliere" of the Corleone family in *The Godfather* as portrayed by Robert Duvall). Walt exclaims, "I'm no Vito Corleone." Saul replies, "No

shit! Right now you're Fredo!" However, there are many striking similarities between *Breaking Bad* and the blockbuster crime film directed
by Francis Ford Coppola (*Apocalypse Now*) and starring Marlon Brando
as Don Vito Corleone, Al Pacino as Michael Corleone, James Caan as
Sonny Corleone, John Cazale as Fredo Corleone, Diane Keaton as Kay

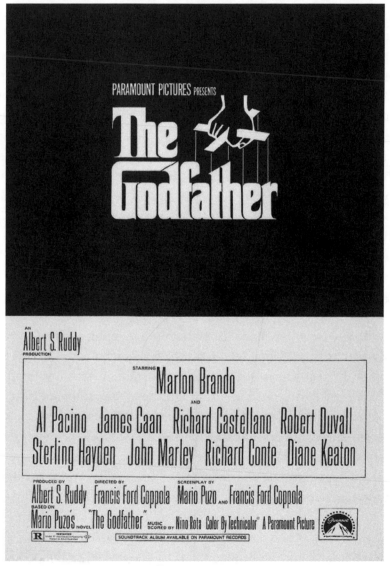

Both *Breaking Bad* and *The Godfather* (1972) focus on a good character turning
bad over the course of the narrative. In the case of the latter, Michael Corleone
transforms from a World War II hero into a cold, brutal mob boss.

Adams-Corleone, and Lenny Montana as Luca Brasi. In fact, both dramas focus on a good character turning bad over the course of the narrative. In the case of *The Godfather*, Michael undergoes a stunning transformation from a naïve college student and World War II hero into a cold, brutal mob boss. Both Walt and Michael descend into various criminal activities by claiming they are doing it for the good of their family. Just like in *The Godfather*, *Breaking Bad* uses the appearance of oranges as a harbinger of death. In addition, the murder of the ten prisoners in *Breaking Bad* echoes the violent ending of *The Godfather* as Michael secures his power by eliminating the heads of the other mob families brilliantly interspersed with scenes from a baptism. *The Godfather* was nominated for seven Oscars and won for Best Picture, Best Actor (Brando), and Best Adapted Screenplay (for Coppola and Mario Puzo). The American Film Institute has ranked *The Godfather* as the second-greatest film in American cinema (behind *Citizen Kane*, Orson Welles's 1941 masterpiece). It was followed by two sequels: *The Godfather: Part II* (1974), which also won a Best Picture Oscar, and *The Godfather: Part III* (1990), which was nominated for Best Picture but lost to *Dances with Wolves*.

Taxi Driver (1976)

"He's a lonely forgotten man desperate to prove that he's alive." Directed by Martin Scorsese (*Raging Bull*), this gritty psychological drama stars Robert De Niro as Travis Bickle, a lonely, unstable Vietnam veteran who takes a night job driving a taxi through the mean streets of New York City. At one point Bickle confesses, "Loneliness has followed me my whole life, everywhere. In bars, in cars, sidewalks, stores, everywhere. There's no escape. I'm God's lonely man." Both Bickle and Walter White are seen initially as sympathetic characters who devolve into total sociopaths over the course of each drama. Walt assumes the evil Heisenberg character, while Bickle also dons sunglasses and sports a rather frightening Mohawk haircut at one point. The scenes where Walt meets with sleazy arms dealer Lawson (Jim Beaver) recall Bickle buying an illegal weapon from equally sleazy gun salesman Easy Andy (Steven Prince). Walt also practices drawing his gun like Travis. In addition, Easy Andy actually offers to sell Travis some crystal meth: "I can get ya crystal meth. Nitrous oxide. How about that? How about a Cadillac?" In 1978, Scorsese directed a fascinating documentary about Prince called *American Boy: A Profile of Steven Prince*.

The Shining (1980)

"You've had your whole fucking life to think things over, what good's a few minutes more gonna do you now?" Just before the Salamanca cousins' murder a police officer with an axe (with definite shades of Jack Torrance) in Episode 3.06 ("Sunset") of *Breaking Bad*, the doomed officer places a call on his radio: "KDK-12 to dispatch." These are the exact call letters for the Overlook Hotel that Wendy repeats multiple times in the classic 1980 horror film *The Shining*. The identically dressed Salamanca twins even call to mind the identically dressed Grady twins ("Come and play with us, Danny. Forever . . ."), who are both murdered with an axe. Just like Walter White transforms from good to evil over the course of *Breaking Bad*, Jack Torrance (Jack Nicholson) makes a startling transformation from struggling writer to total psychopath in *The Shining*. Directed by Stanley Kubrick (*2001: A Space Odyssey*), *The Shining* is based on the 1977 Stephen King novel of the same name and also stars Shelley Duvall, Danny Lloyd, Scatman Crothers, and Joe Turkel. In a 1980 interview with film critic Michel Ciment, Stanley Kubrick remarked, "I think we tend to be a bit hypocritical about ourselves . . . We are capable of the greatest good and the greatest evil, and the problem is that often we can't distinguish between them when it suits our purpose." King, by the way, is a huge fan of *Breaking Bad*.

Scarface (1983)

"He loved the American Dream. With a Vengeance." When Vince Gilligan remarked about transforming Walter White from "Mr. Chips into Scarface," he was referring to the extremely violent 1983 remake of the 1932 Howard Hawks film *Scarface: The Shame of the Nation*. Directed by Brian DePalma (*Carrie*) and scripted by none other than Oliver Stone (*Platoon*), the 1983 version features an over-the-top performance by Al Pacino as Cuban immigrant Tony Montana, who rises to the top of the Miami drug scene with a brutal and reckless abandon. In Episode 5.03 of *Breaking Bad*, Walt and Junior can be seen watching a DVD of *Scarface* during the infamous "Say hello to my little friend!" finale. Walt remarks quite prophetically, "Everyone dies in this movie" (Bryan Cranston reportedly ad-libbed the line), while Skyler looks on in disgust. According to Vince Gilligan in a July 29, 2012, interview with *HuffPost*, "I love *Scarface*, it's one of my favorites. And it's just cool to have it on the show, finally." In the Season Five premiere of *Breaking Bad*, Walt purchases a machine gun, leading to the explosive series finale in "Felina" in which he guns down Uncle Jack's entire crew, just as Tony Montana battles the Bolivian gang at the end of *Scarface*. In addition, Tony Montana's right-hand man, Manny Ribera, is portrayed by Steven Bauer, who plays Don Eladio Vuente in *Breaking Bad*. Last but not least, Mark Margolis—Alberto the Shadow in *Scarface*—portrays the grimacing Hector Salamanca in *Breaking Bad*.

The Terminator (1984)

"The thing that won't die, in the nightmare that won't end." In *Breaking Bad: The Official Book*, Vince Gilligan compared the Cousins (Leonel and Marco Salamanca) in their relentless pursuit of revenge to the Terminator (Arnold Schwarzenegger) in James Cameron's groundbreaking 1984 science-fiction film: "You pay homage to fun characters like that by taking a page from *The Terminator* and have these really scary characters who don't speak their minds . . . and let them be a little *misterioso*." In addition, Gus Fring's partially mutilated face resembles *The Terminator* at the end of the film.

Reservoir Dogs (1992)

"Why can't we pick our own colors?" The *Breaking Bad* character names Walter White and Jesse Pinkman obviously allude to Quentin Tarantino's violent crime thriller *Reservoir Dogs,* which features both a Mr. White (Harvey Keitel) and a Mr. Pink (Steve Buscemi), among other color-coded names. In fact, the standoff scene in *Reservoir Dogs* between Mr. White and Mr. Pink is strikingly similar to the scene in *Breaking Bad* where Jesse holds a gun to Walt. Tarantino's feature-length film debut, *Reservoir Dogs* also stars Michael Madsen, Chris Penn, Tim Roth, Tarantino, Lawrence Tierney, and Edward Bunker. According to the film's tagline, "Seven Total Strangers Team Up for the Perfect Crime. They Don't Know Each Other's Name. But They've Got Each Other's Color." *Empire* film magazine has named *Reservoir Dogs* as the "Greatest Independent Film of All Time."

Pulp Fiction (1994)

"I'm not here to say please, I'm here to tell you what to do and if self-preservation is an instinct you possess you'd better fucking do it and do it quick." Quentin Tarantino's follow-up to *Reservoir Dogs,* this highly influential black comedy/crime thriller features an all-star cast, including Samuel L. Jackson, John Travolta, Uma Thurman, Bruce Willis, Tim Roth, Amanda Plummer, Ving Rhames, Christopher Walken, and Harvey Keitel as a "fixer" named Winston Wolfe, who has been frequently compared to Mike Ehrmantraut, the fixer character from *Breaking Bad*. The scene where Walt and Jesse eat breakfast at Denny's after disposing of Victor's body in *Breaking Bad* echoes a similar scene in *Pulp Fiction* where Jules and Vincent sit down to breakfast at a diner after disposing of Marvin's body. The trunk scene in *Breaking Bad* also pays homage to the trunk scene in *Pulp Fiction*. In addition, several critics have noted that Jesse's girlfriend, Jane, bears more than a passing resemblance to Mia Wallace (Thurman) and both characters overdose.

Fargo (1996)

"A lot can happen in the middle of nowhere." The title of Episode 1.07 ("A No Rough Stuff Type Deal") in *Breaking Bad* alludes to the cult black comedy crime film *Fargo* when the hapless car salesman Jerry

Lundegaard (William H. Macy) exclaims, "This was supposed to be a no-rough-stuff-type deal." Directed by Joel and Ethan Coen, *Fargo* also stars Frances McDormand (who won the Best Actress Oscar), Steve Buscemi, Peter Stormare, and Harve Presnell. The Coen Brothers received the Best Original Screenplay Academy Award for *Fargo*. Interestingly, Jesse Plemons (Todd Alquist in *Breaking Bad*) portrayed butcher Ed Blumquist in the second season of the critically acclaimed *Fargo* TV series, which aired on FX in 2015.

American Beauty (1999)

"Both my wife and daughter think I'm this gigantic loser. And they're right. I have lost something. I'm not exactly sure what it is, but I know I didn't always feel this . . . sedated. But you know what? It's never too late to get it back." Several *Breaking Bad* scholars, most notably Lara C. Stache, the author of *Breaking Bad: A Cultural History*, have drawn interesting parallels between Walter White and Lester Burnham (Kevin Spacey), the burnt-out advertising executive in the critically acclaimed 1999 film *American Beauty*, which was directed by Sam Mendes (*Road to Perdition*). A self-described loser, forty-two-year-old Burnham has reached a dead end on the road of life just like Walter White at the outset of *Breaking Bad*. His wife Carolyn (Annette Bening) can't stand him, his daughter Jane (Thora Birch) ignores him, and he is trapped in a boring and mean-ingless job. Lester's idea of a fun evening is watching the James Bond Marathon on TNT. The highlight of his day is jerking off in the shower; after that, "it's all downhill from here." Things change the minute Lester eyes his daughter's best friend, a beautiful young cheerleader named Angela (Mena Suvari), and becomes immediately obsessed with her. Soon thereafter, he scores some pot from a neighborhood kid, Ricky Fitts (Wes Bentley), who also happens to be obsessed with Jane. One night at dinner, Lester calmly informs his family: "I quit my job, told my boss to fuck him-self and blackmailed him for $60,000." He then takes a job flipping burg-ers at Mr. Smiley's fast-food restaurant (shades of Los Pollos Hermanos?) and starts hanging out in the garage, listening to Dylan's "All Along the Watchtower," pumping iron, and smoking pot. In a yearning to return to the happiness of youth, Lester also purchases a bright red 1970 Pontiac Firebird. In other words, just like Walt, Lester forges ahead with reckless abandon, thoroughly recognizing the futile and ridiculous aspects of his quest but enjoying the ride nevertheless.

Fight Club (1999)

"It's only after we've lost everything that we're free to do anything." Parallels can be drawn between Walter White and his alter ego Heisenberg to the unnamed protagonist (Edward Norton) and his alter ego Tyler Durden (Brad Pitt) in *Fight Club*, the 1999 film adaptation of Chuck Palahniuk's 1996 cult novel of the same name. In *Fight Club*, which was directed by David Fincher (*The Social Network*), Norton portrays a lonely, depressed insomniac who becomes addicted to attending support groups. He soon discovers an alternative view of life through the help of Durden, a free-spirited, eccentric (and ultimately nihilistic) soap salesman. The inseparable duo eventually start their own extremely unconventional "support group"—an underground chain of clubs where the participants simply beat the living shit out of each other. Fight clubs soon become the rage across the country, and the participants start focusing their energies into even darker, more sinister goals. Legendary movie critic Roger Ebert called *Fight Club* "the most frankly and cheerfully fascist big-star movie since *Death Wish*, a celebration of violence in which the heroes write themselves a license to drink, smoke, screw and beat one another up."

23

A Man Provides

Breaking Bad vs. The Sopranos

All due respect, you got no fuckin' idea what it's like to be Number One. Every
decision you make affects every facet of every other fuckin' thing. It's too much
to deal with almost. And in the end you're completely alone with it all.

—*Tony Soprano*

Without the success of a groundbreaking show like *The Sopranos*
paving the way, subsequent long-form dramatic series like
Breaking Bad, The Wire, Six Feet Under, Deadwood, Dexter, Mad Men, and
Boardwalk Empire would most certainly never have been produced. *The
Sopranos* aired on HBO for six seasons between 1999 and 2006 with a total
of eighty-six episodes, changing all the rules of what a dramatic series
should be in the process. In fact, the two award-winning series share a lot
of similarities, including great writing (although *Breaking Bad* was much
more tightly plotted) and direction, well-developed characters along with
amazingly talented casts, high production values, incredible soundtracks,
generous doses of dark humor, inventive cinematography, and the perfect
locales that almost became like characters in their own right (northern New
Jersey in the case of *The Sopranos*).

In 2003–04, *The Sopranos* became the first cable television series to win
an Emmy Award for Outstanding Drama Series (beating out *24, CSI: Crime
Scene Investigation, Joan of Arcadia*, and *The West Wing*). *The Sopranos* was
also the first cable television series to win a Golden Globe Award for Best
Television Series—Drama in 1999 (beating out *ER, Once Again, The Practice*,
and *The West Wing*).

Both series also served as ongoing commentaries on the American Dream, with David Remnick of *The New Yorker* (June 4, 2007) commenting, "Like John Updike's Rabbit series or Philip Roth's novels of the past decade, 'The Sopranos' teems with the mindless commerce and consumption of modern America." At one point, a somewhat despondent Tony Soprano even remarks, "It's good to be in something from the ground floor. I came too late for that and I know. But lately, I'm getting the feeling that I came in at the end. The best is over." Interestingly, *Breaking Bad* contains at least two references to *The Sopranos*: The character Juan Bolsa of the Mexican drug cartel translates to Johnny Sack (the New York City mob boss in *The Sopranos*), and the fifth-season opening episode of *Breaking Bad*, "Live Free or Die," was also the name of the sixth episode of the sixth season of *The Sopranos*.

In terms of viewing habits in general, *Breaking Bad* held a distinct advantage over *The Sopranos* due to the rise of Netflix and other binge-watching options. According to Vince Gilligan in a May 12, 2013, *Vulture* interview, "I am grateful as hell for binge-watching . . . In its third season, *Breaking Bad* got this amazing nitrous-oxide boost of energy and general public awareness because of Netflix." However, *The Sopranos* is a clear winner in the category of profanity, with the word "fuck" said more than 3,500 times during the duration of the series, while *Breaking Bad* creator Vince Gilligan claimed that AMC only allowed one "fuck" per season— the most memorable being when Walt exclaims to Bogdan, "Fuck you and your eyebrows!"; when a dying Mike tells Walt, "Shut the fuck up and let me die in peace"; and when Hank (knowing he is doomed) addresses Uncle Jack, "My name is ASAC Schrader and you can go fuck yourself."

So which is the greatest dramatic television series of all time? For the record, most polls over the last decade have placed *Breaking Bad*, *The Sopranos*, and *The Wire* in various places near the top of their list. In 2016, *Rolling Stone* published its list of the "100 Greatest TV Shows of All Time," with *The Sopranos* at No. 1, *The Wire* at No. 2, and *Breaking Bad* at No. 3. Someday, a new drama will come along influenced by one or all three of these top-rated shows and manage to bump them all down the list. Meanwhile, here's the tale of the tape:

Vince Gilligan vs. David Chase

It seems that behind every successful dramatic television series is an individual creative vision such as Vince Gilligan for *Breaking Bad* and David Chase for *The Sopranos*. Growing up in northern New Jersey, Chase had a somewhat dysfunctional childhood (the character of "Livia Soprano" was reportedly based on his mother!). Just as Gilligan honed his skills as a writer and producer on *The X-Files*, Chase spent years as a story editor, writer, and producer in the television industry on such popular shows as *The Rockford Files*, *I'll Fly Away*, and *Northern Exposure*, as well as more obscure shows like *Kolchak: The Night Stalker* (which served as an influence on *The X-Files*) and *Almost Grown*.

However, after twenty years in the television business, Chase was desperate to break out and create his own show that would leave a lasting imprint and soon started shopping the pilot for *The Sopranos* at various networks until HBO picked it up (Chase reportedly originally envisioned *The Sopranos* as a feature-length film about a mobster who visits a psychiatrist—basically the plot of the 1999 comedy *Analyze This*, which was directed by Harold Ramis and starred Robert De Niro and Billy Crystal). However, the network originally wanted to change the name of the series to something like *New Jersey Blood*, *Made in New Jersey*, or *Family Man* because they thought *The Sopranos* would make people think it was about opera singers! Inevitably, both Chase and Gilligan refused to accept the limits of the television medium, and both stretched the limits of what a television dramatic series could be. Interestingly, both Gilligan and Chase wrote and directed their respective series finales: "Felina" and "Made in America."

Chase has remarked that classic gangster films like *The Public Enemy* (1931), which starred James Cagney, and the TV crime series *The Untouchables* (1959–63) heavily influenced *The Sopranos*. In addition, Chase has cited playwrights Arthur Miller (*Death of a Salesman*) and Tennessee Williams (*A Streetcar Named Desire*) as influences on the show's writing, while the films of Federico Fellini (*La Dolce Vita*) influenced the show's cinematic style. In addition, Chase was influenced by Martin Scorsese's classic 1994 gangster film, *Goodfellas*, and several cast members from the movie also showed up on *The Sopranos* such as Lorraine Bracco (Karen Hill), Michael Imperioli (Spider), Tony Sirico (Tony Stacks), Frank Vincent (Billy Batts), and Tony Lip (Frankie the Wop), among others. In addition, Ray Liotta, who portrayed Henry Hill in *Goodfellas*, was reportedly seriously considered for the role of Tony Soprano. Interestingly, in a December 15, 2013, interview with *The Independent*, Scorsese remarked, "I don't have time to watch any other shows, the famous ones. I've seen a few episodes of some, in fact. I only watched *The Sopranos* once or twice. I just couldn't connect with it. People wonder why I can't do something with that world now, but it was a different situation to when I was growing up fifty years ago, a different world."

Last but not least, Chase (as well as Gilligan) was inspired by *Twin Peaks* (1990–91), David Lynch's totally offbeat dramatic series. According to James Parker in an article in *The Atlantic* titled "How Twin Peaks Invented Modern Television" (June 2017), "Without *Twin Peaks*, and its big-bang expansion of the possibilities of television, half your favorite shows wouldn't exist. The absorptive, all-in serial, sonically and visually entire, novelistically cantilevered with deep structure and extending backwards into the viewer's brain, was simply not a thing before Lynch and [series co-creator Mark] Frost."

In a January 20, 1999, *Salon* interview, Chase remarked, "I want to tell a story about this particular man. I want to tell the story about the reality of being a mobster—or what I perceive to be the reality of life in organized crime. They aren't shooting each other every day. They sit around eating baked ziti and betting and figuring out who owes who money. Occasionally, violence breaks out—more often than it does in the banking world, perhaps."

Walter White vs. Tony Soprano

Both Walter White and Tony Soprano (expertly portrayed by the late, great James Gandolfini) are flawed antiheroes, but the former undergoes a drastic transformation throughout the series (from "Mr. Chips to Scarface," according to Gilligan), while the latter only makes halfhearted attempts to change his way of life as an Italian-American mobster based

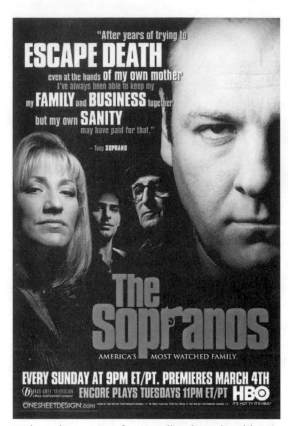

"After years of trying to **ESCAPE DEATH** even at the hands **of my own mother** I've always been able to keep my **FAMILY** and **BUSINESS** together but my own **SANITY** may have paid for that."
— Tony SOPRANO

The Sopranos

AMERICA'S ■ MOST WATCHED FAMILY.

EVERY SUNDAY AT 9PM ET/PT. PREMIERES MARCH 4TH
ENCORE PLAYS TUESDAYS 11PM ET/PT HB☉

ONESHEETDESIGN.com

Without the success of a groundbreaking show like *The Sopranos* paving the way, subsequent long-form dramatic series like *Breaking Bad* would most certainly never have been produced.

out of northern New Jersey. (While Bryan Cranston sat in on high school classrooms to develop his character, Gandolfini reportedly sought out real-life "wise guys" to give him advice on how to portray a mobster.) In a September 16, 2013, *Forbes* article titled, "Why 'Breaking Bad' Is the Best Show Ever and Why That Matters," Allen St. John wrote, "Tony Soprano was a man who didn't change, couldn't change . . . Whereas Tony Soprano spent seven seasons running errands around North Jersey, Walter White embarked on an epic journey, tracing an arc reserved for iconic characters of literature and cinema like Jay Gatsby and Michael Corleone. As he morphed Mr. Chips into Scarface, Gilligan wrote his own version of the Great American Novel. On steroids." Walt had to go through "a bit of a learning curve" toward becoming a criminal mastermind, while Tony was already entrenched as a mobster at the beginning of the series. In fact, Tony was pretty much the same character viewers saw feeding ducks in the series premiere as the guy sitting down at the diner eating onion rings with his family in the series finale.

Both characters try unsuccessfully to balance the stresses of their family life with the increasing demands of their various criminal enterprises. Walt discovers he has lung cancer, while Tony suffers from panic attacks that cause him to seek weekly sessions with psychiatrist "Jennifer Melfi" (Lorraine Bracco), who was reportedly modeled after Chase's own therapist. Both characters frequently get let down by their often drug-addled sidekicks: Jesse Pinkman for Walt and Christopher Moltisanti (Michael Imperioli) for Tony. In addition, Tony's crew is full of much more hardened criminals with the likes of Paulie "Walnuts" Gualtieri (Tony Sirico, who reportedly had compiled quite a rap sheet in his younger years and served time in prison before becoming an actor), Silvio Dante (Steven Van Zandt, a member of Bruce Springsteen's E Street Band who originally auditioned for the part of Tony), and Sal "Big Pussy" Bonpensiero (Vincent Pastore). Both characters eliminate a series of rivals in order to solidify their power. In Tony's case, he must battle against members of his own family, including his domineering mother, Livia Soprano (Nancy Marchand, formerly best known from her role as Margaret Pynchon on the TV drama *Lou Grant*), and uncle, Corrado "Junior" Soprano (Dominic Chianese, who had portrayed Johnny Ola in *The Godfather: Part II*), as well as Richie Aprile (David Proval), Ralph Cifaretto (Joe Pantoliano), Feech LaManna (Robert Loggia), John "Johnny Sack" Sacramoni (Vince Curatola), and Phil Leotardo (Frank Vincent), among others. However, Tony never faced a rival quite as diabolical as Gus Fring.

Both Walt and Tony justify violence and murder as a way to protect their families. However, Tony gets away with murder in multiple instances, whereas *Breaking Bad* showcases the notion that all actions eventually have consequences. In addition, Tony differs from Walt in the fact that he actively engages in a wide variety of vices, including adultery, drugs, alcohol, and gambling, while Walt singularly pursues his goal of expanding his drug empire.

According to cultural scholar Ann Larabee in a 2013 article, "The New Television Antihero," which appeared in the *Journal of Popular Culture*, "The new television narratives speak of fragmentation, desperation and violence of tragic, atomized figures whose only meaning lies in narcissistic projects"—perfectly describing both Walter White and Tony Soprano. Curiously, as flawed and sociopathic as both these characters inevitably are, a sizable contingent of the audience of both shows continued to root for them however despicable their actions. In the end, no one character in either series manages to escape the black hole of corruption surrounding both Walt and Tony (with the possible exception of Walt Jr.). In a March 29, 2001, interview with *Rolling Stone*, Gandolfini

Both Walter White and Tony Soprano are flawed antiheroes, but the former undergoes a drastic transformation throughout the series while the latter only makes halfhearted attempts to change his way of life as an Italian-American mobster.

remarked, "I heard David Chase say one time [*The Sopranos* is] about people who lie to themselves, as we all do. Lying to ourselves on a daily basis and the mess it creates." In fact, both series reveal that actions have consequences: Walt loses everything he cared about by the end and dies alone, while Tony (whether he died in the end or not) finds his whole crew pretty much decimated and his power structure shaken to the core.

Skyler White vs. Carmela Soprano

Both Skyler White and Carmela Soprano (Edie Falco) from *The Sopranos* are reluctant accomplices in their husband's criminal enterprises.

However, Carmela and Tony were actual high school sweethearts, so she knew exactly the lifestyle she was getting into when she married the crime boss. Just like Skyler, Carmela is very protective of the couple's two children: Meadow (Jamie Lynn Sigler) and A. J. (Robert Iler). Both Skyler and Carmela separate from their husbands on occasion, but the latter is much more prone to accepting expensive gifts such as jewelry and furs that keep her frequently reconciling with Tony.

Both Skyler and Carmela feel trapped by the illicit lifestyles made possible by the web of criminal activities surrounding them. Skyler finds a release in the form of her brief fling with Ted Beneke, while Carmela tests the waters with her flirtation with Tony's associate, Furio Giunta (Federico Castelluccio). Perhaps because she has tolerated Tony's excesses for so long, Carmela didn't seem to face nearly the same backlash as Skyler for holding Walt back from his dreams of a criminal empire (it also didn't help Skyler's cause that there were so many new social media avenues for angry, misogynistic fans to vent their rage against the character!).

New Mexico vs. New Jersey

Just as Albuquerque, New Mexico, becomes almost like another character in *Breaking Bad*, who could imagine *The Sopranos* without its northern New Jersey locale? In fact, who can forget the title sequence set to "Woke Up This Morning" by UK band Alabama 3 as Tony Soprano emerges from the Lincoln Tunnel, drives through a tollbooth for the New Jersey turnpike, and passes numerous landmarks on the way to his McMansion on a cul-de-sac in the suburbs? Most of the exterior shots in the entire series took advantage of distinctive northern North Jersey locales such as Pizza Land in North Arlington, Vesuvio restaurant (Manolo's in Elizabeth, New Jersey), and the Bada Bing strip club (the now-defunct Satin Dolls in Lodi, New Jersey), as well as the easily identifiable Sopranos residence itself (exteriors of which were filmed at a private residence in North Caldwell, New Jersey).

"Felina" Series Finale vs. "Made in America" Series Finale

A sense of closure pervades the ending of *Breaking Bad*: In the series finale, "Felina," Walt manages to tie up just about all of his loose ends, gets his revenge against Uncle Jack's crew and Lydia, and also pays the ultimate price for his vanity and grandiose schemes. In fact, *Breaking Bad* was always moving toward an inevitable conclusion, and "Felina" in general pays off, providing a sense of closure to the series, and was generally well received by fans and critics alike. However, the series finale of *The Sopranos*, "Made in America," which originally aired on June 10, 2007, was (and still is!) mired in controversy for its infamous cut-to-black ending (leaving the viewer to decide if Tony was "whacked" in the diner or that his life simply goes on). At the time, some viewers even believed that their cable or satellite dish had cut out at the most inopportune time! Those who believed that Tony was dead pointed to a number of scenes that foreshadowed his demise such as in the episode "Soprano Home Movies" when he discusses the possibility of getting whacked with his brother-in-law Bobby Baccalieri (Steve Schirripa): "You probably don't even hear it when it happens, right?" Also, in "Made in America," a suspicious character credited simply as Man in Members Only Jacket (Paolo Colandrea) enters the diner, glances at Tony, and later goes to the restroom (perhaps he is a hitman who has a gun planted there just like in the famous scene in *The Godfather*).

In a June 11, 2007, interview with *The Star-Ledger*, Chase remarked about the series finale, "I have no interest in explaining, defending, reinterpreting, or adding to what is there. No one was trying to be audacious, honest to God. We did what we thought we had to do. No one was trying to blow people's minds, or thinking, 'Wow, this'll piss them off. People get the impression that you're trying to fuck with them and it's not true. You're trying to entertain them . . . Anybody who wants to watch it, it's all there." A positive outcome of the ending was the ongoing analysis of clues exploring every angle of the series in defense of either side of the argument. Well over a decade later, fans are still debating the controversial ending, and that definitely says something about the show's ongoing legacy.

In a May 2, 2013, interview with *Metro UK* regarding the *Breaking Bad* series finale, Gilligan commented, "My writers and I worked very hard on these final eight episodes which the world has yet to see and I can tell you for sure it is an ending—people should expect a real, conclusive ending. I thought that the close of *The Sopranos* was very bold and very intriguing and very creative, but we are not taking *The Sopranos* route I can tell you that much." For the record, "Felina" attracted 10.3 million viewers, while "Made in America" had 11.9 million viewers.

24

Lies on Top of Lies

The *Seinfeld* Connection

Hey, who invited you, anyway? You're a troublemaker!
—*Tim Whatley to Jerry Seinfeld*

Every hardcore *Seinfeld* fan knows that Bryan Cranston portrayed slightly demented dentist Tim Whatley, but does anyone remember Anna Gunn as one of Jerry's girlfriends who George "catches" making out with Jerry's "horse-faced" cousin Jeffrey, Bob Odenkirk as a struggling med student who briefly dates Elaine, Jessica Hecht as one of George's girlfriends who discovers he did not actually read *Breakfast at Tiffany's*, or Larry "Old Joe" Hankin as the actor portraying Kramer in the *Jerry* pilot who may or may not have stolen the raisins?

An enterprising YouTuber named David Elmaleh actually went so far as to liven up the *Seinfeld* series finale (which got mixed reviews to say the least!) by morphing Tim Whatley/Walter White into the plot to make it seem that the vengeful-minded dentist actually sabotaged the private plane flying Jerry, Elaine, George, and Kramer to Paris (with a completely inappropriate laugh track to boot!).

Considered one of the greatest and most influential TV sitcoms of all time, *Seinfeld* was created by Larry David and Jerry Seinfeld and ran for nine seasons on NBC for a total of 180 episodes between 1989 and 1998. Often described as a "show about nothing" for its ability to create humorous situations based on the minutiae of daily life, *Seinfeld* starred Jerry Seinfeld as Jerry Seinfeld, Julia Louis-Dreyfus as Elaine Benes, Michael Richards as Cosmo Kramer, and Jason Alexander as George Costanza.

Besides the *Breaking Bad* cast members highlighted below, other future stars to appear on *Seinfeld* include Michael Chiklis as Jerry's wannabe friend from Long Island in "The Stranded" (November 27, 1991), Teri Hatcher as Jerry's girlfriend in "The Implant" (February 25, 1993), Jeremy Piven auditioning for the part of George in "The Pilot" (May 20, 1993), Jennifer Coolidge as the reluctant masseuse in "The Masseuse" (November 18, 1993), Courteney Cox as Jerry's "wife" in "The Wife" (March 17, 1994), Jon Favreau as Eric the Clown in "The Fire" (May 5, 1994), Patton Oswalt as a video store clerk in "The Couch" (October 27, 1994), Rob Schneider as the partially deaf Bob Grossberg in "The Friar's Club" (March 7, 1996), Brad Garrett as an obsessive mechanic in "The Bottle Deposit" (May 2, 1996), Sarah Silverman as Kramer's girlfriend in "The Money" (January 16, 1997), Christine Taylor as one of Jerry's brief flames in "The Van Buren Boys" (February 6, 1997), Kristin Davis as one of Jerry's soon-to-be-ex-girlfriends in "The Pothole" (February 20, 1997), Marcia Cross as a dermatologist in "The Slicer" (November 13, 1997), and Drake Bell as Kenny in "The Frogger" (August 23, 1998), among many others.

Bryan Cranston as Tim Whatley

Between 1994 and 1997, Bryan Cranston appeared as debauched dentist Tim Whatley in five of the most memorable *Seinfeld* episodes: "The Mom and Pop Store" (Episode 6.08, 1994), "The Label Maker" (Episode 6.12, 1995), "The Jimmy" (Episode 6.19, 1995), "The Yada Yada" (Episode 8.19, 1997), and "The Strike" (Episode 9.10, 1997). At one point, Whatley is referred to as "Dentist to the Stars" by George. Cranston has acknowledged in several interviews that *Seinfeld* fans still shout out "Whatley!" to him on the streets.

Tim Whatley makes his first appearance as Jerry's dentist who Elaine desires to date in "The Mom and Pop Store," which originally aired on November 17, 1994. Meanwhile, George purchases a 1989 Chrysler LeBaron Convertible because he believes the vehicle's former owner was actor Jon Voight of *Midnight Cowboy* and *Deliverance* fame. Meanwhile, Jerry doesn't know if he has been invited to Whatley's annual Thanksgiving party (however, he decides to crash the party because he has a toothache and a lot of dentists will be present). George finds a chewed pencil in the glove compartment of the LeBaron, while Kramer

In addition to Bryan Cranston's memorable performance as slightly demented dentist Tim Whatley, *Seinfeld* featured a number of actors who later appeared in *Breaking Bad*, such as Anna Gunn, Bob Odenkirk, Jessica Hecht, and Larry Hankin.

runs into Voight on the street and gets bitten by him (Voight mistakenly takes Kramer for a crazed fan). George devises one of his typical bizarre schemes to find out if any of the dentists at the party can match the chewed pencil with the bite marks on Kramer's arm. It turns out that the previous owner of the car was actually Dr. John Voight, a periodontist friend of Whatley's. The episode ends with a hilarious homage to *Midnight Cowboy* (1969), the only X-rated film to win a Best Picture Oscar.

In "The Label Maker," which originally aired on January 19, 1995, Jerry gives two Super Bowl tickets to Whatley since he cannot attend due to the

Drakes' wedding. Jerry and Elaine believe that Whatley is a "re-gifter" after he gives Jerry the label maker that Elaine gave him for Christmas. After the Drakes' wedding is cancelled due to the Super Bowl, George suggests that Jerry "de-gift" Tim Whatley the Super Bowl tickets. Newman (Wayne Knight) drops by Jerry's apartment and smugly informs Jerry that Whatley gave him one of the Super Bowl tickets. Elaine goes on a date with Whatley to find out if he really re-gifted the label maker, and he takes Newman's ticket and gives it to Elaine. Failing to seduce Elaine, Whatley gives her ticket back to Jerry. Elaine discovers that the label maker was defective. Elaine and Whatley end up making out. Jerry shows up at the Super Bowl to discover Newman sitting next to him.

In "The Jimmy," which originally aired on March 16, 1995, Kramer visits Whatley's dentist office and gets an extraordinary mouthful of novocaine, so much in fact that he is mistaken for a mentally challenged person (he's also wearing special training shoes recommended to him by Jimmy, portrayed by Anthony Starke, who has the obnoxious habit of speaking of himself in the third person). Kramer gets invited as the special guest for an Able Mentally Challenged Adults (AMCA) banquet featuring famous crooner Mel Tormé ("The Velvet Fog"). Jerry visits the dentist office and notices that Whatley keeps *Penthouse* magazines in his waiting area. Whatley also has initiated a new adults-only policy for the dentist office. During Jerry's second dentist appointment, Whatley even takes a hit of laughing gas before sedating Jerry (an ad-lib by Cranston that he credited to the lighting guy on the set and that reportedly made Jerry Seinfeld crack up on every take). As Jerry wakes up with his shirt mysteriously untucked, he believes through his blurred vision that he actually sees both Whatley and his dental hygienist putting their clothes back on. As the credits role, Kramer reads a letter in *Penthouse* about an anonymous dentist who describes an encounter with his hygienist and one of his patients as Jerry reacts in horror.

In "The Yada Yada," which originally aired on April 24, 1997, Whatley converts to Judaism, just so he can tell Jewish jokes, according to Jerry, who confesses to a priest that he is offended by Whatley's behavior—not as a Jewish person but as a comedian. The priest laughs at one of Tim's jokes that Jerry repeats, but gets offended when Jerry tells a joke about a sadistic dentist. Whatley hears about the joke Jerry told the priest and takes revenge by prolonging an uncomfortable dental procedure during Jerry's next appointment. After hearing Jerry complain about Whatley, Kramer calls him an "anti-dentite." At Mickey's wedding, Mickey's dad (portrayed by Robert Wagner), also a dentist, exclaims to Jerry, "Tim Whatley was one of my students, and if this wasn't my son's wedding day, I'd knock your teeth out, you anti-dentite bastard!"

In "The Strike," which originally aired on December 18, 1997, Jerry, Elaine, and George attend Whatley's Hanukkah party. George gets upset when he later receives a gift of a donation in his name from Whatley. George gets the idea to create a fake charity called "The Human Fund" in order to get out of buying gifts for his coworkers. "The Strike" served as Whatley's final appearance on *Seinfeld* and is also famous for the introduction of the holiday "Festivus" (invented by George's father, Frank Costanza, portrayed by Jerry Stiller) to the lexicon.

Anna Gunn as Amy

In "The Glasses" (Episode 5.03, which originally aired on September 30, 1993), Anna Gunn portrays one of Jerry's girlfriends, Amy, who is mistakenly viewed by George (sans his prescription eyeglasses) kissing Jerry's cousin, Jeffrey, who reportedly has a "horse face." Jerry confronts Amy, but she adamantly denies any infidelity. After George mistakes an onion for an apple, Jerry starts to doubt his friend's "eyewitness" account. When George gets his glasses back, he realizes that what he saw was a mounted policewoman affectionately petting her horse. Meanwhile, Jerry and Amy pick up Paul Simon tickets from Uncle Leo, who states that Jeffrey wanted to apologize to him. Jerry mistakenly believes Jeffrey's apology concerns making out with Amy, but it actually involved not getting better seats to the concert. A disgusted Amy storms out of Jerry's life. By the way, the "Blind Man" in the episode is portrayed by Ron and Clint's father, Rance Howard.

Bob Odenkirk as Ben

In "The Abstinence" (Episode 8.09, which originally aired on November 21, 1996), Bob Odenkirk portrays Ben, a struggling medical student who Elaine starts seeing while he is working on passing his medical boards. Elaine, who still introduces Ben as a doctor, becomes suspicious after he is unable to help a fellow diner experiencing a medical emergency. Meanwhile, George has been forced to abstain from sex due to his girlfriend having a case of mononucleosis, allowing him to get more focused and smarter. Elaine tries to apply George's abstinence technique on her new boyfriend, and it works for him but backfires for her as she gradually becomes dumber. After Ben finally gets his medical license, he promptly dumps Elaine. The episode features a cameo by none other than David Letterman.

Jessica Hecht as Lindsay

The actress who portrayed Gretchen Schwartz in *Breaking Bad*, Jessica Hecht, appeared as George's girlfriend, Lindsay, in two back-to-back episodes in 1994: "The Couch" and "The Gymnast." In "The Couch," which originally aired on October 27, 1994, George joins a book club to impress Lindsay. He struggles reading his first book assignment, the 1958 Truman Capote classic *Breakfast at Tiffany's*, and opts to rent the video of the 1961 film version starring Audrey Hepburn and George Peppard instead. When George discovers all of the copies of *Breakfast at Tiffany's* have been rented at the local video store, he sneaks a peek to see who has the rental copy and concocts an elaborate story in order to watch the movie with the renter and his family. However, George gets kicked out of the apartment before the end of the movie after being generally obnoxious and spilling grape juice all over the couch. When the book club meets up again, George remarks that Holly Golightly hooked up with her neighbor in *Breakfast at Tiffany's*, and Lindsay realizes George never read the book. Look for stand-up comedian and actor Patton Oswalt as the video store clerk.

In "The Gymnast," which originally aired on November 3, 1994, George gets another chance with Lindsay, who finds his stupidity "charming." Lindsay takes George to her mother's house, and she is impressed with him until she catches him biting into a partially eaten chocolate éclair out of the kitchen trash can. George apologizes and gets still another chance with Lindsay. However, he later throws a bad cup of coffee into the street and accidentally splashes a nearby car. Lindsay's

Larry Hankin has turned in a host of memorable performances over the years, such as junkyard owner Old Joe in *Breaking Bad*, Tom Pepper in *Seinfeld*, and Doobie in *Planes, Trains & Automobiles* (1987).

mother witnesses George cleaning the windshield at the driver's behest and is once again convinced he is a bum. George apologizes once again to Lindsay and gets one more chance. George attends a small party hosted by Lindsay's mother and becomes mesmerized by a 3-D painting in the bathroom. A dazed George exits the bathroom without his shirt on, stunning the other guests and effectively terminating his relationship with Lindsay.

Larry Hankin as Tom Pepper

Known as crusty junkyard owner Old Joe in *Breaking Bad*, Larry Hankin appears in "The Pilot," the two-part finale of the fourth season of *Seinfeld* that first aired on May 20, 1993. After Jerry and George get the green light to produce the pilot for their sitcom about nothing, simply titled *Jerry*, they take part in the casting process, where they meet Tom Pepper (Hankin), who is auditioning for the role of Kramer (Hankin had actually auditioned for the role of Kramer when *Seinfeld* began production). George becomes obsessed with the idea that Tom may have stolen a box of raisins during his audition and confronts him several times. Tom gets tired of being accused of stealing the raisins and finally threatens George with violence: "How would you like it if I just pulled your heart out of your chest right now, and shoved it down your throat?" Shortly thereafter, Tom scores the role and is later seen eating the raisins before the taping of the pilot.

Hankin is one of those actors everyone seems to recognize because of his typically brief but memorable appearances in a host of popular films over the years (as well as showing up on *Friends* as Mr. Heckles). For instance, Hankin's film credits include Charley Butts in *Escape from Alcatraz* (1979) opposite Clint Eastwood, Circus Hand in *The Jerk* (1979), Trucker in *The Sure Thing* (1985), Ace in *Running Scared* (1986), Kokolovitch in *Armed and Dangerous* (1986), Doobie in *Planes, Trains & Automobiles* (1987) opposite Steve Martin and John Candy, Landlord in *Pretty Woman* (1990), Officer Balzak in *Home Alone* (1990), and Carl Alphonse in *Billy Madison* (1995), among many others.

Mark Harelik as Milos

In the *Breaking Bad* episode "Kafkaesque" (3.09), Mark Harelik portrays Hank's doctor, who informs Marie that her husband may never fully recover. *Seinfeld* fans will recognize Harelik as Milos, the Eastern European salesman at a tennis pro shop who tries to sell Jerry an expensive racquet and who is secretly a terrible tennis player in "The Comeback" (1997), which originally aired on January 30, 1997. Milos agrees to set Jerry up with an attractive woman at the pro shop in order to keep his secret, but the date turns out to be none other than Milos's own wife, Patty (Ivana Milečević). After Patty loses all respect for Milos, Jerry agrees to let him win in a game of tennis to gain back his respect. However, Milos starts gloating on the tennis court, causing Jerry to get angry and play harder. At one point, Milos swings wildly at the ball and loses his racquet, which lands on Kramer's head.

Nigel Gibbs as Tenant No. 2

If you blink, you will miss Nigel Gibbs as Tenant No. 2 in the *Seinfeld* episode "The Doorman" (1995), which originally aired on February 23, 1995. Jerry offends the doorman at Mr. Pitt's apartment building and then tries to do him a favor by watching the door for him while he goes out to buy beer. When Jerry abandons his post, someone steals the couch from the lobby. The doorman in question is portrayed by comedian Larry Miller. In *Breaking Bad*, Gibbs portrays Detective Tim Roberts of the Albuquerque Police Department and one of Hank's colleagues in "Grilled" (2009), "Open House" (2011), "Shotgun" (2011), and "Hermanos" (2011). Roberts investigates Walt's disappearance in "Grilled," tells Marie the homeowners will not press charges after she is caught stealing in "Open House," visits Hank to see if he can assist in the Gale Boetticher murder investigation in "Shotgun," and is among the investigators interviewing Gus Fring in "Hermanos."

25

Yeah, Totally Kafkaesque

Literary References in *Breaking Bad*

Gliding o'er all, through all, Through Nature, Time, and Space, As a ship on the waters advancing, The voyage of the soul—not life alone, Death, many deaths I'll sing.

—*Walt Whitman, "Gliding O'er All," Leaves of Grass*

W ho would have thought that a prime-time dramatic series on AMC would feature allusions to not only literary giants like Walt "the Bard of Democracy" Whitman and Franz Kafka, but even name one of its episodes after a famous poem, "Ozymandias," by English Romantic poet Percy Bysshe Shelley? It's actually not that surprising since many astute observers have labeled long-form series like *Breaking Bad, Mad Men, The Wire,* and *The Sopranos* as the true novels of the twentieth century. In a June 12, 2011, interview with *The Telegraph,* novelist Salman Rushdie (*The Satanic Verses*) stated, "In the movies the writer is just the servant, the employee . . In television, the 60-minute series *The Wire* and *Mad Men* and so on, the writer is the primary creative artist . . . You have control in the way that you never have in the cinema . . . If you have that, then what you can do with character and story is not at all unlike what you can do in a novel."

Ironically, Hank's discovery of the inscribed copy of Walt Whitman's celebration of the freedom of the individual, *Leaves of Grass,* proves to be Walt's undoing in the end. According to Vince Gilligan in a Q&A that appeared on amc.com,

I like the idea of [Gale Boetticher's] poetic justice from beyond the grave. The writers and I love the idea of revisiting previous moments in the show because we love the idea that all actions have consequences. We know that in our day-to-day lives, but very often in television storytelling characters say things or they do things and a particular episode ends and there's not necessarily much in the way of resonance. On this show, we very much like a character's actions to have repercussions in ways that we identify with in real life. And to that end, we love revisiting these old moments, and Walt Whitman's poetry was something that Gale Boetticher loved. It touched his heart and he wanted to share it with his new friend and mentor Walter White. And unfortunately the sharing of it and Walt keeping this book in hindsight proved to be a bit unwise.

Icarus

At the end of the *Breaking Bad* episode "Hazard Pay" (5.03), Walter White voices to Jesse Pinkman his disgust at the low financial return on their latest batch of meth and the "legacy costs" imposed by Mike Ehrmantraut that were initiated by the late drug kingpin Gus Fring. Walt tells Jesse he has been thinking of Victor's gruesome murder by Gus Fring using a box cutter: "All this time I was sure that Gus did what he did to send me a message. Maybe there's another reason . . . Victor trying to cook that batch on his own? Taking liberties that weren't his to take? Maybe he flew too close to the sun, got his throat cut."

Why does Walt bring up Victor's death at this point? Perhaps he is pondering out loud that Jesse needs to go next because his meth-cooking skills are just as good as Walt's, or maybe he's thinking that Mike Ehrmantraut needs to be eliminated because of his insistence on paying the exorbitant legacy costs. Walt has stated that he is in the "empire business," and the issue of the legacy costs surely hampers that dream by seriously cutting into the profits of the entire meth-producing operation. In the end, however, Walt fails to see that in his own excessive pride he has himself flown "too close to the sun," and his hubris will indeed come back to haunt him.

In highlighting that Victor might have flown "too close to the sun," Walt invokes the legend of Icarus in Greek mythology. Icarus and his father Daedalus, the master craftsman who created the Labyrinth, attempt to escape Crete (where they were imprisoned by King Minos) by use of wings made of wax and feathers. However, Icarus ignores his father's warning not to fly too close to the Sun or the sea. His wings melt and he falls into the sea and drowns—one of the most notable instances of hubris in Greek mythology.

The legend of Icarus has been captured by artists over the centuries with perhaps the most famous example being *Landscape with the Fall of Icarus* (ca. 1558). What is unusual about the painting is that the horrific fall is hardly noticed by anyone—everyone in the vicinity of the tragedy simply continues to go about their own business. Long attributed to Pieter Bruegel the Elder, the painting, which hangs in the Royal Museums of Fine Arts of Belgium in Brussels, is now thought to be a good early copy of Bruegel's lost original by an unknown artist. *Landscape with the Fall of Icarus* has been the subject of several classic poems, including W. H. Auden's "Musée des Beaux-Arts" (1939), William Carlos Williams's "Landscape with the Fall of Icarus" (1960), and Anne Sexton's "To a Friend Whose Work Has Come to Triumph" (1960).

In addition, *Landscape with the Fall of Icarus* is shown among a book of paintings in the 1976 cult film *The Man Who Fell to Earth*, which was directed by Nicolas Roeg (*Performance*) and based on a 1963 science fiction novel of the same name by Walter Tevis. Interestingly, the first section of the novel is titled "Icarus Descending." In the offbeat, surreal, and ultimately bleak film version, rock star David Bowie portrays Thomas Jerome Newton, an alien from a doomed, water-starved planet. Newton rapidly loses sight of his original mission of building a spaceship and shipping back water to his planet, and gradually gets enveloped in a purple haze of sex, booze, and endless hours of television (at one point he even remarks, "the strange thing about television is that it doesn't tell you anything"). Candy Clark (*American Graffiti*) portrays Mary-Lou, a hotel maid who befriends Newton. The cast of *The Man Who Fell to Earth* also includes Buck Henry as patent attorney Oliver Farnsworth and Rip Torn as college professor Nathan Bryce. As a side note, much of *The Man Who Fell to Earth* was filmed in New Mexico, with several scenes shot in Albuquerque.

"Kafkaesque"

In the *Breaking Bad* episode "Kafkaesque" (3.09), Jesse attends a rehab meeting and describes his job to the other attendees as a "corporate laundry" (leaving out several pertinent details of course!): "It's, like rigid. All kinds of red tape. My boss is a dick. The owner, super dick. I'm not worthy to meet him, but I guess everybody's scared of the dude. The place is full of dead-eyed douchebags, the hours suck and nobody knows what's going on." The group leader states, "Sounds kind of Kafkaesque," with Jesse replying, "Yeah. Totally Kafkaesque." It's obvious that Jesse has no idea what "Kafkaesque" means, nor cares in the slightest for that matter. Later, Jesse is hanging out with Skinny Pete and Badger. The discussion quickly moves to the crushed RV, and Jesse comments that "No one misses it more than me. Free to cook anytime, anywhere. No quotas, no one to answer to. What's the point of being an outlaw when you got responsibilities? . . . I gotta pay taxes? What's up with that? That's messed up. That's Kafkaesque."

According to Franz Kafka biographer Frederick R. Karl in a December 29, 1991, interview with *The New York Times*, "What's Kafkaesque . . . is when you enter a surreal world in which all your control patterns, all your plans, the whole way in which you have configured your own behavior, begins to fall to pieces, when you find yourself against a force that does not lend itself to the way you perceive the world." Certainly many of the bizarre aspects of *Breaking Bad* could be labeled Kafkaesque according to this definition.

One of the most influential writers of the twentieth century, Franz Kafka was born on July 3, 1883, in Prague, Bohemia, and grew up in a middle-class Jewish family with a domineering father. After he received a law degree in 1906, Kafka was employed at the Worker's Accident Insurance Institute, which must have been a dreary bureaucracy if in any way reflected by some of his better-known writings. Kafka's major works include short stories such as "In the Penal Colony" (1914), which details the use of an elaborate torture and execution device; "The Metamorphosis" (1915), in which a man turns into an insect (curiously, the *Breaking Bad* episode following "Kafkaesque" is titled simply "Fly"); and "A Hunger Artist" (1922), which portrays a performance artist who employs all of his efforts into public fasting in a cage; as well as the post-humous novels *The Trial* (1925), *The Castle* (1926), and *Amerika* (1927). In *The Trial*, Kafka wrote, "It is often safer to be in chains than to be free." Kafka, who suffered from tuberculosis, spent much of his time after 1917

In episode 3.9, Jesse hears the term "Kafkaesque" (which is also the episode's title) and later repeats the term to his drug-addled buddies without even knowing that it relates to the famous twentieth-century novelist who authored *The Trial*.   *Wikimedia Commons*

in various sanatoriums and health resorts. He died from tuberculosis at the age of forty on June 3, 1924, virtually unknown since none of his novels were printed during his lifetime. Although Kafka instructed that all his manuscripts be destroyed on his death, his friend Max Brod fortunately paid no heed to the request. Kafka was buried in the New Jewish Cemetery in Prague-Zizhov.

"Ozymandias"

By the end of the appropriately titled *Breaking Bad* episode, "Ozymandias" (5.14) Walter White's dream of empire has been reduced to rubble and his family has been ripped apart, leaving him with nothing (except a single barrel of money and a very shaky destiny over which he has totally lost control). The episode's title derives from a famous sonnet written by English Romantic poet Percy Bysshe Shelley (1792–1822) that was first published in the January 11, 1818, issue of *The Examiner* in London. The following year, "Ozymandias" was published in Shelley's collection *Rosalind and Helen, A Modern Eclogue; with Other Poems*.

The poem highlights the story of a traveler in the desert who comes across the ruins of an ancient monument dedicated to "Ozymandias, king of kings." All of the once mighty Ozymandias's accomplishments have fallen into total ruin, and there is no sign left of the great civilization he once ruled ("Nothing beside remains"). Shelley's poem was inspired by a description of the decaying statue of a thirteenth-century B.C. Egyptian Pharaoh called Ozymandias (aka Ramesses II) by Greek historian Diodorus Siculus. During a 2013 trailer to promote the final episodes of the fifth season of *Breaking Bad*, Bryan Cranston performed a dramatic reading of "Ozymandias" in its entirety (the video can be viewed on YouTube).

Shelley was among the famous English Romantic poets of the late eighteenth and early nineteenth centuries who rebelled against the intellectualism of the Enlightenment—cultivating individualism and favoring more natural, emotional, and personal artistic themes. Other prominent English Romantic poets included William Blake (*The Marriage of Heaven and Hell*), William Wordsworth (*The Prelude*), Samuel Taylor Coleridge (*The Rime of the Ancient Mariner*), Lord Byron (*Don Juan*), and John Keats ("Ode on a Grecian Urn").

Shelley, who drowned while sailing off the Italian coast, was cremated on the beach near Viareggio, Italy, and his ashes were sent to the Cimitero Accattolico in Rome for burial. His epitaph reads "Cor Cordium" ("Heart of Hearts"), along with several lines from "Ariel's Song," which appeared in William Shakespeare's play *The Tempest*: "Nothing of him that doth fade / But doth suffer a sea-change / Into something real and strange." According to legend, Shelley's heart survived cremation and was given to his widow, Mary (best known for her Gothic novel *Frankenstein*). It was reportedly buried with the couple's child, Sir Percy Florence Shelley, in 1889.

Shakespeare

In his 1949 essay on the modern theater, "Tragedy and the Common Man," playwright Arthur Miller (*Death of a Salesman*) writes, "I believe that the common man is as apt a subject for tragedy in its highest sense as kings were . . . if the exaltation of tragic action were truly a property of the high-bred character alone, it is inconceivable that the mass of mankind should cherish tragedy above all other forms, let alone be capable of understanding it." In *Breaking Bad*, Walt starts out as an ordinary Joe—but by taking his fate in his own hands (for good and bad) he becomes somewhat of a tragic hero along the same lines as William Shakespeare's Hamlet, Othello, and especially Macbeth. In fact, *Breaking Bad* was broken into five seasons, mirroring the five-act structure of Shakespeare's plays. Just as Macbeth becomes totally consumed by ambition, Walter White becomes obsessed with building an empire at all costs. In the *Breaking Bad* episode "Rabid Dog" (5.12), Skyler even takes on the role of Lady Macbeth, urging Walt to kill Jesse Pinkman. When Walt exclaims that Jesse isn't just some "rabid dog," Skyler replies, "We've come this far. For us. What's one more?"

Unlike Shakespearean tragic heroes, however, Walt is able to tie up all of his loose ends and get his revenge in the series finale, "Felina," before succumbing to his inevitable fate. *Breaking Bad* is also full of Shakespearean-style villains, most notably Gus Fring. In a September 19, 2011, *Salon* article, TV critic Matt Zoller Seitz remarked, "Giancarlo Esposito, with his haunted eyes and droopy-faced, Chuck Jones reactions, gives Gus an almost Shakespearean richness. I could picture this character sitting across a table from Macbeth or Shylock and having plenty to talk about."

The Tragedy of Macbeth is believed to have been first performed in 1606. Shakespeare's shortest tragedy, *Macbeth* was first published in *Mr. William Shakespeare's Comedies, Histories, & Tragedies* (aka "First Folio") of 1623. In the superstitious world of the theater, there is a strong belief that the play is cursed and therefore it is not wise to name the title aloud but instead simply refer to it as "the Scottish Play." Echoing the poem "Ozymandias," the famous line from Macbeth highlights the futility of human ambitions: "Life's but a walking shadow, a poor player / That struts and frets his hour upon the stage / And then is heard no more. It is a tale / Told by an idiot, full of sound and fury / Signifying nothing."

Walt Whitman

"I sound my barbaric yawp over the roofs of the world." The specter of acclaimed American poet Walt Whitman, known as the "Bard of Democracy," who celebrated American individualism in his masterpiece, *Leaves of Grass*, permeates *Breaking Bad*. Not only does Walter White share Whitman's initials, he becomes an avid reader of his poetry. In the *Breaking Bad* episode "Sunset" (3.06), Walt's new lab assistant, Gale Boetticher, shares his mentor's enthusiasm for Whitman and even recites the poem "When I Heard the Learn'd Astronomer" to Walt from memory upon their first meeting in the superlab. According to Vince Gilligan in *Breaking Bad: The Official Book*, "It's a poem in which the poet states his appreciation of the world more than the dry scientific explanation, and I knew it was the perfect poem for that particular moment of the story." Both Walt and Gale agree that chemistry is "magic." Ironically, Gale considers Walt a mentor and a path to discovering "freedom" through chemistry, while Walt actually sees Gale as a threat to his freedom (if Gale manages to absorb Walt's meth-cooking knowledge, then Walt is expendable to Gus Fring).

Tragically, Walt distorts Whitman's grandiose vision by believing that the creation of an empire will lead to freedom and a better life for him and his family, and he eventually discovers it does the exact opposite. Shortly after Gale's murder, in the episode "Bullet Points" (4.04),

Ironically, Hank's discovery of the inscribed copy of Walt Whitman's celebration of the freedom of the individual, *Leaves of Grass*, proves to be Walt's undoing in the end.

George C. Cox/Library of Congress/Wikimedia Commons

Hank Schrader reads through Gale's lab notebook and notices the line, "To W. W. My star, my perfect silence." Hank turns to Walter and asks rhetorically, "W. W. I mean, who do you figure that is, y'know? Woodrow Wilson? Willy Wonka? ... Walter White?" Walt jokingly replies, "Heh. You got me." Walt quickly attributes "W. W." to Walt Whitman, thus briefly throwing Hank off the trail once again.

Ironically, it is inevitably Whitman (and Gale reaching out from beyond the grave!) who leads Hank to discover Walt's identity as Heisenberg. In the episode "Gliding Over All" (5.08), whose title is actually named after a famous Whitman poem, Hank sits on the toilet during a barbecue at the White household, leafing through Walt's copy of *Leaves of Grass* when he stumbles upon Gale's inscription: "To my other favorite W.W. It's an honor working with you. Fondly G.B." Walt's hubris has finally made him careless enough to display a major piece of evidence in plain sight.

Known for his spirited celebration of individualism and nature, Walter "Walt" Whitman was born on Long Island, New York, on May 31, 1819. *Leaves of Grass* was first published with just twelve poems in 1855 at Whitman's own expense, but the poet continually revised and enlarged his masterpiece right up to his death. According to critic Mark Van Doren, "Whatever the cause, Whitman changed between 1848 and 1855 from a commonplace man to one of the most remarkable men we know: to be more precise, he changed into a person who understood how to talk as if he were Adam reborn." Upon reading *Leaves of Grass*, author Ralph Waldo Emerson sent Whitman a letter on July 31, 1855, exclaiming, "I find [*Leaves of Grass*] the most extraordinary piece of wit and wisdom that America has yet contributed."

However, *Leaves of Grass* had its fair share of critics, such as the *Boston Intelligencer*, which declared the book a "heterogeneous mess of bombast, egotism, vulgarity, and nonsense. The author should be kicked from all decent society as below the level of a brute—it seems he must be some escaped lunatic, raving in pitiable delirium." In 1882, *Leaves of Grass* was banned in Boston after Boston district attorney Oliver Stevens, who claimed that it was "obscene literature," demanded that some of the poems be excised in the new edition. Fortunately, Whitman refused.

Whitman died on March 26, 1892, in Camden, New Jersey, at the age of seventy-two. He is buried in Harleigh Cemetery in an impressive granite mausoleum that he commissioned himself. Adjacent to the mausoleum lies a stone plaque inscribed with a famous excerpt from Whitman's "Song of Myself" from *Leaves of Grass*: "I bequeath myself to the dirt to grow from the grass I love, If you want me again look for me under your bootsoles."

26

Nothing but Chemistry Here

Scientific Allusions and Accuracy

> My God, the universe is random; it's not inevitable, it's simple chaos. It's sub-atomic particles and endless pings, collision—that's what science teaches us.
>
> —*Walter White*

It definitely seems preposterous—a bland high school chemistry teacher with a very distinguished science background transforming into a meth cook and drug kingpin? However, *Breaking Bad* makes it all seem believable by starting with its attention to detail and a consistently accurate depiction of the science itself throughout the entire series. *Breaking Bad* even employed a scientific advisor, University of Oklahoma chemistry professor Donna J. Nelson, to bolster the show's scientific accuracy. According to *Breaking Bad* series creator Vince Gilligan in a September 19, 2011, NPR interview, "[Because] Walter White was talking to his students, I was able to dumb down certain moments of description and dialogue in the early episodes which held me until we had some help from some honest-to-god chemists. We have a [chemist] named Dr. Donna Nelson at the University of Oklahoma who is very helpful to us and vets our scripts to make sure our chemistry dialogue is accurate and up to date. We also have a chemist with a Drug Enforcement Association based out of Dallas who has just been hugely helpful to us."

Nelson, who specializes in organic chemistry, served as the 2016 president of the American Chemical Society. She even filmed a cameo on *Breaking Bad* as a Casa Tranquila nursing home attendant, but unfortunately the scene was cut. In a September 25, 2013, *io9* interview, Nelson remarked, "To us who are educated in science, whenever we see science presented inaccurately [in previous TV shows], it's like fingers on a blackboard . . . It just drives us crazy, and we can't stay immersed in the show . . . It's great to have a hit show . . . a hit Hollywood show that covers chemistry at this level." Interestingly, Gilligan has admitted that he never even took a high chemistry course and that he only has a "layman's love" for science from reading *Popular Science* magazines.

Blue Meth

In the *Breaking Bad* episode "A-No-Rough-Stuff-Type-Deal" (1.07), Tuco Salamanca examines Walt and Jesse's latest batch of meth and asks, "What is this? This is blue." Walt replies, "We used a different chemical process, but it is every bit as pure." Jesse adds, "It may be blue, but it's the bomb." After Tuco samples the product, he exclaims, "Tight! Tight, tight, yeah! Oh, blue, yellow pink. Whatever, man. Just keep bringing me that." Indeed, Walt's signature meth is 99.1 percent pure and goes by several street names, including "Blue Sky," "Big Blue, "Blue Magic," or simply "Blue." Walt's post-Jesse lab assistant Gale Boetticher was the only cook who could even come relatively close to Walt's purity percentage, but only after studying under the master cook himself.

One of the keys to achieving the purity of Walt and Jesse's meth derived from Walt's choice to steal a large drum of methylamine from the outset of the meth-cooking operation instead of going the usual route of acquiring pseudoephedrine (they later even resort to robbing a train to ensure that the methylamine keeps flowing). Walt tells Jesse, "We're not going to need pseudoephedrine. We're going to make Phenylacetone in a tube furnace, then we're going to use reductive amination to yield methamphetamine." Jesse exclaims, "So you do have a plan! Yeah Mr. White! Yeah science!" When Hank reviews the surveillance video of Walt and Jesse's methylamine heist, he exclaims, "P2P—they're cooking old school biker meth." Later, the purity of Walt's meth is enhanced even further by utilizing the state-of-the-art equipment in Gus Fring's underground superlab.

However, in reality, even the purest meth would not appear blue in color but as colorless or white crystals. However, blue methamphetamine does exist in the real world, usually because it is tinted with a dye and is sometimes referred to as "smurf dope," but it is not highly pure. During the flashback in the episode "Box Cutter" (4.01) when Gale is setting up the equipment in the superlab, he informs Gus, "I cannot as of yet account for the blue color," although he guarantees his boss that a sample of Walt's meth was 99 percent pure and "maybe even a touch beyond that." Jesse is later able to cook a meth that is 96.2 percent pure for the Mexican cartel, while Todd's meth is only 76 percent pure. By the end of the series, with Walter, Gale, and Victor all dead, Jesse is the only living person left who knows how to cook the signature blue meth at a high purity level (whether he ever does hit the lab again, we will never know!).

Fulminated Mercury

In the *Breaking Bad* episode "Crazy Handful of Nothin'" (1.06), Walt sneaks a bag of mercury fulminate disguised as meth into Tuco Salamanca's hideout and causes a significant explosion. Tuco reacts, "Are you fucking nuts?" He then asks, "Hey, what is that shit?" Walt replies, "Fulminated mercury. A little tweak of chemistry." Ironically, the psychopathic Tuco admires Walt because he has "balls" and decides to work with him, adding, "That crystal your partner brought me, it sold faster than $10 ass in T.J."

Highly explosive, mercury fulminate, or $Hg(CNO)_2$, was first discovered by British chemist Edward Charles Howard (1776–1816) in 1800. In *Breaking Bad*, Walt first demonstrates the explosive effect of fulminated mercury in his high school chemistry class (a demonstration that would *never* be done in real life!). In *Breaking Bad: The Official Book*, Vince Gilligan states that he was relieved to discover that mercury fulminate "kinda sorta" looked like crystal meth. However, the 2013 *Mythbusters: Breaking Bad Special* debunked the effect using a fifty-gram piece of fulminated mercury that failed to explode. Once the *Mythbusters* crew fitted the fulminated mercury with a blasting cap, it did explode but nowhere near like the explosion created by Walt.

Hydrofluoric Acid

In the *Breaking Bad* episode "Cat's in the Bag . . ." (1.02), Jesse's attempt to dispose of Emilio's body using hydrofluoric acid in the upstairs bathtub goes horribly wrong (Walt had warned him to pour the acid into a plastic container). The hydrofluoric acid ends up eating its way through the tub and floor, depositing a colossal mess in the first-floor hallway of Jesse's house. After the ceiling caves in, Walt remarks to Jesse sarcastically, "I'm sorry, what were you asking me? Oh, yes, that stupid plastic container I asked you to buy. You see, hydrofluoric acid won't eat through plastic . . . it will however dissolve metal, rock, glass, ceramic . . . so there's that."

Walt and Jesse later dispose of several corpses using hydrofluoric acid such as Krazy-8, Victor, one of Gus's unnamed henchman killed by a sniper, Drew Sharp, and Mike Ehrmantraut. In regard to Victor, Mike asks, "I've never used this stuff. Are you sure it will do the job?" A world-weary Jesse replies, "Trust us."

Composed of hydrogen fluoride in water, hydrofluoric acid (HF) is extremely corrosive. However, the 2013 *Mythbusters: Breaking Bad Special* also debunked the effects of hydrofluoric acid in the bathtub. The *Mythbusters* crew tested the potency of HF using an entire pig carcass in six gallons of acid (Jesse had only used two gallons). Although the pig carcass disappeared, the bathtub and floor beneath remained intact.

Werner Heisenberg

Walt first uses his alter ego, Heisenberg, when he confronts Tuco Salamanca in his hideout in the *Breaking Bad* episode "A No-Rough-Stuff-Type-Deal" (1.07). The name Heisenberg refers to Werner Karl Heisenberg, an acclaimed German theoretical physicist who was a key figure in the development of quantum mechanics and considered one of the important physicists of the twentieth century. Born on December 5, 1901, in Würzburg, Heisenberg studied physics at the University of Munich. In 1926, he served as Lecturer in Theoretical Physics at the University of Copenhagen under legendary Danish physicist Niels Bohr (1885–1962).

The following year, Heisenberg was appointed Professor of Theoretical Physics at the University of Leipzig.

Heisenberg's name will always be associated with his theory of quantum mechanics, published in 1925, when he was only twenty-three years old. Heisenberg's "Uncertainty Principle" states that "The more precise the measurement of position, the more imprecise the measurement of momentum, and vice versa." Heisenberg was awarded the Nobel Prize for Physics for 1932—"for the creation of quantum mechanics, the application of which has, inter alia, led to the discovery of the allotropic forms of hydrogen."

During World War II, Heisenberg was appointed Professor of Physics and Director of the Kaiser Wilhelm Institute of Physics at the University of Berlin. He served as a principal scientist in the Nazi German nuclear weapon project. At the end of the war, Heisenberg was briefly taken prisoner by American troops and sent to England. He soon was allowed to return to Germany, where he helped reorganize the Institute for Physics at Göttingen (later renamed the Max Planck Institute for Physics).

The Fifth Solvay International Conference on Electrons and Photons featured the world's most notable physicists, including Albert Einstein, Marie Curie, Niels Bohr, Max Born, and Werner Heisenberg (top row, third from the right). *Benjamin Couprie/Institut International de Physique de Solvay/Wikimedia Commons*

Heisenberg was also a talented pianist who enjoyed playing classical music. He and his wife Elisabeth Schumacher had seven children. On February 1, 1976, Heisenberg died of cancer of the kidneys and gall bladder at the age of seventy-four. Believe it or not, Heisenberg was memorialized by Doctor Manhattan in the comic book *Watchmen* (1987): "We gaze continually at the world and it grows dull in our perceptions. Yet seen from another's vantage point, as if new, it may still take our breath away. Come . . . dry your eyes, for you are life, rarer than a quark and unpredictable beyond the dreams of Heisenberg."

Antoine Lavoisier

In the *Breaking Bad* episode "Say My Name" (5.07), Walt begins teaching his new lab assistant Todd Alquist how to cook meth. He tells the young upstart, "Look, Todd, I don't need you to be Antoine Lavoisier. Uh, what I do need is your full effort and attention. Listen and apply yourself. If you do that, we just might have a fighting chance here, okay." An influential French chemist, Antoine-Laurent Lavoisier (1743–1794) is widely considered the "father of modern chemistry." In 1768, he was elected to France's elite Academy of Sciences at the tender age of twenty-five. A central figure in the eighteenth-century Chemical Revolution, Lavoisier was most noted for his discovery of the role oxygen played in combustion. At the height of the French Revolution, Lavoisier was charged with tax fraud and guillotined on May 8, 1794. Noted Italian mathematician and astronomer Joseph-Louis Lagrange remarked of Lavoisier's death, "It took them only an instant to cut off that head, and a hundred years may not produce another like it."

Lily of the Valley

A poisonous flowering plant found in temperate areas of the Northern Hemisphere, lily of the valley (*Convallaria majalis*) was used by Walt to poison Andrea's young son, Brock. His goal was to get Jesse to believe that Gus Fring had poisoned him and thereby enlist his help in eliminating

LAVOISIER.

While teaching Todd the ropes as his new meth assistant, Walt drops the name of influential French chemist, Antoine-Laurent Lavoisier (1743–1794), who is widely considered "the father of modern chemistry".

Line engraving by Nargeot after J. Boilly/Wikimedia Commons

the drug kingpin. However, in the last scene of the *Breaking Bad* episode "Face Off" (4.13), a lily of the valley plant can be seen in Walt's backyard near his pool. The poisoning of Brock reveals the pure evil of Walt's methods as he pursues the consolidation of his drug empire (although many fans inexplicably continued to rally in support of Walt and justify his actions).

Makeshift Battery

In the *Breaking Bad* episode "4 Days Out" (2.09), Walt and Jesse are stranded in the desert after the RV's battery dies out during a lengthy meth cook. Jesse claims it wasn't his fault since "the buzzer didn't buzz." Walt replies sarcastically, "I should have known to say 'Jesse, don't leave the keys in the ignition the entire two days!" Jesse urges Walt to "think of something scientific . . . How about you pick some of these chemicals and mix up some rocket fuel? That way you could just send up a signal flare. Or you make some kind of robot to get us help, or a homing device, or build a new battery . . . What if we just take some stuff off of the RV and build it into something completely different? You know, like a . . . dune buggy." Without food or water, the duo come close to total despair until Jesse eventually inspires Walt to build a makeshift battery using found materials such as screws, coins, washers, nuts and bolts, brake pads, copper wire, and a sponge soaked in potassium hydroxide.

Phosphine Gas

In the "Pilot" episode (1.01) of *Breaking Bad*, Walt traps the two low-level drug dealers, Emilio and Krazy-8, in the RV with phosphine gas, a colorless, flammable, toxic gas. A panicked Emilio tries to shoot his way out, leaving five permanent bullet holes in the RV's door. Walt later explains to Jesse that "red phosphorus in the presence of moisture and accelerated by heat yields phosphorus hydride. Phosphine gas." To their horror, Walt and Jesse discover that Krazy-8 has survived the phosphine gas attack. As a side note, one of Antoine Lavoisier's students, Philippe Gengembre (1764–1838), first obtained phosphine in 1783.

Ricin

Highly toxic, ricin is used as an ongoing plot device in Seasons Two, Four, and Five of *Breaking Bad*. A naturally occurring protein derived from the beans of the castor oil plant, ricin (*Ricinus communis*) is highly poisonous if inhaled or injected, but somewhat less so when ingested. Ricin was famously used by the KGB to assassinate Bulgarian defector Georgi Markov in 1978 (a modified umbrella was used to inject a tiny pellet dosed with ricin into his bloodstream).

Walt initially creates the ricin in Season Two to use as a way to eliminate Tuco Salamanca, but the plan falls through (the first time Tuco refuses to snort the ricin-tainted meth because Jesse says it's mixed with his signature chile powder and the second time because his Uncle Hector prevents him from eating a ricin-laced burrito). In Season Four, Walt tries to get Jesse to poison Gus Fring with the ricin (he conceals it within a cigarette), but Jesse is unsuccessful. When Andrea's son, Brock, gets severely ill, Jesse discovers the ricin cigarette missing and suspects that Walt poisoned him. Walt manages to convince Jesse that it was actually Gus who poisoned Brock (although we later find out it was indeed Walt using the poisonous lily of the valley plant instead).

In Season Five, Huell Babineaux lifts the ricin cigarette off of Jesse, and Walt hides the capsule behind an electrical outlet in his bedroom. Walt then hides a fake capsule in a cigarette and plants it in Jesse's Roomba. In "Confessions" (5.11), Jesse is waiting to get picked up by the "relocator" when he realizes that Walt had Saul get Huell to lift the ricin cigarette. He confronts Saul, who eventually confesses. In the series finale, "Felina" (5.16), Walt retrieves the ricin from his abandoned house and slips it into Lydia's tea at the coffee shop. Therefore, Lydia becomes the only victim of the ricin in the entire series (although she hasn't died yet, she has developed the severe flu-like symptoms associated with ricin poisoning).

Gerhard Schrader

Hank and Marie's last name, Schrader, alludes to German chemist Gerhard Schrader (1903–90), who accidentally discovered the first nerve gas in 1936 while working on an insecticide. He is sometimes referred to somewhat dubiously as the "father of the nerve agents." The Nazis eventually stockpiled twelve thousand tons of the nerve agent known as tabun.

The production and/or stockpiling of tabun was finally banned by the 1993 Chemical Weapons Convention.

Thermite

In the *Breaking Bad* episode "A No-Rough-Type-Stuff Deal" (1.07), Walt and Jesse break into a chemical warehouse somewhat clumsily in order to steal a barrel of methylamine. They manage to open the door to the warehouse with a thermite charge using Etch A Sketch drawing toys (which contain aluminum powder). A pyrotechnic composition of metal powder and metal oxide, thermite reacts when ignited by heat.

27

Let Me Clue You In

Popular *Breaking Bad* Fan Theories

> One thing seems clear. [Walt] never made it out of that car in the snow, surrounded by police. That's where he died, his final prayer unanswered.
> —*Tweet from Norm MacDonald, October 2, 2013*

One of the most interesting aspects of social media related to *Breaking Bad* has been the nonstop discussion of fan theories related to the series, most of which were bandied back and forth on great sites such as Reddit (which still offers a quite active *Breaking Bad* discussion page at reddit.com/r/breakingbad that is highly recommended). Here are some of the best, worst, and most bizarre fan theories related to *Breaking Bad*, some of which were even validated or completely struck down by series creator Vince Gilligan, as well as members of the cast:

Breaking Bad Is a Prequel to *The Walking Dead*

A sister show of *Breaking Bad* on AMC, the immensely popular zombie apocalypse drama *The Walking Dead* featured a scene where blue meth appears in the stash bag of Merle Dixon (Michael Rooker). Later, Daryl Dixon (Norman Reedus) discusses his brother's former drug dealer, who sounds somewhat suspiciously like Jesse Pinkman:

> This janky little white guy. A tweaker. One day we were over at his house watching TV. Wasn't even noon yet and we were all wasted. Merle was high. We were watching this show and Merle was talking all this dumb stuff about it. And he wouldn't let up. Merle never could. Turns out it was the tweaker's kids' favorite show. And he never sees his kids, so he felt guilty about it

or something. So he punches Merle in the face. So I started hitting the tweaker, like hard. As hard as I can. Then he pulls a gun, sticks it right here. He says "I'm gonna kill you, bitch." So Merle pulls his gun on him. Everyone's yelling. I'm yelling. I thought I was dead. Over a dumb cartoon about a talking dog."

However, the "tweaker" in question seems way too irrational to be Jesse (and besides, he doesn't have any kids that we know of).

The intriguing blue meth Easter egg led fans to think of a scenario where the blue meth in *Breaking Bad* somehow led to the zombie outbreak in *The Walking Dead* (sort of like the scenario from the little-known but eminently entertaining 1978 movie *Blue Sunshine*). Asked in a Q&A on amc.com about how Jesse Pinkman would fare in the world of *The Walking Dead*, Aaron Paul remarked, "Jesse would probably die of a heart attack in a zombie apocalypse. I think he would go out guns blazing, from all the practice he's had in video games. Norman's character, Daryl, would be a survivor on *Breaking Bad*. He'd be a person to reckon with."

A sister show of *Breaking Bad* on AMC, the immensely popular zombie apocalypse drama *The Walking Dead*, actually featured a scene where blue meth appears in the stash bag of Merle Dixon.

Gale Boetticher Was a Sex Offender

Based on the simple fact that Hank uncovers a karaoke video of Gale singing "Major Tom" with Thai subtitles in the pile of evidence related to the lab assistant's death, some fans came up with the theory that Gale was actually a sex offender who was somehow involved in Bangkok's seedy sex tourism industry. Furthermore, how come a talented chemist like Gale couldn't land a legitimate career if he wasn't on some sort of sex offender registry in the United States?

Gus and Max Were Much Closer Than Business Partners

A flashback in *Breaking Bad* reveals Gus Fring's business partner Max Arciniega getting murdered by none other than Hector Salamanca. Many fans have speculated that Gus and Max were lovers as well as business partners, especially since Gus holds such a long-standing personal grudge against the Mexican cartel. In addition, Gus lives alone and there is no evidence that he has any significant romantic relationships with members of either sex during his entire appearance in the series.

Jesse Will End Up "Breaking Good"

When viewers first meet Jesse Pinkman, he is a small-time drug dealer estranged from his family. Walt is a respectable member of society who gradually descends into a ruthless drug kingpin. Interestingly, Jesse matures over time and becomes a somewhat surprising voice of morality as the series progresses. Some fans believe that the ecstatic Jesse, who manages to escape the compound during the series finale with the help of Walt, will change his ways for good (in a reverse transformation of Walt)—and perhaps go to college and become a respected high school chemistry teacher? How ironic would that be?

Skyler's Smoking Habit Causes Walt's Cancer

Despite being pregnant, Skyler continues smoking cigarettes to relieve stress. Therefore, the fan theory is that Skyler's cigarette smoking habit, however discreet, actually caused Walt's lung cancer, and she is ultimately to blame for his descending into a life of crime.

Ted Is Walt Jr.'s Real Father

Skyler and Ted Beneke engage in a brief affair during the show, but there are also allusions to a previous incident that occurred between the couple at a company Christmas party some years before. In fact, Marie refers to Ted as "Mr. Grabby Hands." Some fans have speculated that Skyler and Ted hooked up years before and that Ted is actually Walt Jr.'s real father—come on, the kid looks nothing like Walt! In addition, at one point Ted asks Skyler about Walt Jr. and she replies that he's "handsome." Ted chuckles, "good genes."

Walt Adopts the Character Traits of His Victims

A widespread theory that actually seems to have merit is that Walt adopts certain characteristics of the adversaries that he eliminates during his quest for power. For instance, an imprisoned Krazy-8 cuts the crust off his sandwiches, and later Walt can be seen doing the exact same thing when he's making a sandwich. In addition, Mike can be seen ordering Scotch on the rocks, which later becomes Walt's drink. Gus drives a Volvo, which is the same model of car Walt can be seen driving on his way back from New Hampshire.

Walt Hallucinates the Series Finale

One popular theory pushed by none other than stand up comedian, actor, and *Breaking Bad* superfan Norm MacDonald along with others is

One popular fan theory pushed by stand-up comedian, actor, and *Breaking Bad* superfan Norm MacDonald along with others is that Walt actually freezes to death in his car in New Hampshire and hallucinates the entire series finale.

that Walt freezes to death in his car in New Hampshire at the end of the episode "Granite State" (5.15) and actually hallucinates the entire series finale, "Felina" (5.16). In fact, all of Walt's loose ends are tied up a little bit tidily, and he easily travels across the country from New Hampshire to New Mexico although he is the subject of a national manhunt. However, Vince Gilligan almost immediately refuted the theory since Walt would have hallucinated events that he would haven't even known about (such as Jesse being held as a meth-cooking slave).

Walt Lives On to Enter the Witness Protection Program

According to this fan theory, Walt did not die that night in the meth lab—he lived on to enter the witness protection program, where he was provided with a new identity as Hal Wilkerson and started over with a new family . . . You know where this is going!

28

Are They Punking Me?

The Dark Humor of *Breaking Bad*

> Spock has total Vulcan control over his digestion! You wanna hear this or not?
>
> *—Badger to Skinny Pete*

Much of the comic relief in *Breaking Bad* comes from members of Jesse Pinkman's dim-witted posse, particularly Badger and Skinny Pete as they humorously rant about such offbeat topics as a *Star Trek* pie-eating contest and video game zombies. In an August 17, 2013, interview with *The Hollywood Reporter*, Charles Baker, who portrayed Skinny Pete, commented, "We were the comic relief or a break from the tension. But we always got these great, epic moments. All of the nerd conversations we've had—we talked about *Star Trek*, *Star Wars*, video games—those have been so fun."

In addition, several *Breaking Bad* cast members have stand-up comedy and comedy-writing credentials such as Lavell Crawford, who portrayed Saul Goodman's bodyguard "Huell Babineaux, and Bill Burr, who portrayed another one of Saul's henchmen, Patrick Kuby. And, of course, Bob Odenkirk himself had served as a writer for *Saturday Night Live* between 1987 and 1991. According to Vince Gilligan in a Q&A that appeared on amc.com, "It wasn't like we went looking to hire comedians, it's just that I've got a theory that if you can do comedy—first of all you have to be able to act, and there are plenty of stand-up comedians who are not actors—but if you are an actor at heart and you are also a comedian, you can also do drama. People like Bob Odenkirk and Bill and Lavell who happen to be very funny also happen to be very good for the roles that we hired them for."

Below are some of the funniest moments in the history of *Breaking Bad*—from *Star Trek* to zombies and everything in between:

Badger Scripts *Star Trek*

In the *Breaking Bad* episode "Blood Money" (5.09), Badger informs Skinny Pete about his *Star Trek* script (which he has yet to write down, of course!), which essentially boils down to an intergalactic pie-eating contest: "They're eating tulaberry pies . . . From Gamma Quadrant, yo." According to Badger, Chekov is winning the contest because "every time Chekov eats a pie, Scotty beams it right out of him." However, Scotty gets distracted by Lieutenant Uhura's "big pointies," causing him to beam Chekov's "guts into space."

Bogdan's Eyebrows

In the "Pilot" episode, Walt has taken on a second job at A1 Car Wash to help make ends meet. It's a demeaning experience, and his boss, Bogdan, is a major-league asshole with very distinctive furry eyebrows. After Walt learns that he has lung cancer, he informs Bogdan that he can take his job and shove it in his own style, exclaiming, "Fuck you and your eyebrows!" Walt follows his atypical outburst by grabbing his crotch and bellowing, "Wipe this down!"

Cow House

After they park the RV in a desolate location to embark on their first meth cook in the "Pilot" episode, Jesse stands on some boulders surveying the surrounding area. He informs Walt that there is "some big cow house out that way." Walt exclaims to himself, "Cow house . . . God help me."

Death Star

In the episode "Kafkaesque" (3.09), Jesse complains to Badger and Skinny Pete about all the stress associated with working for Gus Fring at the underground meth superlab: "What's the point of being an outlaw when you got responsibilities?" Badger responds with a tangent on *Star Wars*, "Darth Vader had responsibilities. He was responsible for the Death Star."

Funyuns

Stranded in the desert during a meth cook due to the RV's dead battery (following Jesse's negligence) in the episode "4 Days Out" (2.09), Walt takes stock of what food they have left and notices in disgust that Jesse has brought along three bags of Funyuns (junk food in the form of onion-flavored rings). Jesse comments, "Funyuns are awesome . . . More for me." Walt replies, "How about something with some protein, maybe? Something green, huh? How are you even alive?"

Gale Does Karaoke

As he investigates Gale Boetticher's murder in the episode "Bullet Points" (4.04), Hank scours through piles of evidence and locates a hilarious video of Gale singing karaoke (Japanese for "empty orchestra") to Peter Schilling's 1983 hit "Major Tom (Coming Home)." Gale apparently made the subtitled video—which can be viewed on YouTube, by the way—during a trip to Thailand (leading to all sorts of fan theories).

Hank Sings "Eye of the Tiger"

In the episode "Bug" (4.09), Walt and Hank drive to Los Pollos Hermanos to remove the bug from underneath Gus Fring's car. Hank takes the opportunity during the ride to sing an absolutely horrid, cringe-inducing, but hilarious version of Survivor's "Eye of the Tiger," the theme from the

While investigating Gale's murder, Hank comes across a hilarious video of the lab assistant singing karaoke to Peter Schilling's hit song, "Major Tom," which appeared on the 1983 album, *Error in the System*.

soundtrack of *Rocky III* (1982). Meanwhile, a very stressed and noticeably distracted Walt observes that Tyrus Kitt has been tailing them all along. As a side note, Sylvester Stallone initially intended to use "Another One Bites the Dust" as the theme of *Rocky III*, but was denied permission by Queen.

Hitmen

In the series finale, "Felina" (5.16), Walt intimidates Elliott and Gretchen Schwartz by paying Badger and Skinny Pete to pose as hitmen using nothing but laser pointers. After accomplishing the deed, Skinny Pete suggests that "the whole thing felt kind of shady, you know, like, morality-wise." Walt then hands both of them bundles of money for their services and asks, "How do you feel now?" Skinny Pete replies, "Better."

In "Bug," Hank sings a cringe-inducing but hilarious rendition of Survivor's "Eye of the Tiger" as he and Walt head to Los Pollos Hermanos.

"Home Alone" in the Meth Lab

With Walt at the hospital checking on Hank's condition in the episode "I See You" (3.08), a bored Jesse decides to go apeshit in the meth superlab during a humorous montage (even inflating his yellow hazmat suit, making him look just like Violet from the 1971 film *Willy Wonka & the Chocolate Factory*) accompanied by the sounds of Prince Fatty's version of "Shimmy Shimmy Ya." The party ends upon the arrival of Victor, who asks angrily, "Why isn't there anything cooking?"

Huell's Money Mattress

In the episode "Buried" (5.10), Saul Goodman's henchmen, Huell Babineaux and Patrick Kuby, visit Walt's storage unit, which contains a massive pile of cash, with instructions from their boss to place the money into eight separate barrels (which Walt will later bury in the desert). Huell exclaims, "I gotta do it, man," and lies down on the immense pile, prompting Patrick to react, "We're here to do a job, not channel Scrooge McDuck." However, Patrick eventually succumbs to the temptation himself and leaps onto the pile of money as well. When Huell suggests "Mexico," Kuby wisely reminds him of the incident where Walt had ten prisoners murdered in a span of just two minutes.

Jesse Dines with the Whites

Guess who's coming to dinner? Jesse pays a visit to the White household to discuss meth business with Walt, who insists that he stay for dinner when Skyler arrives in the episode "Buyout" (5.06). So Jesse sits down for the most awkward meal in *Breaking Bad* history up to that time (possibly surpassed by the tableside guacamole fiasco in "Confessions" with Walt, Skyler, Hank, Marie, and an overly enthusiastic waiter). There is complete silence at the dinner table until Jesse decides to break the ice. When Jesse compliments Skyler on the green beans, she replies that she picked them up "from the deli at Albertsons." Jesse then goes into a brief overview of his own eating habits: "I eat a lot of frozen stuff. It's usually pretty bad. I mean, the pictures are always so awesome, you know? It's like, 'Hell yeah, I'm stoked for this lasagna!' And then you nuke it and the cheese gets all scabby on top and it's like you're eating a scab." Jesse then tries to compliment Skyler by saying he has heard from Walt that she is running the car wash "like a machine. Like, well-oiled. Yeah." Before she abruptly excuses herself from the table in disgust, Skyler asks Walt, "Did you also tell him about my affair?" Walt turns to Jesse and says, "You know my kids are gone?" to which he replies, "Thank God!"

Ken Loses

An obnoxious yuppie with a shiny BMW convertible, a Bluetooth headset, and a vanity plate that reads "KEN WINS" steals Walt's parking space at the Mesa Credit Union in the episode "Cancer Man" (1.04). Walt later crosses paths with "Ken" outside of a gas station and, when Ken goes inside, rigs his car battery so it will burst into flames upon ignition. A total douchebag, Ken resurfaces in *Better Call Saul* ("Switch," 2.01) as the victim of Jimmy and Kim's scam to get him to buy a round of extremely expensive tequila.

Kevin Costner Pickup Line

In the "Abiquiu" (3.11) episode, Saul Goodman is driving along with Walt and informs him, "If you're committed enough, you can make any story work. I once told a woman I was Kevin Costner, and it worked because I believed it." In *Better Call Saul* ("Marco," 1.10), viewers get the opportunity to meet the woman in question, who berates Saul (then known as Jimmy McGill) after a drunken one-night stand: "Hey! You are *not* Kevin Costner!" Jimmy replies defiantly, "I was last night."

Pain Is Weakness

Also in the episode "Abiquiu" (3.11), Marie tries to encourage a bedridden Hank, who has become frustrated with his physical therapy, by telling him "It's supposed to hurt. Pain is weakness leaving your body." Hank replies flippantly, "Pain is my foot in your ass, Marie." However, Marie has the last word when she fires back, "Hey, if you could get your leg up that high, I say go for it."

Plane Crash Pep Talk

Feeling perhaps somewhat responsible for the airline collision that killed 167 people, Walt attends a school assembly in the high school gymnasium in the episode "No Más (3.01) and tries to actually downplay the catastrophe that has shaken the entire community: "I guess what I would want to say is to look on the bright side. First of all, nobody on the ground was killed . . . Plus, neither plane was full . . . what you're left with casualty-wise is just the fiftieth-worst air disaster. Actually, tied for fiftieth. There are, in truth, fifty-three crashes throughout history that are just as bad or worse." From a dark humor perspective, this absolutely cringeworthy moment may place No. 1 in *Breaking Bad* history.

Rice and Beans

In episode "Seven-Thirty-Seven" (2.01), Walt comes up with the brilliant idea to use castor beans to create ricin and slip the poison to total psycho Tuco Salamanca. Jesse inquires about the beans and asks Walt, "Are we just gonna grow a magic beanstalk? Huh? Climb it and escape?" Walt replies, "We are going to process them into ricin." Jesse asks, "Rice 'n' Beans?"

Roof Pizza

Walt shows up with a large pizza as a peace offering in the episode "Caballo Sin Nombre" (3.02), but Skyler refuses to let him in. "I've got dipping sticks," Walt protests to no avail. On his way to the car, Walt heaves the uncut pizza onto the roof of the house (believe it or not, Bryan Cranston accomplished this in one take!). As crazy as it sounds to anyone who has never watched *Breaking Bad*, this is truly one of the most memorable scenes in the entire series! In fact, so many hardcore fans tried to duplicate the pizza toss at the house in Albuquerque where exterior shots of the White house were filmed that Vince Gilligan himself felt compelled to publicly remind them that it was a private residence whose occupants did not appreciate all of the uncut pizzas ending up on their roof!

Skinny Pete Plays *Solfeggietto* in C Minor

Badger and Skinny Pete are in a music store in the episode "Hazard Pay" (5.03) when the latter sits down at a keyboard and knocks out a perfect rendition of *Solfeggietto* in C minor by C. P. E. Bach—much to every viewer's astonishment and amusement. It turns out that Charles Baker, the actor who portrayed Skinny Pete, is actually a talented musician. The scene "apparently threw a lot of people for a loop," remarked Baker in a Q&A on amctv.com. Baker admitted he "practiced like a madman" for a month before filming the scene. In real life, he admits to being "more of an acoustic folk kind of dude." In an August 17, 2013, interview with *The Hollywood Reporter*, Baker added, "One of the most endearing moments was the piano thing. It's kind of weird being locked in a character who is such a lowlife—who is dumb, inarticulate and illiterate, and seems like your basic scumbag. To be able to jump out and throw this at people and go 'oh, yeah, he used to be this'—it was really endearing to me. That was a beautiful moment."

Sleestak

During Jesse's nonstop party phase in the episode "Thirty-Eight Snub" (4.02), he tries to persuade Badger to continue hanging out and partying with him. Badger responds, "Jesse, I've been awake for like three straight days. Turning into a Sleestak . . . I think I got like this cat. Think I'm supposed to feed it." As anyone who grew up in the 1970s is aware, Sleestak refers to the hostile green lizard-men who live in the underground "Lost City" from the cheesy 1970s TV series *Land of the Lost*.

Slingin' Mad Volume

In the otherwise dreary episode "Peekaboo" (2.06), Skinny Pete gives Jesse a sheet of paper with the name and address of the couple that jacked him. Jesse calls him out for spelling "street" with an "a". A defensive Skinny Pete replies, "Hey, man, I'm slingin' mad volume and fat stackin' benjis, you know what I'm sayin'? I can't be all about, like, spelling and shit." Skinny Pete then tells Jesse that they call the guy who jacked him "Spooge." Jesse exclaims, "Spooge? Not Mad Dog? Not Diesel? So lemme get this straight, you got jacked by a guy named Spooge?"

Tableside Guacamole

While Walt and Skyler sit down to an extraordinarily tense meal with Hank and Marie at a Mexican restaurant (the latter two now know that Walt is Heisenberg) in the episode "Confessions" (5.11), the waiter cheerfully tries to promote the tableside guacamole: "Welcome to Garduno's! My name's Trent. I'll be taking care of you today. Can I start anybody off with some beverages? Margarita? How about some tableside guacamole?" The terribly awkward situation is reminiscent of the scene in *Office Space* (1999) that takes place at Chotchkie's with an overly enthusiastic waiter named Brian (Todd Duffey): "So can I get you gentlemen something more to drink? Or maybe something to nibble on? Some Pizza Shooters, Shrimp Poppers, or Extreme Fajitas?" Believe it or not, following the *Breaking Bad* scene, Garduno's, the Mexican restaurant in question, reported a dramatic increase in orders for tableside guacamole.

Talking Pillow

In the episode "Gray Matter" (1.05), Walt undergoes an intervention after he refuses to seek further medical treatment for his cancer. It's a very tense scene, lightened quite a bit by the presence of the ridiculous "Talking Pillow," which designates who should speak next and embroidered with the phrase, "Find Joy in the Little Things." Gripping the Talking Pillow, Walt remarks, "Sometimes I feel like I never actually make any of my own. Choices, I mean. My entire life, it just seems I never . . . you know, had a real say about any of it. Now this last one, cancer ... all I have left is how I choose to approach this." Of course, the *Breaking Bad* intervention scene doesn't match the intensity or dark humor of a similar scene in *The Sopranos* ("The Strong, Silent Type," 4.10), which starts out as an intervention for Christopher Moltisanti (Michael Imperioli) and devolves into an out-and-out brawl.

Walt Confronts Ted

After Skyler confesses her affair with Ted Beneke to Walt, the latter storms over to Beneke Fabricators and attempts to confront the former in the episode "Green Light" (3.4). With Ted locked in his office, Walt even tries to throw a massive potted plant through his inside window, but it bounces off harmlessly. Walt is soon tossed out of the building by security guards. Skyler runs downstairs and asks Walt, "What are you doing?" Walt exclaims, "I'm trying to talk to Ted."

"Yeah, Bitch! Magnets!"

Faced with finding out a way to destroy the information on Gus Fring's laptop that is now in police custody in the episode "Live Free or Die" (5.01), Jesse comes up with the creative idea of using a powerful magnet to erase the information. After testing out the magnet theory in the junkyard, Jesse can't contain his exuberance, yelling "Yeah, bitch! Magnets!" It's definitely one of his most triumphant scenes in the entire series.

Zombies

It's only fitting to bookmark a chapter on the dark humor of *Breaking Bad* with the best of Skinny Pete and Badger's dialogue—in this case a lengthy discussion in the episode "Thirty-Eight Snub" (4.02) about video game zombies, specifically comparing *Left 4 Dead*, *Resident Evil 4*, and *Call of Duty: World at War—Zombies*. According to Badger, *Call of Duty* is "the bomb, man. Think on it, bro. They're not just zombies . . . they're Nazi zombies." Skinny Pete responds, "Zombies are dead, man! What difference does it make what their job was when they was living?" Badger replies, "Dude, you are so historically retarded! Nazi zombies don't wanna eat ya just cause they're craving the protein. They do it cause, they do it cause they hate Americans, man. Talibans. They're the Talibans of the zombie world."

29

All the Sacrifices

Top Fifteen Most Disturbing Scenes in the Series

> I know you're a lying, evil scumbag, that's what I know. Manipulating people. Messing with their heads.
>
> —*Jesse Pinkman to Walter White*

Walter White's incredible journey from unremarkable high school chemistry teacher to meth kingpin in *Breaking Bad* left a trail of death and destroyed lives in its wake. Here's a look at some of the most disturbing moments in the series:

Emilio's Remains Fall Through Ceiling

In the episode "Cat's in the Bag" (1.02), Jesse ignores Walt's advice to dispose of Emilio's body using a plastic bin and instead opts to fill his upstairs bathtub with hydrofluoric acid, resulting in a gloopy mess that eats its way through the floor and onto the downstairs hallway. Walt reacts sarcastically to Jesse, "I'm sorry, what were you asking me? Oh, yes, that *stupid plastic container* I asked you to buy. You see, hydrofluoric acid won't eat through plastic; it will however dissolve metal, rock, glass, ceramic . . . so there's that." Although the show *Mythbusters* later disproved that such an incident was possible, it certainly made for one of the truly grossest scenes in television history.

Tuco Beats No-Doze to Death for No Good Reason

In the episode "A No-Rough-Stuff-Type Deal" (1.7), Walt and Jesse find out how unprepared they are for the dark side of the drug business after they witness Tuco Salamanca brutally beat his associate, No-Doze, to death for absolutely no good reason in the junkyard. After Tuco has worked out a deal with Walt and Jesse to cook more meth for him, No-Doze innocently says, "Just remember who you're working for." The remark sends Tuco off in an inexplicable rage that culminates in the deadly assault.

Hector Relieves Himself

In the episode "Bit by a Dead Bee" (2.03), Hank and his fellow DEA agents bring Hector Salamanca in for questioning following the death of his nephew, Tuco. Hector, who has even more contempt for the authorities than for his own nephew's killer, proceeds to noisily shit himself as a message to the DEA agents that he is not about to inform on anyone. Hank turns to Gomie and remarks, "I guess that's a 'no'. . . ."

Spooge's House

Nothing prepares Jesse for the house of horrors that he encounters in the episode "Peekaboo" (2.06) after Walt insists that he take care of the Spooge problem—the old tweaker who jacked Skinny Pete. Walt is scared that if word gets out that their meth operation is "soft" dealing with such issues, they will not be able to make collections as they will lose credibility among blue meth buyers. However, Jesse is totally horrified when he breaks into Spooge's house and discovers the truly deplorable living conditions, along with the fact that there is a little boy just sitting on the couch amid the total ruin, vacantly staring at television tuned to a home shopping channel. It's one of the most heartbreaking scenes in the series and one of the few times that viewers are confronted with the actual cost of meth abuse and the effects of Walt's superior "product" on society in general.

Tortuga's Severed Head

In the episode "Negro y Azul" (2.07), Hank joins the El Paso task force and interrogates an informant named Tortuga (Spanish for "turtle"). The agents later come upon Tortuga's severed head attached to a tortoise in the desert. Hank is visibly aghast, and he immediately backs away from the scene, much to the amusement of the other agents. However, an explosive detonates and kills an agent, while severely wounding several others. A visibly shaken Hank, who is never quite the same again, returns to his old job in Albuquerque.

Danny Trejo's character Tortuga was killed with a machete. Interestingly, Trejo appeared in the films *Machete* (2010) and *Machete Kills* (2013), both of which were directed by his second cousin, Robert Rodriguez.

Tomas Kills Combo on Street Corner

Just before he is gunned down on a street corner by a young kid on a bike in the episode "Mandala" (2.11), Christian "Combo" Ortega phones Skinny Pete and exclaims, "Yo, Skinny. I'm up here on Second and Hazeltine, getting eyeballed hard." Combo had noticed a couple of rival drug dealers driving by, so he did not expect that his death would come at the hands of a kid, who is ultimately identified as Jesse's girlfriend Andrea's brother, Tomas, who later gets killed by the same drug dealers. Skinny Pete attends Combo's funeral and relates the scene back to Jesse: "And you should've seen the coffin. It was like this shiny white pearlescence, like I'm pretty sure I seen the exact same paint job on a Lexus, right? So we're definitely talking high end."

Jane's Death

Bryan Cranston has admitted that the truly disturbing scene in the episode "Phoenix" (2.12) where Walt stands over Jane, who has overdosed and is choking on her vomit, deeply affected him. During a 2015 appearance on *Inside the Actors Studio*, Cranston got choked up reminiscing about filming the scene, remarking, "[Jane's] a little girl—she's young enough be my daughter . . . And then, I see the face of my own daughter in her place. I didn't want to, I didn't plan on it . . . What civilians don't understand, that we do, is that actors need to be willing to pay a price for it . . . It's an emotional price that you need to be willing to pay."

Plane Crash

Foreshadowed in four cold opens throughout Season Two of *Breaking Bad*, the airplane collision caused by Jane's grieving father, an air traffic controller, in the episode "ABQ" (2.13) scatters human remains and debris over Albuquerque, some of which (like the haunting one-eye pink teddy bear) ends up in the White household's pool. All in all, 167 innocent victims are dead indirectly due to Walt's callous indifference to Jane dying from an overdose in the previous episode, "Phoenix."

The Cousins Blow Up a Truck Full of Illegal Immigrants

In the episode "No Mas" (3.01), the Cousins travel across the Mexican border with a truck full of illegal immigrants and then proceed to shoot all of the passengers. They then blow up the entire truck because they may or may not have been identified by one of the passengers. As the truck explodes, the Cousins walk away casually, totally unscathed, and determined to complete their mission of eliminating Heisenberg. The incident revealed for the first time just how totally ruthless the Cousins were and how overmatched Walt will be in dealing with these Terminator-like assassins.

Jesse Kills Gale

A true free spirit, Gale Boetticher engages in illegal activity in the meth superlab, but outside of that he is one of the kindest individuals in the series and truly doesn't have any animosity toward anyone. Even when Walt replaces Gale with Jesse as his lab assistant, Gale is more hurt and baffled by the move than truly angry about it. However, in the episode "Full Measure" (3.13), Gale gets caught up innocently as a pawn in the diabolical chess game between Gus Fring and Walt. Realizing Gus is going to eliminate him and replace him with Gale, Walt knows his only move is to make a frantic phone call to Jesse requesting that he kill Gale first. By killing Gale in cold blood, Jesse also loses a bit of his humanity and resorts to his usual fallback of turning to drugs to help ease the pain.

Gus Uses a Box Cutter on Victor

In "Box Cutter" (4.01), Gus Fring proves to be even more of a ruthless badass than anyone would have ever suspected as he enters the meth superlab after the death of Gale Boetticher, changes into a red hazmat suit, and coolly and deliberately slashes Victor's throat with a box cutter. He then calmly tells Walt and Jesse to "get back to work," and exits the lab with the same stoic demeanor that he had when he entered it.

Gus Loses Face

In the episode "Face Off" (4.13), Gus Fring proves too clever to be eliminated until Walt discovers a way to exploit his one true weakness: the drug kingpin loathes aging gangster Hector Salamanca, who years before had killed his business partner (and possible lover), Max Arciniega. Disregarding the strong possibility that an explosion in the Casa Tranquila nursing home could produce collateral damage and kill many innocent people along with Gus, Walt convinces Hector to allow him to equip his wheelchair with a homemade bomb activated by the signature bell that Tio uses to communicate.

The result is one of the most horrifying images in the series as Gus casually strolls out of Hector's room to leave viewers reacting in horror that half of his face has been blown off (a special effect achieved with the help of some of the expert makeup personnel from *Breaking Bad's* sister show on AMC *The Walking Dead*).

Todd Guns Down the Dirt Bike Kid

In the episode "Dead Freight" (5.05), Walt and his gang pull off an audacious train heist to seize thousands of gallons of methylamine, and everything goes off without a hitch until an innocent kid on a dirt bike arrives on the scene. Mindlessly following the rigid instructions Jesse gave him that no one else find out about the heist, Todd Alquist casually guns the kid down. He later informs Jesse that "shit happens," whereupon Jesse punches him out. Equally horrifying, Walt and Mike outvote Jesse and allow Todd to remain working in the meth-cooking operation.

Jailhouse Slaughter

With the assistance of Uncle Jack Welker and his neo-Nazi associates, Walt manages to orchestrate a calculated and efficient assassination of ten prisoners in a matter of minutes in the episode "Gliding Over All" (5.08). It is an extremely violent and disturbing montage, and evidence that Walt has been totally consumed by his Heisenberg persona and there will be no turning back.

Todd Casually Kills Andrea

In the episode "Granite State" (5.15), Todd Alquist casually shoots Jesse's girlfriend, Andrea, in the back of the head on her doorstep, after telling her, "Just so you know, this isn't personal." A horrified Jesse looks on from the car. Todd decided to kill Andrea as punishment for Jesse attempting to escape Uncle Jack's compound, where he is being held as a meth-cooking slave.

Todd Alquist (Jesse Plemons) is responsible for several of the most disturbing scenes in *Breaking Bad* such as gunning down the dirt bike kid and killing Jesse's girlfriend, Andrea.
Andrew Walker/Wikimedia Commons

30

Just Marking Time

Greatest Songs from the *Breaking Bad* Soundtrack

Our son doesn't know who Boz Scaggs is. We have failed as parents.
—*Walter White to Skyler*

Eclectic and quirky, the *Breaking Bad* soundtrack perfectly comple-
ments the tone of the entire series—from the amazing original score
composed by Dave Porter first heard in the "Pilot" episode to the use of two
classic songs in the season finale, "Felina," Marty Robbins's "El Paso" and
Badfinger's "Baby Blue." And who could ever forget the novelty songs such
as the "Ballad of Heisenberg" narcocorrido (drug ballad) by Los Cuates
de Sinaloa or Gale Boetticher's hilarious karaoke version of "Major Tom
(Coming Home)" by Peter Schilling? Or the very amusing but ultimately disturbing montage of a day in the life of Wendy the Meth Whore accompanied
by the Association's relentlessly cheesy 1967 hit "Windy"?

Let's face it—every track was meticulously utilized to the utmost effect
throughout the series, and much credit goes to series creator Vince Gilligan
and his music supervisor Thomas Golubić. In a November 27, 2013, *HuffPost*
interview, Golubić remarked, "*Breaking Bad* is ultimately a show about
change. (Creator) Vince Gilligan's line is that he's 'taking Mr. Chips and
turning him into Scarface.' Because of that premise the show itself shifts
and changes . . . [and] the music ideas that we deliver have to change as
well. Ideas during season one or two were no longer viable as the characters
changed in seasons three, four, and five." Therefore, without further ado,
here is a selection of the greatest songs from the *Breaking Bad* soundtrack:

"Tamacun"—Rodrigo y Gabriela ("Pilot," 1.01)

The energetic "Tamacun" by Rodrigo & Gabriela plays during the "Pilot" episode as Walter White accompanies his brother-in-law Hank Schrader on a DEA raid and watches in astonishment as one of his former students, Jesse Pinkman, escapes the scene. A Mexican classical guitar duo, Rodrigo (Sanchez) y Gabriela (Quintero), have been influenced by a number of diverse genres, including nuevo flamenco, rock, and heavy metal. "Tamacun" first appeared on Rodrigo y Gabriela's 2006 self-titled album, which was released in 2006 and debuted at No. 1 on the Irish Albums Chart (the duo began their career with an eight-year stint in Dublin before returning to Mexico). The album also features scintillating covers of Led Zeppelin's "Stairway to Heaven" and Metallica's "Orion." Rodrigo & Gabriela have contributed to several other soundtracks, including *Pirates of the Caribbean: On Stranger Tides* (2011) and *Puss in Boots* (2011). The duo even performed on the South Lawn of the White House for President Barack Obama following a State Dinner with Mexico in 2010.

"Out of Time Man"—Mick Harvey ("Pilot," 1.01)

The final scenes of the "Pilot" episode are perfectly accompanied by Mick Harvey's mesmerizing rendition of "Out of Time Man" with its prophetic lyrics, "I'm walking bad really down" and "No use in waiting no more." An Australian singer-songwriter, Harvey is a frequent collaborator with legendary musician Nick Cave. Together, the duo formed the Boys Next Door, the Birthday Party, and Nick Cave and the Bad Seeds. "Out of Time Man," which was first recorded by now-defunct French rock band Mano Negra (who are considered pioneers in world fusion), appeared on Harvey's fourth solo studio album, *Two of Diamonds*, in 2007.

"Who's Gonna Save My Soul"—Gnarls Barkley ("A No-Rough-Stuff-Type Deal," 1.07)

Gnarls Barkley's "Who's Gonna Save My Soul" perfectly highlights the closing scene of "A No-Rough-Stuff-Type Deal" as Walt and Jesse stand in the junkyard, stunned and horrified by Tuco Salamanca's brutality toward his associate No-Doze. An American soul duo, Gnarls Barkley features singer-songwriter CeeLo Green (Thomas DeCarlo Callaway) and Danger Mouse (Brian Joseph Burton). "Who's Gonna Save My Soul" was released on Gnarls Barkley's second studio album, *The Odd Couple*, in 2008. The accompanying music video was nominated for a Grammy Award for Best Music Video (losing out to "Pork and Beans" by Weezer). In a *Billboard* magazine interview, CeeLo remarked that the song was written about the "Godfather of Soul" himself, James Brown, "from an admirer's perspective . . . someone who had truly personified everything that we are."

"Negro y Azul: The Ballad of Heisenberg"—Los Cuates de Sinaloa ("Negro y Azul," 2.07)

The cold open for "Negro y Azul" features the novelty of a "narcocorrido" (drug ballad)—"Negro y Azul: The Ballad of Heisenberg"—performed by Mexican trio Los Cuates de Sinaloa. The song relates the story of the "gringo boss" known only as "Heisenberg" who now "controls the market" with his infamous blue meth. The song also foreshadows the ultimate fate of Heisenberg: "This homie's already dead/He just doesn't know it yet." According to *Breaking Bad* music supervisor Thomas Golubić in *Breaking Bad: The Official Book*, "These [narcocorrido] videos are all over YouTube . . . They're homemade, cobbled together from news report images of cocaine seizures, discoveries of machine gun stockpiles, and dead bodies. They're real-life outlaw ballads and they're absolutely fascinating. It seemed appropriate for *Breaking Bad* because we're dealing with the same world, just on the other side of the border." Some of the most infamous narcocorridos include "Contrabando y Tradicion" (Angel Gonzalez), "El

Mas Bravo de los Bravos" (Tucanes de Tijuana), "A Mis Enemigos" (Valentin Elizade), "Los Duros de Columbia" (Gerardo Ortiz), and "El Corrido de Juan Ortiz" (Oscar Ovidio), among others.

One of the most unusual cold opens in *Breaking Bad* involves the narcocorrido (aka drug ballad) music video, "Ballad of Heisenberg," by Los Cuates de Sinaloa in "Negro y Azul."

"DLZ"—TV on the Radio ("Over," 2.10)

In the "Over" episode, "DLZ" by TV on the Radio, an indie rock band from Brooklyn, New York, can be heard as Walt confronts the two wannabe meth cooks outside the hardware store and threatens them to "stay out of my territory." In 2008, "DLZ" first appeared on *Dear Science*, the band's third album. "DLZ" was also featured in episode 2.12 ("The Descent") of *The Vampire Diaries* in 2011.

"Zungguzungguguzungguzeng"—Yellowman ("Over," 2.10)

As their relationship starts getting serious, Jesse shows Jane some of his comic book sketches accompanied by the immensely popular reggae song "Zungguzungguguzungguzeng" by Yellowman. Considered Jamaica's first dancehall superstar, Yellowman (aka King Yellowman) was born with albinism in Kingston in 1956 and grew up in Alpha Boys School, a Catholic orphanage. Known for his sexually explicit lyrics (a style of dancehall known as "slackness"), Yellowman made his album debut with *Mister Yellowman* in 1982, followed by *Zungguzungguguzungguzeng* in 1983. Yellowman was featured in the 1983 video, *Jamaican Dancehall Volcano Hi-Power*, along with other popular dancehall artists such as Josey Wales, Massive Dread, Eek-A-Mouse, and Burro Banton. He also recorded a popular version of Fats Domino's "Blueberry Hill" in 1987. Quoted in *The Illustrated Encyclopedia of Music* (2003) by Paul Du Noyer, Yellowman exclaimed, "I never know why they call it slackness. I talk about sex, but it's just what happens behind closed doors. What I talk is reality."

"Enchanted" by the Platters ("Mandala," 2.11)

Jane introduces Jesse to heroin for the first time accompanied by the 1959 song "Enchanted" by the Platters—creating the perfect dreamlike quality of the scene as he drifts away from reality into a seemingly enchanted but ultimately dangerous journey. The Platters achieved forty charting singles on the *Billboard* charts between 1955 and 1967, including four No. 1 hits: "The Great Pretender," "My Prayer," "Twilight Time," and "Smoke Gets in Your Eyes." In 1990, the Platters were inducted into the Rock and Roll Hall of Fame, along with Hank Ballard, Bobby Darin, the Four Seasons, Four Tops, the Kinks, Simon & Garfunkel, and the Who. According to the group's official Rock and Roll Hall of Fame biography, "The Platters were one of the top vocal groups of the Fifties, delivering smooth, stylized renditions of pop standards . . . Like the Ink Spots a decade earlier, they were the most popular black group of the time, achieving success in a crooning, middle-of-the-road style that put a soulful coat of uptown polish on pop-oriented, harmony-rich material."

"Magic Arrow"—Timber Timbre ("Caballo Sin Nombre," 3.02)

Mike Ehrmantraut bugs the White household under the instigation of Saul Goodman and narrowly avoids detection by Walt to the accompaniment of Timber Timbre's "Magic Arrow." A Canadian music group, Timber Timbre blends the musical talents of Taylor Kirk, Simon Trottier, Mathieu Charbonneau, and Mark Wheaton. "Magic Arrow" appears on the band's self-titled third studio album, which was released in 2009. The song also made its way onto the soundtrack of the episode "Bitcoin for Dummies" on the TV series *The Good Wife* in 2012. *Fast Forward Weekly* has described Timber Timbre's sound as "an aesthetic rooted in swampy, ragged blues" and "beautifully restrained blues from an alternate universe."

"A Horse with No Name"—America ("Caballo Sin Nombre," 3.02)

The episode title "Caballo Sin Nombre" is Spanish for "Horse with No Name," and Walt sings along to the hit 1971 song by folk-rock band America as he drives his Pontiac Aztek to work. At the end of the episode,

The title of episode 3.02, "Caballo Sin Nombre," is Spanish for "Horse with No Name," and Walt sings along to the hit 1971 song by folk-rock band America as he drives his Pontiac Aztek to work.

Walt again mindlessly sings the song in the shower while the Salamanca twins wait patiently for him outside in the bedroom with an axe. America was formed in England in 1970 by Dewey Bunnell (who wrote "A Horse with No Name"), Dan Peek, and Gerry Beckley—all of whom were the sons of U.S. Air Force personnel stationed in London. "A Horse with No Name" (originally known as "Desert Song") appeared on the band's self-titled debut album in 1971, and Bunnell has described the song as "a metaphor for a vehicle to get away from life's confusion into a quiet, peaceful place." In addition, Bunnell has admitted the song was strongly inspired by the playing style of Neil Young: "I know that virtually everyone, on first hearing, assumed it was Neil . . . I never fully shied away from the fact that I was inspired by him. I think it's the structure of the song as much as in the tone of the voice. It did hurt a little, because we got some pretty bad backlash. I've always attributed it more to people protecting their own heroes more than attacking me."

Ironically, it was "A Horse with No Name" that knocked Young's "Heart of Gold" out of the No. 1 spot on the U.S. charts. Since "horse" is a common slang word for heroin, several U.S. radio stations refused to play "A Horse with No Name." America won a Grammy Award for Best New Artist in 1973. Other notable America songs include "Ventura Highway," "I Need You," "Tin Man," "Lonely People," "Sister Golden Hair," and "You Can Do Magic." In 2006, America was inducted into the Vocal Group Hall of Fame along with Billy Ward & the Dominoes, Bread, the Byrds, Deep River Boys, the Duprees, the Fleetwoods, Haydn Quartet, the Hi-Lo's, the Hollies, Journey, the Lovin' Spoonful, the Moody Blues, the Shangri-Las, and Simon & Garfunkel.

"Timetakesthetimetimetakes"—Peder ("Mas," 3.05)

Gus Fring gives a very impressed Walt a grand tour of the superlab accompanied by "Timetakesthetimetimetakes" by award-winning Danish musician Peder (full name: Peder Thomas Pedersen). The song first appeared on Peder's 2007 album *And He Just Pointed to the Sky*. A member of the hip hop production team the Prunes, Peder has worked with a variety of artists, including DJ Krush, the Beastie Boys, the Roots, and DJ Vadim.

"Ginza Samba"—Vince Guaraldi ("Sunset," 3.06)

An upbeat montage that depicts Walt and new apprentice Gale's "honeymoon phase" in the superlab is accompanied by "Ginza Samba" by Vince Guaraldi. According to an August 30, 2012, article by Patrick Bowman that appeared on mtv.com, "the whole sequence seems like it's taken from a *Breaking Bad* spin-off where Walter and Gale are obliviously happy as lab partners playing chess, doing chemistry things in unison, making weird coffee in Gale's Rube Goldberg device, and churning out the best crystal meth in the world." Born Vincent Anthony Dellaglio, Guaraldi

(1928–76) was an American jazz pianist best known for composing the soundtrack that accompanied TV adaptations of the *Peanuts* comic strip such as *A Charlie Brown Christmas* (1965) and *It's the Great Pumpkin, Charlie Brown* (1966), as well as the 1969 film *A Boy Named Charlie Brown*. In 1996, pianist George Winston released a Guaraldi tribute album, *Linus and Lucy—The Music of Vince Guaraldi*.

"Shimmy Shimmy Ya"—Prince Fatty ("I See You," 3.08)

With Walt away at the hospital checking on Hank's condition, Jesse just hangs out goofing off in the superlab like a kid in a candy store to the accompaniment of the upbeat, reggae version of "Shimmy Shimmy Ya" by British dancehall musician Prince Fatty (Mike Pelanconi). The song was originally recorded by Ol' Dirty Bastard (Russell Tyrone Jones) and first appeared on his 1995 album *Return to the 36 Chambers: The Dirty Version*. VH1 ranked "Shimmy Shimmy Ya" No. 59 on its list of the "100 Greatest Songs of Hip Hop."

"Windy"—the Association ("Half Measures," 3.12)

A humorous but eminently disturbing montage that depicts a day in the life of meth-addicted Wendy the Whore is accompanied by the carefree hit "Windy" by 1960s California pop group the Association. According to an August 11, 2013, *Complex* article, "In what must be some kind of record for most blow jobs depicted in a single two-minute sequence, Wendy serves her clients so she can get served." In a Q&A session with *Breaking Bad* fans on amc.com concerning the soundtrack, Vince Gilligan remarked, "Every now and then we'd have an idea for a song in advance while writers and I were all putting our heads together to figure out the story at hand. That didn't happen that often, but one example of that is when we came up with the teaser set to the song 'Windy,' by The Association. We had a teaser with Wendy the loveable meth whore going through an average day at work and servicing a lot of Johns and the whole time this bubbly 60s pop song is playing."

The Association's second No. 1 hit (after "Cherish"), "Windy" reached No. 1 on the charts in July 1967. The song was later covered by various artists, including Gary Lewis and the Playboys, Astrud Gilberto, Andy Williams, Billy Paul, and Barry Manilow. Interestingly, "Windy" also appeared on the soundtrack of Bryan Cranston's former TV series *Malcolm in the Middle* ("Butterflies," 6.17) in 2005. Nearly forgotten today, the Association served as the lead-off band at the legendary Monterey Pop Festival in 1967 that also featured the talents of Jefferson Airplane, the Who, the Grateful Dead, the Jimi Hendrix Experience, Big Brother and the Holding Company (featuring the vocals of Janis Joplin), Eric Burdon and the Animals, Otis Redding, Ravi Shankar, and the Mamas & the Papas, among others. One notable band missing from the lineup was the Doors, with keyboardist Ray Manzarek later remarking, "We were quite angry wondering why the Association was at the Monterey Pop Festival, and the Doors were not." Other hits from the Association include "Never My Love" and "Along Comes Mary."

"Crapa Pelada"—Quartetto Cetro ("Full Measure," 3.13)

Just prior to an unexpected visit by Gus Fring, the very meticulous Gale Boetticher tidies up his apartment and sings along to the catchy "Crapa Pelada" by Quartetto Cetro (Italian for Cithara Quartet), an Italian vocal quartet that was formed in the 1940s. "Crapa Pelada" translates into English as "Bald Head." The next time Gale responds to a knock on the door of his apartment in this episode he will be murdered by Jesse Pinkman.

"Truth"—Alex Ebert ("Box Cutter," 4.1)

The closing montage of "Box Cutter," where Walt makes his way back to his condo, is accompanied by "Truth" by singer-songwriter Alex Ebert, lead singer of American bands Ima Robot, and Edward Sharpe and the Magnetic Zero. "Truth" first appeared on Ebert's 2011 solo album

Alexander, which *Rolling Stone* gave just two-and-a-half stars, calling "the dream-catcher naiveté he tries on here seems genuine. It's also kind of annoying: 'Would you call the Earth an asshole for turning round and round?/Ya know it never, ever stays in just one place.' We wouldn't, because unlike some people, we weren't skipping out of science class to do 'shrooms." In 2013, Ebert (full name: Alexander Michael Tahquitz Ebert) won a Golden Globe Award for Best Original Score for the adventure thriller *All Is Lost*, which stars Robert Redford as an unnamed man who is lost at sea aboard a heavily damaged sailboat.

"Hoochie Mama"—2 Live Crew ("Thirty-Eight Snub," 4.02)

2 Live Crew's raunchy tune "Hoochie Mama" accompanies Badger and Skinny Pete's scintillating discussion of zombie video games. "Hoochie Mama" had previously appeared on the soundtrack for the 1995 stoner comedy *Friday*, which was directed by F. Gary Gray and starred Ice Cube, Chris Tucker, and Nia Long. The stellar *Friday* soundtrack, which reached No. 1 on the *Billboard* charts, also features "Friday" by Ice Cube, "Keep Their Heads Ringin'" by Dr. Dre, "Roll It Up, Light It Up, Smoke It Up" by Cypress Hill, "Take a Hit" by Mack 10, "Mary Jane" by Rick James, "Superhoes" by Funkdoobiest, and "Blast If I Have To" by E-A-Ski. The success of *Friday* led to two sequels: *Next Friday* (2000) and *Friday After Next* (2002).

Miami-based rap group 2 Live Crew (which initially consisted of Luke Skyywalker, Fresh Kid Ice, Mr. Mixx, Amazing V, and Brother Marquis) managed to generate a significant amount of controversy by padding their 1989 album *As Nasty as They Wanna Be* with plenty of sexually explicit lyrics in such "classic" songs as "Me So Horny," "Put Her in the Buck," "The Fuck Shop," "Dick Almighty," "Bad Ass Bitch," and "Dirty Nursery Rhymes." The album caught the attention of a Christian-based group called the American Family Association, and various lawsuits started flying around in an attempt to ban the "vile filth" from record stores. An obscenity verdict banning the album was eventually overturned by the United States Court of Appeals in 1992. However, the controversy generated much interest in the album, and 2 Live Crew laughed all the way to the bank. In a July 25, 1990, interview with *The Los Angeles Times*, Campbell stated, "A lot of people have gotten the impression that I'm this rude sexual deviant or something . . . But contrary to what has been printed about me in the papers, I'm no moral threat to anybody. I'm just a hard-working guy marketing a new product." As an amusing side note, filmmaker George Lucas successfully sued Campbell for using the name "Skywalker" from the *Star Wars* films for his record label, Luke Skyywalker Records (Campbell simply changed the label's name to Luke Records).

"Major Tom (Coming Home)" by Gale Boetticher ("Bullet Points," 4.04)

As he reviews evidence related to Gale Boetticher's mysterious death, DEA agent Hank Schrader discovers a hilarious DVD with Thai subtitles of Gale singing a trippy karaoke version of "Major Tom (Coming Home)," a song by German musician Peter Schilling, which first appeared on the 1983 album *Error in the System*. The song peaked at No. 14 on the U.S. charts. The fictional astronaut character of Major Tom first appeared in the 1969 David Bowie song "Space Oddity." Bowie later featured the character in his songs "Ashes to Ashes" (1980), "Hallo Spaceboy" (1995), and "New Killer Star" (2003), along with possibly the music video "Blackstar" (2016), which depicts a dead astronaut. Tragically, Bowie died on January 10, 2016, just two days after the release of the "Blackstar" music video. Considered a one-hit wonder (at least in the United States), Schilling remixed "Major Tom" several times, including "Major Tom 94" in 1994 and "Major Tom 2000" in 2000.

"1977"—Ana Tijoux ("Shotgun," 4.05)

Mike and Jesse make pickups while a disgruntled Walt cooks alone during a montage that is accompanied by Ana Tijoux's "1977," a single from her second studio album of the same name that was released in 2010. The album itself received a Grammy Award nomination for Best Latin Rock/Alternative Album (losing out to *El Existential* by Grupo Fantasma). The single "1977" was later featured in the EA Sports video game *FIFA 11* in 2010. A French-Chilean musician, Tijoux once served as the MC of hip-hop group Makiza during the late 1990s.

"Tidal Wave"—Thee Oh Sees ("Salud," 4.10)

The appropriately titled "Tidal Wave" by Thee Oh Sees plays as Gus Fring poisons the Mexican cartel (along with himself!). According to H. Drew Blackburn in a September 30, 2013, *Complex* article, the psych-garage rock band Thee Oh Sees "are one of the most entertaining bands out right now because thankfully, they always come to fuck shit up and we need that in rock music." Blackburn goes on to refer to "Tidal Wave" as "a hyperactive and contemporary take on danceable retro-surf rock complete with distorted vocals." Formed in 1997 out of San Francisco, Thee Oh Sees currently consists of John Dwyer, Tim Hellman, Dan Rincon, and Paul Quattrone. The band has changed its lineup and name several times over the years, having once been known as Orinoka Crash Suite, OCS, Orange County Sound, the Ohsees, the Oh Sees, and Oh Sees.

"Goodbye"—Apparat ("Face Off," 4.13)

As Gus enters Casa Tranquila for his final meeting with Hector, "Goodbye" by German electronic musician Apparat (Sascha Ring) appropriately plays on the soundtrack: "Find out/I was just a bad dream." Apparat frequently collaborates with the German electronic music duo Modeselektor under the name "Moderat."

"Black" by Danger Mouse and Daniele Luppi, featuring Norah Jones ("Face Off," 4.13)

The closing scene of the Season Four finale features "Black" as Walt informs Skyler that "I won" after he eliminates Gus Fring. Featuring a collaboration between Danger Mouse and Daniele Luppi (along with vocals by Norah Jones), "Black" first appeared on the 2011 album *Rome*, which took five years to complete and was reportedly inspired by the soundtracks of such classic Spaghetti Westerns as Sergio Leone's *The Good, the Bad, and the Ugly* (1966). Danger Mouse (Brian Joseph Burton) first came to prominence in 2004 when he released *The Grey Album*, which blended Jay-Z's vocals from *The Black Album* (2003) with instrumentals from the Beatles' 1968 self-titled album (aka the White Album). In 2003, Danger Mouse formed Gnarls Barkley with CeeLo Green, a collaboration that resulted in two immensely popular studio albums: *St. Elsewhere* (2006) and *The Odd Couple* (2008).

"Stay on the Outside"—Whitey ("Madrigal," 5.02)

Whitey's "Stay on the Outside" can be heard as Walt and Jesse search for the ricin cigarette. An English songwriter and multi-instrumentalist, Whitey (Nathan Joseph White) released his debut album, *The Light at the End of the Tunnel Is a Train*, in 2005. "Stay on the Outside" first appeared on the 2007 album *Kitsuné Maison Compilation 4*. In addition to *Breaking Bad*, Whitey's songs have appeared in episodes of *The Sopranos*, *One Tree Hill*, *The O.C.*, *Kyle XY*, *Entourage*, and *CSI*.

"On a Clear Day You Can See Forever" by the Peddlers ("Hazard Pay," 5.03)

A meth-cooking montage featuring Walt and Jesse utilizes the mellow sounds of the Peddlers performing "On a Clear Day You Can See Forever" from the popular Broadway musical of the same name. A British soul/jazz trio, the Peddlers formed in Manchester in 1964 with Trevor Morais,

Tab Martin, and Roy Phillips. The version of "On a Clear Day You Can See Forever" highlighted on *Breaking Bad* first appeared on the Peddlers' 1968 album *Three in a Cell*.

"Knife Party"—Bonfire ("Fifty-One", 5.04)

Bonfire's "Knife Party" can be heard as Walt and Junior gleefully rev up their new cars in the driveway. An Australian electro house duo, Bonfire consists of Rob Swire and Gareth McGrillen (both of whom were in the band Pendulum). The duo has collaborated with a variety of other artists, including Tom Morello, Tom Staar, I See MONSTAS, Foreign Beggars, MistaJam, Steve Aoki, and Swedish House Mafia. "Knife Party" first appeared on the 2012 album, *Rage Valley*.

"Crystal Blue Persuasion"—Tommy James & the Shondells ("Gliding Over All," 5.08)

The perfect song to go with a classic meth-producing montage, "Crystal Blue Persuasion" was originally released by Tommy James and the Shondells on their 1969 album *Crimson & Clover*. The song reached No. 2 on the U.S. charts behind "In the Year 2525" by Zager and Evans. In a 1985 interview with *Hitch* magazine, James claimed he came up with the song's title after reading the Book of Revelation: "The words jumped out at me, and they're not together; they're spread out over three or four verses. But it seemed to go together, it's my favorite of all my songs and one of our most requested." Rock critic Dave Marsh described the song as "a transparent allegory about James's involvement with amphetamines." Other memorable songs from Tommy James and the Shondells include "Hanky Panky" and "Crimson and Clover" (both of which reached No. 1 on the U.S. charts, as well as "I Think We're Alone Now, "Mirage," "Mony Mony," and "Sweet Cherry Wine."

"Pick Yourself Up," by Nat King Cole ("Gliding Over All," 5.08)

The violent prison murder montage is accompanied by (what else?) the smooth sounds of crooner Nat King Cole's version of "Pick Yourself Up," which was composed by Jerome Kern with lyrics by Dorothy Fields and appeared in the 1936 musical *Swing Time*, which was directed by George Stevens (*Giant*), and starred Fred Astaire and Ginger Rogers. Cole's version of the song first appeared on his 1962 album *Nat King Cole/George Shearing Plays*, which features the talents of pianist George Shearing and peaked at No. 27 on the U.S. charts.

"Pick Yourself Up" has also been recorded by such legendary entertainers as Ella Fitzgerald, Frank Sinatra, Peter Tosh, Natalie Cole, and George Shearing, among many others. During his inauguration speech on January 20, 2009, President Barack Obama quoted the song's lyrics, remarking, "Starting today, we must pick ourselves up, dust ourselves off, and begin again the work of remaking America."

"Take My True Love by the Hand"—The Limeliters ("Ozymandias," 5.14)

Walt desperately rolls his remaining money barrel full of approximately $11 million in cash through the desert to the accompaniment of "Take My True Love by the Hand" by the Limeliters. Formed in 1959, the Limeliters were a folk trio composed of lead vocalist/guitarist Glenn Yarbrough, bassist/vocalist Lou Gottlieb, and banjoist/vocalist Alex Hassilev. The group was named after a club they worked at in Aspen, Colorado, called The Limelight. For several years, the Limeliters served as the musical representatives of Coca-Cola and recorded a popular jingle called "Things Go Better with Coke."

"Breaking Bad Title Theme (Extended)"—Dave Porter ("Granite State," 5.15)

The extended version of the "Breaking Bad Title Theme" can be heard after Walt talks to Junior briefly in the New Hampshire bar and then glimpses Elliott and Gretchen Schwartz being interviewed by Charlie Rose on the TV. The *Breaking Bad* theme was created by Los Angeles-based composer Dave Porter, who went on to compose music for *Better Call Saul* and the NBC crime thriller *The Blacklist*, among others. In *Breaking Bad: The Official Book*, Porter remarked, "My idea behind the theme was that it would be representative not of where Walter White is at the beginning of the series, but what he is to become. To that end the theme is intentionally brash and aggressive."

Porter attended Sarah Lawrence College, where he studied both classical and electronic music composition. According to Bryan Cranston in a 2014 *HuffPost* interview, "With his music, Dave Porter has created another character for *Breaking Bad*. Evocative and meaningful, Dave's work is an essential part of the storytelling." In 2013, Porter was awarded the inaugural ASCAP Composer's Choice Award as Best Television Composer for his work on *Breaking Bad*. Porter also composed the score for the 2017 film *The Disaster Artist*, which was directed by James Franco and also starred Franco as director Tommy Wiseau, the "genius" behind the 2003 cult drama *The Room*, known as "the *Citizen Kane* of Bad Movies."

"El Paso"—Marty Robbins ("Felina," 5.16)

"Out in the west Texas town of El Paso/I fell in love with a Mexican girl." As Walt makes his way back to New Mexico to settle various scores in the series finale, he listens to the classic country and western ballad "El Paso" by Marty Robbins (1925–1982). "El Paso" was first released on Robbins's 1959 album *Gunfighter Ballads and Trail Songs*, reached No. 1 on both the country and pop charts, and won the Grammy Award for Best Country & Western Recording in 1961. In addition, "El Paso" was named one of the

"Top 100 Western Songs of All Time" by members of the Western Writers of America. The song features a first-person narrative from a cowboy that details an ill-fated love triangle centering around a young Mexican dancer named "Faleena." The Grateful Dead often performed "El Paso" during their live concerts.

"Baby Blue"—Badfinger ("Felina," 5.16)

The closing scene of the *Breaking Bad* series finale features "Baby Blue" by British rock band Badfinger. "Baby Blue" first appeared on Badfinger's 1971 album *Straight Up*. Originally known as the Iveys, Badfinger became the first band signed by the Beatles' Apple label. In fact, Paul McCartney wrote their first hit, "Come and Get It," and George Harrison produced their biggest hit, "Day After Day." Badfinger's Pete Ham cowrote "Without

The closing scene of the *Breaking Bad* series finale features–quite appropriately–"Baby Blue" by British rock band Badfinger. The song first appeared on the band's 1971 album, *Straight Up*.

You," which was covered by Harry Nilsson in 1972 and years later became a hit for Mariah Carey. Ham, who struggled with financial difficulties, hanged himself in the garage of his Surrey, England, home in 1975, just four days before his twenty-eighth birthday. His blood alcohol level at the time of his death was .27 percent. Ham's suicide letter read "I will not be allowed to love and trust everybody. This is better." In 1983, Badfinger band member Tom Evans, who reportedly never got over his friend's death, hanged himself in his backyard.

31

Like the Rest of Us

Breaking Bad and the American Dream

> It's called the American Dream, 'cause you have to be asleep to believe it.
> —*George Carlin*

In *The Hawk Is Dying*, a critically acclaimed 1973 novel by Harry Crews (1935–2012), the protagonist, George Gatling, exclaims, "I'm at the end of my road. I was warned about everything except what I should have been warned about. I was warned about tobacco and I don't smoke. I was warned about whiskey and I don't drink except when I can't stand it. I was warned about women and I never married. But I was never warned about work. Work hard, they say, and you'll be happy. Get a car, get a house, get a business, get money. Get get get get get get get. Well, I got. And now it's led me here where everything is a dead-end." Walter White faces a similar predicament at the outset of *Breaking Bad*. Caught in a true suburban nightmare, he has reached a total dead end on the road of life.

As James Meek in the *London Review of Books* writes: "Albuquerque is presented in bleak terms: the faded, badly lit, over-upholstered clutter of ugly furniture in middle-class homes, Walter's mean little swimming pool in which no one ever swims but which will over time receive all kinds of substances (money, vomit, a false eyeball from an exploding plane), the cold carpet-tiled fluorescent barns of office space, the strip malls . . . The only haven against the man-made desert of Gilligan's Albuquerque is the beauty of the actual desert, criss-crossed as it is by drug dealers, drug makers, killers and illegal migrants."

Although *Breaking Bad* subtly alludes to the failure of the American Dream on many occasions (remember the show launched in 2008 amid the

Known as the "Crystal Palace," the infamous Crossroads Motel is where meth-addicted hooker Wendy turns tricks and where Hank lectures Walt Jr. about the dangers of drugs. It represents the dark side of the American Dream.   *Courtesy of Ben Parker*

housing bubble burst and stock market crash), it's curious to note that no significant political issues of any kind are raised by Walt or any of the other characters, nor do we even know who the president is or anything about the party in power. In the Introduction to *Breaking Bad: The Official Book*, critic David Thomson remarked, "We are the slaves in the land of the free who sustain the 1 percent who've made it. That's what happens if you build a society on desire and advertising, fear and loathing, and unregulated banking . . . Walter is fifty as the story begins, and it's easy to see fifty as the border between hope and despair."

In an August 10, 2015, article in *The Guardian*, Thomas Batten even compared the nature of Walter White's appeal to audiences to the improbable rise of then-presidential candidate Donald Trump: "Walter White won hearts by going into the meth trade after the American Dream let him down. He decided to go against the law because the law didn't seem to have his best interests at heart, and however horrible his crimes became, fans never forgot, or stopped identifying with, the frustration that set everything into motion. So maybe that's why Trump has some segment of the population so excited. He's running his campaign like he's getting away with something."

Downward Mobility

Before receiving his lung cancer diagnosis, Walt has apparently played by all of society's rules and gotten exactly nowhere as a result. A high school chemistry teacher who earns just $43,500 per year, he is forced to take a demeaning second job at a car wash just to make ends meet. In addition, the Whites' residence has seen better days and is in drastic need of repairs and updates. In the article "Breaking Bad's Failed American Dream," which appeared in *The Nation* on July 11, 2012, Max Rivlin-Nadler comments, "*Breaking Bad* dismisses the idea that your blue-collar job will provide for you, that, if needed, the State will, too, and that doing the right thing will be its own substantive reward. The show doesn't aim to moralize or assign blame; it works to deconstruct these little fallacies that keep the poor from demanding dignity." Being a member of the middle class in the United States is often precarious, and financial ruin can occur with just one simple health-care diagnosis. Indeed, Walt only achieves financial independence by becoming a meth dealer and destroying the lives of not only those closest to him, but also the anonymous drug users who clamor for his signature product.

Drug War

Breaking Bad makes clear that the so-called "War on Drugs" has totally failed. For example, the DEA spends all of their time busting low-level drug dealers like Badger while a true drug kingpin like Gus Fring "hides in plain sight" and distributes millions of dollars in meth unimpeded using his fast-food chain as a cover. Meanwhile, drugs move freely back and forth over the border with relative ease. The true cost of the drug war is reflected in the episode "Peekaboo" (2.06) as Jesse visits Spooge's house and witnesses the little boy sitting alone with vacant eyes inside the dilapidated home of his absent, drug-addled parents.

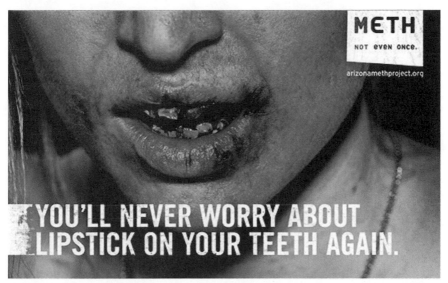

The true coast of meth addiction is reflected in "Peekaboo" as Jesse visits Spooge's house and witnesses the little boy sitting alone with vacant eyes inside the dilapidated home of his absent, drug-addled parents.

Education

Walt's high school chemistry classes are full of bored, distracted students who would rather be anywhere else. In fact, he is totally disrespected as a teacher. Ironically, Jesse Pinkman, one of his worst former students, becomes a top-rate meth cook only under Walt's tutelage. In addition, higher education is out of the question with college tuition costs continuing to skyrocket, reaching as high as $60,000 a year. What hope is there if Walt cannot even pay his health-care bills for Walt Jr. to strive for any higher education beyond maybe that of a community college?

Health Care

In a YouTube parody video titled "Breaking Bad: Canada Edition," the doctor informs Walt that since his health-care costs will be covered, he "won't need to do anything crazy like selling crystal meth to pay for it."

In the United States, the majority of personal bankruptcies are driven by exorbitant medical expenses, according to a recent study published on cnbc.com. Faced with a diagnosis of lung cancer, Walt is looking at extensive health-care treatments that will bankrupt himself and destroy his family's future. Health insurance won't even cover Walt Jr.'s physical therapy. In Walt's mind, the only reasonable solution is to put his chemistry skills to good use and compile the $737,000 necessary to provide for his family when he's gone.

Rampant Materialism

The empty materialism of our times is symbolized by the arrogant yuppie in the expensive red BMW convertible with a vanity license plate that reads "KEN WINS" who Walt gets a satisfying revenge on in the episode "Cancer Man" (1.04). It's interesting to note that even when Walt rises to become a drug lord, he remains unsatisfied with his life. He has accumulated over $80 million, which is stacked in a storage unit and then discreetly buried in eight huge barrels in the desert. When Uncle Jack Welker steals Walt's drug money, leaving him with a single barrel full of about $11 million, Todd convinces his uncle to start up the meth-cooking operation, exclaiming, "No matter how much you got, how do you turn your back on more?" In "Walter White's Dream," which was published in *The New York Times* on October 1, 2013, Ross Douthat remarks, "Ultimately, all of these themes [in *Breaking Bad*] converge to raise the most harrowing questions of all—the taboo questions about whether we should really cherish the desperation, the greed and the every-man-for-himself ideologies that drive Walter White and that make American the industrialized world's exception."

32

The Study of Change

Dissecting the *Talking Bad* Aftershow

All right, I've got the Talking Pillow now. Okay? We all, in this room, love each other. We want what's best for each other and I know that.

—*Walter White*

An immensely popular television aftershow that discussed the last eight episodes in the fifth and final season of *Breaking Bad*, *Talking Bad* was hosted by Chris Hardwick and featured cast and crew members, along with celebrity superfans such as Samuel L. Jackson, Julie Bowen, Don Cheadle, and Bill Hader. Broadcast live from August 11 to September 29, 2013, *Talking Bad* followed in the footsteps of *Talking Dead* (also hosted by Hardwick), which serves as a companion to that other hit AMC series *The Walking Dead*. *Talking Bad* segments included "Respect the Chemistry" (a "periodic table character study"), a "fix" from Vince Gilligan to preview the following episode (with Gilligan wearing a different *Breaking Bad* T-shirt for each segment), an online poll, and episode trivia, as well as questions taken from fans via phone, the official *Talking Bad* website, and social media.

"We have had so much success with Chris Hardwick and *Talking Dead*, the show-talking-about-a-show that attracted five million viewers after last season's *The Walking Dead* finale," remarked Joel Stillerman, AMC's EVP of original programming, production, and digital content, announcing the show on amc.com. "An aftershow hosted by Chris seemed like the perfect way to pay homage to and countdown the final eight episodes of *Breaking Bad*, giving fans the opportunity to come together and talk about the end of this iconic series brought to life by creator Vince Gilligan and his amazing cast and crew."

In a July 21, 2013, AMC press release to introduce the host of *Talking Bad*, Hardwick remarked,

> *Breaking Bad* will go down as one of the best shows in television history. Obviously, it's tonally much different than *The Walking Dead*, and I will strive to give *Breaking Bad* the send-off it deserves. I am honored to be able to give fans a peek behind the curtain for the last eight episodes so we can all say goodbye to it together. AMC will tell you that it's because of the success of *Talking Dead* or my friendship with the *BB* cast that they asked me to host this, but I maintain it probably has more to do with my unmistakable resemblance to Jesse Pinkman, BITCH."

Born on December 23, 1971, in Louisville, Kentucky, Hardwick is chief executive of Nerdist Industries, the digital division of Legendary Entertainment. His film credits include *Beach House* (1996), *Courting Courtney* (1998), *Art House* (1998), *Jane White Is Sick & Twisted* (2002), *House of 1000 Corpses* (2003), *Terminator 3: Rise of the Machines* (2003), *Spectres* (2004), *Johnson Family Vacation* (2004), *The Life Coach* (2005), *Halloween II* (2009), *Me Him Her* (2015), and *The LEGO Ninjago Movie* (2017).

Episode 1 ("Blood Money"): Aired on August 11, 2013

The debut *Talking Bad* show featured *Breaking Bad* creator Vince Gilligan, along with actress and "superfan" Julie Bowen, who portrays Claire Dunphy on the award-winning sitcom *Modern Family*, to discuss episode 5.09, "Blood Money." Gilligan, who wore a Heisenberg T-shirt that included the "Br" and "Ba" symbols, remarked that he was aware of the "blue meth" homage to *Breaking Bad* that appeared in a *Walking Dead* montage. In fact, the *Breaking Bad* prop department actually lent the "blue meth" to their sister show. Gilligan also claimed the fake meth "smells like cotton candy." Hardwick brought up the fan theory that *Breaking Bad* is actually a prequel to *The Walking Dead*, and Bowen exclaimed, "The blue meth makes them crazy trying to eat each other's brains!" Both Gilligan and Bowen admitted the character they missed

Talking Bad followed in the footsteps of *Talking Dead* (both hosted by Chris Hardwick), which serves as a companion to that other hit AMC series, *The Walking Dead*.

most was Gale Boetticher, who was according to Gilligan, "the sweetest, kindest, most nonfitting [individual] in the meth business. He didn't deserve it."

Episode 2 ("Buried"): Aired on August 18, 2013

Actor and comedian Bill Hader (*Documentary Now!*) was scheduled to appear with Anna Gunn on this episode to discuss "Buried" (5.10), but dropped out when Aaron Paul became available. Hader would later appear on the September 15 show to discuss "Ozymandias." Gilligan wore a "Say My Name" T-shirt during his "fix" segment. Paul was asked by Hardwick what is worse for Jesse to find out: Walt's role in Jane's death, Walt poisoning Brock, or Walt murdering Mike? Paul replied, "I mean all of them are so terrible, but I think it would be such a slap in the face if he found out about Jane. It's just so terrible . . . Jane died . . . it was really the first love of his life and Walt took her away from him." Asked how much Jesse has matured over the course of the series, Paul responded, "In Season One when we first met him I don't think he even truly knew who he was. He was just dressing in this ridiculous attire. He still wears his terrible bedazzled T-shirts but at least the clothes are a little bit, you know, more fitted and I think he kind of knows where he's at right now, but he's in a much darker, sadder place, so I don't know if he's going to climb out of that dark rabbit hole that he's in."

Asked if Skyler feels trapped by Walt, Gunn replied,

> I think Skyler has felt trapped by him for a long time. But I do think that now she feels a little bit like she understands fully that she has involved herself in this and she's culpable and she's complicit. So she's living in a little bit of a place [where] there is two things going on: which is that he has forced her against the wall and he's put her in a corner and he's held her hostage, but at the same time she has a full awareness of the decisions and the choices that she's made. And that she's lost her moral compass. And I don't think that Walt knows that about himself. I think he's in denial about everything that he's done. She really understands what's she has done.

Episode 3 ("Confessions"): Aired on August 25, 2013

Actor Samuel L. Jackson (*Pulp Fiction*), a huge fan of *Breaking Bad*, appeared with Bob Odenkirk to discuss episode 5.11, "Confessions." Jackson wore a porkpie hat, dark sunglasses, and a *Breaking Bad* T-shirt that featured a beaker of blue liquid along with the image of Heisenberg. Vince Gilligan wore a "Better Call Saul" T-shirt that featured Saul's business card: "I Can Make It Legal!" Odenkirk was asked who Saul is more afraid of: Walt sending him to Belize, Todd and Lydia paying him a visit, or Hank kicking in his door? "Walt can hunt you down almost wherever you go," replied Odenkirk. "And he's incredibly devious . . . Walt is the scariest thing of all." Odenkirk added that Saul was not sad to see Mike Ehrmantraut go: "Mike became such a pain in the ass . . . Saul realized that Mike was not going to work for him, really, ever." Jackson commented that "Mike was also part of that tug for Jesse's soul too . . . He actually saw some good in that kid. And he was trying to give him some survival skills."

Episode 4 ("Rabid Dog"): Aired on September 1, 2013

Betsy Brandt and RJ Mitte guest-starred on Episode 4 to discuss Episode 5.12, "Rabid Dog." Vince Gilligan wore a "Heisenberg College School of

Chemistry" T-shirt with the motto "Respiciunt Chemiae" ("Respect the Chemistry"). Brandt joked that Hank had to deal with all of Marie's craziness: "Look at all the purple he puts up with! I mean that's like taking his balls and putting them in a little handbag. He lets it go . . . God love him . . . he lets it go." Hardwick told Mitte that he "keeps hoping that Walt Jr. is the ultimate mastermind behind everything, pulling the strings the entire time." Brandt chimed in, "No one would suspect him." Brandt was asked that if Hank was Heisenberg, would Marie have stood by him as long as Skyler stood by Walt? She replied, "I think she would back him up. It's easy when he's a good guy. Hank's such a good guy. I think that Marie just believes in him so much that whatever he's saying she would think that's the right thing to do."

Episode 5 ("To'hajiilee"): Aired on September 8, 2013

Actor, writer, and director Don Cheadle (*Avengers: Infinity War*) joined Steven Michael Quezada and Bryan Cranston (appearing via satellite from Boston) to discuss Episode 5.13, "To'hajiilee." During his "fix" segment, Vince Gilligan wore an "I Am the One Who Knocks" T-shirt. Cranston remarked that portraying Walter White was "the ultimate role" and "an amazing journey for me." When asked whether he continues to enjoy playing Walt even after all of his truly despicable acts, Cranston replied, "When you're playing a character, you don't want to judge the character. You want to live it. We're so used to in television liking the main character, but not so anymore. That's what makes great television . . . it creates controversy." Responding to Jesse's collaboration with Hank to bring Walt down in "To'hajiilee", Cranston said with a smile, "He's a rat. He broke the code. We fully embraced our criminality and so now all of the sudden that's the one thing you don't do. You don't rat and he ratted. He's a filthy little rat!" Cranston also remarked that fans "won't be disappointed" by the series finale: "It ends in a very unapologetic, *Breaking Bad* way."

Episode 6 ("Ozymandias"): Aired on September 15, 2013

Dean Norris appeared to discuss episode 5.14, "Ozymandias," as well as his last day on the *Breaking Bad* set. Norris, who wore a Schraderbrau T-shirt (the name of Hank's home brew), was joined by actor and comedian Bill Hader (*Saturday Night Live*). During the "fix" segment, Vince Gilligan wore a "Pollos Hermanos" T-shirt. Regarding his character's demise, Norris commented, "We originally had the discussion about a year and a half ago, and [Vince Gilligan] told me about what episode [Hank would] be dying in . . . But at the beginning of the season, he sat me

32-02   In addition to host Chris Hardwick and guest appearances from *Breaking Bad* cast and crew members, *Talking Dead* featured celebrity superfans such as Samuel L. Jackson, Julie Bowen, Don Cheadle, and Bill Hader.   *Gage Skidmore/Wikimedia Commons*

down and said, 'I'm going to tell you what happens.' So we sit down in a room. It takes a half hour, and he really got to those last few lines and I was just [makes crying sound]. But it was great, and he knew it. They knew it." According to Norris, filming the scene took "shorter than we expected. We ended up shooting that scene, my final scene, the close-ups were all shot in one take, which takes quite a few takes . . . Literally, we did it in one take. Rian Johnson, the director, said, 'That's how you die on TV.'" Norris added, "Getting shot in the head is a great ending . . . I thought it was a proper ending. I'm glad he got to say the F-word. We always battle for that. We get one F-word a season."

Episode 7 ("Granite State"): Aired on September 22, 2013

Actor Adam Scott (*Parks and Recreation*) joined Matt L. Jones (Badger) and Bryan Johnson of *Comic Book Men/Tell 'Em Steve-Dave!* fame to discuss Episode 5.15, "Granite State." During his "fix" segment, Vince Gilligan wore a *Breaking Bad* T-shirt that featured blue blocks around the "Br" and "Ba". Asked about Todd's murder of Jesse's girlfriend, Andrea Cantillo, Johnson commented, "If I were Jesse at this point, if I made my escape, I would never date another girl. Jane dies. Now Andrea dies. I mean how do you ever recover from something like that?" Jones added that he believes that Andrea's death was Jesse's fault: "With the botched escape, the reason he didn't get out is because he never thinks with his head. He's the heart and Walt's the brains, right? So he does everything very impulsively and he does whatever he feels at that moment. So at the moment with Andrea he wasn't thinking correctly. He just ran away so they brought him to the house and the reason why she's dead is because he's weak . . . But everything that's bad that's happened to Jesse is because he's weak and Walt is strong. And that doesn't mean it's not evil." Scott countered that "Everything that's happening is ultimately Walt's fault." Jones replied, "Jesse could have walked away so many times. And he didn't because he wanted to be hardcore."

Episode 8 ("Felina"): Aired on September 29, 2013

Late-night TV host Jimmy Kimmel joined an all-star cast featuring Vince Gilligan, Aaron Paul, Anna Gunn, RJ Mitte, Giancarlo Esposito, and Jonathan Banks for an extended one-hour episode of *Talking Bad* to discuss the series finale, "Felina" (5.16). Gilligan, who wore a Heisenberg "Monopoly" T-shirt, explained that the reason Walt left his watch on top of the payphone had nothing to do with symbolism, but rather it was to avoid a continuity error (he wasn't wearing the watch in the flash-forward of him at Denny's in Episode 5.01, "Live Free or Die"). Paul (who sported a Vamonos Pest Control jumpsuit) explained why Jesse wouldn't shoot Walt during the final standoff: "The more episodes that were revealed, I realized I didn't want Jesse to take another life . . . besides Todd." Gilligan remarked that the classic 1956 John Wayne/John Ford Western *The Searchers* influenced the final standoff between Walt and Jesse.

Gunn stated that in the final scene between Skyler and Walt, she wore oversized clothing to make her appear like a "shrunken person" and a "shadow of her former self." It was also revealed that a scene was cut from the season finale script due to time and budget reasons. The scene involved one of Walt's former students recognizing him and Walt asking him, "What kind of teacher was I?" The student replies, "You were good" and then relates the time Walt sprayed a host of chemicals at a flame and created different colors. Asked about the legacy of *Breaking Bad*, Gilligan alluded to his favorite TV show, *The Twilight Zone* (1959–64): "You want to have that kind of immortality with your work." Asked to describe his portrayal of Gus Fring, Giancarlo Esposito commented that Gus masqueraded as a "mild and meek servant of the people at Los Pollos Hermanos . . . hiding in plain sight . . . pretending to be that kind and wonderful human being which was a part of him. There was a part that we didn't see that was a darkness and a part that [sought] revenge, and a part that was ambitious. So I think the combination of both dark and light, black and white, were the reasons why Gus became a fan favorite somewhere in the middle of Season Four."

In a review of "Felina," *Variety* praised the series finale but slammed the aftershow: "AMC does deserve one demerit for its companion program, 'Talking Bad.' While the tag-along talk hour introduced with 'The

Walking Dead' certainly represents a shrewd and inexpensive way to maximize profits off a single license fee (it must cost less to produce than the average school play), the network settled for a giddy fan tone that's frankly well beneath the show it's meant to celebrate, as well as the astonishingly detailed and exhaustive recap analysis 'Bad' has inspired."

Talking Saul

Using the same format of *Talking Bad*, *Talking Saul* was a live aftershow also hosted by Chris Hardwick to discuss the *Breaking Bad* spin-off prequel, *Better Call Saul*. *Talking Saul* first aired after the Season Two premiere, "Switch," on February 15, 2016, and featured special guests Vince Gilligan, Peter Gould, Bob Odenkirk, and Rhea Seehorn. The second *Talking Saul* aired on April 18, 2016, after the Season Two finale, "Klick," and featured special guests Jonathan Banks, Vince Gilligan, and Peter Gould. The third episode of *Talking Saul* aired on April 10, 2017, after the Season Three premiere, "Mabel," and featured special guests Vince Gilligan, Peter Gould, Jonathan Banks, and Rhea Seehorn. The fourth episode of *Talking Saul* aired on June 19, 2017, after the Season Three finale, "Lantern," and featured special guests Peter Gould, Patrick Fabian, Michael Mando, and Michael McKean (via satellite).

33

We Live to Fight Another Day

Better Call Saul

I'm not good at building shit, you know? I'm excellent at tearing it down.
—Jimmy McGill

Before Saul Goodman (Bob Odenkirk) ever even met Walter White, helped drug dealers evade the law, laundered money, and ended up managing a Cinnabon in Omaha, Nebraska, he was simply Jimmy McGill, a struggling attorney who lived in the shadow of his brilliant older brother, Chuck (Michael McKean).

Created by Vince Gilligan and Peter Gould, the *Breaking Bad* prequel *Better Call Saul* traces McGill's evolution from Slippin' Jimmy, who originally hails from Cicero, Illinois, to become Albuquerque's most notorious criminal lawyer. *Better Call Saul* is set in 2002–03, six years before Goodman meets White in *Breaking Bad* (he was first introduced on that show in Episode 2.08, "Better Call Saul,"). Believe it or not, *Better Call Saul* producers considered making the show a half-hour sitcom but fortunately decided on an hour-long drama with plenty of comic overtones.

In an August 14, 2017, *Vice* interview, Odenkirk remarked, "In America, we can reinvent ourselves—we're encouraged to. Jimmy's trying to reinvent himself from a con man to a respected lawyer. He feels entitled to do that, and a lot of the characters in his world feel he's entitled to do that as well. But his brother doesn't believe he should be allowed to reinvent himself, and he refuses to allow him to have the respect that he's desperately trying to earn."

Better Call Saul traces Jimmy's journey as he moves to Albuquerque, starts working in the mailroom of Chuck's law firm, and struggles to escape his brother's shadow. He eventually obtains a law degree via correspondence

Better Call Saul producers actually considered making the show a half-hour sitcom but wisely opted for an hour-long drama along with the right mix of comic overtones.

from the University of American Samoa Law School. However, at every turn, Chuck tries to block Jimmy's progress as a lawyer. At one point Chuck exclaims, "Slippin' Jimmy with a law degree is like a chimp with a machine gun." *Better Call Saul* has completed three seasons of thirty episodes. A fourth season of ten episodes began to air in fall 2018.

Better Call Saul Cast

Michael McKean is perfectly cast as Charles "Chuck" McGill Jr., a partner at Hamlin, Hamlin & McGill (HHM), one of the most prestigious law firms in Albuquerque. However, Chuck has been sidelined due to his suffering from "electromagnetic hypersensitivity," leaving him a virtual prisoner in his own house. McKean is perhaps best known for two previous roles: as Lenny Kosnowski in the popular 1970s/1980s sitcom *Laverne & Shirley* and as David St. Hubbins in the hilarious 1984 mockumentary *This Is Spinal Tap*. McKean also had appeared in Gilligan's short-lived spin-off to *The X-Files*, *The Lone Gunmen*, in 2001. Rhea Seehorn portrays Jimmy's law associate, romantic interest, and occasional partner in crime Kimberly 'Kim' Wexler. Previous to *Better Call Saul*, Seehorn has appeared in several recurring roles in TV series such as Charlotte in *The Starter*

Wife (2008), Brooke in *Trust Me* (2009), Roxanne in *Whitney* (2011–13), Cheri Young in *I'm With Her* (2003–04), Nicole Walker in *Head Cases* (2005), Stephanie Vogler in *The Singles Table* (2007), Samantha in *House of Lies* (2014), and Ellen Swatello in *Franklin & Bash* (2011–14). *Better Call Saul* also features the welcome return of Jonathan Banks as Mike Ehrmantraut, a former Philadelphia police officer who we first meet as a courthouse parking lot attendant. The cast also includes Patrick Fabian as slick lawyer Howard Hamlin, Michael Mando as aspiring drug kingpin Ignacio "Nacho" Varga, and Kerry Condon as Mike's struggling daughter-in-law Stacey Ehrmantraut, who has a daughter, Kaylee.

A slew of *Breaking Bad* characters also reappear in *Better Call Saul* during the first three seasons such as Gus Fring (Giancarlo Esposito), Tuco Salamanca (Raymond Cruz), No-Doze (Cesar Garcia), Gonzo (Jesus Payan Jr.), Ken (Kyle Bornheimer), Officer Saxton (Stoney Westmoreland), Lawson (Jim Beaver), Krazy-8 (Maximino Arciniega), Hector Salamanca (Mark Margolis), Fran (Debrianna Mansini), Leonel and Marco Salamanca (Daniel and Luis Moncada), Stephanie Doswell (Jennifer Hasty), Francesca Liddy (Tina Parker), Victor (Jeremiah Bitsui), Tyrus Kitt (Ray Campbell), Dr. Barry Goodman (J. B. Blane), Don Eladio Vuente (Steven Bauer), Juan Bolsa (Javier Grajeda), Huell Babineaux (Lavell Crawford), and Lydia Rodarte-Quayle (Laura Fraser).

SEASON ONE

Episode 1.01: "Uno" (February 8, 2015)

In the second-to-last *Breaking Bad* episode, "Granite State" (5.15), Saul Goodman told Walt as they were both waiting to be relocated, "If I'm lucky, month from now, best-case scenario, I'm managing a Cinnabon in Omaha." The black-and-white cold open of the first episode of *Better Call Saul* features Saul Goodman living under the new identity Gene and indeed managing a Cinnabon in Omaha following his relocation at the end of *Breaking Bad*. After work, he nostalgically watches a tape of the TV ads he made as Albuquerque's most outrageous criminal lawyer.

Flashback to 2002 as Saul, who was then known by his birth name, Jimmy McGill, struggles to get by as an Albuquerque public defender. He lives in the storage room of a Vietnamese nail salon (the same business that Saul tries to sell to Jesse as a money-laundering operation in *Breaking Bad*), drives a rundown 1998 Suzuki Esteem, and takes care of his brother, Chuck, a once-brilliant attorney and partner at Hamlin, Hamlin & McGill (HHM) and now a total recluse due to his belief that he suffers from "electromagnetic hypersensitivity." At one point, Chuck asks Jimmy, "Wouldn't you rather build your own identity? Why ride on someone else's coattails?"

Jimmy enlists two skateboarding twins, Cal and Lars, to help him with an accident scam in order to secure the wealthy Kettlemans as clients. Unfortunately, the wrong car is targeted and the scheme unravels quickly. The episode, which premiered on February 8, 2015, was directed by Gilligan and written by Gilligan and Peter Gould. The writing duo captured the Writers Guild of America Award for Television: Episodic Drama for the pilot episode. With 6.9 million viewers, "Uno" was the second highest debut in cable history behind *Fear the Walking Dead* (10.1 million viewers). As a subtle homage to *Breaking Bad*, look for the familiar jacket and porkpie hat of Heisenberg hanging behind the reception desk in the courthouse.

Episode 1.02: "Mijo" (February 9, 2015)

"I'm a lawyer, not a criminal." In "Mijo," Tuco Salamanca's grandmother returns home, followed by the skateboarding twins, who boldly overstate the nature of their injuries as part of Jimmy's scam. Tuco proceeds to knock them both unconscious with a cane. Jimmy arrives at the home, and Tuco drags him inside at gunpoint. Although Jimmy denies involvement in the scheme, he is outed by one of the twins. Tuco and his henchmen drive Jimmy and the twins out to the desert to eliminate them. Jimmy manages to talk himself out of getting killed, but Tuco states he will have to break one leg on each of the twins as an example for insulting his grandmother. The skateboarding twins call Jimmy "the worst lawyer in the world."

The episode was written by Peter Gould and directed by Michelle MacLaren. The episode's title is a contraction of "mi hijo" ("my son"). Note that Jimmy often uses the phrase "It's showtime, folks!" made popular from the 1979 musical *All That Jazz*, which was directed by Bob Fosse and starred Roy Scheider.

Episode 1.03: "Nacho" (February 16, 2015)

The teaser involves a flashback to a much younger Jimmy incarcerated in the Cook County Jail for an unspecified offense. Jimmy pleads with Chuck to beat the rap, and his older brother agrees under the condition that Jimmy clean up his act. In the present day, Jimmy grows concerned by Nacho's plot to extort the Kettlemans and leaves them an anonymous tip that they are in danger. The next day Jimmy receives word from Kim that the Kettlemans are missing. The police later arrest Nacho, who requests Jimmy as his legal counsel. Jimmy accompanies Kim to the Kettleman home and notices several inconsistencies, leading him to believe they have gone into hiding. Jimmy explores the desert area behind the Kettleman residence and discovers their campsite.

The episode was written by Thomas Schnauz and directed by Terry McDonough, who directed three *Breaking Bad* episodes: "Bit by a Dead Bee" (2009), "Better Call Saul" (2009), and "Bug" (2011). At one point, Mike alludes to the "Pine Barrens" in New Jersey, recalling a hilarious episode of the same name in *The Sopranos* involving Paulie (Tony Sirico), Christopher (Michael Imperioli), and Valery (Vitali Baganov), a member of the Russian mafia. "Pine Barrens" is considered one of the best, if not the best, episode in the history of the series. Also note that Jimmy states that there are only two things he knows about Albuquerque: "Bugs Bunny should've taken a left turn there. And give me a hundred tries, I'll never be able to spell it."

Episode 1.04: "Hero" (February 23, 2015)

The cold open reveals a younger Jimmy and a buddy running a scam in an alley involving "found money." In the present day, the Kettlemans offer Jimmy a bribe to try to prevent him from revealing their theft of the $1.6

million. Jimmy offers to be their legal counsel, but they turn him down. Nacho warns Jimmy that he will face the consequences of warning the Kettlemans. It later turns out that Jimmy has accepted the Kettlemans' bribe and he spends some of his newfound cash on a billboard that strongly resembles an HHM law office ad. Jimmy is ordered to take down the ad, so he creates a publicity stunt where he saves a worker who was physically removing the billboard. The so-called "rescue" makes the front page of the newspaper. The episode was written by Gennifer Hutchison and directed by Colin Bucksey.

Episode 1.05: "Alpine Shepherd Boy" (March 2, 2015)

Chuck gets a visit from two police officers after retrieving his neighbor's newspaper and reading about Jimmy's "rescue" of the billboard worker. Due to Chuck's strange living conditions, the officers first conclude that he must be a meth user or "tweaker." Through his newfound celebrity, Jimmy gets approached by several potential clients, including Big Ricky Sipes, who offers Jimmy $1 million in cash to help him secede from the United States (turns out the $1 million was in his own printed currency!), and Roland Jaycocks, an inventor who needs help getting a patent for his creepy "Tony the Toilet Buddy." However, Jimmy also gets a legitimate lead when he helps an elderly woman named Mrs. Strauss with her estate planning.

The episode was written by Bradley Paul and directed by Nicole Kassell. The title refers to Mrs. Strauss' Hummel figurine collection, which includes an alpine shepherd boy. At one point, Jimmy can be seen at Casa Tranquila nursing home trying to drum up business. Casa Tranquila is the notorious nursing home in *Breaking Bad* where Hector Salamanca resides and Gus Fring gets blown up.

Episode 1.06: "Five-O" (March 9, 2015)

In an opening flashback, Mike first arrives in Albuquerque via train with a fresh bullet wound in his shoulder. He visits his daughter-in-law Stacey and granddaughter Kaylee. He discusses the recent death of his son Matty, who was also a Philadelphia police officer. Mike assures

Stacey that Matty was not involved in anything illegal. Mike later gets his bullet wound treated by a shady veterinarian. Back to the present, two Philadelphia police detectives try to interrogate Mike, but he gives them Jimmy's business card. Mike and Jimmy visit with the detectives, who believe that Mike killed the two dirty cops suspected in his son's murder. Jimmy spills coffee as a diversion, allowing Mike to steal one of the detectives' notebooks. Another flashback reveals that Mike indeed had murdered the two detectives as revenge for the death of his son. Mike reveals the truth to Stacey and his guilt over the fact that he had actually encouraged Matty to be a corrupt cop. The episode was written by Gordon Smith and directed by Adam Bernstein.

Episode 1.07: "Bingo" (March 16, 2015)

Jimmy and Mike return the detective's notebook, claiming they found it in the parking lot. Kim turns down Jimmy's offer to become his law partner due to her loyalty to HHM. The Kettlemans reject Kim's proposal of a plea deal that would only require a sixteen-month prison sentence. The Kettlemans fire Kim and hire Jimmy as their legal counsel. Jimmy later finds out that Kim has been demoted at HHM after losing the Kettlemans as clients. He then has Mike deliver the money to the district attorney. The Kettlemans have no choice but to return to HHM and accept Kim's plea bargain. With Mike's assistance, Jimmy traces the Kettlemans' stolen money to a hidden compartment in their bathroom cabinet. The episode was written by Gennifer Hutchison and directed by Larysa Kondracki.

Episode 1.08: "RICO" (March 23, 2015)

During a flashback, a young Jimmy works in the HHM mailroom. He receives news that he has finally passed the bar exam and delivers the news to Chuck, expecting to be hired by HHM as an attorney. Chuck coldly replies that he must consult his partner first. Howard Hamlin informs Jimmy that he will not be hired immediately but that the firm will reevaluate his application in six months. In the present, Jimmy discovers some shady financial dealings at the Sandpiper Crossing nursing home. He gathers invoices from several residents and discovers that

Sandpiper has been systematically overcharging them. Jimmy does some dumpster diving to retrieve more evidence against Sandpiper. Chuck decides to assist Jimmy with the case. Sandpiper's attorneys deny any fraud at the facility but offer $100,000 to compensate the residents who were overcharged. Chuck counters with a demand that Sandpiper pay $20 million in settlement fees, paving the way for a court case. In order to assist his daughter-in-law and granddaughter financially, Mike visits the "veterinarian" and asks if there is any work available for him. The episode was written by Gordon Smith and directed by Colin Bucksey.

Episode 1.09: "Pimento" (March 30, 2015)

The Sandpiper case becomes too overwhelming in scope for Jimmy and Chuck, who recommends they take it to HHM. During a meeting the next day at HHM, Howard offers Jimmy a counsel fee and percentage of final settlement fees but angers him by stating that he will no longer work on the case or get hired by HHM for that matter. Jimmy checks his phone and discovers that Chuck had called Howard before the meeting. He now realizes that it has been Chuck all along who has prevented him from joining HHM. Jimmy exclaims to Chuck, "So that's it then, right? Keep old Jimmy down in the mail room. He's not good enough to be a lawyer." Chuck replies, "I know you. I know what you were, what you are. People don't change. You're Slippin' Jimmy. And Slippin' Jimmy I can handle fine. Slippin' Jimmy with a law degree is like a chimp with a machine gun. The law is sacred. If you abuse that power, people get hurt. This is not a game." Mike receives a bodyguard job for Pryce, a nerdy and arrogant first-time drug dealer. Mike drives with Pryce to an abandoned factory to help with his drug deal with Nacho. The episode was written and directed by Thomas Schnauz.

Episode 1.10: "Marco" (April 6, 2015)

In an opening flashback, a young Jimmy visits a dive bar in Cicero, Illinois, after getting released from jail with Chuck's assistance. He visits with his old pal Marco, who helps with his cons, and informs him he is moving to Albuquerque to start anew. In the present day, Jimmy visits

Before Saul Goodman (Bob Odenkirk) ever even met Walter White, helped drug dealers evade the law, laundered money, and ended up managing a Cinnabon in Omaha, Nebraska, he was simply Slippin' Jimmy McGill.   *Irmin Wehmeier/Wikimedia Commons*

with Howard at HHM and receives his counsel fee of $20,000 for the Sandpiper case. Jimmy has a mental breakdown while running a bingo game at the nursing home. He decides he needs to take a break and return to Cicero, where he looks up Marco. The duo start running cons again over the next week. During their last con before Jimmy is scheduled to return to Albuquerque, Marco suffers a heart attack. Before dying, he gasps, "I screwed up. Jimmy, you know what, this was the greatest week of my life." Jimmy attends Marco's funeral and inherits his pinky ring. Kim calls Jimmy and informs him that the Sandpiper case is so big that HHM had decided to partner with Davis & Main (D&M), a Santa Fe law firm. In addition, D&M is interested in hiring Jimmy.

The episode was written and directed by Peter Gould. Note that after Jimmy's one-night stand, the waitress he picks up exclaims, "Hey! You are not Kevin Costner!" Jimmy replies, "I was last night!" In the "Abiquiu" episode (3.11) of *Breaking Bad*, Saul had commented to Walt, "If you're committed enough, you can make any story work. I once told a woman I was Kevin Costner, and it worked because I believed it."

SEASON TWO

Episode 2.01: "Switch" (February 15, 2016)

The opening teaser for the Season Two premiere features Gene (Saul's new identity) managing the Cinnabon store and getting locked in the mall's dumpster room after hours. The janitor finally lets him out after a few hours, during which he has carved "SG WAS HERE" on the wall. Back in the present, Jimmy declines D&M's employment offer and convinces Kim to help with a "tequila con" on a businessman named Ken (Kyle Bornheimer) at a hotel bar. Kim enjoys the sordid adventure but admits to Jimmy that she does not want to participate in any of his other illegal schemes. Jimmy thinks it over and decides to join D&M.

Meanwhile, Mike refuses to accompany Pryce on another drug deal since he is now driving a flashy new Hummer. Pryce decides he doesn't need Mike anyway and meets alone with Nacho, who discovers his real name and address by discreetly going through the Hummer's glove compartment. He later ransacks Pryce's home looking for drugs. Pryce actually calls the police after discovering his rare baseball collection has been stolen. However, police are very suspicious about Pryce's story and the fact that he is driving such an expensive vehicle. They also discover a hidden compartment behind the couch that had been broken into by the burglar.

The episode was written and directed by Thomas Schnauz. The total douchebag, "Ken," who Jimmy and Kim pull the tequila scam on in the hotel bar, is none other than "KEN WINS," who steals Walt's spot in *Breaking Bad* (Walt later gets his revenge by rigging Ken's battery to set fire when he starts it up at the gas station). By the way, the tequila in question, Zafiro Añejo ($50 per shot), is the same tequila Gus Fring uses to poison Don Eladio and his crew in *Breaking Bad*. Note that the officer responding to the theft of the baseball cards is the same Officer Saxton (Stoney Westmoreland) who arrives on the scene when Skyler calls the police on Walt in *Breaking Bad*. Note that the first letter of each episode title in Season Two unscrambles to foreshadow "Fring's Back."

Episode 2.02: "Cobbler" (February 22, 2016)

Jimmy and Kim's relationship heats up while Chuck ruminates about Jimmy's new job at D&M. Jimmy receives a Mercedes-Benz as his new company car. Mike strongly recommends to Pryce that he not discuss the burglary of his house with the police, although a clueless Pryce is adamant about getting his baseball cards back. Mike assures him that he will get the cards back for him, so he tracks down Nacho working at his father's car restoration shop. Mike threatens Nacho that he will inform Tuco about Nacho's side deals. Mike works a deal that involves Pryce trading his Hummer to Nacho for the baseball cards and $10,000. Pryce is summoned for an interview with detectives, but Mike hires Jimmy to accompany him. Alone with the detectives, Jimmy claims that his client is embarrassed by fetish videos involving sitting on pies that were hidden in the secret compartment. The story is so outrageous that the detectives actually believe Jimmy.

The episode was written by Gennifer Hutchison and directed by Terry McDonough. Note that Kim wears a University of American Samoa sweatshirt in one scene. It's the law school where Jimmy received his degree.

Episode 2.03: "Amarillo" (February 29, 2016)

Jimmy travels to Amarillo, Texas, and bribes a Sandpiper bus driver to "break down" so he can solicit residents on the bus. At the next Sandpiper strategy meeting, Jimmy proudly announces the success of his outreach to residents, but Chuck voices concern about Jimmy's sleazy methods. Jimmy decides to film his own television ad targeting Sandpiper residents but fails to run his idea for approval by his superiors at D&M. The ad proves to be a huge success but ends up getting Jimmy in trouble. Meanwhile, Stacey informs Mike that she has heard gunshots in the neighborhood and fears for the safety of herself and her daughter. Mike stakes out the scene and realizes there is nothing to her story, but he offers to find her a new place to live anyway. Mike receives a job offer from the "veterinarian," and the client turns out to be Nacho. The episode was written by Jonathan Glatzer and directed by Scott Winant.

Episode 2.04: "Gloves Off" (March 7, 2016)

After the TV ad debacle, Jimmy gets a second chance with the D&M partners. Because she was aware of Jimmy's ad (but not the fact that Jimmy didn't get approval for it), Kim gets demoted by HHM to the basement of the law office for document review. When Jimmy confronts Chuck about the firm's treatment of Kim, Chuck remarks, "See that's your problem, Jimmy . . . thinking the ends justify the means. And you're forever shocked when it all blows up in your face." When Jimmy asks what he did wrong, Chuck replies, "You broke the rules." Mike and Nacho discuss plans to murder Tuco since Nacho is afraid that Tuco will find out about his side deals. Mike decides against the hit, realizing that it would draw the unwanted attention of the Mexican cartel. Instead, Mike sets up a scenario where he provokes Tuco into assaulting him. The episode was written by Gordon Smith and directed by Adam Bernstein. Note that the arms dealer that Mike visits, Lawson (Jim Beaver), is the same guy that Walt buys illegal weapons from in *Breaking Bad*.

Episode 2.05: "Rebecca" (March 14, 2016)

The episode opens with a flashback that shows Jimmy shortly after moving to Albuquerque and visiting Chuck's house, where he meets Chuck's new wife, Rebecca. Chuck gets upset when Rebecca falls for Jimmy's charm. In the present, Kim works overtime to bring a new client to HHM so she can get her old position back. She manages to bring Mesa Verde Bank to HHM, but Howard still keeps her on document review. Chuck informs her that Jimmy embezzled so much money from their father's grocery store that it eventually closed. Chuck confides, "My brother is not a bad person. He has a good heart. It's just . . . he can't help himself. And everyone's left picking up the pieces." Meanwhile, Mike has a run-in with none other than Hector Salamanca (Mark Margolis), who tells him in no certain terms that he is going to have to take the rap for his nephew Tuco's gun charge in order to reduce his sentence. He offers

$5,000 but Mike refuses the request. The episode was written by Ann Cherkis and directed by John Shiban. Note that a bell rings just before Hector approaches Mike in the diner—alluding to the bell on Hector's wheelchair in *Breaking Bad* that he will use for various forms of communication and ultimately to kill Gus Fring.

Episode 2.06: "Bali Ha'i" (March 21, 2016)

Jimmy becomes disenchanted with his new job at D&M and looks for a way out. Although Chuck helps Kim get her old position back, Howard treats her rudely and sends her out to handle unwinnable motions in court. However, she catches the eye of Rich Schweikart, who offers her a position with Schweikart & Cokely (S&C) law firm. Unsure of whether to accept, Kim runs another scam with Jimmy. Mike faces pressure to accept Hector's offer, and eventually even Hector's nephews, Leonel and Marco Salamanca (the Cousins), show up to try to intimidate him. Fearing for the safety of his daughter-in-law and granddaughter, Mike accedes to Hector's deal but manages to raise it to $50,000 (giving half of it to Nacho for failing to uphold his part of the earlier deal).

The episode was written by Gennifer Hutchison and directed by Michael Slovis. The title refers to the Rodgers and Hammerstein show tune from the 1949 Broadway musical *South Pacific* that Jimmy sings on Kim's answering machine. In addition, Jimmy scams a $10,000 check out of his mark made out to Ice Station Zebra Associates (referencing the 1968 film *Ice Station Zebra*, a favorite of billionaire recluse Howard Hughes). The check itself is from Cradock Marine Bank, which also makes an appearance in both *The X-Files* and *Breaking Bad*.

Episode 2.07: "Inflatable" (March 28, 2016)

A flashback reveals ten-year-old Jimmy in his father's store during the early 1970s. A grifter arrives and attempts to con Jimmy's father, who is actually quite gullible. However, an astute Jimmy reads right through the scam. While Jimmy's father is distracted, the grifter informs him that there are only "wolves and sheep" in the world and he has to choose which one he will be. Jimmy decides to be a "wolf" and ends up stealing some money from his father's register. In the present, Jimmy accompanies Mike to the district attorney's office so he can take the rap for Tuco's gun charge. Jimmy finds out he will only get to keep his signing bonus at D&M if he makes them fire him, so he does everything in his power to annoy the firm—including wearing increasingly louder suits and even playing the bagpipes in his office. Jimmy's persistence eventually pays off, and he gets fired. He then approaches Kim and once again tries to convince her to become his partner in their own law firm. Kim refuses after she asks Jimmy if he will play it on the "straight and narrow," and he tells her he can only be himself. Kim later proposes that they start two separate law firms utilizing the same office. The episode was written by Gordon Smith and directed by Colin Bucksey.

Episode 2.08: "Fifi" (April 4, 2016)

Jimmy decides to accept Kim's offer of starting two law firms that share the same office. After Kim resigns from HHM, she secures the Mesa Verde Bank account as her first solo client. Chuck calls a meeting with Mesa Verde where he manages to slyly undercut Kim's abilities, and the bank decides to stay with HHM. However, Chuck collapses after the meeting and is hospitalized. Mike continues his surveillance of Hector and starts constructing a highway spike strip. The episode was written by Thomas Schnauz and directed by Larysa Kondracki.

Episode 2.09: "Nailed" (April 11, 2016)

Mike ambushes one of Hector's trucks and walks away with $250,000. Nacho suspects that Mike was behind the heist and meets with him. He informs Mike that a "Good Samaritan," who came upon the scene and assisted the driver, was later murdered by Hector. Due to Jimmy falsifying some of Chuck's Mesa Verde documents, the grand opening of their newest branch will have to be delayed six weeks. Chuck believes that Jimmy is responsible for the sabotage, which leads to Mesa Verde dumping HHM and re-signing with Kim. The episode was written and directed by Peter Gould.

Episode 2.10: "Klick" (April 18, 2016)

A flashback reveals Jimmy and Chuck sitting beside a hospital bed, where their comatose mother lies. After Jimmy leaves to get some sandwiches, his mother wakes up and calls out his name twice before dying. However, Chuck later denies to Jimmy that their mother had any last words. In the present, Jimmy visits Chuck in the hospital (he had passed out in the copy store while investigating if Jimmy sabotaged the Mesa Verde deal). Mike buys a rifle from Lawson with the intent of killing Hector. He positions himself at a distance but cannot get a clear shot. Just then, Mike hears his horn blaring, and when he returns to his car finds a note that simply reads "Don't." After getting a CT scan, Chuck devolves into a "self-induced catatonic state," according to his doctor. Jimmy assumes temporary guardianship of Chuck. Howard advises Jimmy that Chuck has quit the law firm. Jimmy arrives at Chuck's house and discovers his brother covering everything with foil. Chuck explains that the electro-magnetic radiation caused him to screw up the Mesa Verde files. Jimmy ends up confessing that he sabotaged the documents, just like Chuck had originally suspected. After Jimmy leaves, Chuck reveals a tape recorder that had been running for Jimmy's entire visit. The episode was written by Heather Marion and Vince Gilligan, and directed by Gilligan.

SEASON THREE

Episode 3.01: "Mabel" (April 10, 2017)

As with both the Season One and Season Two opening episodes, "Mabel" opens at the mall where Gene works as the manager of a Cinnabon. He helps mall security capture a shoplifter and then advises him to hire a lawyer. Gene collapses when he returns to work. Back to 2003, Jimmy assists Chuck in removing the foil from the walls of his house. Chuck tells Jimmy that his actions will never be forgiven. Bewildered by the thwarted killing of Hector, Mike discovers a tracking device inside his car's gas cap. The episode was written by Vince Gilligan and Peter Gould, and directed by Gilligan.

Episode 3.02: "Witness" (April 17, 2017)

Chuck consults with a private investigator. Mike requests Jimmy's assistance in helping him identify the individual (Victor from *Breaking Bad*, portrayed by Jeremy Bitsui) that attached a tracking device to his vehicle. Mike and Jimmy are watched from a distance by none other than Gus Fring (Giancarlo Esposito in his first appearance on *Better Call Saul*). Jimmy breaks into Chuck's house and destroys the tape of his confession. However, both the private investigator and Howard witness the break-in. The episode was written by Thomas Schnauz and directed by Vince Gilligan. Note that Saul meets Gus for the first time in this episode (interestingly, they never meet in *Breaking Bad*). "Witness" also marks the first appearance of Francesca (Tina Parker) on *Better Call Saul*. She makes a reappearance as Saul's secretary in *Breaking Bad*.

Episode 3.03: "Sunk Costs" (April 24, 2017)

Gus and Mike come to an understanding that Gus will stop tracking Mike and Mike will not kill Hector. Mike, however, decides to continue trying to get Hector apprehended by the police. Mike creates an elaborate plan to dump cocaine on one of Hector's trucks. A drug-sniffing dog discovers the cocaine at the border, and DEA agents arrest Hector's men. Meanwhile, Jimmy gets arrested for breaking into Chuck's house. He chooses to represent himself and pleads not guilty. When informed that Jimmy might get disbarred due to the break-in, Kim pleads with Jimmy to let her help with the case. The episode was written by Gennifer Hutchison and directed by John Shiban.

Episode 3.04: "Sabrosito" (May 1, 2017)

Gus humiliates Hector by sending a larger tribute than he did to Don Eladio. Hector visits Los Pollos Hermanos and threatens Gus. Meanwhile, Jimmy hires Mike to pose as a handyman and photograph the interior of Chuck's house in order to document his brother's truly strange living conditions. Gus visits Mike and asks to hire him. He also explains to Mike why he prevented him from killing Hector—"a bullet to the head would have been far too humane." Kim learns from Chuck that he has a copy of the taped confession. The episode was written by Jonathan Glatzer and directed by Thomas Schnauz. The title, "Sabrosito," means "tasty" in Spanish. For the first time in the series, there is no cold open in this episode. Steven Bauer appears in *Better Call Saul* for the first time in "Sabrosito" as Don Eladio and is seen diving into his swimming pool (the same pool he will later die in after being poisoned by Gus in *Breaking Bad*).

Episode 3.05: "Chicanery" (May 8, 2017)

During an opening flashback, Chuck invites Rebecca to dinner and creates an elaborate lie on why there is no power in the house. She gets very suspicious, however, when she attempts to answer her cell phone and a distressed Chuck proceeds to knock it out of her hands. In the present, Jimmy prepares for his hearing to take place in front of the New Mexico Bar Association. The tape is played during the hearing, but during Jimmy's cross-examination of the recording, he reveals that Huell has planted a cell phone battery on Chuck, suggesting that his symptoms actually show signs of mental illness. Chuck then embarks on a diatribe against Jimmy that shocks everyone at the hearing. The episode was written by Gordon Smith and directed by Daniel Sackheim. "Chicanery" represents the first appearance in the series by Huell Babineaux (Lavell Crawford), Saul's burly bodyguard from *Breaking Bad*. Note that Mike does not appear in this episode.

Episode 3.06: "Off Brand" (May 15, 2017)

After the hearing, Jimmy is handed a one-year suspension from practicing law. While Jimmy and Kim celebrate the verdict, Rebecca pleads with Jimmy to help with Chuck, who has barricaded himself within his house. Howard visits Chuck and tells him that he has to move on and forget about Jimmy. Gus works out a deal with Hector, who wants to use Nacho's father's business as a front for drug activity. Jimmy poses as a new character, Saul Goodman, for a series of TV commercials.

The episode was written by Ann Cherkis and directed by Keith Gordon. "Off Brand" marks the first appearance of Lydia Rodarte-Quayle (Laura Fraser) from *Breaking Bad*. Note that Gus and Lydia share a scene together in this episode, which they never do in *Breaking Bad*.

Episode 3.07: "Expenses" (May 22, 2017)

After being suspended from practicing law for a year, a depressed Jimmy runs out of money. Kim starts feeling regret over what happened to Chuck at the hearing. Nacho approaches Pryce with a pill he stole from Hector and offers the novice drug dealer a new opportunity in a plot to kill Hector. Pryce tries to procure Mike's bodyguard services in his dealings with Nacho (Mike initially declines but later changes his mind). Mike learns about Nacho's plan to replace Hector's medication with fake pills. Jimmy deliberately lets it slip to an insurance agent that Chuck is suffering from mental illness. The episode was written and directed by Thomas Schnauz.

Episode 3.08: "Slip" (June 5, 2017)

In a flashback, Jimmy and Marco prepare for yet another con. In the present, Chuck consults with Dr. Cruz and finally admits that his condition may be partly psychological. Chuck is able to visit the grocery store, but he sees Howard, who informs him that there are issues with his malpractice insurance. Kim attempts to repay her law school loans to Howard but he refuses, telling her she betrayed the firm. Jimmy uses a "slip and fall" con. Nacho successfully replaces Hector's heart medication pill with a placebo. Mike starts doing business with Gus. The episode was written by Heather Marion and directed by Adam Bernstein.

Episode 3.09: "Fall" (June 12, 2017)

Jimmy discovers that the Sandpiper settlement deal would give him more than $1 million if accepted by both HHM and D&M. He attempts to get Howard to approve the deal, but Howard refuses. Chuck decides to fight the insurance company in court due to his malpractice issues. Howard informs Chuck that he will be forced to retire, prompting Chuck to sue HHM for $8 million. Mike is hired to work as a security consultant" for Madrigal based on a recommendation by Gus. Nacho informs his father that he works for Hector and pleads with him to follow Hector's orders. Nacho's father responds by kicking him out of the house. Through a series of unethical moves, Jimmy manages to help the Sandpiper settlement move forward. An exhausted Kim falls asleep at the wheel and drives her car off the road, crashing it into a boulder. The episode was written by Gordon Smith and directed by Minkie Spiro.

Episode 3.10: "Lantern" (June 19, 2017)

In a flashback, young Chuck reads young Jimmy a story using the light of a lantern. In the present, Kim has a broken arm as a result of her car crash. Chuck is finally forced out of HHM with a $9 million buyout paid for by Howard. Hector meets with Nacho's father and bribes him for his loyalty. After being told by Juan Bolsa that Don Eladio has requested that Gus handle all smuggling operations, an enraged Hector suffers a heart attack. Jimmy attempts to reconnect with Chuck but is strongly rebuffed by his older brother, who remarks, "Why don't you skip the whole exercise? In the end, you're going to hurt everyone around you. You can't help it. So stop apologizing and accept it. Embrace it. Frankly, I'd have more respect for you if you did." Chuck reveals to Jimmy that "Hey, I don't want to hurt your feelings, but the truth is, you've never mattered all that much to me." While attempting to remove the wiring out of the walls of his home, Chuck knocks the gas lantern over, starting a fire while he is trapped inside. The episode was written by Gennifer Hutchison and directed by Peter Gould.

34

Never Give Up Control

Merchandising, Homages, and Parodies

> Not only is the story compelling—it's a really interesting story—
> but the acting is superb.
>
> *Warren Buffett on* Breaking Bad

So you've watched every episode of *Breaking Bad* along with all the DVD commentaries and you still need a fix? Want to gift something more original than a Los Pollos Hermanos T-shirt, Heisenberg "I am the Danger" phone case, or a Saul Goodman action figure? How about getting your hands on some Blue Sky Rock Candy, *Breaking Bad* board game, or even an authentic Goorin Bros Heisenberg Hat (good luck with that one)?

Not everyone is happy with the glut of somewhat tasteless merchandising that continues to be churned out in the wake of both *Breaking Bad* and *Better Call Saul.* For example, a Florida mom even went so far as to start a petition to get *Breaking Bad* action figures removed from Toys R US shelves (the now-defunct company removed the offensive merchandise after she gathered more than nine thousand signatures). In a September 11, 2014, *Vice* article titled "*Breaking Bad* Merchandise Is Cheapening the Show's Legacy," Jack Murray writes, "[T]he merchandising of *Breaking Bad* leaves the gruesome undercurrent of the show lost in a gaudy, tacky selection of collectables that color the series as a lightweight cartoon. The narrative is diluted from a bleak tale of economic strife, drugs and terminal illness and reworked into travel mugs and a throwaway fashion line."

Below is a compilation of offbeat *Breaking Bad* merchandise, as well as some fascinating homages and parodies to the series that, in some cases, really have to be seen to be believed:

Blue Sky Rock Candy

Wandering around Albuquerque visiting famous *Breaking Bad* locales and seeking a knockoff of the blue stuff? Just stop by the Candy Lady (aka Debbie Ball), a landmark Albuquerque candy restaurant at 424 San Felipe NW. The Candy Lady actually created crystal rock candy that was used as prop meth in Seasons One and Two of *Breaking Bad*, and visitors can take home a few bags of the Blue Sky Rock Candy as a souvenir. The blue ice candy was even featured on the *Late Show with David Letterman* after guest Bryan Cranston presented it as a gift to Letterman. A disclaimer on the thecandylady.com website reads, "The Candy Lady does not endorse recreational and illegal drug use. Here we encourage people to use the show's popularity and events to teach others about the Real Consequences, Life Cost and Danger of 'Meth' and other illicit drug use." Got that?

"Breakbad Mountain"

In a Q&A that appeared on amc.com, Aaron Paul remarked, "I love the little mock-up videos people have made using clips from the show. There's one called 'Breakbad Mountain.' It puts together all these clips and makes it seem that Walter White and Jesse Pinkman are having a secret love affair, and it is incredible. It really looks like an amazing movie." A spoof on the critically acclaimed 2005 film *Brokeback Mountain*, which was directed by Ang Lee and starred Heath Ledger and Jake Gyllenhaal, "Breakbad Mountain" was designed as a mock trailer with the tagline, "It was a friendship that became a secret. There are lies we have to tell." Designed by Eric Posen and Jason Mittleman, "Breakbad Mountain" can be viewed on YouTube.

"Breaking Bad: 1995 Style"

What if *Breaking Bad* had aired in the 1990s as a cheesy family drama along the lines of *Party of Five*, *Picket Fences*, or *Beverly Hills, 90210*?

Here's about what viewers could have expected if *Breaking Bad* was produced long before the spate of spectacular antihero dramas that came about in the late 1990s and early 2000s such as *Oz*, *The Wire*, and *The Sopranos*. Check it out on YouTube.

Breaking Bad: All Bad Things

The twenty-page digital comic version of *Breaking Bad* was released in August 2013. The comic "recaps the first four-and-a-half seasons of Walter White's descent from mild-mannered chemistry teacher to drug kingpin." The cover of *Breaking Bad: All Bad Things* features Heisenberg standing alone in a junkyard amid iconic artifacts from the show such as the one-eyed pink teddy bear, a Los Pollos Hermanos cup, methylamine barrels, a "Better Call Saul" matchbook, and even a tarantula in a glass jar. *Breaking Bad: All Bad Things* can be viewed at www.amc.com/shows/breaking-bad/exclusives/all-bad-things.

Breaking Bad: Alternate Dream Ending

In a hilarious homage to the series finale of *Newhart*, which aired in 1990, Bryan Cranston as Hal Wilkerson from the popular sitcom *Malcolm in the Middle* (2000–06) wakes up in bed from a nightmare and relates to his wife Lois (Jane Kaczmarek) that he dreamt he was a drug kingpin. Hal describes Jesse, the meth-cooking partner in his dream, like "he was wearing his older brother's clothes . . . He would use the b-word a lot. He would say, 'Yo, b-word! Yah science b-word!'" He also refers to his brother-in-law Hank as looking "like the guy from *The Shield*."

In the season finale of *Newhart*, "The Last Newhart," Bob Newhart reprises his role as Dr. Bob Hartley from *The Bob Newhart Show* (1972–78), waking up in bed and revealing to his wife, Emily (Suzanne Pleshette), that he had just dreamt that he was an innkeeper in Vermont surrounded by a slew of wacky characters. In a 2013 television interview with David Steinberg, Newhart credited his wife, Ginnie, for coming up with the idea for the dream sequence (a notion that was later dismissed by the show's

Breaking Bad: All Bad Things, a twenty-page digital comic version of the series, was released in 2013 and highlighted "Walter White's descent from mildmannered chemistry teacher to drug kingpin."

executive producers). *Entertainment Weekly* named the *Newhart* episode as No. 1 on its list of the "20 Best TV Series Finales Ever." The *Breaking Bad* alternate ending can be found on the final-season Blu-ray/DVD set and *Breaking Bad: The Complete Series Barrel Set*.

Breaking Bad: The Board Game

In this intriguing idea for a board game that "propels you into the treacherous underbelly of Albuquerque," players can choose to join one of three criminal factions—Heisenberg, Los Pollos Hermanos, or the Juarez Cartel—and try to "amass a fortune" while "eliminating rivals." Or they can simply join the DEA and try to put everyone else behind bars.

Breaking Bad: The Complete Series Barrel Set

On November 26, 2013, the complete *Breaking Bad* series (all sixty-two uncut, uncensored episodes) was released on DVD and Blu-ray within a collectible box shaped like one of the barrels Walt uses to bury his $80 million worth of meth earnings in the desert. In addition to a two-hour documentary, the set features an alternate *Newhart*-inspired ending (see above entry), more than fifty-five hours of special features, commemorative challenge coin designed by Vince Gilligan, Los Pollos Hermanos apron, and "Better Call Saul" matchbook 4GB flash drive. It's simply a must-own for every hardcore *Breaking Bad* fan!

Breaking Bad Fest

The first (and apparently last!) Breaking Bad Fest took place November 7–8, 2014, at the Albuquerque Convention Center. Highlights included the Geeks Who Drink Breaking Bad Trivia Contest at Tractor Brewery, Karting Bad go-kart races at Albuquerque Indoor Karting (where Jesse used to hang out!), a Behind the Scenes panel discussion with *Breaking Bad* crew, Costume Contest, and a *Breaking Bad* cast panel featuring

Steven Michael Quezada (Gomie), Charles Baker (Skinny Pete), Jeremiah Bitsui (Victor), Luis and Daniel Moncada (the Cousins), and Max Arciniega (Krazy-8).

"Breaking Bad Meets Malcolm in the Middle"

Before his five-season stint as Walter White in *Breaking Bad*, Bryan Cranston portrayed Hal Wilkerson on the immensely popular sitcom *Malcolm in the Middle* between 2000 and 2006. This fairly amusing clip addresses the possibility that Walter White and Hal Wilkerson are actually the same person. It can be viewed on YouTube.

"Breaking Bad: The Middle School Musical"

In this hilariously clever spoof of both *Breaking Bad* and middle school musicals in general, a group of child actors embark on a musical recap of the entire series featuring a more innocent drama that replaces meth with blue rock candy, and features "I Am the One Who Knocks" and other humorous tunes. "Breaking Bad: The Middle School Musical" was created by Rhett McLaughlin and Link Neal (aka Rhett & Link). The duo also has created middle school musical versions of *Star Trek* and *Superman*. All of their videos can be found on YouTube.

Breaking Bad: The Movie

In March 2017, two French superfans of *Breaking Bad*—film director Lucas Stoll and graphic designer Gaylor Morestin—released a two-hour feature-length film online called *Breaking Bad: The Movie* that was culled from the entire series (an absolute dream for the binge watcher with a short attention span!). According to the film summary: "It's not a fan-film, hitting the highlights of show in a home-made homage, but rather a re-imagining of the underlying concept itself, lending itself to full feature-length treatment. An alternative *Breaking Bad*, to be viewed with fresh eyes." Good luck finding *Breaking Bad: The Movie* anywhere online—it has apparently been removed due to copyright issues.

"Breaking Bad Sadness"

An amusing online parody that applies *Breaking Bad* dialogue to "Summertime Sadness," Lana Del Rey's hit ballad, "Breaking Bad Sadness" was written and produced by comedian Beth Crosby, the co-creator of the popular web series *Jessica and Hunter*. "Breaking Bad Sadness" can be viewed on YouTube.

"The Breaking Bad Show"

Originally aired at the Emmy Awards on September 24, 2012, and introduced by host Jimmy Kimmel (with Bryan Cranston and Aaron Paul in the audience), this short parody morphs the series with the whimsically wholesome classic *The Andy Griffith Show* (1960–68) to see how it may have fared as a 1960s sitcom. Dressed in full meth-cooking gear, Cranston and Paul stroll along the river with fishing poles. They then shoot Barney Fife. A voice-over states, "Brought to you by meth." Look for "The Breaking Bad Show" on YouTube.

"Breaking Bread"

Another rather amusing online video parody, "Breaking Bread" features "Walter Wheat," a home economics teacher who is diagnosed with Type 4 Diabetes and teams up with his former student "Jesse Pinkberry" to create an addictive cupcake. "Breaking Bread" was created by Tucker Matthews and Mark Nager.

"Breaking Nye"

Imagine Bill Nye the Science Guy as drug kingpin Walter White and you can just imagine where this clever parody video from collegehumor.com is going. "Breaking Nye" can be viewed on YouTube.

"Breaking Swift"

Created by Israel Curtis and Eddie King of Somakat.com, "Breaking Swift" features the duo revisiting the exploits of Walt and Jesse set to Taylor's Swift's hit 2012 song "We Are Never Ever Getting Back Together."

"Do You Want to Build a Meth Lab?"

Ever wonder what would happen if *Breaking Bad* clashed with Disney's 2013 animated classic *Frozen*? Neither do I, but those who are truly interested can check out this mishmash video that parodies the *Frozen* song "Do You Want to Build a Snowman?" and features such compelling lyrics as "It gets a little lonely/In this empty lab/Just watching that fly whiz by."

Dumb and Dumber To (2014) with Bill Murray as Ice Pick

An underwhelming sequel to the 1994 box-office hit *Dumb and Dumber* starring Jim Carrey as Lloyd Christmas and Jeff Daniels as Harry Dunne, *Dumb and Dumber To* features at least one bright spot in an over-the-top cameo by Bill Murray as Harry's meth-cooking roommate, Ice Pick. In an obvious homage to *Breaking Bad*, Ice Pick wears a yellow hazmat suit and cooks up meth as a clueless Harry introduces him to an equally clueless Lloyd. During a typically idiotic verbal exchange, Harry tells Lloyd, "Pick cooks up a rock candy that'll make you dizzy. Folks come from all over the city to buy it." Lloyd replies, "It's burning my eyes. Must be Cajun style."

Esurance Commercial featuring Walter White

Just one week before the premiere of *Better Call Saul*, Bryan Cranston turned up as Walter White in an Esurance commercial that aired just once during Super Bowl XLIX (New England Patriots vs. Seattle Seahawks) on February 1, 2015. A woman arrives to visit her pharmacist and instead encounters Walter White behind the counter. According to Cranston in his 2016 memoir *A Life in Parts*, "It was funny, and it paid a lot. A ridiculous amount. I thought I would be a fool not to take it. Accepting a commercial like that makes it possible for me to do super-low-budget-passion projects."

According to a lukewarm review of the Esurance commercial in the *HuffPost*, the "awkward 60-second spot . . . lacked any sort of direction. Its closing seconds—which felt more like an underdeveloped *SNL* skit feeling around in the dark for an ending—couldn't have come soon enough. But like always, Cranston was great. Even when he doesn't have to be."

Family Guy Spoofs *Breaking Bad* Fans

Instead of parodying *Breaking Bad* directly, *Family Guy* decided to spoof fans of the series in a 2013 episode titled "Space Cadet" that features "Peter" getting brainwashed while watching TV. While lying in bed watching the show, Peter starts getting ordered to "recommend *Breaking Bad* to everyone you know. *Breaking Bad* is the best show you've ever seen, except maybe *The Wire*. You will never stop talking about *Breaking Bad* or *The Wire*."

Goorin Bros Heisenberg Hat

Why settle for a cheap knockoff porkpie Heisenberg hat when you can get the real deal from San Francisco-based hat maker Goorin Bros? Good luck finding these classic, best-selling hats in stock!

Heisenberg Chronicles

Literally thousands of posters, T-shirts, articles, and other tributes inspired by both *Breaking Bad* and *Better Call Saul* can be found at the Heisenberg Chronicles (heisenbergchronicles.com). It's all here, including a rendition of Walt and Skyler posing as the couple from Grant Wood's famous 1930 *American Gothic* painting (complete with a midair collision in the background).

Heisenberg *Saturday Night Live* Skit

Bryan Cranston hosted the December 12, 2016, episode of *Saturday Night Live* and participated in a rather clever skit involving newly elected president Donald Trump tapping Walter "Heisenberg" White (complete with signature porkpie hat) to head up the Drug Enforcement Administration: "I know the DEA better than anyone, inside and out." White informs the interviewer that he was selected by controversial Trump advisor Steve Bannon, who found him "on the comment section of Breitbart." White also smirks, "I also like that wall [Trump] wants to build. Nothing comes in from Mexico, meaning a lot less competition for the rest of us." The clip can be viewed on YouTube.

"Joking Bad"

In line with his string of TV parodies such as "Downton Sixbey" and "Game of Desks," Jimmy Fallon offered the ambitious parody "Joking Bad," which features the late-night talk host in a bald cap and goatee who partners with his assistant, "Higgins." The 2013 sketch, which can be viewed on YouTube, features cameos by Bryan Cranston, Aaron Paul, and Bob Odenkirk.

"LEGO Breaking Bad: The Video Game (Parody)"

"LEGO Breaking Bad" was created by animator and designer Brian Anderson, who remarked, "I started thinking of other movies with fairly shocking moments that would be funny if they were acted out by LEGO characters—the ear scene from *Reservoir Dogs*, the shower scene from *Psycho*." It's just too bad this game isn't real—yet!

Metástasis (Spanish remake of *Breaking Bad*)

A joint project between Sony Entertainment Television and Colombian production company Teleset, the Spanish version of *Breaking Bad* stars Diego Trujillo as meth cook/drug kingpin Walter Blanco and Roberto Urbina as his sidekick, José Miguel Rosas. In the United States, *Metástasis* aired on Univision in 2014. *Metástasis* was relatively faithful to the original series with a few exceptions such as the locale being moved to Bogotá, Columbia; Walter teaching at a private school; a school bus replacing the

One of the most fascinating aspects of the *Breaking Bad* craze is the incredible fan art that can be found in some of the least likely places around the world (in this case as graffiti on a wall in Valencia, Spain).   *Joanbanjo/Wikimedia Commons*

mobile meth lab RV; and sleazy lawyer Saul Bueno being the host of a late-night legal talk show.

The Mob Museum *Breaking Bad* Exhibit

The National Museum of Organized Crime and Law Enforcement (aka the Mob Museum) in downtown Las Vegas offers a permanent display featuring a growing collection of artifacts from popular movies and TV shows such as *Breaking Bad* that portray organized crime. *Breaking Bad* items on display include Walter White's yellow hazmat suit, gas mask, and rubber apron, among other artifacts. The Mob Museum first opened its doors on February 14, 2012, the eighty-third anniversary of the St. Valentine's Day Massacre, and also features artifacts related to real-life gangsters such as Al Capone, Dion O'Bannion, George "Bugs" Moran, Charlie "Lucky" Luciano, Meyer Lansky, Benjamin "Bugsy" Siegel, Sam Giancana, Joe "Joe Bananas" Bonanno, Frank "Lefty" Rosenthal, Mickey Cohen, Moe Sedway, Tony "the Ant" Spilotro, and John "the Dapper Don" Gotti, among others.

Mock Obituary and Funeral Procession for Walter White

On October 4, 2013, a *Breaking Bad* fan club placed a paid obituary for "Walter White" in the *Albuquerque Journal* that read: "WHITE, WALTER aka 'Heisenberg,' 52 of Albuquerque, died after a long battle with cancer, and a gunshot wound. A co-founder of Gray Matter, White was a research chemist who taught high school chemistry and later founded a meth manufacturing empire. He is survived by his wife, Skyler Lambert; son Walter 'Flynn' Jr.; and daughter Holly. A private memorial was held by his family. In lieu of flowers, donations can be made to drug abuse prevention charity of your choice. He will be greatly missed."

A mock funeral procession followed on October 19, 2013, that featured a hearse and meth lab RV replica, along with services and even a headstone with a photo of "White" displayed at Sunset Memorial Park

Cemetery in Albuquerque. Tickets for the mock funeral raised approximately $17,000 for a local charity, Healthcare for the Homeless.

The Office Halloween Party

In *The Office* episode "Spooked" (2011, 8.05), Ryan (B. J. Novak) dresses as Jesse Pinkman for the office Halloween party, complete with yellow hoodie and beanie. For the record, Dwight dresses as Sarah Kerrigan from the StarCraft video game series; Angela dresses as a cat; and Jim, Kevin, and Darryl dress as then-Miami Heat basketball players Chris Bosh, Dwayne Wade, and LeBron James.

Preacher Easter Egg

Preacher is a TV series that airs on AMC and has been renewed for a third season in 2018. An adaptation of the comic book series of the same name, *Preacher* stars Dominic Cooper in the title role. In the "Finish the Song" episode (1.09), the scene where Fiore and DeBlanc await their "charter bus to Hell" is the same filming locale, John B. Robert Dam, where both Jesse Pinkman and Walter White wait for Ed to pick them up and whisk them off to a new life (Jesse ends up backing out, while Walt relocates briefly to a snowy New Hampshire cabin).

Samuel L. Jackson Reads

Everyone knows actor Samuel L. Jackson (*Pulp Fiction*) is a *Breaking Bad* superfan, so it was no surprise when the actor created a series of recorded monologues, including Walter White's infamous "I am the danger" speech, in order to raise funds for the Alzheimer's Association. One Reddit user suggested that Bryan Cranston should return the favor and record himself reciting the "Ezekiel Speech" from Jackson's character Jules Winnfield in *Pulp Fiction* (1994). We're still waiting, Mr. Cranston!

SaveWalterWhite.com

In Season Two of *Breaking Bad*, Walt Jr. creates a cheesy but heartfelt website, SaveWalterWhite.com, in an attempt to raise money to help pay for his father's medical bills (Saul Goodman soon transforms the site into a money-laundering operation). The site can still be visited today and features a rambling discourse on how great (but nerdy) Walt Jr.'s dad is, followed by a desperate plea for support: "What a wonderful dad I have. But he is in trouble. It's Lung Cancer. He needs an operation. Now!" Visitors to the site who hit the "Click Here to Donate" button are redirected to amc.com/shows/breaking-bad.

The Simpsons Parody of *Breaking Bad*

Homer Simpson assumes the Heisenberg persona in a hilarious montage accompanied by "Crystal Blue Persuasion" by Tommy James and the Shondells during the "What Animated Women Want" episode of *The Simpsons* that originally aired on April 14, 2013.

The Walking Dead Connection

One of the most intriguing fan theories circulating out there is that *Breaking Bad* serves as a prequel to *The Walking Dead* (see Chapter 27). In fact, several Easter eggs related to *Breaking Bad* can be found in *The Walking Dead* such as in the episode "Bloodletting" (2.02), where blue meth can be seen in Daryl's stash of meds, and the episode "Indifference" (4.07), where Daryl relates a story about some dirtbag drug dealer he once knew who sounds suspiciously like Jesse Pinkman.

Warren Buffett—Superfan?

Billionaire investor Warren Buffett has admitted to being a huge fan of *Breaking Bad* and even visited the set in one instance to tape a funny sketch of himself playing a version of Heisenberg that included cameos by Bryan Cranston and Aaron Paul, and was later screened at his annual gathering of stockholders. Buffett later described Walter White as a "good businessman" and added that Heisenberg "would be my guy if I ever had to go toe-to-toe with anyone."

Zootopia Easter Egg

Disney's 2016 animated comedy *Zootopia* features a lab scene inspired by *Breaking Bad* in which bunny cop Judy Hopps (Ginnifer Goodwin) and her crime-solving partner, Nick Wilde (Jason Bateman), discover an underground flower-harvesting operation featuring a ram in a yellow jumpsuit named Woolter cooking up a blue serum with his assistant Jesse that makes animals go wild. Directed by Byron Howard and Rich Moore (and co-directed by Jared Bush), *Zootopia* also features the vocal talents of Idris Elba, Jenny Slate, Nate Torrence, Bonnie Hunt, Don Lake, Tommy Chong, J. K. Simmons, Octavia Spencer, Alan Tudyk, and Shakira. *Zootopia* received an Oscar for Best Animated Feature Film.

35

Any Future That You Want

Whatever Happened to . . .

Charles Baker (Skinny Pete)

Baker appeared in several feature films in 2018—including Robinson Devor's *You Can't Win*, which is based on the groundbreaking 1926 work of hobo literature of the same name by Jack Black, a legendary hobo, opium addict, convict, and professional thief. Baker also has a recurring role as Grey on the NBC TV series *The Blacklist*, which stars James Spader and Megan Boone.

Jonathan Banks (Mike Ehrmantraut)

Banks appeared (as a character named Walt!) in the 2018 action thriller *The Commuter*, which starred Liam Neeson. Banks returned as Mike Ehrmantraut in the fourth season of *Better Call Saul*, which made its debut in the fall of 2018. He also appeared as Pepin Herstal, Lord of the Franks in *Redbad*, a Dutch historical epic directed by Roel Reine.

Jeremiah Bitsui (Victor)

Bitsui has reprised his role as Victor in five episodes of *Better Call Saul*: "Witness," "Sunk Costs," "Sabrosito," "Off Brand," and "Fall." In an August 28, 2017, interview with *Indian Country Today*, Bitsui remarked, "I feel like I've been blessed with these opportunities. I just want to continue to make good work."

Michael Bowen (Uncle Jack Welker)

Since *Breaking Bad* ended, Bowen has made guest appearances in several TV series, including as Mullet in *Raising Hope*, Matches Malone in *Gotham*, and Vin in *Animal Kingdom*.

Betsy Brandt (Marie Schrader)

Brandt currently costars as Heather Hughes in the CBS sitcom *Life in Pieces*, which was created by Justin Adler and also features Colin Hanks, Thomas Sadowski, Zoe Lister-Jones, Dianne Wiest, and James Brolin. In a November 2, 2017, interview with CBS Los Angeles, Brandt commented, "I love playing Heather on *Life in Pieces* . . . I love being part of that family. It's such a talented group of actors and nice people." She also appeared in the 2018 drama, *Just a Little Bit Longer*.

Ray Campbell (Tyrus Kitt)

Campbell has reprised his role as Tyrus in two episodes of *Better Call Saul*: "Sunk Costs" and "Off Brand." In addition, he has appeared on several other TV series such as *The Gifted, SEAL Team, Colony, NCIS: New Orleans, Coconut Hut, For Better or Worse, Supergirl, NCIS: Los Angeles, Brooklyn Nine-Nine,* and *Gang Related.*

David Costabile (Gale Boetticher)

In 2012, Costabile appeared as Republican Congressman James Ashley of Ohio in Steven Spielberg's epic historical drama *Lincoln,* which starred Daniel Day-Lewis in the title role, as well as Sally Field, Tommy Lee Jones,

David Strathairn, Joseph Gordon-Levitt, James Spader, and Hal Holbrook. The film was nominated for twelve Academy Awards (Day-Lewis won Best Actor and the film won Best Production Design). Costabile also appeared in the films *Side Effects* (2013), *Runner Runner* (2013), and *13 Hours: The Secret Soldiers of Benghazi* (2016). In addition, he has had recurring roles on several post-*Breaking Bad* TV series such as Simon Boyd in *Low Winter Sun*, Tad Billingham in *Dig*, Daniel Hardman in *Suits*, and Mike "Wags" Wagner in *Billions*.

Christopher Cousins (Ted Beneke)

Cousins has kept very busy appearing in a variety of TV series over the past few years such as *The Mentalist, CSI: Crime Scene Investigation, Twisted, Revolution, Matador, Glee, The Vampire Diaries, CSI: Cyber, Bosch, UnReal, Training Day, Designated Survivor*, and *The Exorcist*, among others.

Bryan Cranston (Walter White)

In 2013 and 2014, Cranston portrayed President Lyndon B. Johnson in the critically acclaimed Broadway play *All the Way*. He won a Tony Award for Best Actor for the role, which he reprised in the 2016 HBO movie of the same name. Cranston received a Best Actor Oscar nomination (losing out to Leonardo DiCaprio in *The Revenant*) for his role as blacklisted screenwriter Dalton Trumbo in *Trumbo* (2015). Cranston's other post-*Breaking Bad* acting credits include *Godzilla* (2014), *Kung Fu Panda 3* (2016), *Get a Job* (2016), *The Infiltrator* (2016), *Wakefield* (2016), *In Dubious Battle* (2016), *Why Him?* (2016), *The Upside* (2017), *The Disaster Artist* (2017), and *Last Flag Flying* (2017). In 2017, Cranston portrayed Howard Beale in a stage adaptation of *Network* at the Royal National Theatre in London. He is currently the executive producer and star of the popular Amazon Video series *Philip K. Dick's Electric Dreams*.

Breaking Bad garnered an impressive nineteen Primetime Emmy Awards, eight Satellite Awards, two Golden Globe Awards, two Peabody Awards, two Critics' Choice Awards, and four Television Critics Association Awards.   *Peabody Awards/Wikimedia Commons*

Lavell Crawford (Huell Babineaux)

In 2017, Crawford reprised his role of Huell Babineaux in the "Chicanery" episode of *Better Call Saul*. He also served as the voice of LeDante in the animated TV series *Legends of Chamberlain Heights* and portrayed Gus Patch in the 2015 movie *The Ridiculous 6*. Crawford will appear as Brother Winters in the 2018 Netflix original comedy *Love Is Not Enough*.

Raymond Cruz (Tuco Salamanca)

Cruz reprised his role as Detective Julio Sanchez in *The Closer* spin-off *Major Crimes*, which ran six seasons between 2012 and 2018. He also

Raymond Cruz left *Breaking Bad* to assume the role of "Detective Julio Sanchez" in the TV series *The Closer*. *RedCarpetReport/ Wikimedia Commons*

reprised his role as Tuco Salamanca in three episodes of *Better Call Saul*: "Uno," "Mijo," and "Gloves Off." In addition, Cruz appeared as Che "Padre" Romero in the *Sons of Anarchy* spin-off *Mayans MC*, which first aired in the fall of 2018.

Laura Fraser (Lydia Rodarte-Quayle)

Post-*Breaking Bad*, Fraser has reprised her role as Lydia" n two *Better Call Saul* episodes ("Off Brand" and "Fall") and appeared in several other TV series, including as Reagan Black in *Black Box*, Juliet in *One of Us*, Eve Stone in *The Missing*, and Detective Sergeant Annie Redford in *The Loch*.

John de Lancie (Donald Margolis)

Best known as Q in the *Star Trek* franchise, De Lancie has voiced the character Discord in the animated series *My Little Pony: Friendship Is Magic* since 2010.

Giancarlo Esposito (Gus Fring)

Esposito has reprised his role as Gus Fring in nine *Better Call Saul* episodes: "Witness," "Sunk Costs," "Sabrosito," "Chicanery," "Off Brand," "Expenses," "Slip," "Fall," and "Lantern." In addition, he has appeared in a host of films and TV series, including *Community* (2012–13), *Revolution* (2012–14), *Allegiance* (2015), *Maze Runner: The Scorch Trials* (2015), *The Jungle Book* (2016), *The Get Down* (2016–17), *Dear White People* (2017), *Once Upon a Time* (2011–17), *Rebel* (2017), and *Dallas & Robo* (2018). In January 2018, he reprised his role as Jorge in *Maze Runner: The Death Cure*.

Vince Gilligan (Creator/Executive Producer/Writer/Director)

Post-*Breaking Bad*, Gilligan has served as co-creator and executive producer of *Better Call Saul*, which debuted its fourth season in the fall of 2018. Gilligan also served as the co-creator (with David Shore) of the short-lived comedy-drama *Battle Creek* in 2015.

Adam Godley (Elliott Schwartz)

A Tony Award nominee and three-time nominee for the Olivier Award, Godley has frequently appeared in TV series, including *A Young Doctor's Notebook & Other Series* (2012–13), *Perception* (2014), *Manhattan* (2014), *Homeland* (2014), *Powers* (2015–16), *The Blacklist* (2016), *Fallet* (2017), and *Lodge 49* (2019).

Anna Gunn (Skyler White)

In 2016, Gunn starred in the drama *Equity*, which premiered at the Sundance Film Festival. The following year she had a recurring role as Julia Ayres in the TV series *Shades of Blue*. Gunn is set to appear in the 2018 comedy *You Can Choose Your Family*. Her film and TV credits include *The Mindy Project* (2014), *Gracepoint* (2014), *Portlandia* (2015), *Criminal Minds* (2015), *Chunk & Bean* (2016), and *Sully* (2016).

Jessica Hecht (Gretchen Schwartz)

Hecht has performed to critical acclaim in several Broadway plays including *Harvey* (2012) and *Fiddler on the Roof* (2015). She also had a recurring role in the TV series, *Person of Interest*. Her TV and film credits include *Person of Interest* (2013–15), *Manhattan* (2014), *Jessica Jones* (2015), *Falling Water* (2016), *Red Oaks* (2016–17), *Madam Secretary* (2017), and *Blindspot* (2017).

Matt Jones (Badger)

Since his frequently hilarious turn as Jesse's sidekick, Badger, Jones has appeared in a variety of TV series, including *NCIS* (2011–15), *Deadman* (2013), *Sanjay and Craig* (2013–16), *Mom* (2013–18), and *Let's Get Physical* (2018), among others. Jones also starred in the 2018 comedy *Corpse Tub*.

Daniel and Luis Moncada (the Cousins)

Both Daniel and Luis Moncada have stayed quite busy since bursting onto the scene as the Terminator-like Cousins in *Breaking Bad*. Daniel's TV and film credits include Lobo Soldier in *Sons of Anarchy* (2014), Perp No. 2 in *Brooklyn Nine-Nine* (2014), Eddie in *McFarland, USA* (2015), Thug One in *Scorpion* (2016), Triumph Seeker No. 1 in *Lopez* (2017), Bloody Man in *Fear the Walking Dead*, and Cartel Thug in *The Night Shift* (2017). Luis's film and TV credits include Grueso in *Chop Shop*, Gnomo Pinzeta in *Gang Related* (2014), Randall in *Brooklyn Nine-Nine* (2014), Roberto in *Key and Peele* (2013–14), Manny in *NCIS: Los Angeles* (2015), Paco in *Lethal Weapon* (2016), Hector Pedroza in *Criminal Minds: Beyond Borders* (2017), and Romero in *The Night Shift* (2017). The Moncada brothers also have reprised the roles as the Cousins in *Better Call Saul* (episodes "Bali Ha'i" and "Klick").

Mark Margolis (Hector Salamanca)

Margolis reprised his Hector character in ten episodes of *Better Call Saul* and has also appeared in *Law & Order: Special Victims Unit* (2011), *Person of Interest* (2011–12), *Fairly Legal* (2012), *American Horror Story* (2012), *Constantine* (2015), *Gotham* (2015), *You Bury Your Own* (2015), *The Affair* (2015), *Broken Soldier* (2016), *My Big Fat Greek Wedding 2* (2016), *A Remarkable Life* (2016), *One Fall* (2016), and *Valley of Bones* (2017).

RJ Mitte (Walter White Jr.)

Mitte appeared in the 2012 thriller *House of Last Things*, and also can be seen in Hollywood Undead's 2013 music video for "Dead Bite." He also had a recurring role in the ABC drama *Switched at Birth*. His film credits include *Dixieland* (2015), *Who's Driving Doug* (2016), and *Time Share* (2018).

Dean Norris (Hank Schrader)

After his five-season stint as Hank in *Breaking Bad*, Norris jumped right into another series, starring as town councilman James "Big Jim" Rennie on the CBS series *Under the Dome* (2013–15). He later appeared in the TV series *The Big Bang Theory* (2016–17) as Colonel Richard Williams. Ironically, he currently portrays mob boss Clay "Uncle Daddy" Husser in the TNT series *Claws*. Norris's filmography includes *The Counsellor* (2013), *Small Time* (2014), *Men, Women & Children* (2014), *Secret in Their Eyes* (2015), *Sons of Liberty* (2015), *Fist Fight* (2017), and *Death Wish* (2018).

Bob Odenkirk (Saul Goodman)

Odenkirk reprised his role as Jimmy McGill/Saul Goodman in the fourth season of *Better Call Saul*, which made its debut in the fall of 2018. In addition, he has joined the cast of *Incredibles 2* (2018), the sequel to the hit 2004 Disney film *The Incredibles*. His recent film credits include *Hell and Back* (2015), *Freaks of Nature* (2015), *Girlfriend's Day* (2017), *The Disaster Artist* (2017), and *The Post* (2017). He also appeared in a recurring role as Bill Oswalt in the *Fargo* TV series in 2014.

Tina Parker (Francesca Liddy)

Saul Goodman's good-natured secretary in *Breaking Bad*, Tina Parker reprised her role as Francesca in *Better Call Saul*. Her TV and film credits include *Rectify* (2014), *Salem* (2015), *The Ridiculous 6* (2015), *Walk of Fame* (2017), *One Mississippi* (2017), *The Middle of X* (2018), and *Sleeping in Plastic* (2018).

Aaron Paul (Jesse Pinkman)

Paul served as the voice of Todd Chavez on the Netflix animated series *BoJack Horseman* (2014–17) and also appears as Eddie Lane on the Hulu drama *The Path* (2016–18). His film credits include *Hellion* (2014), *Need for Speed* (2014), *A Long Way Down* (2014), *Eye in the Sky* (2015), *Exodus: Gods and Kings* (2014), *Central Intelligence* (2016), and *Come and Find Me* (2016).

Jesse Plemons (Todd Alquist)

Plemons portrayed butcher Ed Blumquist in the second season of *Fargo*, an FX anthology series. His recent filmography includes *Battleship* (2012), *The Master* (2012), *Black Mass* (2015), *Other People* (2016), and *American Made* (2017). In addition, Plemons was considered for the role in *Star Wars: The Force Awakens* (2015) that eventually went to John Boyega. Plemons is engaged to actress Kirsten Dunst (*Melancholia*).

Ian Posada (Brock Cantillo)

Known as the child actor who portrayed Brock, the kid poisoned by Walt with lily of the valley berries, Posada also has appeared in the 2014 short *Heirloom* and in the feature *Sicario* (2015) as Fausto's Son No. 2.

Steven Michael Quezada (Steven Gomez)

A native of Albuquerque, Quezada appeared in two films that were released in 2018: *Wish Man* and *Duke City*. His post-*Breaking Bad* film and TV credits also include *Light from the Darkroom* (2014), *The Mindy*

Project (2014), *Hermanos* (2014), *Foreseeable* (2015), *Outlaws and Angels* (2016), *Fender Bender* (2016), *Girlfriend's Day* (2017), *The Night Before* (2017), and *Kepler's Dream* (2017), among others.

Emily Rios (Andrea Cantillo)

Since portraying Jesse's other, also doomed, girlfriend Andrea, Rios has appeared in several TV series, including as Adriana Mendez in *The Bridge*, as Betty Chessni in *True Detective* (2015), as Ximena Vasconcelos in *From Dusk till Dawn: The Series* (2015–16), and as Lucia Villanueva in *Snowfall* (2017–18).

Krysten Ritter (Jane Margolis)

In addition to her portrayal of Jesse's doomed girlfriend Jane in *Breaking Bad*, Ritter is well known for her role as superheroine Jessica Jones in both the *Jessica Jones* (2015–18) and *The Defenders* (2017) TV series. She also has appeared in *Gravity* (2010), *Robot Chicken* (2013), *The Cleveland Show* (2013), *Don't Trust the B---- in Apartment 23* (2012–13), and *The Blacklist* (2014).

Krysten Ritter currently stars as the title character in the highly popular Netflix series, *Jessica Jones*.

Carmen Serano (Carmen Molina)

Serano has made appearances in several TV series since her stint as Assistant Principal Carmen Molina in *Breaking Bad*, such as *Switched at Birth* (2014), *Chop Shop* (2014), *The Comedy Get Down* (2017), and *Runaways* (2017–18). Her film credits include *Distortion* (2016) and *Silverdome* (2016).

Michael Shamus Wiles (ASAC George Merkert)

In addition to his role as George Merkert, Hank's boss in *Breaking Bad*, Wiles had a recurring role as Jury White in another immensely popular TV series, *Sons of Anarchy*, a crime drama about an outlaw motorcycle club that ran between 2008 and 2014. His film credits include *K-11* (2012), *Saving Lincoln* (2013), *Iron Man 3* (2013), *The Lost One* (2015), *Let Me Make You a Martyr* (2016), *Lake Alice* (2017), and *Death Note* (2017).

Selected Bibliography

Abbott, Stacey, ed. *The Cult TV Book: From Star Trek to Dexter, New Approaches to TV Outside the Box*. New York: Soft Skull Press, 2010.

Armstrong, Jennifer Keishin. *Seinfeldia: How a Show About Nothing Changed Everything*. New York: Simon & Schuster, 2016.

Arp, Robert, and David R. Koepsell, eds. *Breaking Bad and Philosophy: Badder Living Through Chemistry*. Chicago: Open Court, 2012.

Atwood, Blake. *The Gospel According to Breaking Bad*. Dallas: AtWords Press, 2013.

Batten, Thomas. "Mad Men: How Don Draper and Walter White Prepared Us for Donald Trump." *The Guardian*. August 10, 2015.

Bianculli, David. *The Platinum Age of Television: From I Love Lucy to The Walking Dead*. New York: Doubleday, 2016.

Bland, Archie. "Breaking Bad: Why Life Won't Be the Same Without This Radical American Television Drama." *The Independent*. August 8, 2013.

Brown, Lane. "In Conversation: Vince Gilligan on the End of Breaking Bad." *Vulture*. May 12, 2013.

Castle, Alison, ed. *The Stanley Kubrick Archives*. Cologne: Taschen, 2008.

Clem, Carren LeAnn, and Ronald B. Clem. *Loss of Innocence: A Family's Journey with Meth*. London: Virgin Books, 2007.

Coppola, Francis Ford. *The Godfather Notebook*. New York: Regan Arts, 2016.

Couch, Aaron. "'Breaking Bad' Sets Guinness World Record." *The Hollywood Reporter*. September 5, 2013.

Cranston, Bryan. *A Life in Parts*. New York: Scribner, 2016.

Crease, Robert P., and Alfred Scharff Goldhaber. *The Quantum Moment: How Planck, Bohr, Einstein, and Heisenberg Taught Us to Love Uncertainty*. New York: W. W. Norton & Company, 2014.

Crumb, Robert, and David Zone Mairowitz. *Kafka*. Seattle: Fantagraphics Books, 2007.

Cyriaque, Lamar. "We Talk to the Cast of Breaking Bad about Science, Swearing and Saul Goodman. *io9*. July 14, 2012.

Douthat, Ross. "Good and Evil on Cable." *The New York Times.* July 28, 2011.

Ebert, Roger. *Life Itself: A Memoir.* New York: Grand Central Publishing, 2011.

Frayling, Christopher. *Sergio Leone: Something to Do with Death.* Minneapolis: University of Minnesota Press, 2012.

Gajanan, Mahita. "Donald Trump Picks Walter White to Head DEA on 'Saturday Night Live.'" *Time.* December 11, 2016.

Ginsberg, Merle. "'Breaking Bad' Star Bryan Cranston on Walter White: 'He's Well on His Way to Badass' (Q&A).". *The Hollywood Reporter.* July 16, 2011.

Gomez, Adrian. "'Breaking Bad' Fan Group Places Paid Obituary for Walter White." *Albuquerque Journal.* October 4, 2013.

Goodman, Tim. "'Breaking Bad': Dark Side of the Dream." *The Hollywood Reporter.* July 13, 2011.

Grillo, Ioan. *El Narco: Inside Mexico's Criminal Insurgency.* New York: Bloomsbury Press, 2011.

Guffey, Ensley F. and Koontz, K. Dale. *Wanna Cook? The Complete, Unofficial Companion to Breaking Bad.* Toronto: ECW Press, 2014.

Hickey, Walter. "Breaking Bad Is the Greatest Show Ever Made." *Business Insider.* September 29, 2013.

Hilton, James. *Goodbye, Mr. Chips.* London: Hodder & Stoughton, 2016.

Jeffery, Morgan. "Bryan Cranston on 'Breaking Bad' End: 'There's No Redemption.'" *Digital Spy.* February 25, 2013.

Jones, Jenny M. *The Annotated Godfather: The Complete Screenplay.* New York: Black Dog & Leventhal Publishers, 2007.

Kelley, Seth. "'Breaking Bad' Creator Urges Fans to Stop Throwing Pizzas on Walter White's Roof." *Variety.* March 11, 2015.

Keslowitz, Steven. *Why You Better Call Saul.* Tucson, AZ: QuillPop Books, 2017.

King, Stephen. "Stephen King: I Love 'Breaking Bad'!" *Entertainment Weekly.* March 6, 2009.

Klosterman, Chuck. "Bad Decisions: Why AMC's *Breaking Bad* Beats *Mad Men, The Sopranos,* and *The Wire. Grantland.* July 12, 2011.

Labuza, Peter. "'Breaking Bad' Director of Photography Michael Slovis Talks About Shaping the Look of the Most Cinematic Show on Television." *Indiewire*. September 5, 2012.

Larabee, Ann. "The New Television Antihero." *Journal of Popular Culture* 46, no. 6. 2013.

Lowry, Brian. *The Truth Is Out There: The Official Guide to The X-Files*. New York: Harper Prism, 1995.

Marcus, Greil. *The Doors: A Lifetime of Listening to Five Mean Years*. New York: PublicAffairs, 2013.

Martin, Brett. *Difficult Men: Behind the Scenes of a Creative Revolution: From The Sopranos and The Wire to Mad Men and Breaking Bad*. New York: Penguin Books, 2014.

Martin, Brett. *The Sopranos: The Complete Book*. New York: Liberty Street, 2007.

Meslow, Scott. "On 'Breaking Bad,' Family Is a Motivation and a Liability. *The Atlantic*. July 23, 2013.

Moaba, Alex. "Anthony Hopkins' 'Breaking Bad' Fan Letter to Bryan Cranston Is Awesome." *The Huffington Post*. October 15, 2013.

Peary, Danny. *Guide for the Film Fanatic*. New York: Simon & Schuster, 1986.

Pressler, Jessica. "Cranston Comes Alive." *Esquire*. October 17, 2017.

Price, V. B. *Albuquerque: City at the End of the World*. Albuquerque: University of New Mexico Press, 2003.

Rhodes, Joe. "Shattering All Vestiges of Innocence: 'Breaking Bad' Returns and Walter White's Descent Continues." *The New York Times*. July 15, 2011.

Rich, Nathaniel. "William Faulkner's Tragic Air Circus." *The Daily Beast*. May 30, 2015.

Rothman, Lily. "Breaking Bad: What Does That Phrase Actually Mean?" *Time*. September 23, 2013.

San Juan, Eric. *Breaking Down Breaking Bad: Unpeeling the Layers of Television's Greatest Drama*. North Charleston: CreateSpace, 2013.

Segal, David. "The Dark Art of 'Breaking Bad.'" *The New York Times*. July 6, 2011.

Sepinwall, Alan. *The Revolution Was Televised: How The Sopranos, Mad Men, Breaking Bad, Lost, and Other Groundbreaking Dramas Changed TV Forever.* New York: Touchstone, 2015.

Sheffield, Rob. "100 Greatest TV Shows of All Time." *Rolling Stone.* September 21, 2016.

Shields, Michael. "Walter White vs. Walt Whitman." *Across the Margin.* August 4, 2012.

St. John, Allen. "Why 'Breaking Bad' Is the Best Show Ever and Why That Matters." *Forbes.* September 16, 2013.

Stache, Lara C. *Breaking Bad: A Cultural History.* Lanham, MD: Rowman & Littlefield, 2017.

Stanyard, Stewart T. *Dimensions Behind The Twilight Zone.* Toronto: ECW Press, 2007.

Stevenson, Damian. *Scarface: The Ultimate Guide.* North Charleston, SC: CreateSpace: 2014.

Stopera, Dave. "Was the 'Breaking Bad' Finale All Just a Fantasy in Walter White's Head?" *BuzzFeed.* October 2, 2013.

Thomson, David. *Television: A Biography.* New York: Thames & Hudson, 2016.

Thomson, David, ed. *Breaking Bad: The Official Book.* New York: Sterling Publishing, 2015.

Valdez, Marc P. *A Guidebook to 'Breaking Bad' Filming Locations.* North Charleston, SC: CreateSpace, 2016.

Van Doren, Mark, ed. *The Portable Walt Whitman.* New York: Penguin Books, 1977.

Vulliamy, Ed. *Amexica: War Along the Borderline.* New York: Farrar, Straus and Giroux, 2010.

Wallach, Jason. "A Comprehensive Guide to Cooking Meth on 'Breaking Bad.'" *Vice.* August 11, 2013.

Weingus, Leigh. "'Breaking Bad': John Cusack, Matthew Broderick Turned Down Walter White Role." *The Huffington Post.* July 16, 2012.

Westenfield, Adrienne. "The Great Oz." *Esquire.* November 2017. Woodward, Richard B. "Breaking Bad: Better Television Through Chemistry." *The Huffington Post.* July 20, 2011.

Zicree, Marc Scott. *The Twilight Zone Companion.* West Hollywood, CA: Silman-James Press, 1992.

Index

THE FAQ SERIES

AC/DC FAQ
by Susan Masino
Backbeat Books
9781480394506...$24.99

Armageddon Films FAQ
by Dale Sherman
Applause Books
9781617131196.........$24.99

The Band FAQ
by Peter Aaron
Backbeat Books
9781617136139 ....$19.99

Baseball FAQ
by Tom DeMichael
Backbeat Books
9781617136061........$24.99

The Beach Boys FAQ
by Jon Stebbins
Backbeat Books
9780879309879..$22.99

The Beat Generation FAQ
by Rich Weidman
Backbeat Books
9781617136016 ....$19.99

Beer FAQ
by Jeff Cioletti
Backbeat Books
9781617136115 ....$24.99

Black Sabbath FAQ
by Martin Popoff
Backbeat Books
9780879309572....$19.99

Bob Dylan FAQ
by Bruce Pollock
Backbeat Books
9781617136078 ....$19.99

Britcoms FAQ
by Dave Thompson
Applause Books
9781495018992 ....$19.99

Bruce Springsteen FAQ
by John D. Luerssen
Backbeat Books
9781617130939.......$22.99

Buffy the Vampire Slayer FAQ
by David Bushman and Arthur Smith
Applause Books
9781495064722.....$19.99

Cabaret FAQ
by June Sawyers
Applause Books
9781495051449......$19.99

A Chorus Line FAQ
by Tom Rowan
Applause Books
9781480367548 ...$19.99

The Clash FAQ
by Gary J. Jucha
Backbeat Books
9781480364509 ..$19.99

Doctor Who Faq
by Dave Thompson
Applause Books
9781557838544....$22.99

The Doors FAQ
by Rich Weidman
Backbeat Books
9781617130175........$24.99

Dracula FAQ
by Bruce Scivally
Backbeat Books
9781617136009 .....$19.99

The Eagles FAQ
by Andrew Vaughan
Backbeat Books
9781480385412.....$24.99

Elvis Films FAQ
by Paul Simpson
Applause Books
9781557838582.....$24.99

Elvis Music FAQ
by Mike Eder
Backbeat Books
9781617130496......$22.99

Eric Clapton FAQ
by David Bowling
Backbeat Books
9781617134548 ......$22.99

Fab Four FAQ
by Stuart Shea and Robert Rodriguez
Hal Leonard Books
9781423421382.......$19.99

Fab Four FAQ 2.0
by Robert Rodriguez
Backbeat Books
9780879309688...$19.99

Film Noir FAQ
by David J. Hogan
Applause Books
9781557838551......$22.99

Football FAQ
by Dave Thompson
Backbeat Books
9781495007484 ...$24.99

Frank Zappa FAQ
by John Corcelli
Backbeat Books
9781617136030 ....$19.99

Godzilla FAQ
by Brian Solomon
Applause Books
9781495045684 $19.99

The Grateful Dead FAQ
by Tony Sclafani
Backbeat Books
9781617130861........$24.99

Guns N' Roses FAQ
by Rich Weidman
Backbeat Books
9781495025884 ..$19.99

Haunted America FAQ
by Dave Thompson
Backbeat Books
9781480392625.....$19.99

Horror Films FAQ
by John Kenneth Muir
Applause Books
9781557839503....$22.99

Jack the Ripper FAQ
by Dave Thompson
Applause Books
9781495063084....$19.99

James Bond FAQ
by Tom DeMichael
Backbeat Books
9781557838568.....$22.99

Jimi Hendrix FAQ
by Gary J. Jucha
Backbeat Books
9781617130953.......$22.99

Johnny Cash FAQ
by C. Eric Banister
Backbeat Books
9781480385405.. $24.99

KISS FAQ
by Dale Sherman
Backbeat Books
9781617130915........$24.99

Led Zeppelin FAQ
by George Case
Backbeat Books
9781617130250 ......$22.99

Lucille Ball FAQ
by James Sheridan and Barry Monush
Applause Books
9781617740824.......$19.99

MASH FAQ
by Dale Sherman
Applause Books
9781480355897.....$19.99